Motae Jeromi Wada

# HISTORY OF
# JAPANESE RELIGION

# HISTORY OF
# JAPANESE RELIGION

With Special Reference to the Social
and Moral Life of the Nation

By MASAHARU ANESAKI

CHARLES E. TUTTLE COMPANY
*Rutland, Vermont & Tokyo, Japan*

*Representatives*
*Continental Europe:* BOXERBOOKS, INC., *Zurich*
*Canada:* HURTIG PUBLISHERS, *Edmonton*
*Australasia:* BOOK WISE (AUSTRALIA) PTY. LTD.
*104-108 Sussex Street, Sydney 2000*

*Published by the Charles E. Tuttle Company, Inc.*
*of Rutland, Vermont & Tokyo, Japan*
*with editorial offices at*
*Suido 1-chome, 2-6, Bunkyo-ku, Tokyo, Japan*

© *1963 by Masaharu Anesaki*

*Library of Congress Catalog Card No. 63-19395*

*International Standard Book No. 0-8048-0248-3*

*First edition published 1930 by Kegan Paul, Trench,*
*Trubner & Co., London*
*First Tuttle edition, 1963*
*Ninth printing, 1977*

PRINTED IN JAPAN

# PREFACE

IN putting this book before the Occidental public, the author, an Oriental, wishes to acknowledge his indebtedness to the modern science of the Occident. For it is modern science that has trained his mind in its methods and scope, and opened his eyes to many aspects of the present subject which otherwise would have remained unnoticed. At the same time gratitude is due to the sages and saints of the Orient whose souls and spirits have inspired and moulded the author's spiritual life, however meagre and unworthy it be.

The original draft of the present book was an outcome of the author's lectures at Harvard University during the years 1913-15, when he had the honour of occupying there the chair of Japanese Literature and Life. In response to the encouragement given by several friends at Harvard, the author tried to put the material of the lectures into book form and redrafted it from time to time. Some parts were translated into French for a series of lectures at the Collège de France, in 1919, and the result was *Quelques pages de l'histoire religieuse du Japon*. Another invitation, from the Pacific School of Religion in 1921, gave occasion for preparing lectures on the contemporary religious movements, and the results were published in *The Religious and Social Problems of the Orient*. In fact, the years after the Great War saw more unrest and turbulence in the moral and spiritual life of Japan, and the author was sometimes at a loss to grasp the situation. Yet the drafting was never given up. Then came the great earthquake and fire of 1923, which not only destroyed a large part of the author's manuscripts but brought a change in his life. The work of reconstructing the destroyed library of his University fell upon his shoulders. The preparation of the present draft has been done during five years of stress; and now that the new library building is nearly ready for dedication, thanks to the generosity of Mr John D. Rockefeller, Jr., the author feels a special pleasure in sending the rearranged manuscripts to the press.

The work of reconstructing the lost library, though it has little to do with the present subject, needs special mention on the part of the author. It was, indeed, by a mere chance that he was compelled to take up the library work, but when he started it, three months after the disaster, he began to realize the deeper significance of his new task. Innumerable expressions of sympathy and helpfulness came from all sides, both at home and abroad; and offers of donations poured in, manifesting a spirit of international helpfulness and co-operation in the cause of science and education. This is no occasion to enter into the details of that help and sympathy; but it must be mentioned that the author, in taking up the responsibilities of reconstruction, was profoundly impressed with the international significance of his task. The realization of this has been a great encouragement and inspiration during the years of hardship in which the author has been able to rewrite this book, which, as he hopes, may serve the cause of interpreting the Orient to the Occident.

The author in no way cherishes the idea of being an apologist or a propagandist, but has ever been eager to be a scientific historian, whose function it is to weigh the balance of data and to obtain truthful insight into the movements of the human soul. Any degree of success he achieves, in carrying out this ambition, the author owes to his predecessors and teachers in this new branch of the science of religion and religious history. On the other hand, if there be any trace of undue estimation or reverence towards the religious leaders treated of in the book, he asks the reader's generosity to tolerate it, while critically weighing the circumstances, as it comes from the author's own religious heritage.

The long history of the making of the present book has involved many persons to whom thanks are due, and the author feels sure they will excuse his not mentioning their names here.

MASAHARU ANESAKI,

*Tokyo, Oct. 5, 1928,*
*the forty-seventh Anniversary of*
*his father's death.*

# CONTENTS

## INTRODUCTORY

## BOOK I

### THE SHINTO RELIGION AND THE COMMUNAL SYSTEM, EARLY STAGES AND SURVIVAL

## BOOK II

### INTRODUCTION OF BUDDHISM AND ITS ESTABLISHMENT (about 600–800)

## BOOK III

## THE PERIOD OF HEIAN, AN AGE OF PEACE
## AND EASE (about 800–1200)

## BOOK IV

## THE AGE OF FEUDAL STRIFE AND RELIGIOUS STRUGGLE (about 1200–1600)

## BOOK V

### THE TOKUGAWA RÉGIME OF PEACE AND ORDER (1600–1868)

# CONTENTS

## BOOK VI

## THE ERA OF MEIJI AND THE PRESENT, AN AGE OF PROGRESS AND PROBLEMS (1868–1928)

# LIST OF ILLUSTRATIONS

# NOTES ON PROPER NAMES AND TRANSLITERATION

IN transliterating Japanese, Chinese and Sanskrit names and terms, no rigid scientific method has been observed, but the conventional methods in common use. Japanese plural forms, without *s*, have been retained.

Both Japanese and Chinese write their family names first, followed by their personal names, and this method is followed in this book, except for names appearing in the sixth book, *i.e.* after the opening of Japan to foreign intercourse. Thus, in cases like *Sugawara no Michizane* or *Yamazaki Ansai*, the first part is the family name and the second personal, while in cases like *Joseph Neesima* or *Yukichi Fukuzawa*, the second is the family name.

Before 1869, no Buddhist monk or priest was called by his family name, but by his Buddhist name; since that year every Buddhist priest has been required to bear a family name, so that in the sixth book the Buddhists are mentioned by their family names.

# PRINCIPAL WORKS BY THE SAME AUTHOR

*Ancient Religions of India.* Tokyo, 1900.

*The Dawn of Resurrection.* Tokyo, 1904.

*Buddha's Person in its Historical and Religious Aspects* (Thesis). Tokyo, 1904.

" How Christianity Appeals to a Japanese Buddhist " (Article in the *Hibbert Journal*). 1905.

*Religious History of Japan, an Outline* (for private circulation). Tokyo, 1907.

*The Four Buddhist Agamas and their Pāli Counterparts* (TASJ). Tokyo, 1909.

*Flowers of Italy, Diaries of a Pilgrimage.* Tokyo, 1909.

*Buddhism in its Fundamental Features as a Religion.* Tokyo, 1910.

*Buddhist Art in its Relation to Buddhist Ideals.* Boston, Houghton-Mifflin, 1916.

*Nichiren, the Buddhist Prophet.* Harvard University Press, 1916.

*Nichiren, the Man who Lived the Life of the " Lotus of Truth."* Tokyo, 1916.

*Quelques pages de l'histoire religieuse du Japon.* Paris, Musée Guimet, 1921.

*The Religious and Moral Problems of the Orient.* New York, Macmillan, 1923.

*The Extermination of Kirishitans and their Survivals.* Tokyo, 1925.

*The End of the Persecution of Kirishitans.* Tokyo, 1926.

" Japanese Mythology " (in Vol. VIII of *Mythology of all Races*). Boston, Marshall Jones, 1928.

* In Japanese.

xxi

*A Concordance to the History of Kirishitan Missions* (Supplementary volume to the *Proceedings of the Imperial Academy*).   Tokyo, 1930.

Besides, several articles, particularly in *Hastings' Encyclopædia of Religion and Ethics :*

" Docetism " (Buddhist) ; " Ethics and Morality " (Buddhist) ;   " Hymns " (Japanese) ;   " Life and Death " (Japanese) ;   " Missions " (Buddhist) ;   " Philosophy " (Japanese) ;   " Prayer " (Buddhist) ;   " Transmigration ' (Buddhist) ;   " Vows " (Buddhist).

* *History of Kirishitan Missions,* 1549-1715.   Tokyo, 1930.

**INTRODUCTORY**

**THE PEOPLE AND THE PHASES OF THEIR
CIVILIZATION**

# INTRODUCTORY

## THE PEOPLE AND THE PHASES OF THEIR CIVILIZATION

### General Remarks on the Japanese People

A S the destiny of an individual is a mystery to himself,
so it is with a nation. When the forefathers of the
Japanese lived in an immemorial past along the coast
of the Pacific Ocean in the land of " Sun-facing " [1] and enjoyed nature's bounteous gifts, little did they dream of the
struggles their descendants would have to pass through in
the course of their national life, and of the results that would
be attained. Again, when the Buddhist missionaries of the
seventh and eighth centuries introduced the civilization of the
Asiatic continent into these islands, how could they foresee
the future of their religion, which after almost perishing in its
home, has been preserved in the island empire and remains a
living force of new Japan? The Pacific Ocean which once put
a check on emigration and adventure is now a great highway
which links the nation with the wide world. The Sea of Japan
and the Yellow Sea, which once presented obstacles to invaders
from the continent and gave security to the archipelago, are
nowadays the avenue of the nation's intercourse with the
neighbours across the waters. How should we regard the
vicissitudes and achievements of the nation—as the work of
a blind fate or of an intelligent Providence?

However this may be, the Japanese were ever a virile

---

[1] " Hi-mukai," now known as Hiuga, a province in the island of Kyūshū facing
the Pacific. There are numerous mounds indicating the ancient home of the people.

people who knew how to make the most of native forces and foreign contributions.   Concerted effort was a conspicuous feature, the numerous clans and tribes were practically united in early times under the rule of one powerful family; thus there was a basis for ordered progress.   The advance of civilization, however, was made possible chiefly by the universal religion of Buddhism, together with its arts and literature, and by the civic morality of Confucian ethics, with their educational methods and legal institutions, all introduced from the Asiatic continent.   Chance may have played a great part in the entrance of these inspiring and civilizing influences from the outside, but equally, perhaps more, important was the rôle played by the people themselves in receiving these importations with an open mind, tempering and refining them and stamping them with the mark of the Japanese genius.   The nation passed through the vicissitudes of its history not in blind submission to chance or fate but in an inspired enthusiasm and with keen insight.   It was the ambition and aspiration of the national leaders and the plasticity of the people that made possible a long record of national effort and achievement.

The people now known as the Japanese have inhabited, ever since the dawn of their history, the group of islands skirting Eastern Asia.   When they first appear on the stage of history they are fairly united as a people, though still crude in civilization.   The people were not a homogeneous group. The aborigines, the hairy and deep-eyed Ainus, seem once to have extended over nearly the whole archipelago, but were driven farther and farther to the east and north by immigrants or invaders.   The origin of these latter is still obscure : they were probably not of one stock.   One strong group of them settled down first in the island of Tsukushi (now Kyūshū) and along the northern coasts of the main island.   This group was destined to become the rulers of the whole country and the chief stock of the people. They were of a higher type than the aborigines, having middle-sized stature, oblong face, dark hair and eyes, and usually an aquiline nose. In addition to these there came invaders from the south, probably Malayans, by way of the Black Stream or along the chain of small islands. These flat-faced people of quick temper thrust themselves among the earlier occupants of the archipelago and finally succeeded in establishing themselves along the southern coasts at various points.

During this period of the subjugation of the aborigines and the struggles in the south, the pressure of migration in northern Asia and the dynastic changes in China and Korea drove other immigrants and invaders over to the islands. The immigrants were peaceful Chinese and Koreans who became useful instruments in the civilizing work of the chief stock. The invaders who came later were barbarians from the forests and coasts of Siberia. They attacked the islands in the Sea of Japan and the northern coasts, but were repulsed or finally assimilated.

In spite of diverse elements and the constant influx of new blood, the people of Japan were able to achieve national unity comparatively early in their history, and a noteworthy fact is that there exists among them hardly any sense of race division or antagonism.[1] This is partly due to the geographical features of the country—the rough seas surrounding it, and its long and narrow shape divided into numerous valleys and plains by mountain ranges. Sailing was far too difficult for new-comers to arrive in large numbers; the few who came at one time were readily assimilated; and on the main island the rulers were able to drive the unruly tribes farther and farther along the length of the island, and so gradually to unify the territory.

[1] One exception is a group known as *Eta*, living scattered in Central and Western Japan. Their origin and history are obscure. In recent times they organized a nation-wide movement demanding equal treatment.

By far the more important factor, however, in the attainment of national unity was the character and ability of the chief stock. They were strong and daring and were united by the belief that they descended from the heavenly gods, among whom the supreme deity, the Sun-goddess, was believed to be the ancestral protectress of the royal family and the nation. The direction of the people's migration seems always to have been to the east, and it is said that in battle they avoided facing the sun. In their progress, the victorious race established the cult of their gods among the conquered, and embraced these into the communion of worship. Ardour and ability, daring spirit and versatile temper, military valour with religious fervour, these qualities can be seen throughout their history and remain in some degree the heritage of the people.

The sympathetic heart of the people is shown in their sentiment for nature and in their love of order in communal life. Close affinity with nature is shown in their life and poetry. This may be due partly to the influence of the land and climate and partly to the early attainment of settled agricultural civilization. Traversed everywhere by passable mountain ranges, rich in streams and lakes, the land was favourable to settled abodes and the development of communal life. The mild climate, the variety of scenery, the rich flora and sea-products, and the remarkable absence of beasts of prey, contributed greatly to the development of a peace-loving disposition and ability to establish order and attain solidarity.

In the earliest period of Japanese history the chief scene of action was the Pacific coast, which is blessed with almost perpetual spring. Although this side of the country is visited by typhoons, and the sea is sometimes rough, the life of the people is passed much in the open air, and the fields are bright throughout the year with grasses and flowers. A feeling of

idyllic peace comes over anyone looking at the farmers
working among the yellow blossoms of the rape, or hearing
the songs of the fishermen rowing their boats on the calm
sea-water reflecting the golden purple of the setting sun.
Such are the scenes to-day ; in olden times they were surely
not essentially different. The blue waters of the many bays
and inlets, the gentle slopes of the mountains, the graceful
curves of the volcanoes, and the abrupt promontories over-
grown with fantastic trees, these picturesque scenes cannot
fail to awaken in a responsive heart a tender love for nature.
These natural blessings remain ever a benignant influence
upon the sentimental life of the nation.

The sympathetic response of the heart, the receptive
movement of thought, and the flexibility of mind were fostered
by the influence of the physical environment and quickened
by frequent contact with other civilizations. The course
and destiny of Japanese civilization were determined, then,
by the inherent character of the people, combined with external influences. The people were able to assimilate new-
comers, as well as to adapt the various streams of civilization
and religion which were introduced one after another from
the Asiatic continent. Not only undisturbed by these importations and impacts, but ever turning them to their own
advantage, the people made vigorous efforts towards progress.
The incessant impact of new influences sometimes dazzled
their minds, but equilibrium was soon restored ; the Japanese
proved themselves able to handle the new problems, adapting
the foreign civilization to their own genius and to the needs
of circumstance.

The island empire in this way became a repository for the
various arts, religions, and literatures of the Asiatic continent,
and has preserved many things which have been lost in their
continental homes. A large part of the interest in Japanese
history lies in the variety of these importations and in the

modes of the people's reaction towards them.  The whole
history is a record of these actions and reactions, which produced varieties of culture, rich in struggles and compromises,
conflicts and combinations.  To-day it is hardly possible to
distinguish exactly what was original and what foreign, yet
the fundamental character of the people seems to have
remained fairly unchanged, highly responsive but hardly
penetrating, active and seldom pensive.  On the other hand,
while a completely free and independent development of
the people's faith and ideas was made impossible by the
powerful foreign influences, the latter always invigorated
and elevated the indigenous qualities.  It is not otherwise
even to-day, when Japan is no more an isolated nation of the
Far East but a world-power playing her political and cultural
rôles in various ways, when her ancient heritage of civilization in all its phases is facing the impact of the tremendous
forces of modern civilization.

### Religions in Japan

Speaking in a general way, Shinto, the indigenous religion,
was an outcome of the people's life and temperament, closely
connected with national traditions and social institutions.
Shinto was originally an unorganized religion, having hardly
any system of doctrine; but its cult well embodied the nation's
ideas and sentiments, and its influence has persisted throughout the vicissitudes of the nation's history.   National unity
and  social  solidarity  were  always  maintained  by  the
reverence towards the ruling family, belief in the divine origin
of the Throne being inseparable from the worship of the
Sun-goddess.  This notion of the divine dignity of the Throne
has its historical development, but has always played an
integral part in political and social institutions, together with
the related cult of ancestral deities and national heroes.  The

idea of family perpetuation and the importance of communal life played no less important parts ; the virtues of valour and fidelity, as well as the faithful observance of family traditions, were always integral factors of the indigenous religion. The fate of this ancestral religion in an industrial régime like the present is a grave question, yet the part that Shinto still plays in the ideas and life of the nation must be fully reckoned with.

Confucianism, the ethical system of the northern Chinese, came into Japan and gave impetus to the further development of her national life. Its teaching furnished materials for social institutions, political organization, the systematization of moral precepts. Early Shinto had no clear conception of loyalty or filial piety, the virtues which played so important a part in the moral life of the people. The very names for these were supplied by Confucianism, giving a systematic teaching of morality and supplying the methods of instruction. Chinese metaphysics and religious practices played some part, but they degenerated into methods of divination. When, later on, Japan received Confucian ethics furnished with a metaphysical background, it was in the form of Chinese ideas modified by Hindu speculation. The Confucian influence in Japan was always more conspicuous in the sphere of legal and educational institutions than in the domain of religious sentiment; civic institutions and moral teaching were the Chinese contributions to Japan.

In addition to these influences, Buddhism served to consummate and give vitality to the religious life of the Japanese by stimulating universal ideals and refining their religious and æsthetic sentiments. The religion of Buddha was first adopted by the people to satisfy their yearnings for a beyond, and it supplied abundant material for transcendental speculation. It guided the mind of the people to broader visions and deeper mysteries than had ever been dreamt of by them.

The arts and literature were vigorously stimulated, methods of spiritual training elaborately worked out, ecclesiastical institutions organized, a system of cosmology and eschatology taught, with scenes of the future life delineated graphically, and, too, occult practices introduced by Buddhism.

The Buddhism introduced into Japan was *Mahāyāna*, or the Broader Communion, together with its many-sided cults and philosophical systems.   This form of Buddhism had absorbed various ideas and practices with which it had come into contact in Central Asia and China, and it brought over to Japan all those manifold elements.   However, the Japanese were always prone to neutralize extremes and extravagances and to adapt the various phases of Buddhism to their own needs.   Thus Japanese Buddhism is quite a distinct branch of Buddhism differing from any of the Continental types. Another point to be noted is that not a few scriptures and traditions lost in India and China have been preserved in Japan, and that through them a continuous development of the different forms of Buddhism can be traced.

The history of Japanese religions and morals shows in this way the interaction of various forces which manifested their vitality more in combination than in opposition.   A saying ascribed to Prince Shōtoku, the founder of Japanese civilization, compares the three religious and moral systems found in Japan to the root, the stem and branches, and the flowers and fruits of a tree.   Shinto is the root embedded in the soil of the people's character and national traditions ; Confucianism is seen in the stem and branches of legal institutions, ethical codes, and educational systems; Buddhism made the flowers of religious sentiment bloom and gave the fruits of spiritual life.   These three systems were moulded and combined by the circumstances of the times and by the genius of the people into a composite whole of the nation's spiritual and moral life.   In the fifteenth century, however, the line between Buddhism and the other systems became marked, and finally the combination broke up in the course of the following centuries. Nevertheless, the three systems have been so intricately and delicately interwoven in the head and heart of the people, that the Japanese even to-day are, consciously or unconsciously, followers of these various teachings at the same time, no one system being absolutely excluded.

A point to be noted in this process of amalgamation is the tolerance displayed; throughout the whole history of the contact and combination there are only exceptional instances of persecution and religious wars. This was largely due to the pragmatic nature of the people, which restrained them from running to extremes and bigotry. Another cause is to be sought in the nature of the imported religions themselves. Confucianism was a system of practical ethics caring little for creed and dogma, while Buddhism was a religion preeminently idealistic and tolerant. These two systems never came into conflict until the bigoted Confucianists of the seventeenth century began to attack Buddhism, for a motive which was not purely religious.[1] However, we may say on the whole that tolerance prevailed, while the contact never resulted either in full harmony or in complete absorption of one by another. The comparative absence of antagonism may partly be due to the tendency to keep apart the transcendental aspects of religious ideal and the practical morality of daily life, as if there were a division between the two phases of life. Solution was always sought in practical compromise, not in speculative or logical pursuit of consequences.

Another point to be noted in connection with tolerance is the relationship between the State and religion. Shinto was always supported by the Government and the community,

---

[1] Similarly, the persecution of Catholics in the seventeenth century pursued with fierce vigour to their practical extermination was motivated not so much by religious considerations as political and social.

having its place of worship in every locality, but it never achieved the organization of a State church. Buddhism, on the other hand, for some time secured the power of a State church and its prelates attained the dignity of State functionaries, yet it never attempted to suppress other religions but always endeavoured to absorb them. Confucianism played the rôle of a useful instrument of government, but seldom claimed exclusive authority. In this way the Government kept the reins of control over religious institutions, while the people, including the clergy and laity, followed the lead of the governing classes. This condition prevailed so long as the nation was ruled by a central Government and the Throne was regarded as the highest authority in religion and morality. But when the country was divided into feudal states, the religious bodies began to combat one another, meddling in the strife for feudal territories. Thus, in the age of warfare lasting through the fifteenth and sixteenth centuries, bloody battles were fought among Buddhist sects, while at the same time the Catholic missions were involved in the confusion of the day and were finally expelled.

In this way, the voice and interests of the central government in the first stage, and of the predominant clans or of feudal lords in the latter stage, determined the fate of religious institutions and missionary movements. Government control, patronage by the nobles, or the lead taken by the upper classes, almost always guided the sentiment and conscience of the people at large. There were, of course, exceptional instances when a strong personality asserted himself or the common people raised their voice, as was the case in the thirteenth century. Moreover, conditions are now changing rapidly, and the moral and religious life of the nation is entering on a new stage of personal freedom and individual choice. This struggle for freedom and self-assertion on the part of the people is a result of new conditions brought about by the impact of a new civilization, especially the industrial régime ; though the outcome is yet to be seen, the current will never flow towards the old régime of mere subserviency. It remains still a question what rôle will be played by the newly introduced Christianity, which is itself facing a crisis in its home as a result of the problems of modern civilization.

## Epochs of Religious History

(1) The original religion of the Japanese was an unorganized worship of the deities and spirits, both of nature and of the dead. At the dawn of history this religion, known by the name of Shinto, was beginning to develop more or less articulate expressions of hero and ancestor worship, with a background of nature worship. The cult of heroes and ancestors was an integral part of social tradition, and the clan or communal life of the people derived its sanction and solidarity from the worship of those divinities. When the tribes and clans were gradually amalgamated under the power and prestige of a ruling family who were believed to have descended from the Sun-goddess, this goddess was revered as the supreme deity of Shinto, and her worship became the central feature of the national cult. These two aspects of the Shinto religion, communal and national, were gaining in force at the dawn of the historical age, and that tradition plays even nowadays a considerable part in the social and spiritual life of the nation.

(2) The gradual introduction of Chinese civilization, dating from about the third century of the Christian era, and that of Buddhism in the sixth century, were concomitant with a vigorous social growth and the progress of national unity. The nation was beginning to learn new things from the then flourishing culture of the Asiatic continent, and Buddhism

gave a vital impetus to the development of civilization by inspiring higher ideals and encouraging the arts and literature. The new religion imported arts and science, letters and philosophy, all working as instruments of its propagation, and through the astounding progress of its missionary work the whole country was almost transformed into a Buddhist land in the course of the seventh century. A close alliance was established between the throne and the religion, since the consolidation of the nation under the sovereignty of the ruler was greatly supported by the fidelity of the imported religion to the Government, while the works of Buddhist propaganda were much extended and facilitated by the encouragement of the ruling classes. Thus in the course of about three hundred years after its introduction, Buddhism became firmly established in the national life of Japan and manifested the glories of its culture in many ways.

(3) Marked national unity and centralized government had been achieved at the turn of the eighth and ninth centuries. The mutual assistance of the Buddhist hierarchy and the court bureaucracy was the leading feature of the social, religious, and political life throughout the following three centuries. This period, called the reign of " Peace and Ease," was indeed the classical period of Japanese culture. A deep inspiration derived from Buddhism marked the sentiment and life of the people, so that we could date from the tenth century the ripening of national literature profoundly tinged with Buddhist sentiment. The over-refined teaching of Buddhism, with its mysteries and artistic displays, transformed the aristocrats, the chief patrons of this religion and its hierarchy, into effeminate and decadent sentimentalists. This degeneracy of the court nobles weakened the central Government, and the end of the bureaucratic régime was concurrent with the strong reaction of military men, who lived in the provinces and were little touched by sentimentality.

The change consummated in the last part of the twelfth century signalized a revival of the native vigour of the provincial people, which led to the establishment of a feudal régime ûnder a military dictatorship.

(4) The thirteenth century marks a significant epoch in the history of Japan. Together with the political and social changes which occurred in that century, new religions or new forms of Buddhism arose in response to the spiritual demands of the people at large. Buddhism ceased to be an affair of national polity and became the question of individual piety. The warlike spirit of the age found its reflection in religion too, and militant leaders of Buddhism appeared side by side with masters of spiritual training adapted to the life of the warriors. Institutions gave way to individual character, and strong men carried out missionary work, not only apart from the authorities but often against them. In this respect the thirteenth century saw a new trait in the religious movement, and this new spirit manifested its vigour in artistic and literary movements also.

Further changes occurred in the fourteenth century. A political revolution and civil wars leading to dynastic division took place. This crisis of imperial prestige gave impetus to a revival of national Shinto ideas, which found their mouthpiece in some patriots who attempted to concentrate all the moral ideas and religious teachings existing in Japan in the adoration of the Throne. But the trend of the times ran against the patriotic moralists, while the signs of moral degeneration and social disintegration became more and more evident. Religious strife raged side by side with feudal wars. The confusion lasted over two hundred years, until the middle of the sixteenth century, when prospects for peace began to dawn. Confusion was aggravated by the arrival of the Jesuit missionaries in the middle of the fifteenth century, which was followed by the rapid progress of their propaganda, the bloody persecution of the converts, and the final expulsion.

(5) The restoration of peace and political unity at the beginning of the seventeenth century was followed by the extermination of Catholic propaganda and foreign intercourse. This policy of seclusion produced far-reaching results in the political, social, intellectual, moral, and religious life of the nation during the following three centuries. Buddhism, now made a useful tool against Christianity, enjoyed various privileges, and its clergy lived in ease and luxury. The military Government established a State orthodoxy of moral teaching, and the social order was firmly established and maintained by the combined power of these orthodox ethics and the strong feudal Government. The reign of feudalism in national seclusion made possible strict rules for class distinction, rigid enforcement of the laws that made for peace, a peace which tended to stagnant formalism in all phases of national life. Refinement and over-refinement of life and sentiment within the prescribed limits were the result, which finally provoked a spirit of revolt and desire for change on the part of vigorous minds. Meanwhile, towards the end of the eighteenth century, Occidental powers, then aiming at the Pacific Ocean, began to knock at the door of the secluded nation, and the pressure from the outside worked to accelerate revolutionary movements arising within. These combined forces finally overthrew the feudal régime in the middle of the nineteenth century and restored the imperial authority, which was regarded as the essential condition for national unity in an age of international intercourse and competition.

(6) The opening of the country to foreign intercourse in 1859, and the restoration of the imperial régime in 1868, led to the shaking off of all the restraints that had made for peace. The Government and the people, in the frenzy of entering into a new era, gave indiscriminate welcome to Western civilization.

The foundation of new institutions, the growth of industry and commerce, the inauguration of constitutional government, the prospects and problems consequent upon two foreign wars, all contributed to the rise of many problems quite new to the nation's experience. Social life was full of vigour but everything was passing through the difficulties of transition, caused by the time-honoured inheritance of Oriental culture coming into conflict with the new civilization introduced from the Occident. The contact and reaction betweeen the various religions, old and new, was bewildering, and the struggle between conservative reaction and radical extremes was very fierce. Just as the tide of these difficulties was ominously rising, the death of the great ruler in 1912 was followed by the World War. The changing and conflicting currents cannot fail to affect all phases of the nation's life. Now the imminent problems of social and political situations, the conflicts between capital and labour, the cleavage between the old and new generations as regards their attitudes towards life, these seem to overshadow the questions of religious piety or moral ideals. Japan is facing the double difficulties of going through a transition from the feudal régime, with its ideas and forces still persisting more or less, to the industrial régime of modern civilization, and of setting all the problems arising out of the anomalies consequent upon the rapid infusion of imported culture which is in itself being questioned as to its destiny. Religion is naturally involved in this perplexing situation, and no one would dare to foretell the outcome; yet the past experiences and achievements of the Japanese nation may point to the possibility of a certain way of establishing harmony.

BOOK I

THE SHINTO RELIGION

AND

THE COMMUNAL SYSTEM
EARLY STAGES AND SURVIVAL

# GENERAL FEATURES OF SHINTO

" In that Land there were numerous deities (or spirits) which shone with a lustre like that of fireflies, and evil deities which buzzed like flies. There were also trees and herbs which could speak." [1] This is said of the Japanese archipelago when the founder of the nation meditated descending from heaven to the country. And it is said in another connection : " The God who originally founded this country is the God who descended from Heaven and established this State in the period when Heaven and Earth became separated, and when the trees and herbs had speech." Imagine a religion amounting to the worship of these deities or spirits and lacking almost any system of moral teachings or metaphysical doctrines. It cannot but be called " primitive," if not in a strictly anthropological sense. Certain systems have, from time to time, been established on the basis of those primitive ideas, and indeed attempts, more or less successful, have been made to lay the foundation of a national life on the worship of the " Deity who originally established this State." The beliefs and practices pertaining to those deities and spirits remain even in these days of the twentieth century a living force among the people, and represent the basic elements of their religious and social life, out of which new offshoots of religion or quasi-religion may and do arise. The whole complex of beliefs and worship is known by the name of *Shinto*, which means the " Way of the Gods (or Spirits)," and it may be

[1] *Nihon-gi, Chronicles of Japan* (tr. by W. G. Aston, London, 1896), vol. i, p. 64 and vol. ii, p. 77.

called the national or popular religion of the Japanese, as it was their ancient and indigenous religion.

The designation was, however, made in the sixth century in order to distinguish the native religion from Buddhism, and its being called a " Way " may be due to the influence of Taoism, the Chinese religion of the " Way." Now the latter is a religion which regards supernormal attainments in corporeal life as the ideal aim or ultimate potentiality of human beings, in contrast to the social and moral teachings of Confucianism. A combination of naturalism and supernaturalism, it exercised a great influence upon popular beliefs in China and Korea, and it is no wonder that the Shinto theorists found in it congenial features and adopted some Taoist ideas and practices.[1] However this may be, Shinto is fundamentally not so much a religious system as a complex of ancient beliefs and observances which have remained comparatively unchanged through the vicissitudes of history, despite the impacts of foreign systems like Buddhism and Confucianism. Thus it is not quite unnatural that the advocates of Shinto even nowadays call their religion " The Way after the manner of the Gods," or " as it was practised by the Gods " (*Kami nagara no Michi*). But on the other hand we must not forget that attempts have repeatedly been made to organize these primitive beliefs into a national or State religion centred round the adoration of the sovereign as the descendant of the " Deity who established the State," particularly the Sun-goddess, the supreme deity of the Shinto religion. Though a clear line of demarcation can never be drawn between these two aspects of Shinto, the primitive and popular on the one side, and the national and official on the other, the distinction and connection between them can

---

[1] In fact there are many common traits in the popular beliefs among peoples of the Far East. It remains still to be investigated whether this is due to mutual influence, or to the universal prevalence of primitive beliefs, or to a common origin of their religions.

be compared to those between the mystery gods and the Olympian gods of the Greeks, as shown by Miss Harrison in her *Themis*.   The history of Shinto is a series of reactions between these two factors, to speak in a broad way, as influenced by the development of the national life in its social and political organization, and also in reaction to the overwhelming influence of Buddhism and Confucianism.

Now, the deity or spirit is called *Kami* which, though of disputed etymology, means " superior " or " sacred " or " miraculous."   Any object or being which evoked a thrill of emotion, whether affectionate or awe-inspiring, appealing to the sense of mystery, might be regarded as a Kami and accorded due respect.   Some of the Kami were thought to reside in the heavens, others to sojourn in the air or in the forests, to abide in the rocks, in the fountains, or to manifest themselves in animals or human beings.   Princes and heroes were Kami manifest in human form, or any person might become a Kami by exhibiting supernormal powers.   These gods were, as a later Shinto theorist said, men in the age of the gods, while human beings are gods in the age of men. As a matter of fact, only an aritificial line can be drawn between the Age of the Gods and that of Men, and gods, spirits, men, and any natural objects or phenomena pass easily, even in the later age of men, from one realm to the other.   " In the beginning " men and animals were gods, and plants and rocks had speech ;  but even now, according to the Shinto conception, it is not entirely otherwise.   Thus it is no wonder that out of this stuff any sort of gods can be enthroned, and that crude mysteries, often vigorous in their nascent state, come to command a certain amount of influence.

These deities or spirits were more or less personified and called such-and-such *Mikoto* (August One), or *Nushi* (Master), *Hiko* (Lord) or *Hime* (Lady), but their individuality was not always distinct.   In some cases a person or an object was regarded as a Kami in itself, but in many other cases men or objects were respected as Kami on account of their having been possessed by a certain divinity or spirit. Here again no clear distinction can be drawn between these two categories of sacred beings, nor was personification necessary in worshipping a divinity. It is also to be noted that sex distinction never played a very important part either in worship or in mythology, and that the attributes and functions of the deities were easily variable and interchangeable.[1]

In short, Shinto as a religion was an unorganized worship of spirits. It was rooted in the instinctive being of human nature feeling itself in communion with the living forces of the world and showed its vitality in the communal cult. For the worship was often connected with local legends and communal customs, and the deities thus worshipped were mostly considered to be the ancestral or tutelary spirits of the communes. Thus the communal cult was the pivot upon which the traditions and life of the people moved, wherein gods or spirits, animals and trees, even rocks and streams, were believed to be in living communion with men. In some cases, however, stories of the Kami were told as mere stories or poetic fancies about the occurrences of nature related in the fashion of human events. There were awesome mysteries in the worship side by side with playful elements in the myths; traditions and conventions played as great a part as the basic manifestations of passions and instincts, and all these factors were often so mixed that Shinto comprises religion and customs, poetry and folklore, politics and magic, among other things.

But one point to be specified in conclusion is that it was pre-eminently the religion of an agricultural people. The frequent manifestation of spirits of plants and corn, the

---

[1] On this and the following, cf. Anesaki, *Japanese Mythology*, in vol. viii of *The Mythology of all Races*. (Boston, 1928.)

intimate relationship existing between the people and the communal deities, the close ties binding the divinities with things of nature, all this indicates the life of an agricultural people settled down in close communities.  And when it had been more or less organized in the course of several centuries up to the eighth, emphasis was laid on the supremacy of the Sun-goddess, who was naturally adored as the protectress of agriculture and as the ancestress of the ruling family.  Thus the Shinto religion is not a primitive one in the strict sense, but has the traits of national religion glorifying the unity of the nation under the rulership of the emperor identified with the guardianship of the great goddess.

# SHINTO MYTHOLOGY

## *The Primordial Chaos and the Growth of Life*

神経病学

THERE was no definite theogony in Shinto, yet a certain cycle of cosmological myths may be discerned. Three deities are said to have sprung out of the primeval chaos which was like an ocean of mud veiled in darkness. The head of the triad was the Heavenly-Central-Lord (*Ame-no-minaka-nushi*), or the Eternal-Land-Ruler (*Kuni-toko-tachi*), while the two subordinates were the High-Producing (*Taka-mi-musubi*), and the Divine or Mysterious-Producing (*Kami-mi-musubi*). This latter couple seem to have symbolized the male and female principles of generation and are sometimes identified with the Divine-Male (*Kami-rogi*) and the Divine-Female (*Kami-rami*), *i.e.*, the Divine-Father and the Divine-Mother who are constantly invoked in the rituals.[1] This first triad, however, vanished without leaving posterity, and was followed by a series of similar ones, who were generated spontaneously independently from one another. All of them came out of the primeval chaos and vanished without trace. However, their titles indicate that they were intended to personify powers of spontaneous generation, such as mud, vapour, germs, were thought to be.

These deities are called the celestial deities in seven generations, in distinction from those who are said to have worked on earth, the earthly deities. It is an interesting

[1] Cf. Aston, *Shinto*, p. 35. He thinks that the primal triad is but an adoption of the Chinese triad of the ultimate reality and its two principles, *Yin* and *Yang*. It is also disputed among Japanese scholars whether Ame-no-minaka-nushi and Kuni-toko-tachi were one deity or two.

24

question whether the former belonged to the category of those deities no more worshipped, forgotten deities, or were mere abstractions borrowed from outside. Though a conclusive solution of the problem can perhaps never be expected, the present writer inclines to the former alternative, from some analogies in other religions.

The last couple of the series were the Male-who-Invites (*Izana-gi*) and the Female-who-Invites (*Izana-mi*). They are said to have descended to earth by order of the celestial deities, in order to produce the terrestrial world. Most probably they were conceived to be the earthly manifestations of the male and female principles in the primeval triad. They united and gave birth to many things, to the Japanese archipelago, first of all, and to things or spirits, such as waters, winds, mountains, fields, mists, foods, fire, and so on. This was evidently conceived as sexual generation, while on the other hand a belief in spontaneous generation and metamorphosis is betrayed even in the stories of the birth of their children; these two modes of generation were believed to exist side by side. All things produced were called Kami, deities or spirits, though only a few of them were actually worshipped. Sex distinction is made among them, but it plays no important part in the mythology and cult, probably because the Japanese mind had not yet attained a state of definite personification.

Finally, the divine couple begat the rulers of the world, the Heaven-Illumining Goddess (*Ama-terasu Ohmi-kami*), the Moon-Ruler (*Tsuki-yomi*) and the Valiant-Swift-Impetuous Hero (*Takéhaya Susanowo*).[1] The realm of light, including heaven and earth, was assigned to the Sun-goddess, the

---

[1] Another tradition is that these deities were given birth by the Male alone, when he was washing away the stains he had got in his visit to the subterranean world. This difference has no great bearing upon the cycle of myths as a whole, but it is interesting to see that, in this latter version, the sun and moon were born from the eyes and the storm-god from the nostrils.

reign of night to the Moon-god, while the ocean, together with
the domain of hidden things, was entrusted to the rule of the
Swift-Impetuous.  The Moon-god never played a prominent
part ;  the rule of the universe was divided between the two
others, a division which was to have very great importance
in mythical narratives where it is possible to discern a reflection of some political and social events, as we shall see
further.

Thus the divine couple were the originators of life on
earth, but life was associated with its necessary counterpart,
death.  The mythology tells us how the Female deity came
later to be the genius of evil and death, having died
on giving birth to fire and gone to a subterranean abode
where death and darkness prevailed.  Death in this case was
apparently conceived as through fever, and considered to be
the first instance of mortality.  The Male deity, like Orpheus,
pursued his lamented consort to her dark abode, tried to look
at her by lighting a torch, to the dismay of the Female,
because decomposition was taking place in her body.  This
act of impudence enraged the Female, and she caused the
hosts of evil spirits and furies to pursue the Male in order to
confine him in the realm of death and darkness.  Having
repulsed the pursuers, the Male reached the boundary between the dark world and the realm of light, there he blocked
up the passage with a huge rock, and the two deities exchanged
words across the barrier.  The Female threatened to kill a
thousand people in his domain, while the Male retorted by
saying that he would give birth to five hundred more than
that every day.  This story was evidently intended for an
explanation of the proportion of births and deaths in the
human world.  Thus, after all, death was unable to super-
sede life, yet the fear of death is expressed in the story, and ills
and dangers are therein identified with pollution, to be expiated by purification.  The act of purification is said to have

been inaugurated then by the Male deity who, having escaped the snare of death, washed himself in the sea. Various kinds of evil spirits came out of the dirt and stain which he had brought from the dark region. These evil spirits are believed to be still lingering among men and to cause all kinds of evil and trouble.

### The Two Rulers of the World

We hear nothing definite about the end of the Male progenitor, except that he finally hid himself, or is abiding in the Solar Palace of Youth (*Hi-no-waka-miya*).[1] After the disappearance of the primeval couple the world was transferred to the dual rule of the Sun-goddess and the Swift-Impetuous, the latter of whom showed many traits of a storm-god. The Sun-goddess, or the Heaven-illumining Lady,[2] was bright and beautiful in features, unrivalled in dignity, benign, honest, and meek in temper. She ruled wisely and brilliantly the realm assigned to her, giving light and life to all, and she also protected the rice-fields by constructing irrigation canals. Besides, she is represented as the organizer of religious rites, especially those in observance of the rules of purity. In short, she was the presiding deity of peace and order, of agriculture and the food supply. Herein we can detect a representation of the rôle womanhood played in the early rise of peaceful social order and agricultural pursuits. On the other hand, her brother, the Swift-Impetuous, was wild, arrogant, and disobedient. He cried in wild fury, disregarded all his duties, and raged in the air between heaven and earth. The details of his atrocities against his sister in heaven remind us strongly of storm-gods in other mythologies. His cry and fury are said to have been instigated by his longing for the abode of

---

[1] The shrine of Taga, in the province of Ōmi, is the chief site of his worship. There he plays the rôle of guardian of female chastity, as shown in a curious festival observed there.

[2] She is also called *Oh-hiru-me-muchi*, the Great Mistress of the Day.

his mother, who had become the genius of death and darkness. In this respect the Storm-god is often identified with the mighty evil spirit ruling the invisible world—a feature which, as we shall presently see, is inherited by his posterity.

The contest of the two deities is depicted in two scenes, one on the Heavenly River-basin of Peace (*Ama-no-Yasu-gawara*) and the other in the arbour where the Sun-goddess was preparing for the great feast of harvest, the foremost of Shinto festivals. The former can be taken as symbolic of the contest between sun and storm, and yet each of the deities is said to have given birth to children by the " inspiration " of the other, or by exchanging respiration and jewels. The latter story of sacrilege represents evidently a conflict in social order, but the story culminates in a scene reminding us of a solar eclipse. It runs as follows :

The Swift-Impetuous ravaged the domain of his sister by destroying the rice-fields cultivated by her, and finally by an act of sacrilege, polluting the sacred observance instituted by her. The Sun-goddess, greatly distressed by the wanton acts of her brother, but not combating him, hid herself in a cave, whereby the entire world was deprived of light, and disorder ran riot. Eight million deities assembled in front of the cave and at last succeeded in inducing her to come out, by performing charms and a ceremonial dance. When light and order had been restored by the reappearance of the goddess, all the assembly burst into a cry of joy, at the resonance of which heaven and earth trembled. This is the climax of the mythical narrative, and therein we see the triumph of light over darkness, of peace and order over savagery and destruction. This triumph of the Sun-goddess over the Storm-god secured her the rule of the world, and the belief in her as the supreme deity was associated with the tradition that the ruling family descended from the Sun-goddess.

The triumph of light over darkness was accomplished by hosts of the Kami, who stood loyally on the side of the Sun-goddess in her resistance against the opposing power. This narrative has two aspects in its bearings upon the belief and life of the people. As a myth of solar phenomena, it represents the beliefs of an agricultural people and their reverence for the sun as the source of life, as well as their practice of exorcism in case of a solar eclipse. Politically, the same beliefs resulted in the predominance of a certain family or tribe, who worshipped the goddess as their progenitrix, and in the allegiance of other tribes to that family. Thus, the Sun-goddess embodied life-giving power and wise rulership at the same time. In the former aspect she is associated with a male counterpart, the High-Producing Deity, who accompanies her as her hidden or higher entity. There is, however, also a female partner, the Abundance-Bounty Goddess (*Toyo-uke no Kami*),[1] who is even to-day worshipped besides her at Isé, the most holy of the Shinto sanctuaries. The political rôle attributed to the Sun-goddess is no less important, the belief in the divine origin of the ruling family being symbolized by the insignia of the imperial throne, a mirror, a sword, and a bead, all believed to have been handed by her to her posterity. We shall see later how these three treasures led Shinto theologians to ethical and cosmological speculations. The Sun-goddess may be called the supreme deity of the Shinto religion, and her worship occasionally gave rise to a kind of monotheism in the course of Shinto history.

On the other hand the outrageous Storm-god was banished to a remote region by the hosts assembled before the " heavenly cave." The place of exile is located in the province of Izumo on the northern coast of Japan, facing the eastern side of the Korean peninsula ; it was there, in fact, that a tribe claiming their descent from the Storm-god

---

[1] No story is told about her in the mythology. Her origin is a disputed question.

established themselves and resisted for a while the rule of
the Solar Race. As the ancestor of the Izumo tribe, the
Swift-Impetuous played the rôle of pioneer and colonizer,
and a story says that he planted, from his hair and beard,
the mountains in the province of Kii on the southern side of
Japan.[1]

The Storm-god and his sons are regarded as rulers of
Izumo and at the same time as agents of mysterious things,
including even evil-doings. This is a natural consequence
of the conception that the Storm-god was an associate or
chief of the spirits inhabiting the subterranean world ; quite
naturally the primitive mind invoked the genius of evil for
the purpose of averting ills and calamities. One of the sons
of the Storm-god was the Great Evil-doer (*Oh-Magatsumi*), the
source of all evils, while another son, the Great Land-master
(*Oh-Kuninushi*), worked for the welfare of the people in
association with his partner, the Small Prince of Renown
(*Sukuna-biko*), who is regarded as the chief of medicine-men.
On this account the deities belonging to the Izumo group
were worshipped when a pestilence raged or any disaster
took place.

The opposition between the contending powers did not,
as we might have expected, develop into a dualism like that
of the ancient Persian religion, to which Shinto has some
similarities. On the contrary, a compromise in the way of a
division of spheres was arranged between the two deities and
their descendants. The rule of the actual world in a theocratic
government was entrusted to the descendants of the Sun-
goddess, while the mysterious side of the religion, including
magic, divination, exorcism, was left to the care of the Storm-
god and his children. This pact of division is said to have

[1] A flower festival is observed in Kii in honour of the Storm-god. He is said
also to have colonized Korea, a story which may have some historical background,
indicating a connection between Korea and Izumo. Cf. Anesaki, *Japanese
Mythology*, p. 248.

been made between the children of the Storm-god and the generals sent to them by the Sun-goddess, that the " realm of the visible " should belong to the latter and the " domain of the invisible " to the Storm-god. Thus, a division between the Olympian gods and the mystery gods, to borrow an analogy from Greek religion, was decided once for all—a division which was destined to determine the nature and function of the official Shinto religion as the worship of the Sun-goddess and other deities believed to care for the welfare of the people in worldly matters. This function of the official cult, national and communal, was a strength in the sense that Shinto worship was ever closely related with the political and social life of the nation, but it was a weakness at the same time, as the official Shinto alienated itself more and more from the mysteries of religious life. The consequence was that Shinto in general has always had a tendency to formalism and officialism, and that, whenever a reaction against this formalism took place, resort was had to the occult side of the religion, and appeal made to the superstitious ideas and practices of the people.

# RELIGION AND SOCIAL LIFE

*National Cult and Communal Life*

THE general tendency of the Shinto religion at the dawn of the historical period was towards the domination of the Sun-goddess over the numerous local deities and miscellaneous spirits. This was made possible by the growing power of the ruling family (the descendants of the Sun-goddess), the several subjugated clans bringing their respective clan cults under the hegemony of the Sun-goddess. Thus the growth of national unity was a political and religious issue, and was symbolized in a central seat of worship dedicated to the Great Deity (*Oh-mi-kami*), which was established at Isé on the sea-coast facing the east. Even to-day Isé remains the holy of holies of the Shinto cult. Moreover, the worship and predominance of the Sun-goddess were accelerated by the progress of agriculture, because she was regarded as the greatest protectress of agriculture, and because the Japanese people seem to have made a rapid transition from a life of hunting and fishing to one of agriculture, especially of rice culture. Herein religious beliefs worked together with political and economic conditions. This connection is best shown in the ritual of the Harvest-prayer Festival (*Toshigoi no Matsuri*). After the invocation of various deities, it says : [1]

> More especially do I humbly declare in the mighty presence of the Great Heaven-shining Deity who dwells in Isé. Because the Great Deity has

---

[1] From Aston, *Shinto*, pp. 283-4, with a few alterations. The codification of this and other rituals dates from early in the ninth century, but they preserve some ancient characteristics in idea and wording.

bestowed on him (the sovereign) the lands of the four quarters over which her glance extends as far as where the walls of Heaven rise, as far as where the bounds of Earth stand up, as far as the blue sky extends, as far as where the white clouds settle down ; by the blue sea-plain, as far as the prows of ships can reach without letting dry their poles and oars ; by land, as far as the hoofs of horses can go, with tightened baggage-cords, treading their way among rock-beds and tree-roots where the long roads extend, continuously widening the narrow regions and making the steep regions level, in drawing together, as it were, the distant regions by throwing over them (a net of) many ropes—therefore let the first-fruits for the Sovran Deity be piled up in her mighty presence like a range of hills, leaving the remainder for him (the sovereign) tranquilly to partake of.

Moreover, whereas you bless the Sovran Grandchild's reign as a long reign, firm and enduring, and render it a happy and prosperous reign, I plunge down my neck cormorant-wise in reverence to you as our Sovran's dear, divine ancestress, and fulfil your praise by making these plenteous offerings on his behalf.

Here we see pictured all the clansmen coming together to pray for harvest and welfare, joining in the worship of the genius of life and growth, the progenitrix of the ruling family. Similarly instituted was the thanksgiving for harvest, the Festival of First Fruits (*Nii-name*), celebrated at midnight in the late autumn, observed annually even to-day. It is the most solemn and mysterious of all the Shinto ceremonies, the deity worshipped being unknown or unmentioned and all the performance being carried on in darkness, except for a few torches in the holy precinct. The Sun-goddess herself is believed to have served in this ceremony as the chief priestess, and hence the Emperor alone always serves as the chief priest. His person is in direct communion with the unnamed Deity, or he is identified with the Deity, and what he performs in the worship remains a sealed mystery to all but himself. Yet all those who participate in the ceremony outside the inner sanctuary are supposed to share the mysterious union, in darkness and to ancient music.

The supremacy of the Sun-goddess had thus been established, but it never suppressed the tribal cults and the com-

munal life of the clans. The whole history of Japan, in its
social and political aspects, exhibits a series of compromises
as well as conflicts of the two forces, union and division,
the national principle and the clan interest. Similarly there
were changes of religious ideas tending alternately to unity
and plurality, or monotheistic and polytheistic tendencies ;
these two phases are indicated by the tenacious persistence
of the tribal and local cults beside the national cult of
the Sun-goddess, while the simple pure faith of the people
often led them to a monotheistic worship of the supreme
deity.

The people settled in agricultural pursuits along valleys
or on lake-sides were separated from one another by hills
and inlets, and the groups made up compact communities
bound by clan kinship and communal traditions. The clan
was called *uji*, which meant birth or blood relationship, and
each of the clans kept to its native soil and communal cult.
The clan deity (*uji-gami*) was conceived as the progenitor of
the *uji*, or as the tutelary spirit of the locality ; in many cases
the local chthonian deity was identified with the ancestral.
Many clans derived their descent from a certain nature-god,
such as the spirit of water or of wind, as there was no sharp
distinction between a deity of nature and a spirit of the dead.
The clan cult was the centre of the communal life, resting on
the communion of the deity and the people, as well as on the
common beliefs, observances, and traditions, all closely knit
into the daily life of the people and their attachment to the
soil they inherited.

The clan deity was usually represented by a symbol and
enshrined in a simple sanctuary erected at a spot commanding the best view of the locality, and in many cases occupying
a strategic point. The sanctified spot was carefully guarded
and kept scrupulously clean. The simple, sober-looking shrine
standing in the dim light of the woods inspired the people

with the presence of a divine spirit. The sacred grove furnished a prominent landmark in every locality and was associated with the legendary lore of the community, its ancestors and heroes, or genii and fairies. The communal sanctuary was also the place where periodical celebrations and social gatherings were held, all connected with various phases of social life as well as with the change of the seasons and the associated festivities. Thus the Shinto religion was deeply rooted in the soil of the national spirit, patriotism in the narrower but original sense. Just as men lived in communion with the gods and they together made up the communal life, so nature and the physical surroundings played a no less important part in moulding religious sentiment.[1] These remarks hold true to a great extent concerning village life in modern Japan. This aspect of Shinto may be called the Hellenic feature in Japanese life, because the religious and social life of the people is manifested in festivities and in connection with the poetry of nature.

Shinto, in this way, derived its continuity largely from its function as a communal cult, in which the observance of rites and customs was supported by the sanction and tradition of the community. The reason for the sanctity of traditional rules was that they were believed to have originated in divine or ancestral ordinances. The most important of the observances was that of purity and ablution in ceremonies as well as in daily life. The worst offence was violation of the rules of purity. Impurities were of various kinds, such as birth, blood, disease, corpses ; contact with any of these required ablution, usually by bathing in a stream, often accompanied by fasting. Unconscious or involuntary offences were washed away, while conscious offences were expiated by penance or fines paid to

[1] This is the reason why local legends play so great a part in Shinto lore. They were collected in the eighth century (beginning in 713), and were called *Fu-do-ki*, " Records of Air and Soil "

the community in the presence of the divine spirit. Cases of
civil and penal offences were decided by ordeal, " divine
punishment," generally banishment. Thus, morality, religious
observances, laws and customs were interwoven, and their
inculcation rested upon the shoulders of the community,
represented by an assembly of priests and elders. Grave
offences on the part of any member of the community were
believed to draw divine wrath upon the whole community,
and therefore propitiation was required from the community
as well as from the individual. However, these ordinances
were rarely formulated but were mostly handed down in
traditional customs. This is one of the reasons why the
priesthood has played little part outside merely ceremonial
observances.

### Tribal Ethics, Authority of the Community

Scrupulous fidelity to tradition is everywhere a characteristic of tribal religion. Its morality is based upon the sanctity
of the communal life amounting to the adoration of blood
kinship and the observance of social rules. The individual is
almost nothing in the face of the community, and unreasoning
submission to social sanction is the essential condition of
individual life. Authority and tradition, not the person and
conscience, are the ultimate foundation of morality which,
though remaining still in force, are being modified by the
influence of modern civilization on village life. This has been
the strength and at the same time the weakness of Japanese
morality. It was the force that solidified the feudal régime
and still sustains the solidarity of the people as a body. On
the other hand, the lack of individual initiative and the
tyranny of the community over the individual have often
produced evils, and the history of the nation has exhibited

in many phases the conflict between group control and individual freedom.[1]

There was in the primitive society of the Japanese no systematic teaching of morality nor any definite codification of social and political institutions. This was yet to be achieved, awaiting the help of Chinese civilization.[2]   Philosophical elaboration of ideas and beliefs was far beyond the ken of the primitive faith, and it was Buddhism that supplemented this defect.

Shinto morality emphasized the virtue of submission, while its aggressive aspect was exhibited in valour and militancy.   Clan division was necessarily associated with strife, even among the clans adhering to the central authority of the ruling family.  Combat was regarded as the affair of the whole clan, and therefore of the clan deity.  Thus people fought with religious zeal, and it was everyone's duty to do his best according to the ordinance of tradition, and to die for the clan or its chief.  Submission was not mere renunciation but demanded action and valour.  The old saying, " Face the flying arrows, never turn thy back towards them," represented this temperament.  A warrior poet of the eighth century sang :—

> Serve our Sovran at sea,
> Our sodden corpses leaving to the salt sea,
> Serve our Sovran by land,
> Our corpses leaving amid the wild-waste bushes ;
> Rejoice to die in our dread Sovran's cause,
> Never looking back from the border of the battles.[3]

This he sang, to be sure, as an old tradition among his clansmen, and the wording is not his own.  Though loyalty

---

[1] Cf. the author's article in the *Open Court* (April, 1917) : *The Idea of Moral Heritage in the Japanese Family.*  We shall return to the point several times in the following chapters.

[2] The chauvinist Shintoists of the eighteenth century boasted that primitiveness was the criterion of holiness, as sanctioned by derivation from the gods, and that the Chinese had needed ethics because they were immoral.

[3] *Mannyō-shū*, Dickins' translation, vol. ii. p. 263.

towards the sole sovereign was a product of gradual growth, service done for the clan and valour in its cause were coeval with the communal cult of the Shinto religion. We shall see later how these militant qualities manifested themselves in the twelfth century, in connection with the rise of the military men in the provinces and the consequent foundation of a feudal régime.

The military aspect of Shinto morality is shown in the instances of swords, spears, bows and arrows being worshipped as deities or as their symbols. Naturally, Susanowo, the raging spirit of Storm, represented this militant aspect, and it is said that he presented to his sister, the Sun-goddess, a sword which he had discovered in the body of the dragon slain by him. This sword is believed to have later been used by Prince Yamato-takeru, or Japan-valiant, in his military expeditions, and it is now enshrined in a sanctuary.[1] More mythical personifications of the warlike spirit are the Sharp-Cutting-Lord (*Futsu-nushi*), and the Valiant-August-Thunder (*Take-mika-zuchi*), who are said to have subjugated the unruly gods of Izumo at the behest of the Sun-goddess. These deities are worshipped at Kashima and Katori in eastern Japan, as the tutelary spirits of outposts against the Ainus in the northeast, and it is possible that they commemorate certain fighters. A rock is shown in Kashima which is said to have been thrust by the August-Thunder deep into earth as the sign of his firm grasp of the country. It is interesting to see that further development of the warlike spirit was always associated with the worship of the patrons of military families, while the Sun-goddess played the rôle of peace-maker, as the

---

[1] This sword is one of the three Insignia of the Throne. The two others are a mirror and a crooked ornamental bead, believed to symbolize the soul of the Sun-goddess, its sagacity and clemency respectively. The mirror is deposited in the sanctuary of Isé and the bead or jewel is in the personal possession of the Emperor. Further on we shall see the symbolic doctrines concerning these three as propounded by the later Shinto theorists.

progenitrix of the ruling family and the presiding deity of agriculture. Thus, the militant aspect of Japanese morality was a manifestation of the Shinto religion as a tribal cult, whereas national unity as embodied in the worship of the Sun-goddess represented the peace-loving disposition of the people and their submission to the sovereign.

### Idea of the Soul

Belief in spirits was the basis of the ancient Shinto religion; but in spite of this, the conception of the human soul and its future conditions was very vague. Yet undoubtedly there existed an idea of the soul and belief in its future life. The Land of Gloom (*Yomotsu-kuni*) or the Bottom-Land (*Sokotsu-kuni*), where the Female-who-Invites reigned as the genius of ills and death, was a kind of Hades. Apparently it was conceived to be somewhere in the subterranean world. In the heavenly world, the Plain of High Heaven (*Takama-no-hara*), celestial beings reside, presided over by the Sun-goddess. Probably the human soul was thought to go after death to one of these regions, but the legends speak of future life only in connection with deities or great men. Possibly the souls of common mortals were believed to vanish sooner or later. Objects excavated from ancient tombs show that various utensils and even human beings were buried beside the remains of a dead lord or lady, undoubtedly with the intention that he or she might enjoy comfort and service in the future life. Only a faint idea of an eternal life is indicated by the name *Toko-yo*, or " Perpetual Country," which is sometimes identified with the heavenly plains, but oftener believed to mean a country beyond the sea where oranges grow. At any rate, the soul, if it continued to exist at all, was believed to sojourn among its former fellow-beings for an indefinite period, and both the Heavenly Plain and the

Bottom-Land were considered to be not very far away from this world.

Perhaps more important than the question of the future life was the activity of the soul apart from its bodily confine- ment. The soul was believed to be composed of two parts, one mild, refined, and happy, the other rough, brutal, and raging (the mild, *nigi-mitama*, and the rough, *ara-mitama*). The former cares for its possessor's health and prosperity, while the latter performs adventurous tasks or even malicious deeds. Either of them can leave the body and appear to the astonishment of its possessor himself. The *nigi-mitama* is also designated as, or subdivided into, *saki-mitama* (happy, prosperous) and *kushi-mitama* (wondrous, mysterious). This is the ordinary interpretation, but the author is inclined to identify this dual division with the one stated above. It is not clear whether every deity or human being was believed to possess double souls, or powerful persons only. Certain, however, it is that the idea of the soul was associated with breathing, and it is called *tama*, which means a precious or mysterious thing (globular in form as a rule). Another name for the soul, *tama-shii*, seems to mean " mysterious breathing ", and probably the word *shinu*, to die, the departure of breath.[1] According to the popular belief, which prevails even nowadays, the soul quits the body at the moment of death ; it may often be seen lingering as a pale fire-ball flying in darkness.

### Cult and Priesthood

The Shinto sanctuary was very simple, as was quite natural in a rather primitive religion, yet remarkably simpler than in many other religions. Its simplicity is due not merely to the preservation of its primitive character, but in many

---

[1] The derivation of the word *shinu* from *sugi-inu,* "to pass away," is far- fetched or betrays a rationalist bias. The philologists who insist on this ex- planation overlook the ancient word for wind, which is *shi*, as in the case of *Shinatsu-hiko*, the god of wind

PLATE I

A

B

**A SHINTO TEMPLE, KAMI-GAMO NEAR MIYAKO**
Note the combination of Nature and Architecture

A. Seen through the woods
B. Nearer the buildings, representing Syncretic Shinto Architecture

cases to deliberate purity and intentional austerity. The deity was worshipped, in the remote ages of prehistoric antiquity, at a hallowed ground enclosed by trees or fences planted around a square and marked off by a sanctified rope of straw. The enclosure was either temporary or permanent and called *himorogi*, which is explained in various ways, often in mystic interpretations by later Shintoists, but it seems to have meant an abode of the deity. There were also sacred grounds surrounded by stones, like Stonehenge of the Druids (they were called *iwa-ki*, stone enclosure, or *kōgo*, divine abode), the remains of which are found mostly in western Japan. These primitive sanctuaries were gradually replaced by the shrines which mark the Shinto sanctuaries of to-day. But these shrines are mostly built in wooded places and preserve the atmosphere of primitive nature-worship.

The construction of the shrine is extremely simple— straight pillars thrust into the earth, covered by a thatched roof. There is no decorative effect, except the conventional- ized ends of the beams projecting in an oblique cross over the angle of the roof. A shrine of this kind is called *yashiro*, *i.e.*, miniature of a dwelling-house, and its model is evidently taken from a human abode. The architecture can hardly be called artistic, yet the unvarnished pillars exhibit a singularly attractive simplicity and the whole structure an archaic sobriety. The situation of the sombre-looking shrine among old trees in the dim light of wooded places contributes very much to the austerity of the sanctuary. This sequestered solemnity is characterized by words such as *kōgōshi*, " god- like, very godlike," or *kami-sabi*, " divinely serene." The Shinto Japanese have never built a stone cathedral ; their holy places were temples of nature wherein a group of huge trees rivalled a Gothic tower.[1]

[1] Cf. Lafcadio Hearn, *Gleanings in Buddha-fields*, chapter on " A Living God." See Plate I.

Every hallowed spot of ground or sanctified object is marked off by a straw rope, as referred to above, from which pieces of paper hang. It is called *shime-nawa*, or demarcation rope, and its purpose is to keep off evil influences. Another symbol of sanctity is a small pole of wood or bamboo, in which is inserted a piece of paper or cloth, so cut that the two parts hang down on the two sides of the pole and each part looks plaited. This is called *nusa* (or *gohei*) and was originally an offering of cloth, which was converted to a symbol of sanctity or divinity. Another sign of a Shinto sanctuary is the *tori-i* which stands at the entrance to every sanctuary. It is a simple structure, either in wood or stone, made up of two quadrangular beams laid horizontally above the head and supported by two round columns. This is the portal, and it stands at the entrance to a long avenue of trees, and at intervals as well as in front of the shrine. A temporary entrance is occasionally constructed by making a large ring by binding sheaves of a kind of reed. Thus, the portals, the avenue, and the woods, together with the shrine and various sacred symbols, make up a Shinto sanctuary. A well or rock is sanctified within the precinct for the use of the deity; and similarly a fountain is provided for the purification of the worshippers.

Equally simple, austere, and quiet are Shinto ceremonials. In the shrine there is no image but only a symbolic representation of the deity called " spirit-substitute " (*mi-tama-shiro*), usually a mirror or a *nusa*. The offerings consist of food stuffs, such as fish, fowl, cereals, vegetables, always uncooked—arrayed together with *saké* drink and some other objects. No flower is offered but green leaves of the tree *sakaki*—probably in contradistinction to the abundant flowers of Buddhist rites. There are traces of human sacrifice both in the ceremonies and in the legends, but it ceased to be practised long before the historical period, and any bloody sacrifice is carefully avoided, because it means pollution.

The ceremony proper consists of bringing offerings one after another, reciting a ritual, and then taking away the offerings. Private prayers may be offered, but the regular ritual is always public. The priests serving in these ceremonies glide in and out of the sanctuary with quiet footsteps, silence being strictly observed. Besides these austere services, however, dances are performed with songs and musical accompaniment in a separate building, in the presence of the worshippers. The dance is either a simple movement or it portrays scenes from myths. The motion of the dancer is usually horizontal and a jump or other abrupt movement is scarcely ever seen—although it is a feature of most of the secular dances. The representation of the stories gave rise, as in other countries, to dramatic performances, while the primitive dances are carefully preserved. Torches are used in festivals, but exclusively for light, no kind of explosive fireworks being used. In this way Shinto ceremonial is peculiarly pure and solemnly quiet. These features give to it an archaic sobriety, and the Shintoists are proud of this as an evidence of its direct derivation from the celestial world. But as a matter of fact there are some boisterous services in local performances, and the quiet feature of the official rites was chiefly derived from the solemnity of court ceremonies.

There were periodical festivities as well as occasional ceremonies performed in front of a shrine or in the family. The greatest of the public festivals are those of the Harvest and the Purification. At the Feast of Harvest, offerings from the new crops are made every autumn to the Sun-goddess and once after the coronation ceremony of each reign. The Harvest is the most solemn ceremony, being celebrated at midnight at a fixed date in late autumn, now the 23rd of November.   The rice to be offered on this occasion is taken from a special rice-field, sanctified by ritual, and cultivated by hallowed virgins.   The Purification is performed twice a year, for the purpose of washing away the pollution, physical and moral, incurred during the preceding half-year.   This was, in the ancient days, performed at the court by the priestly family Nakatomi, and the ritual is known by that name—the Naka-tomi Ritual.   But the ceremony may be performed in any other place, within a sacred precinct or on the river-bank, and the members of the community are expected to attend it.   The performance consists in sprinkling water, reciting the ritual, and swinging the symbolic *nusa*, while human figures made of rice-straw are thrown into the stream, the effigies representing the stained substance of the attendants. The *nusa* was, as we have said, originally an offering, but it was adapted to symbolize the deity and to represent the divine potency, therefore evil influences were averted by swinging it.

The Nakatomi Ritual recited on the occasion of the periodical ablution is a good example of the religious and moral sentiments of Shinto.   We cite some passages :

Give ear, all ye Imperial Princes, Princesses, Ministers of State, and functionaries who are here assembled, and hearken every one to the Great Purification by which at this year's interlune of the sixth (or twelfth) month he deigns to purge and absolve all manner of faults and transgressions which may have been committed by those who serve in the Imperial Court . . . all those who do duty in the various offices of State.

Now of the various faults and transgressions to be committed by the celestial race destined more and more to people this land of his peaceful rule, some are of Heaven, to wit, the breaking down of divisions between rice-fields, filling up of irrigation channels, removing water-pipes, sowing seed over again, planting skewers, flaying alive, flaying backwards.   These are distinguished as Heavenly offences.

Earthly offences which will be committed are the cutting of living bodies, the cutting of dead bodies, leprosy, *kokumi*,[1] incest of a man with his mother or daughter, with his mother-in-law or step-daughter, bestiality, calamities

---

[1] Its meaning is uncertain, but it seems to have meant a certain kind of skin disease.

from creeping things, from the high gods and from high birds, killing animals, bewitchments.

Whensoever they may be committed, let the Great Nakatomi, in accordance with the customs of the Heavenly Palace, cut Heavenly saplings at the top and cut them at the bottom, and make thereof a complete array of one thousand stands for offerings. Then let him recite the mighty ritual words of the celestial ritual.

When he does so, the Gods of Heaven, thrusting open the adamantine door of Heaven and cleaving the many-piled clouds of Heaven with an awful way-cleaving will lend ear. The Gods of Earth, climbing to the tops of the high mountains and to the tops of the low mountains, sweeping apart the mists of the high mountains and the mists of the low mountains, will lend ear.

When they have thus lent ear, all offences whatsoever will be annulled, from the Court of the Sovran Grandchild to the provinces of the four quarters of the Under-Heaven.

As the many-piled clouds of Heaven are scattered by the breath of the Wind-Gods ; as the morning breezes and the evening breezes dissipate the dense morning vapours and the dense evening vapours ; . . . as yonder thick brushwood is smitten and cleared away by the sharp sickle forged in the fire, so shall all offences be utterly annulled.

Therefore he (the Mikado) is graciously pleased to purify and cleanse them away. The Goddess called *Se-oritsu-hime* (The-Lady-who-descends-the-Rapids), who dwells in the rapids of the swift streams whose cataracts tumble headlong from the tops of the high mountains and from the tops of the low mountains will bear them out into the great sea-plain. Thereupon the Goddess called *Haya-aki-tsu-hime* (Rapid-Open-Channel-Lady), who dwells in the myriad meetings of the tides of the myriad brine-paths of the myriad ways of the currents of the boisterous sea will swallow them up. And the God *Ibukido-nushi* (Breath-Blowing-Lord), who dwells in the Breath-blowing-place, will puff them away to the Root-country, the Bottom-country. Then the Goddess *Haya-sasura-hime* (Swift-Banishment-Lady), who dwells in the Root-country, the Bottom-country, will banish and abolish them. When they have been so destroyed, every one, from the servants of the Imperial Court to the four quarters of the Under-Heaven, will remain void of all offences whatsoever.[1]

Here we see the offences " of Heaven," that is, pertaining to agriculture, and those " of Earth," mostly physical pollutions, enumerated side by side with offences connected with sexual relations. This list of offences clearly shows the rather primitive stage of social and ethical ideas ; the method

---

[1] The translation is by Satow and Florenz, cited in Aston, *Shinto*, pp. 296-302. The English equivalents of the deities invoked are the author's.

of casting out those pollutions is correspondingly naïve, consisting simply in performing a ceremony believed to have magical efficacy.

Besides the public ceremonies and the private prayers, spells and charms were much in vogue, and divination and augury were practised.  The divine and magical efficacy of objects connected with the ceremonies was believed in and made use of, mostly against evil spirits.  Swinging the *nusa*, making fire of wood used in the ceremonies, partaking of food or drink offered to the gods—these were believed to confer miraculous powers.  Certain austerities were practised with the intention of expelling evils and purifying oneself, such as bathing in cold streams, hard mountain climbing, or abstaining from sexual intercourse.  Magic, exorcism, and other occult practices were performed by persons who had passed certain stages of ascetic training.  These practices were later combined with and elaborated by Buddhist occultism and gave impetus to many superstitious beliefs and customs.  We shall see (in the third period) the rise of the mountaineer priests, who still later became promulgators of the various forms of popular Shinto in which reverence towards invisible spirits and devils played a large part.

Priestly families have existed from an unknown antiquity, the Nakatomi and the Imbé being the foremost.  Whatever these names may have meant,[1] most probably the former performed public services in the court and represented the bright side, so to speak, of the Shinto religion, while the latter attended the propitiatory services and practised occultism.  The chief priest at a service was, and is, called *kan-nushi*, the " god-man " or the chief of the priests, and he presided over the ceremonies ; under him there were *negi*, reciters, *hafuri*, service-men, and *kan-nagi*, dancers.  Women

[1] Cf. Aston, *Nihon-gi*, vol. i, p. 56.

also served as priestesses and they were expected to be virgins, though not necessarily for life. The most important of the priestesses was a royal princess who served the Sun-goddess at Isé. There were similar priestesses in other sanctuaries recruited from noble families, while the dancers were women of no rank.

The Shinto priest is to-day clad in a broad mantle-like costume, with large sleeves, usually white, and the dancing virgins are clad in white robes with long red skirts. These are of later origin, being the court dresses dating from the tenth century; the ancient priestly robes are entirely lost.

In spite of the existence of the priestly families and professional priests, sacerdotal services were not limited to them, but every ruler or patriarch played a priestly rôle. Another point to be noticed here is that the Shinto priests seldom played such a prominent part in politics as the Buddhist. The descendants of the Nakatomi became, after the seventh century, ministers of State and majordomos of the ruling family; this was not because of their priesthood, for in fact they had abandoned their priestly function when they began to control politics. To-day the Shinto priest is often chauvinist and his ambition is rising under the protection of the reactionary government.

# BOOK II

## INTRODUCTION OF BUDDHISM
## AND ITS ESTABLISHMENT
### (ABOUT 600-800)

# SPREAD OF BUDDHISM AND ITS ARRIVAL
# IN JAPAN

AT the beginning of our history we see a powerful ruling family established in the central part of the main island and many tribes attached to it, joined in the cult of the Sun-goddess. Her shrine had been detached from the residence of the ruler and erected on the eastern coast, in the province of Isé, which became thenceforward the central seat of the national worship. Military expeditions to the east and to the west were followed by the establishment of Shinto worship, including the cult of those heroes and deities who were believed to have served the Sun-goddess and her descendants. Many important seaports and strategic points were occupied by clansmen of the ruling family, and there they established Shinto sanctuaries. Although the progress of national unity was often disturbed by the incursion of invaders and immigrants coming from the south-west and by uprisings of the aborigines in the north-east, those unruly elements were gradually brought under the military and religious influence of the dominating clans.

While in this way a central authority was being established and the clans and tribes of the numerous islands were being welded into a nation, communication with the Korean peninsula provided a continual stimulus to change and movement. The establishment of Japanese colonies in the southern part of Korea, probably in the early centuries of the Christian era, military and diplomatic engagements with the principalities of Korea, the perpetual influx of Chinese and Korean immigrants, the impact of the continental civilization, all these made impossible an isolated development of the island nation. The ambitious plan of a Chinese ruler early in the fifth century to extend his influence to the east and the consequent rise and propagation of the Buddhist religion in the Korean peninsula changed the life of the Koreans. Japan could not remain unaffected by this movement. Moreover, Japan was still backward, first in the lack of the writing art, and more important, in the still prevailing system of separate clans and internecine strife. The Koreans were much in advance of the Japanese as a result of their better acquaintance with Chinese civilization, and consequently their resistance to Japanese penetration grew in the course of the sixth century. These circumstances awoke the leaders of Japan to the necessity of adopting many features of the civilization of their continental neighbours.

It was chiefly Korean immigrants and some Chinese who introduced the various arts of civilization, and these artisans and scholars greatly contributed to the rise of the ruling family, in whose service most of them worked. The importation of useful and decorative commodities was followed by the introduction of writing and learning, and these were finally consummated by the adoption of Confucian ethics and the Buddhist religion. In many cases the immigrant artisans and scholars worked as missionaries. The first name we have of a prominent Buddhist in Japan is that of Shiba Tachito, a refugee from the eastern coast of China, who arrived in Japan in 522, probably through Korea. He is well remembered as a leader of the new movement, for his family later produced eminent Buddhist workers, the first Buddhist nun and the greatest artist of the seventh century.[1]

After these preliminaries the new religion was presented

[1] The artist was Tori, the first Buddhist artist in Japan. His works are preserved even to this day.

to the court of Yamato [1] by a delegation sent by the Prince of Kudara (or Pakchoi, a principality in the south of Korea) as a sign of homage and friendship. This took place in 538 (or in 552 as is usually assumed). The delegation was accompanied by Buddhist priests, and the objects presented were statues of Buddha and his saints, copies of scriptures, banners and other ceremonial articles.[2] The message accompanying the presents said :

This religion (hō, Sanskrit *dharma*) is the most excellent of all teachings, though difficult to master and hard to comprehend ; even the sages of China would have found it not easy to grasp. It brings endless and immeasurable blessings and fruits (to its believers), even the attainment of the supreme enlightenment (*Bodhi*). Just as the *Chintā-mani* jewel is said to fulfil every need according to desire, so the Treasures of the glorious religion will never cease to give full response to those who seek for it. Moreover, the religion has come over to Korea far from India, and the peoples (in the countries between these two) are now ardent followers of its teaching, and none are outside its pale.

These statements, backed by fine statues and exquisite works of art, were a marvellous revelation to a people who knew only how to invoke deities conceived as not very much superior to mankind.

Buddhism is usually known in the Occident as a religion of ascetic practice and atheistic ideas. Whatever the Western critics may say, the influence Buddhism exerted everywhere lay in its practice of love and equality, which was an outcome of its fundamental teaching of the unity of all beings, and of its ideal of supreme enlightenment (*Bodhi*) to be attained by all. This *Bodhi* amounts to realizing, in the spirit and in life, the basic unity of existence, the spiritual communion pervading the whole universe. This was exemplified by the person of Buddha, not only in his teaching

[1] Yamato is now a province in central Japan, but it meant in those days central Japan. The Imperial residence and the seat of government were always in that part of Japan until 1869, when the capital was removed to Tokyo.

[2] These were meant to embody the " Three Treasures " of Buddhism, to be referred to below, Buddha in his image, his Dharma in the scriptures, and his Sangha in the priests.

of all-oneness but in his life of all-embracing charity.  Those united in the faith in Buddha and his teaching form a close community of spiritual fellowship, in which the truth of oneness is embodied and the life of charity is practised.  In short, the principle of the Buddhist religion amounts to faith and life in the Three Treasures (*Ratna-traya*), which means oneness of the Perfect Person (*Buddha*), the Truth (*Dharma*), and the Community (*Sangha*).[1]

Now the Buddhism brought over to Japan was a developed form of this religion, demonstrated artistically in ceremonies and supported by a system of idealistic philosophy.  The Japanese learned for the first time through this religion that there was a deity or superman who looked after the welfare and salvation of all beings without regard to clan or nationality.  The people saw, to their astonishment and admiration, the figure of a divine being represented in beauty and adored by means of elaborate rituals.  This was, indeed, a new revelation which was destined to rule the faith and sentiment of the nation.

When the Buddhist gifts from Korea were officially presented, the court circles were divided into two parties, the one favouring acceptance and the other opposing it.  Ostensibly their dispute was as to whether or not the newly offered deity was superior to the native deities.  But the hidden and more vital motive lay in the strife among various clans for political supremacy, combined with their conflicting interests in Korea and several other issues.  The anti-Buddhist party was led by the Mononobe, the military clansmen, who were blind to general tendencies in the continent and stood for high-handed measures towards foreign countries.  The priestly family, the Nakatomi, naturally stood on this side, though their descendants later became ardent Buddhists.  Against this combined force stood the Soga family, who were administrators and

---

[1] Cf. Anesaki, *Buddhist Art*, pp. 2-6 ; Anesaki, *Nichiren*, pp. 138-147.

diplomats and fully recognized the necessity of a progressive policy. Thus the dissension was a manifestation of the antagonism between two tendencies and temperaments with a difference of interests, which was a natural outcome of the nation's internal development as well as of contact with her continental neighbours.

The strife lasted about fifty years, during which time the fate of the new religion seemed at times doubtful, endangered as it was by the threats and attacks of the military party and by the superstitious dread of the wrath of the native gods prevailing among the people at large. On the other hand, however, the first presentation of Buddhist objects was followed by a continual influx of missionaries, artisans, and other immigrants, reinforcing the influence of the new religion. The introduction, furthermore, of the medical science, of Chinese arts and sciences, especially of writing and astronomy, was always identified with Buddhist missions, and even the conservatives gradually gave in to the irresistible force of these importations. It was quite natural that the display of ritual and the practice of medical arts were most effective in inducing a people like the Japanese of that time to receive civilization.

Thus in spite of opposition the new religion gradually took hold of the hearts of the people, and many nobles accepted it although in some cases they were not bold enough to profess it in public. Strife continued and became finally so vehement that the succession to the throne and other important State affairs became involved, and even the life of the sovereign was threatened. But the opposition gradually waned, and the military party succumbed in their final desperate attempt, in 587. This marked a decided turn in the movement of the time, and a Buddhist temple was built in commemoration of the event, named Hōkō-ji, the " Temple of the Rise of Truth." This and other foundations caused an increasing importation of Buddhist statues, instruments, manuscripts, accompanied by missionaries and artisans. Their displays were assisted by organizations for charity and public benefit, and the nation entered the path of civilization, undergoing at the same time the conversion of her heart and faith. All this was certainly due to the irresistible force of the tide of civilization and propaganda from the Asiatic continent, but the changes might have remained mere importations and imitations if there had not appeared a strong personality who guided and consolidated the movement by his wisdom and insight. This man was the Prince-Regent Shōtoku, the son of a Buddhist ruler and his pious consort, and therefore himself a Buddhist of the second, or possibly third, generation.

# THE PRINCE-REGENT SHŌTOKU
## HIS IDEALS AND WORK

THE triumph of the Buddhist party was strengthened by the accession of Prince Shōtoku to the regency under his pious aunt, in 593.[1] He was born in 574, thirty-six years after the public introduction of Buddhism, and he was only nineteen years old when he became the actual ruler, with the title of regent, supported by the progressive party. His reign of thirty years was the most epoch-making period in Japanese history, and it was marked by the striking advance of Buddhist influence and continental civilization. He became the founder of Japanese civilization as well as of a united Japanese nation. But his achievements are not to be credited to his personal merit alone, because his insight and wisdom so well embodied the highest ideals of Buddhism that his work amounted to founding a national life on the basis of spiritual unity and moral edification as inspired by Buddhism.

The first act of the prince as regent was the public proclamation of Buddhism as the religion of State, and the foundation of a grand Buddhist institution. This was composed of four establishments : the temple proper, an asylum, a hospital, and a dispensary. The temple proper served not only for the performance of Buddhist worship but it included departments for the study of Buddhist philosophy and sciences, for a disciplined order of monks, and their training in arts

---

[1] " Shōtoku " is a title given the prince by his admirers, probably his contemporaries, and means " Holy-Virtuous." His real name was " Umayado," which meant the " Stable " or " Born in the Stable." The hypothesis that this name betrays the influence of Christian legend is unwarranted. See Plate II.

and ceremonies. The three other institutions were the first establishments of the kind and became models for the coming ages. Thus the institution, called Tennō-ji, was a group of religious, educational, and philanthropic organizations. But there was something more in the idea of the prince embodied in this foundation. Its site was selected at the seaside, on a slope leading to the beach of the seaport now known as Osaka. It was the port for the capital in the interior, lying at the eastern end of the Inland Sea, on the main maritime route connecting the central provinces with the western and therefore with the continent. The main temple building faced south, but there was an entrance facing west towards the sea, and it was there that the embassies, missionaries, and immigrants were admitted and welcomed to the country, through the gateway of Buddhist communion. This fact alone eloquently declared the high idealism of the prince's statesmanship and spiritual leadership.

During the first ten years of his regency the prince was chiefly occupied with reforms in internal administration and the diplomatic relations with Korea. Then he extended diplomatic relations to the court of China, to which an envoy was sent in 607. This was the beginning of Japan's direct official communication with China, which was destined to play a very great rôle in the development of Japanese civilization during the following three centuries. The primary purpose of the envoy was to learn more from China of religion, sciences, and government institutions, thus proving that the prince was not content with being a diplomat but used the occasion to serve his aspirations. The letter addressed to the Chinese Emperor opened with the following words : " The Ruler of the Land of Sunrise sends his message to the Ruler of the Land of Sunset ". China, which had ever regarded her neighbours as inferiors, was much displeased not only with the tone of equality but with the contrast between sunrise and sunset. The Japanese ambassador explained to the Chinese court that the Prince-regent regarded the Chinese Emperor as a Bodhisattva, one striving for Buddhist perfection, who was ruling his country in accordance with the moral ideals of the religion, that it was the aim of the prince also to rule his own country as a Bodhisattva, and thus the ties connecting them were not merely diplomatic but moral and spiritual.[1] If not quite satisfied with this explanation, the Chinese Emperor despatched an embassy replying to the message with the words : " The Emperor speaks to the Prince of Yamato ". The second envoy from Japan brought the words : " The Heavenly Ruler[2] of the East speaks to the Emperor of the West." In this way diplomatic communication with China was opened by insisting on terms of equality, a manifestation of the prince's conviction of the equality of nations in the light of Buddhist faith.

The envoys to China took with them monks and students, who there studied religion and science, and later worked for reform and civilization. Besides these Japanese students, more Chinese and Koreans were induced to come and work in Japan, and all of them were instrumental in the further progress of religion and civilization. The times were favourable to these schemes of the prince, because China had just then (in 590) been unified under the powerful government of the Sui dynasty, after a long period of division and confusion, and culture was blooming with fresh vigour. Moreover, various new schools of Buddhist philosophy were arising, and their teachings were later introduced into Japan one after another. The prince himself was educated in the

---

[1] This is not recorded in Japanese annals but in the Chinese.

[2] Japanese *Tennō*, the official title of the Emperor, which is kept to the present. Most probably it was an invention of Prince Shōtoku occasioned by the communication with China. The appellation *Mikado*, so well known in the Occident was not used before the tenth century. It meant " The August Port," *i.e.*, of the palace.

philosophy of the Sanron [1] school, and as we shall presently see, became the pioneer of philosophical thinking in Japan.

When the prince had succeeded in introducing and carrying out various plans of reform, he made, in 604, a proclamation summing up his idea of administration and declaring the fundamental principles of State organization. It was called a " Constitution " (*Kempō*), and known as the " Constitution in Seventeen Articles." Though the document bears the traits of a moral treatise rather than of a legal decree, it was in fact intended to be a formulation of the State constitution. This very fact, that political principles are interwoven with moral ideas and religious ideals, shows the ideal nature of the prince's statesmanship, and it is no wonder that in later ages this document was regarded as the formulation of the fundamental principles of national life.

The Constitution laid special stress upon moral and spiritual harmony between sovereign and subjects, between the superior and his subordinates, which was propounded to be the essential basis of national life and government. The rulership of a single monarch implied the equality of all people, just as faith in the unique personality of Buddha as the saviour of all mankind presupposed the intrinsic value and destiny of every individual to be in communion with him. The prince expressed his high aim by saying at the opening of the first article : " Harmony is to be valued, and discord is to be deprecated." In saying this he had before his eyes the actual conditions of clan division, and so added : " All men are influenced by partisanship, and there are few who have wide vision." His purpose was to rectify the evils of division and strife by the highest ideal of moral and spiritual life.

[1] The school adhering to the philosophy of Nāgārjuna, the Indian patriarch of the second century, so named because the school bases its theories on the three treatises of Nāgārjuna, Sanron meaning the " Three Sāstras." The general tendency of the school is a transcendental idealism.

Further, in the second article he enunciated the fundamental principle of spiritual harmony as follows :

Sincerely revere the "Three Treasures." The Three Treasures are Buddha, Dharma, and Sangha, the final resort of all beings and the supreme object of faith for all peoples. Should any age or any people fail to revere this truth? There are few men who are utterly vicious. Every one will realize it (truth) if duly instructed. Could any wickedness be corrected without having resort to the Three Treasures?[1]

We have seen the Buddhist idea of the triune relationship between the Buddha, the Truth, and the Community : statesmanship was to the prince nothing but an application of the truth of the Three Treasures to every phase of national and individual life. Thus, he further inculcated the virtues of propriety, justice, faithfulness, and the like, and added provisions for applying them to the management of State affairs. All this was meant to emphasize the foundation of life upon the Buddhist ideal of the oneness of being, and to work out the edification of national life by realizing the universal communion of faith and charity. On the other hand, we have to note that the prince was not a mere idealist but a statesman who struggled to build a nation out of a people divided into clans and who carried out numerous practical reforms in government and social work. Besides being an organizer of charitable work, as we have seen, he was also the first road-maker of Japan, he directed building work, and greatly promoted agriculture.

A national leader striving for the moral elevation of the people, the prince was also a man of pious devotion and speculative mind. Not content with his proclamation of the Constitution, he endeavoured to explain his ideals and to instruct his people by giving lectures on the Buddhist scriptures in the palace and in the temples. The texts selected for this purpose were three, and in the selection the prince

---

[1] Aston, *Nihon-gi*, vol. ii. pp. 129-32. His translation is too literal in some passages.

showed the depth and breadth of his ideas.  The books
were : (1) the *Hokke-kyō*, or the Lotus of Truth, expounding
the all-embracing scheme of Buddhist salvation ; (2) the
*Yuima-gyō*, the discourses of the lay Buddhist sage, Yuima
(Vimalakīrti), an elder of the city republic Vaisālī and the
ideal model of Buddhist citizenship ; and (3) the *Shōman-gyō*,
discourses between Buddha and the Queen Shōman (Srīmālā)
of Benares, the ideal representative of Buddhist womanhood.[1]

The " Lotus " is a gospel of universal salvation and its
purpose is to interpret the life and personality of the historical
Buddha Sākya-muni as a manifestation of eternal truth
(*Dharma*), working ever to bring all beings without exception
into the all-embracing way (*Eka-yāna*) of salvation and enlightenment.  His power of saving all is likened to the rain-
water which, being one and homogeneous in itself, nourishes
all plants and herbs of diverse sorts according to their
respective natures and capacities.  Not only was Buddha
himself an example of Buddhist perfection but he also guides
and inspires every one who is ready to follow him.  His
working is not limited to his lifetime, he is an eternal and
omnipresent Lord of the Universe, and besides his own
direct instruction and inspiration, he sends innumerable
saints, *Bodhisattva*, for the salvation of all throughout the
ages.  Thus we can see why Prince Shōtoku selected this
book as the central theme of his lectures.  His life was an
emulation of this work of Buddha, and considering himself

[1] In Buddhism there were various triads of sacred books selected and grouped
according to the views and purposes of different thinkers, such as the three texts
of Shingon mysticism, of Jōdo pietism.  Even later Buddhists in Japan mostly
followed Chinese examples in the grouping of triads, but the present grouping by
the prince was his own selection.

*Hokke-kyō* is the Japanese equivalent of the Sanskrit *Saddharma-pundarīka ;*
see Kern's English translation in SBE, vol. xxi, and Burnouf's French translation
entitled *Le Lotus de la Bonne Loi.*  Cf. Anesaki, *Nichiren*, pp. 19-32 ; K. Saunders,
*The Gospel for Asia* (London, 1928).

Of the *Yuima-gyō* an incomplete English translation was published in the
*Hansei Zasshi* (Tokio, 1896), which is out of print and very scarce.

PLATE II

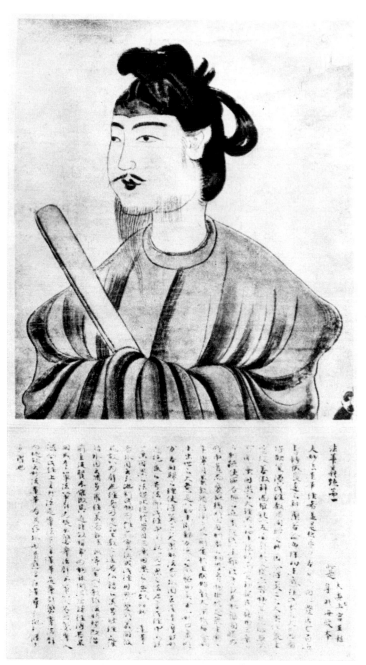

PORTRAIT OF PRINCE SHŌTOKU
Work of the Seventh Century, handed down in Hōryū-ji

Below: The opening passage of his Commentary on the Lotus of
Truth, his Holograph

to be a Bodhisattva, he derived inspiration from those passages where Buddha's saints were depicted as working incessantly for perfecting themselves by saving others and inducing others to take the same way to perfection.

Similarly, we can see how the prince was inspi·ed by the high type of moral and spiritual life exemplified by the virtuous elder of Vaisālī, and also how earnestly he wished to see in his aunt, the reigning sovereign, another Queen of Benares. Now, the life of the ideal Bodhisattva embodied in the person of Yuima is described in one passage of the text as follows :

His mother is Wisdom, his father Tactfulness, his kinsmen All-being, his abode Vacuity, his wife Joy, his daughter Love, his son Truthfulness. Thus he is living the life of a householder, yet it does not fetter him to worldly existence.

And in the introduction to his commentary the prince says :

Yuima was a great sage who reached the height of Buddhist perfection, being equal to Buddha himself in enlightenment. In its metaphysical entity his person was identical with the Ultimate Reality (*Tathatā*), but in its manifestations his life was identified with all beings. . . . His spiritual life had for ever overcome the boundaries of intentions and volitions and his mind was not trammelled by affairs of State and Society. . . . Yet being moved by an unintermittent compassion, he worked perpetually for the benefit of the people, in living himself the life of a householder.

This was, in fact, the prince's own ideal.

The heroine of the Shōman-gyō, the Queen Srīmālā, was a model of womanhood. Pious to her mother and devoted to her husband, and living the life of a queen, she dedicated her life to the Buddhist cause, and the vows taken by her before Buddha were a fervent expression of charity and self-denial. Her vows to dedicate all her possessions to the poor, to serve the helpless and needy by all means, her readiness even to sacrifice her life—the spirit of these vows was to a great degree carried out by Prince Shōtoku in his organization of charitable institutions, and finally, as we shall presently see, by the practice of non-resistance. Another point of inspiration which the prince evidently derived from the discourses of the Indian queen was the distinction between the persuasive method of inducing others to lead a virtuous life and the repressive method of combating sin and vice. In fact, the statesmanship of the prince exhibited tactful applications of the two methods according to the objectives and circumstances.

The union of religious ideals and national life thus proclaimed, expounded, and carried out by the prince, became once for all the aim of the greatest Buddhists and the aspiration of the best statesmen in Japan. Through the broad vision and high idealism of his leadership, Buddhism was able to influence the Japanese extensively and profoundly ; it was largely due to Buddhist inspiration that the wise prince was able to handle successfully the difficult situations of his government and to lead his people to a high level of culture and spiritual edification. The prince's lectures on the three books were written down in terse and expressive Chinese, and the volumes are preserved to this day as the first books written by a Japanese—one of them even in the prince's original manuscript.[1] They testify to the prince's thorough acquaintance with Buddhist philosophy, and also to his high aspiration of enlightening his people by the wisdom and morality of Buddhism.

Besides this, however, the prince showed his religious spirit in pious devotion and mystic contemplation. There stands in the precinct of Hōryū-ji,[2] which was his college and sanctuary, an octagonal shrine called *Yumé-dono* (Vision Chapel), where he used to retire to meditate and is said to have entered into spiritual communication with Buddha and Buddhist saints. In the shrine there stands a statue of Kwannon, the all-compassionate Lord of Mercy, before whom the prince used to sit in meditation, and in the somewhat

[1] See Plate II.                    [2] See Plate III.

dreamy expression of the statue we may imagine how the prince was immersed in spiritual communion with the deity.

In conclusion, it is remarkable that Japan produced a man of such extraordinary genius at that critical juncture of her history. He laid the foundation of national unity, guided and inspired the nation with the spiritual ideals of Buddhism, educated the people in arts, sciences, and other works of civilization. Not unnaturally, later Buddhists, and probably his contemporaries too, considered him as an incarnation of Kwannon, the Lord of Mercy. His achievements and ideal aims, his talent and wisdom, are to the credit of his personal genius ; but credit is to be rendered also to the Buddhist religion, that it inspired, educated, and developed this man's genius, and thereby helped him in laying the foundation of national life on the basis of high ideals.

# BUDDHIST INSPIRATION AND ITS MANIFESTATIONS

*The Ideal of Universal Salvation and the Deed of Dedication*

THE central idea in Buddhist teaching is the gospel of universal salvation based on the idea of the fundamental oneness of all beings. There are in the world, Buddhism teaches, manifold existences and innumerable beings, and each of these individuals deems himself to be a separate being and behaves accordingly. But in reality they make up one family, there is one continuity throughout, and this oneness is to be realized in the attainment of Buddhahood on the part of each and all, in the full realization of the universal communion. Individuals may purify themselves and thereby escape the miseries of sinful existence, yet our salvation is imperfect so long as and so far as there remain any who have not realized the universal spiritual communion, *i.e.*, who are not saved. To save oneself by saving others is the gospel of universal salvation taught by Buddhism. A prayer commonly used by Japanese Buddhists is :

> " There are beings without limit,
> Let us take the vow to convey them all across.
>
> There are depravities in us without number,
> Let us take the vow to extinguish them all.
>
> There are truths without end,
> Let us take the vow to comprehend them all.
>
> There is the Way of Buddha without comparison,
> Let us take the vow to accomplish it perfectly."

Hereby it is emphasized that without striving to fulfil the first vow, of saving fellow beings, the other three are vain,

even if they could be achieved. Another prayer more frequently recited at the conclusion of the ritual says :

> " Let these merits (now performed) universally pervade all,
>     And let us, together with all beings, soon accomplish the way of
>     Buddha."

The characteristic feature of Buddhism in Japan consists in
the emphasis laid on the universal communion to be realized
and the dedication of one's own wisdom and merit to one's
fellow beings.  This universalism was indeed an ideal never
dreamt of before by the Japanese, and this religion of all-
embracing love and salvation gave the people a wider and
deeper comprehension of human life, an aspiration for an
incomparably broader communion than had been taught by
Shinto or Confucianism.  These teachings of communion and
salvation were, of course, not appreciated by the people in
general in metaphysical terms as they were used by Buddhist
doctors, but they appealed to the people as a promise of
eternal life to be enjoyed in community with kinsmen and
fellow people in Buddha's paradise.

The ideal of universal fellowship and the practice of
dedication are but two aspects of the fundamental unity of
existence, and this teaching always encouraged acts of piety
and meritorious work, not only for the doer's sake but on
behalf of others—of the doer's own kinsmen first, and then
of all fellow beings.  Works done for this purpose may be
the celebration of a religious ceremony, or the building of a
temple, the making of a statue, making copies of sacred texts,
charitable work of any kind.  When a deed or work is performed with the intention and pious desire of dedicating it
to the soul of a certain person, its efficacy will establish a
closer communion between the dedicator and the objective.
If the soul to whom it is dedicated is travelling in the inferior
resorts of transmigration, the piety and virtue of the dedication
will help it along its way towards a better resort and finally

to Buddhahood.    If it has already attained a certain height
of spiritual enlightenment, the dedicator himself will be led
up more closely to the realm of bliss.    Since the connection
between the two is not merely based on their relationship
during earthly existence but is in fact a partial manifestation
of the universal nexus binding all beings, the dedication may,
nay must, at the same time be directed to all fellow beings
and the merit thereof will be participated in by them all.

   This idea and practice of dedication [1] had far-reaching
effects upon the religious sentiment of the people, extending
the conception of fellowship and stimulating charitable deeds.
Indeed, the works achieved by Prince Shōtoku were intended
by him to be dedications made for the sake of his people,
including past and coming generations.    The same spirit was
expressed by his princess-consort, when she caused, in dedication to the deceased prince, a bronze statue of Buddha to be
made by the greatest artist of the time, Tori, and when she
herself worked on a tapestry depicting scenes of the blissful
life in the Land of Heavenly Life (*Tenju-koku*).[2]    Of the
latter only fragments remain but the beautiful colours and
careful needlework bear witness to her pious sentiments and
ideal aspiration.    The former, the statue,[3] is preserved intact
in the Golden Hall of Hōryū-ji, and the inscription on the
back of its aureole expresses the ideal which inspired the
execution of that work.    The inscription says in part :

   Here we have reverently caused a statue of Buddha Sākya-muni with his
attendant Bodhisattvas to be made and the associate decorative work to be

   [1] Sanskrit *parināmanā*, Japanese *ekō*.    Cf. Suzuki, *Outlines of Mahāyāna
Buddhism*, pp. 283-86.    He gives this word by a Sanskrit word *parivarta*, but it is
unwarranted.
   [2] It is an unsettled question whether this paradise meant the Land of Bliss
(Sukhāvatī) of the Buddha Amita, to which reference occurs frequently in the
Middle Ages.    The tapestry is preserved in the nunnery Chūgu-ji in the precinct of
Hōryū-ji.    The nunnery was the one established on the site of the residence of Prince
Shōtoku's mother in her memory.    The statue of Kwannon, the central figure in
the chapel, is said to have been executed by the prince himself.    *Cf.* Plate IVA.
   [3] See Pl. IIIA.

executed. Let us, by the virtue of this modest merit, advance on the way of faith and wisdom ; let us live in safety in the present life and finally be released from rebirth and attain the final destiny. Let us, by following the steps of the deceased, contribute to the rise of the Three Treasures and ultimately join them (the deceased) in the life beyond. Let (the merit) pervade universally the six resorts (of transmigration) and let all living beings in the whole universe be emancipated from their woeful abodes and attain Bodhi together with us.

We see here the intention of the dedicatory work clearly stated in terms of Mahāyāna Buddhism. This practice became thenceforth a great force among Japanese Buddhists, and we cannot overestimate the influence it exercised in broadening sympathy and in refining religious sentiment. The history of Japanese Buddhism abounds in instances of similar works of dedication ; memorial stones and tablets recording them with prayers for the sake of the dead are seen everywhere throughout the country.[1]

Now it was quite natural that the spiritual communion taught by Buddhism was made to embrace the souls of ancestors, and the practice of dedication was adapted to the cult of the dead. This was an accommodation of Buddhism to the animistic religion of the people, but it nevertheless elevated their spiritual level to a higher plane, the ideal of universal fellowship. The cult which had been performed as a request for favour or for propitiation was now combined with the new conception of spiritual fraternity. Japanese Buddhists even nowadays observe strictly the periodical services in memory of the deceased members of the family. This is a family cult and ancestor-worship, as it is called, but the spiritual communion intended in the cult may be extended indefinitely to the whole cosmos. Medieval legends are full of instances of the souls of those who had died in battle being consoled and saved from the torment of revengeful

[1] Besides building temples and similar practices, relief for sick travellers was organized, their bodies buried ; services were held for those who had died by flood or earthquake ; the dead on battle-fields were given funeral services, and so on. In short, any charitable deed was regarded as dedicatory work in the Buddhist sense.

spirits by the virtue of a religious dedication performed by monks or laymen. There is an All Souls' Day of Japanese Buddhism observed in the middle of the year, and on this occasion the family as well as the community, or the church, calls on all souls.[1] It is intended to benefit the dead, and prayers are said for their spiritual welfare, not to them. It is called ancestor-worship, but it is rather services for their sake as well as for the celebrants. Besides its influence on their sentimental life, the cult plays a great part in the social life and daily usage of the Japanese.

### The Teaching of Karma and its Effects

Another important factor of Buddhist teaching is the doctrine of *Karma*,[2] *i.e.*, moral causation of the continuity of existence through successive births and deaths. The inscription referred to above, concerning the dedication in memory of Prince Shōtoku, says as regards the intention of the dedicators while the prince was ill :

In our deep distress we made a vow, putting our faith in the Three Treasures, to cause a statue of Buddha to be made, equal in stature to the Prince. By virtue of this vow, our desire was that his illness be cured and his life prolonged, and that welfare in this life be secured for him. Yet if the inexorable Karma should not allow this, if he must pass away from this world, we earnestly desired that he be soon induced to the Land of Purity and finally attain the perfect fruit (of Bodhi).

---

[1] This festival is called *Bon*, a word derived from the Skt. *Udlambana*, a Hindu Buddhist festival. For the ancestor worship of the Japanese, cf Lafcadio Hearn, *Japan, an Attempt at Interpretation*, pp. 49-56, 210-15, 220, etc.

In the words of Lafcadio Hearn, ancestor worship in Japan is not so much "praying to the dead" as "praying for the dead." This trait makes the cult practised by the Japanese comparatively free from superstitious elements found among the Chinese, such as the idea of appeasing the spirits or extravagances in the cult of the dead.

[2] Japanese, *ingwa* or *shikugō*, or often simply *gō*. *Ingwa* means causation but is used also to designate fate, while *gō* means deed or work, and *shikugō* is the deed done in the past, *i.e.*, "inherent Karma." In mediæval Japanese literature this idea of moral causation was applied to explaining the irresistible force of affection between loving persons—the word used being *sukuse*, *i.e*, the connection established in a past life, implying its continuity in the present.

The illness had proved fatal and yet those who remained behind found a great consolation in seeing the statue made and imagining the deceased prince accepted into the communion of the saints in the Realm of Buddha. This is an outcome of the belief in Karma associated with the aspiration for the salvation of all.

The well-known but often misunderstood doctrine of Karma amounts to this, that no man's life is a product of the present only but is the result of a long chain of moral causation, in which the quality of his deeds and character bears the fruits deserved. It teaches that there is a necessary course of life and fortune for every one, which is determined by his or her moral disposition tantamount to the merit or demerit of the past and present deeds. The doctrine sounds like fatalism, yet the intention was to admonish every one to do his best in endeavouring to free himself from vicious Karma and to advance on the way to Buddhist perfection. The causal nexus was conceived not to involve reward and penalty imposed from outside but to consist solely in natural consequences of the inherent character or Karma of each person or being.[1] This teaching impressed the minds of the people with a sense of their own sinful nature and of the predetermined nature of their life ; it aroused a strong yearning to overcome the fetters of Karma, either by self-purification or by the grace of Buddha. It was one of the

---

[1] The cardinal vices are three : Greed, which is the inclination towards pleasure and satisfaction ; Hatred or Arrogance, which is repugnance against pain and displeasure ; and Stupidity, indolent Stolidity. Various combinations of these three qualities make up the resorts of transmigration, which are enumerated as six, or ten, including the lives of higher attainment. The six are : The *Deva,* or celestial existence of pleasure and satiation but subject to decay ; the Human existence, furnished with all the three qualities and therefore standing in the middle scale of transmigration ; the Animal, the embodiment of greed and stupidity ; the *Preta,* or ghostly existence perpetually tormented by thirst and hunger, the embodiment of insatiable greed ; the *Asura,* or fierce spirit perpetually overtaken by hatred and engaged in combat ; and the *Naraka,* or infernal existence characterized by endless torment and vain struggle against it.

chief factors by which Buddhism influenced the Japanese
extensively and profoundly.  The first conspicuous confession
of faith in it was made in the inscription cited above.[1]

The doctrine of Karma influenced the life and sentiment
of the Japanese people in two ways.  One was an extension
in the conception of life and the other was a fostering of the
mood of self-renunciation.  Human life, according to the
teaching of Karma, is an endless continuity of deeds and
retributions extending to the infinite past and to the future
far beyond the ken of any mortal being, and including the
existences in all possible realms, celestial, human, bestial,
infernal, and so on.  Moreover, the bond of Karma is not
limited to the continuity of one's individual life, but extends
to the ties of association binding fellow beings together in
a group or realm of existence.  The relationship of parents
and children, of husband and wife, of any social, racial, or
national groups, all are manifestations of Karma working to
perpetuate the inherited links of deeds and dispositions.[2]
This sense of continuity, both serial and collateral, made a
deep impression upon the moral and sentimental life of the
people, and extended and deepened the delicate, affectionate
attachments to fellow beings in all directions, strengthening
the sense of mutual indebtedness.  The sentimental life
refined and deepened by the sense of continuity found expressions especially in poetry and romantic literature, as
well as in the love of nature, in which the animistic traits of
Shinto religion found a modified expression.  The morality
of mutual indebtedness joined hands with the old communal
ethics and strengthened family integrity, especially during
the Middle Ages, and all was supported by Confucian ethics.

[1] The existence of not a few inscriptions of similar intent dating from the seventh
century shows that the teaching of Karma found easy acceptance and speedy
propagation.

[2] This is the doctrine of the *Dhātu*, for which see the *Samyutta-Nikaya*, 14—
a doctrine which was developed by Mahāyāna into a system of Buddhist sociology.
Cf. Anesaki's article on "Buddhism" in the *Encyclopedia of Social Sciences*,
edited by E. R. A. Seligman and Alvin Johnson.

The doctrine of Karma brought to Japan a religion of tender sentiment and broad sympathy, tending frequently to an extreme of sentimentalism or fatalism.[1] The belief in Karma, in this latter respect, induced the people to submit themselves to the necessity of fate or to renounce self in face of irremissible retribution. It amounted, in its extreme, to a teaching of non-resistance towards any ill, because every occurrence in life, whether human or physical, was considered to be an irresistible consequence of one's own Karma.[2] The remote causes of a present ill may be wholly unknown, but there must be causes of which present conditions are the effects. One can never escape the results of Karma but is responsible for them even without knowing it. Moral responsibility in the Buddhist sense in no way depends upon our own recognition of it, which is usually based on the continuity of memory. To say that we did not know its sinfulness when we committed an act, or to argue that we do not remember it, is simply an evasion, or at least forgetfulness or delusion. Indeed none of us remember all our past deeds, still less our past lives, yet we are thereby not released from responsibility ; the chain of Karma continues and its effects persist in the present life, despite our own ignorance or forgetfulness.

Now to confess one's Karma and to live a life of repentance are necessary preliminaries to Buddhist training, which consists in an endeavour to overcome the iron fetters of Karma as manifested in weal and woe, in births and deaths. Belief in Karma is not a blind submission to fate, but a step towards a strenuous effort to overcome selfish motives and to emerge from the vicious narrowness of individual life into broad

[1] Cf. Lafcadio Hearn, *Japan, an Attempt at Interpretation*, p. 216 f.

[2] However, this is not so much the case in present-day Japan. The change is due to the influence of industrial and scientific civilization, a change significantly illustrated by the attitude of the people towards the recent earthquake and consequent disasters. Though not losing at all an attitude of renunciation, very few thought or talked of Karma or fate in those terrible days.

communion with other beings, especially with enlightened spirits. The doctrine of Karma works, negatively, to relieve one from distress and remorse, and, positively, to arouse a sense of oneness and continuity of life. Buddhist fatalism, as it is often called, teaches how to renounce self for a broader selfhood and a higher cause. It was this virtue of self-renunciation that produced noteworthy moral effects in association with the Confucian morality of obedience. It trained the Japanese in the practice of forbearance and toleration, which were exhibited in various aspects of their life, though not infrequently verging on slavish yielding to circumstances.

Here again we can cite the life of Prince Shōtoku as exemplifying Buddhist influence exerted by the doctrine of Karma. The spirit of revenge was always a powerful factor in tribal morality, and the prince lived in the midst of tribal and factious strifes. How much he stood apart from the enmity of the contending clans can be seen from his conciliatory attitude towards the Soga family, who were believed to have instigated the murder of his uncle.[1]    Later Confucianists and Shintoists accused him, on this account, of lack of the sense of justice, but we must recognize, at any rate, that tolerance was on the part of the prince a stronger motive than revenge or strict justice. One evil or wrong is not remedied by another, to take revenge is to perpetuate evil Karma—that was the creed of the prince due to Buddhist inspiration.[2]

A further instance of tolerance and meekness was shown by the family of the prince in their practice of non-resistance. Eleven years after the death of the prince, his eldest son was besieged, together with his whole family, by the Soga, because the prestige of the prince's family was an obstacle to the

[1] Cf. Arthur Lloyd, *Creed of Half Japan*, p. 180.
[2] Cf. the case of Hōnen, below pp. 171-72.

political ambition of the Soga clan. The besieged prince, faithful to his father's legacy, observed the virtue of non-resistance, rejecting his retainers' advice to raise an army in his defence. There are several instances in the history of the time of similar practices of meekness, wherein we can discern the effects of the teaching of Karma.

However these cases may be criticized, Prince Shōtoku and his family testified to the rapid progress of Buddhist influence, which so refined the sentiments of its followers that some of them carried out the teaching of non-resistance even in face of the utmost peril. Nevertheless, the prince was not a weakling, but a man resolute in purpose and strong in action.[1] It still remains a general question how far non-resistance can be carried out in human life, but we see that the spiritual legacy left by the prince, supported and per-petuated by Buddhism, has borne fruits in the moral life of the Japanese. We shall see in the Middle Ages how many warriors exhibited the strength of their character in deter-mined indifference to weal and woe, in a peculiar combination of dauntless spirit and calm resignation, in all of which the Buddhist teaching of Karma manifested its great influence.

### Buddhist Art and Résumé

Among the achievements of Prince Shōtoku, those in the sphere of the fine arts stand out most conspicuously, not because the prince was himself an artist, but because he inspired the artists of his time in a manner unparalleled in

---

[1] Buddhist morality distinguishes, as referred to above, the repressive (*pradhāna*), and the persuasive (*sangraha*) methods in counteracting evil and vice. Prince Shōtoku explains this distinction in his commentary on *Shōman-gyō* as follows: "Extreme vices should be repressed by force, while light vices are to be remedied by the power of moral persuasion." Further he comments on the meaning of the persuasive method: "Since the mind which persuades and that which is persuaded are one in their basic unity, true persuasion consists in revealing the truth (of the oneness of existence)."

our history.   Buddhist art was the most effectual means of
attracting the people's admiration and reverence to religion.
It was a synthetic art based on ceremonies, architecture
playing the chief part in it.   Ritual with musical accompaniment was performed in temples decorated with mural
paintings.   These paintings, together with the decorations on
panels, ceilings, and pillars, constituted the setting for the
ceremonials, which were conducted around the statue of
Buddha standing in the middle of the dais.   The temple
buildings were mostly grouped together, and the central
building, usually called *Kondō* (Golden Hall), was surrounded
by shrines, pagodas, a bell-tower, and a drum-tower.   The
whole group was enclosed by quadrangular galleries, with an
imposing gateway at the south.[1]   The beauty of this architecture consisted in the combined effects of roofs, eaves,
gables, and pillars.   The whole plan was meant to represent
the communion of all beings gathering around Buddha and
making up a realm of spiritual enlightenment.   Another
feature in the Buddhist architecture of Japan is that the
background of nature is always taken into consideration,
both in the selection of sites and in effecting a harmonious
configuration of buildings and natural surroundings.[2]

Next to architecture, sculpture was a great manifestation
of religious faith as well as a powerful source of inspiration.
Buddhist sculpture flourishing in northern China and Korea
in the fifth and sixth centuries was marked by charming
naïveté and serene purity ; it was an art of contemplative
inwardness, well in accord with the transcendental idealism
of its doctrinal background.   Japan imported this art first
through Korea and later from China.   Most of the works

---

[1] The best example of the architecture of the sixth century is Hōryū-ji, near
Nara, erected by Prince Shōtoku as a college of Buddhist learning.   The mural
paintings in the Golden Hall there, dating from the end of the sixth century, represent various Buddha-lands with the figures of Buddhas and Saints.

[2] See Plates III, VII, XIX.

PLATE III

A

A. THE SĀKYA-MUNI
TRIAD
Work of Tori
Dedicated in memory of Prince
Shōtoku, dated 623
(installed in the Golden Hall
of Hōryū-ji)

B

B. THE HŌRYŪ-JI BUILDINGS
(7th century)
The Golden Hall on the left.   The Pagoda on the right.
The Main Gateway in the middle

PLATE IV

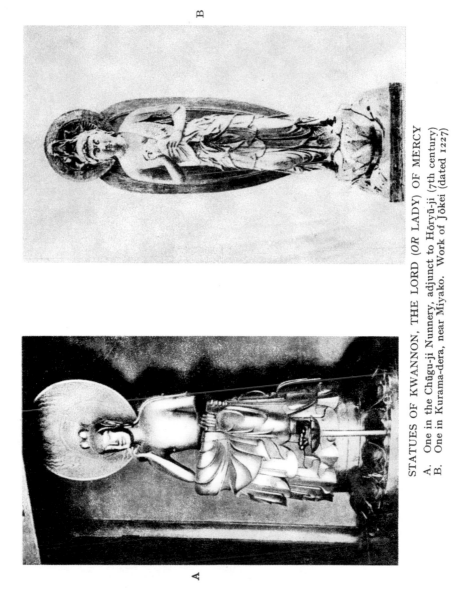

B

A

STATUES OF KWANNON, THE LORD (*OR LADY*) OF MERCY

A.   One in the Chūgu-ji Nunnery, adjunct to Hōryū-ji (7th century)
B.   One in Kurama-dera, near Miyako.   Work of Jōkei (dated 1227)

preserved from the sixth century are bronze statues, in which delicacy of line and charm of expression are gracefully combined with dignified serenity of posture. The people, newly awake to the profundity of Buddhist teaching, must have looked at these statues in piety and admiration, with a sense of a new revelation. We can well imagine how the pious prince, more than all others, used to sit immersed in profound meditation in the presence of these statues of Buddha and his saints, entering into spiritual communication with those celestial beings manifesting themselves in the mysterious beauty of sculpture. Indeed, the statue of Kwannon in the Vision Chapel, referred to above, is said to have been executed by the Prince himself. If the tradition were not quite true, it is possible that he caused his vision to be embodied in this statue.[1] Although many of the statues dating from his time seem to have been importations from the continent, there was then at least one great artist born in Japan—Tori, the grandson of the first Buddhist leader, Tachito, referred to above.

In sum, the turn of the sixth and seventh centuries marked the first epoch-making juncture of Japanese history, when the nation emerged from the primitive stage of its existence. The establishment of the central authority was a decided advance and a united national policy was inaugurated, although the clan division still continued to exist. Buddhism brought a marvellous revelation to the islands ; its philosophy was eagerly studied, monastic institutions were established, temple buildings arose to command admiration ; various sciences were introduced, orchestral music was played, and elaborate religious dances were cultivated. The country, at least the central part of it, was almost transformed into a Buddhist land.[2] Court nobles wore coronets and uniforms of

[1] Cf. further : Anesaki, *Buddhist Art*, chap. i and ii, also Plate IVA.

[2] In the year following the death of the prince there were in the central provinces 46 *tera*—temples and monasteries, with 816 monks and 569 nuns.

brilliant colours, church prelates in broad robes marched in religious processions, and the Prince-regent himself appeared as lecturer wearing a crown and monastic robes. Foreigners were welcomed in state with musical accompaniment and introduced into the country through the gateway of a Buddhist temple. Embassies were sent to the courts of Korea and China, and students brought back useful knowledge and high ideals from abroad. In all these reforms and in all phases of the national life Buddhism was the chief factor and source of inspiration, and the Prince-regent the leader, instructor, patron, and organizer. Indeed, his regency of thirty years (593-622) marked a highly significant epoch in the social and religious development of the nation.

# REFORMS AND PROGRESS

### The " Great Innovation " and Buddhist Work

THE seventh century witnessed further progress in the reforms inaugurated by Prince Shōtoku. The powerful clan oligarchy of the Soga was given the *coup de grâce* (in 645), and the way was thus opened to further reforms, which were signalized by the motto of the time, *Taikwa*, the " Great Innovation," the name of the era inaugurated in 645. The main aim of the reforms was to abolish the privileges and properties of the semi-independent clans and to make all the people directly subject to the Throne, pursuing the policy introduced by Prince Shōtoku. The scheme was framed by former students who had been sent to China by the prince, while it was supported by the Fujiwara family, who were the descendants of the old Shinto priestly family Nakatomi and were ardent Buddhists and progressives. The programme of reforms was not carried out at one stroke ; half a century more was required for its full execution. The rights of the chiefs of the clans over the lives and properties of their respective clansmen were gradually suppressed by repeated measures, yet the distinction between nobility, free people, and serfs, remained. The fundamental principle was made clear and largely respected, that the unit composing the nation was not the clan but the family and that the sole rulership rested with the Throne.

The political and social reforms were supported by moral instruction, chiefly based on Confucian ethics, that the virtues of justice, propriety, faithfulness, harmony were to be observed by ruler and ruled alike. Judiciary procedure was readjusted and instructions were given by the Government to the officials and through them to the people. The reforms marked a decided step in the advance of the influence of Chinese institutions and Confucian ideas, but it was at the same time a national renovation aiming at the unity and integrity of State organization. However, in all this the people at large remained passive and the leadership was taken by the Throne and nobility.

Naturally, Buddhism played a great part in the reforms. A religion emphasizing the ideal of equality, Buddhism always stood for national unity as opposed to the tribal idea, and its propaganda was conducted in co-operation with the united national scheme of government. In order to secure the efficiency of the Buddhist clergy, the Government established a system of supervision over the monks and priests by appointing " Religious Teachers," particularly of discipline, and also civil officials for the administration of ecclesiastical affairs. Buddhist missionaries were sent among the aborigines in the north-east and to the islands in the south-western seas. The zeal of Buddhist leaders in the capital and the activity of missionaries in the provinces during this and the following centuries were indeed admirable. Their influence made itself felt throughout the country. By their efforts roads were built, rivers bridged, the water supply secured, fruit-trees planted, alms-houses constructed for travellers, mountainous regions made passable and forests cleared. Not only did the religious propaganda assist the political scheme, but Buddhism thereby became more closely interwoven with the interests of the central government. Thus, the consolidation of the nation under a strongly centralized government increased in association with the penetration of Buddhist influence, and Buddhism became a State organization.[1]

A mysterious and yet conspicuous figure among these Buddhist workers was En-no-Otsunu (also called Shōkaku—died 701), better known as the *Gyōja*, or " Austerity Man." He was never ordained to the regular priesthood but lived a solitary life, unmarried, with only his mother. The mother died when he was about thirty years old, and thence he lived thirty years among the mountains practising austere discipline, and is said to have travelled much in the provinces, where his miracle-working is recorded in legends. Though we cannot ascertain whether he was a Buddhist or Taoist, he is regarded as the pioneer of the Buddhist mountaineer priests, a special order of priests who played an important rôle in the social and religious life of the following centuries, to be referred to several times in the Middle Ages.

The most prominent leader of the Buddhist movements in the seventh century was Dōshō (629-700) who had studied in China under the greatest Buddhist scholar of that time, Yuan-chang, and brought back with him the new translations of Buddhist books produced by his master. Through these Dōshō introduced the religious philosophy of the Hossō school, which was destined to exercise great influence, as we shall presently mention.[2] Dōshō also practised the Buddhist method of spiritual exercise and is said to have attained a high degree of divine vision. Though he left no writings, he was a pioneer of Buddhist philosophy, including logic and

[1] The rise of Buddhist influence is instanced, among other matters, by a limitation put on entombment, decreed in 645. Shinto, as a cult of the dead, was solicitous concerning the services rendered to the dead. It required enormous mounds to be erected for tombs and many things to be buried with the corpse. The new decree reduced the size of the mounds, and prohibited extravagant burial of treasures. This measure against gigantic entombment was only a preliminary step to the further simplification which culminated in the predominance of cremation, preeminently a Buddhist practice.

[2] Hossō, Skt. *Dharma-lakshana*, the " Criteria or Marks of Laws and Truths." It was a realistic philosophy of analytical tendency. See below, pp. 95-96.

other sciences. After having instructed his disciples in philosophy and in mystic meditation, he spent the last years of his life visiting the provinces, building monasteries and alms-houses, making ferries, constructing bridges and the like.[1] Thus he became a model for the Buddhist leaders of the following century. He was also a pioneer in the practice of cremation, for he gave an order that his own ashes were to be scattered to the winds.

Thus Buddhism rendered great services to the Government, in working to confirm the belief that the peace of the country and the security of the Throne depended upon the guardianship of Buddha and his saints. Temples were dedicated to Buddhist deities, rituals were organized in the court and official buildings ; copies of the sacred texts were distributed in the provinces, because the benefit of the celestial protection was believed to be secured where there existed copies of the scriptures or where they were recited. At the time of the foundation of the Court Chapel (*Nai-Dōjō*, or Inner Sanctuary), an order was issued in 655 to set up a similar place of Buddhist worship in every household throughout the country.[2] Whenever a case of illness occurred in the noble families, a state ceremony was carried out in Buddhist temples and various offerings were made. New temples were built and new statues made for special purposes of this kind.[3] These occasions were not only stimulating to Buddhist art, but to superstitious practices too. Taoist beliefs and

[1] At Uji, near Kyōto, there is a bridge first built by Dōshō, and his work is commemorated by a stone pagoda erected by him in the river basin, now excavated and re-erected.

[2] We cannot ascertain how far this order was carried out at that time, but we know that the Buddhist family sanctuary later became almost universal in Japan. But vigilance against Christianity, first adopted in the seventeenth century, was another powerful factor for promoting this practice, because every household had to be examined periodically by the parish priest to see if it had a proper place of Buddhist worship.

[3] We owe to the occasion of the illness of an Empress-consort (in 680) one of the finest groups of bronze statues that exists in Yakushi-ji near Nara.

Chinese traditions also supplied superstition ; the appearance
of lucky omens was celebrated, such as a white pheasant or
a pink sparrow, clouds of extraordinary forms or an alleged
transformation of waterfalls into wine.   But on the whole
Buddhism contributed to the material benefit of the people
as well as to the satisfaction of pious desires, because Buddhist
propaganda worked in association with the Government in
educational work, in the relief of famine and pestilence,
distributing medical materials and despatching physicians in
company with preachers.   These were received by the people
with admiration and gratitude, both towards the State and
towards the religion.   In short, the work of civilizing the
country and promoting charitable work lay mainly on the
shoulders of Buddhist workers.


### Further Reforms and the Institutes of Taihō

The progress of Buddhism and civilizing work proceeded
in association with the political consolidation of the country.
After the " Great Innovation," government institutions were
reformed and extended from time to time on models mostly
taken from China, which was then at the zenith of her glory
under the Tang Dynasty.   The seventh century marked in
Japanese history a period of rapid and profound changes,
the significance of which could be compared only with that
of the Meiji era, thirteen hundred years later.   The reformation
of legal and social institutions was consummated in the
codification of the " Institutes of Taihō " (or " Great Treasure ")
which was completed in 701.   The Institutes represented the
acme of Chinese influence upon the political, legal, social, and
moral life of the Japanese, and they were to remain the
standard code of law during the five hundred years of the
imperial régime.

There was one domain which remained comparatively free from Chinese influence, and that was the cult of the national gods, including the worship of the clan and communal deities. The National Cult Department (*Jingi-kwan*), which administered affairs relating to the priests, court ritual, the cult of all the Shinto deities, the Great Offering, propitiation of the spirits, divination and augury, was considered as superior to all the departments of government. Herein is shown the tenacity of the indigenous beliefs, and the special position assigned to the Department played a part in the development of the Shinto religion, especially when the Shinto institutes were re-codified at the beginning of the ninth century.

The most important features of the Taihō Institutes were the bureaucratic organizations of the central government, while the land was made national property of which portions were allotted to each family, the allocation being revised every six years. The unit of social organization was the family, in contrast to the clan in preceding ages, and the family was under the control of its head, the father. No one was allowed to marry without the consent of the head of the family, nor were occupation and habitation left to individual choice. Family continuity was perpetuated by means of adoption in case of necessity, but the adopted person had to be within the fourth degree of consanguinity. In the community five families were organized into a " body " (*ho*) and had to help each other as well as to keep order among themselves under a head, and a group of ten such " bodies " made up a village community. Thus the family and communal system was a legal and moral institution, which replaced the ancient clan grouping. This family system once inaugurated proved a very effective unit in the social and moral life of the nation and remained the vital factor of social organization throughout the imperial and the feudal régimes. It remains a living force even now, but it is facing a grave crisis in face of the industrial régime.

Another important feature of the Taihō Institutes was the inauguration of a system of public education. The institutions for this purpose were a university in the capital and a provincial school in each province. The university consisted of several faculties—Chinese classics, including ethics and law, literature, mathematics, and medicine, together with various applied sciences. The provincial school trained promising boys of the local nobility in Chinese classics, and the best of them were sent to the capital. This system of education, however, aimed exclusively at training for an official career, and only the boys of the noble families were admitted as a rule. The curriculum, which was based almost entirely on Chinese models, was arranged according to this aim ; it was this system that made possible the centralization of the government, which meant at the same time the elaboration of bureaucracy. The most important of its effects was the sharp division between the ruling class and the ruled. The nobles were trained as State functionaries, and Confucianism was the guiding principle in their moral instruction, while the people at large were left to themselves or under the care of Buddhist priests. Thus the class division also meant distinction in culture and sentiment, and this division was to show its effects more and more in the course of centuries. At any rate the fact is important that an educational system was established and that it was dominated by Chinese ideas.

# THE PERIOD OF NARA AND THE GLORIES
## OF THE TEMPYŌ ERA

*Nara, the First Permanent Capital, and the Era of Tempyō*

THE progress of national unity and State organization made it necessary to establish a permanent capital, instead of changing it at every new reign as had been done before. An impetus was also given by the zeal to rival the glories of the Chinese capital, while the progress of architecture made it possible. Preparations went on for years and finally the new capital was founded in 710, in a valley " surrounded on three sides by hills, opening to the south and washed by two streams." [1] The new city was called Nara, the name being interpreted to mean the " Abode of Peace." This event testified to the influence exerted by Chinese and Buddhist ideas, involving as it did a complete suppression of the old Shinto idea that the place where death had taken place was desecrated and must be abandoned—the chief reason for the frequent removal of the capital in previous ages.

The results of the social changes effected since the end of the seventh century were to be seen in the new metropolis, in the splendour of its government buildings and Buddhist temples with their heavy red pillars and green curved roofs and their greater size. The imperial residence was surrounded by " ninefold circles of clouds " and the city flourished like

---

[1] This configuration of hills and waters was considered to be auspicious and essential for the site of a national capital. The idea is of Chinese origin formulated in the theory of " Air and Waters."

" eightfold cherry-blossoms." [1] The glorious period of Nara (710-794) was thus inaugurated, and during its continuation all national movements arose in the capital. The measures adopted and the institutions established by the Institutes of Taihō were vigorously carried out, and every effort was made to centralize national life.

One of the significant achievements at this juncture was the compilation of annals and legends, partly based on the work started by Prince Shōtoku nearly one hundred years before. The compilations are the " Records of Ancient Matters " (*Koji-ki*, finished in 712), said to have been collected from oral traditions, and the " Chronicle of Japan " (*Nihon Shoki* or *Nihon-gi*, finished in 720).[2] These legendary histories contain stories of the gods and their descendants down to certain historical periods. The aim of these compilations was primarily to preserve the memories of ancestral times, but another motive, perhaps more important than the former, was to demonstrate the divine origin of the ruling family and other aristocrats, and also the remote antiquity of the foundation of the State. All this implied a zealous desire to rival the great continental neighbour in the dignity of national history. Naturally, native traditions were carefully recorded, but in many passages Chinese influence can be discerned both in ideas and expressions, though the exact amount of foreign influence cannot be ascertained. At any rate, these writings recorded a climax of the rise of national consciousness, and became the fundamental scriptures of the Shinto religion, though not sacred books in the strict sense of the term. They make up the material with which

[1] The former metaphor is borrowed from Chinese poetry and is often pictorially represented as the variegated clouds surrounding the palace, while the latter is found in Japanese poetry and is actually embodied in the numerous cherry-trees planted in the capital.

[2] B. H. Chamberlain's English translation of the *Koji-ki* forms the supplement to the TASJ (1882) ; W. G. Aston's of the *Nihon Shoki* in the Supplement of the Transactions of Japan Society (London, 1896).

later systematizers of Shinto and patriotic leaders worked to elaborate their ideas and theories. Another of the compilations was the *Fudo-ki*, or the " Records of the Air and Soil," referred to above, composed mostly of geographical descriptions collected according to the provincial divisions. Though they served certain administrative purposes, the legends and folk-lore contained in the writings pertain much to the so-called age of the gods. Thus we see in the beginning of the Nara period an overwhelming influence of Chinese civilization working side by side with the awakening of national pride.

The close connection established between Buddhism and the State was consummated in the first half of the eighth century. The sovereign who played the central part in this was the Emperor Shōmu, who ruled during the years 724-49 and lived a further seven years as ex-emperor in monastic robes. His reign, known as the Era of Tempyō, or Heavenly Peace, marks a climax of glory in religion and art as well as in government institutions. The ideals inspired by the Buddhist religion were put into practice by this ruler, and his work was supported by many able Buddhist leaders who worked not only in the domains of religion and learning but for social welfare and government too.

Indeed, the two centuries from the time of Prince Shōtoku saw a steady progress of Buddhist influence in nearly every branch of social life. Besides the religious functions of numerous temples and monasteries, these institutions also worked for developing the natural resources of the country and in establishing communications. These circumstances caused a steady accumulation of wealth in such ecclesiastical establishments, and while this was freely spent on social and educational work, it proved later to be a cause of corruption of the priesthood, which manifested its evil effects in the latter half of the eighth century. It must be borne in mind, however, that the education and discipline of the clergy were provided for. Archbishops, bishops, disciplinary masters, and other functionaries were appointed by the Government. Examinations for novitiate and priestly ranks were conducted with strictness, and disciplinary rules were rigorously carried out. Early in the eighth century, orders were given to the provincial governors to pay regard to the foundation of provincial monasteries as centres of religious observances and monastic discipline as well as of social work, especially of medical care. This plan was further carried out in the era of Tempyō, and finally the ruler conceived the foundation of a central cathedral which was to be a symbolic display of the Buddhist ideal of universal spiritual communion centred in the person of Buddha, parallel to the political unity of national life centred in the monarch.

The Central Cathedral, later known as Tōdai-ji, was erected in Nara and dedicated to the Buddha Lochana, a heavenly manifestation of the Buddha Sākya-muni, which was believed to have appeared when he remained in spiritual rapture after his attainment of supreme enlightenment under the Bo-tree. As is stated in a scripture [1] with profuse imagination, he was then in the midst of heavenly glories, being surrounded by all varieties of celestial beings, who were in reality but manifestations of his own spiritual illumination. In the Central Cathedral in Nara he is represented in a bronze statue more than fifty feet in height, seated on a gigantic lotus pedestal. The enormous halo is studded with minor statues of Buddhas and saints, while on the petals of the pedestal are engraved scenes of the twenty-five realms of existence with the figures of celestial and terrestrial beings —all united in adoration of the central figure and glorifying the majesty of the Supreme Enlightened. The temple structure covering the gigantic statue was originally sur-

---

[1] *Kegon-kyō*, Skt. *Gandha-vyūha*, see below, p. 93

rounded by pagodas and other minor sanctuaries enclosed in galleries, the whole structure being intended to symbolize the communion of Buddhist saints and at the same time the unity of national life.

The dedication of the completed structure (in 752) was the most brilliant event in the history of Japanese Buddhism. The whole court attended the ceremony and thousands of priests are said to have participated in it. The gilded statue stood in the centre, the ceilings and pillars were lavishly decorated, golden banners and variegated curtains waved in the air, candles illuminated the altars and niches. All sorts of music and dances were performed, introduced from India, Annam, China, and Korea. The richness and splendour of the ceremony can be imagined from the relics of objects used on the occasion, preserved even to this day in the magazine known as Shōsō-in standing near the temple—scores of dance masks, numerous musical instruments elaborately decorated with mother-of-pearl, rich brocades and fine needlework of varied designs, and screens originally decorated with iridescent feathers, which were set up by the roadside leading from the palace to the temple,

Besides these displays of artistic and ceremonial splendour the Emperor Shōmu devoted himself eagerly to ecclesiastical discipline, while the clergy worked for social betterment. The Empress-consort herself organized charitable establishments. A legend says that Buddha disguised himself as a leper and applied for treatment in her hospital, and that when he was being washed by the Empress he resumed his radiant aspect and ascended out of her sight. The conduct of the rulers was emulated by the nobility and people and much wealth was lavished in pious causes. Thus the union of State and religion was well established in the two centuries after the introduction of Buddhism, and its force manifested itself in the elaboration of ecclesiastical institutions, artistic display, and social work, all of which contributed to the glorification of the ruling dynasty.

## Buddhist Works and Buddhist Learning

It is no wonder that in such circumstances Buddhism produced many able leaders and workers. Not only were foreign monks and missionaries induced to come to Japan, but the Japanese themselves exhibited their talents and ardour in various branches of religious and social work. Bodhisena, a Brahman of the Bhāradvāja clan, arrived in Japan in 736, bringing with him learned monks and musicians from Indo-China and China, and he served Buddhism until his death in 760. Kanjin, a Chinese monk of the Disciplinary School (*Rits-shu*), showed indefatigable zeal in his missionary work and came to Japan in 754, after repeated failures in attempting the voyage. His work consisted in introducing a special discipline of monastic life, and he established the central Initiation Hall (Skt. *Sīmā*, Jap. *Kaidan*), an institution which was destined to play a great part in the coming years, because initiation into the mysteries of monastic ordination was regarded as vital for ecclesiastical organization as well as for personal faith and moral life. In addition, Kanjin organized charitable works and founded a botanical garden for medical purposes. He enjoyed the honour of being one of the most revered prelates of the time when he died in 763. Omitting other instances of foreign missionaries, we may add that the cases of these two exemplify the maritime connection of Japan with the Asiatic continent and the South Sea countries.

Among native workers, we may mention the names of three typical men. Giyen (*d.* 728) was an able teacher of Buddhist philosophy and opened the way for philosophic thinking. Though he himself left no writing we may trace to him the beginning of studies in logic, psychology, and metaphysics, which his disciples pursued further. The most eminent of Giyen's disciples was Gyōgi (670-749) who, besides being a philosopher, exerted himself in social work, founded thirty-four monasteries and fifteen nunneries,[1] built many alms-houses along highways, constructed reservoirs and canals for irrigation, planted fruit-trees, made ferries, and constructed harbours along the coast of the Inland Sea. In all this he persuaded the people to participate by preaching to them on the meaning of " meritorious works " (*pūnya* in Buddhist terminology), and thus combined his missions with social work. It is little wonder that the first census in Japan is attributed to him,[2] because he was the man who knew best the conditions and distribution of the people. He also, in co-operation with his fellow-worker Rōben, assisted the Emperor Shōmu in the foundation of the Central Cathedral. Rōben (689-773) was eminent for his learning and inspiration, and educated many disciples.[3]

There was another type of men who worked as pioneers in opening wild regions and in founding Buddhist sanctuaries on mountains, such as Taichō (682-767) and Shōdō (in the latter half of the eighth century). These men trained themselves among the mountains, and the people revered them as wonder-workers—an aspect of Buddhist influence allied with the primitive belief in the mysteries of the wilderness.[4] Thus we may see in all these Buddhist workers a wide extent and variety of work and influence, and both the Government

[1] The number forty-nine was holy to the Buddhists of the Hossō school, because their ideal land, the *Tushita* paradise, was said to contain forty-nine regions furnished with corresponding aspects of blissful conditions.

[2] This census attributed to Gyōgi gives the population at 4,989,658 — 1,994,828 males and 2,994,830 females. This disproportionate number of females is rather a credit to the alleged return than otherwise, because in those ages of corvée, including military service, many males concealed their identity or existence.

[3] His portrait statue in Plate VI

[4] It is an unsettled question whether these men were under Taoist influence, and if so, how much.

and the people showed appreciation of their achievements by generous donations and voluntary co-operation.

Besides the growth of Buddhist institutions, of monastic discipline and learning, influence was exerted by the schools of Buddhist philosophy which had been evolving in China for two or three centuries. As mentioned above, the Chinese monk Kanjin introduced into Japan a system of monastic discipline. It was founded on the basis of Mahāyāna ethics as systematized by Tao-hsuan (596-667). This *Ritsu* school introduced mystic ideas into monastic discipline, elaborating it through the mysteries of the initiation ceremony. Another school known as the *Kegon*, systematized by the Chinese Tu-shun (557-640), was introduced by the Korean Jinjō (*d.* 742) who gave a long series of lectures on the scripture Kegon in the Central Cathedral.

In the scripture Kegon, the Buddha Sākya-muni, or Lochana, is represented at the supreme moment of his great enlightenment. Immersed in deep contemplation under the Bo-tree, he realizes in spiritual vision the inner secrets of all existence. As the book portrays the scene graphically, all celestial beings assemble about the " Seat of Enlightenment " (*Bodhi-manda*) in adoration of the " Supreme Enlightened," every one of them bringing with him his characteristic brilliance and glories, to be fused into the all-illumining radiance of Buddha himself. In other words, the whole cosmos here manifests a grand symphony of spiritual forces mutually pervasive and all joining in glorifying Buddha. Expressed in philosophical terms, every existence is a reality in itself with its own nature and activity ; but these realities, though diverse in individual qualities, can perfect themselves by realizing their ultimate communion with the cosmic soul embodied in Buddha's person, and thereby make up the grand system of the universe. The aim of the Buddhist religion, according to the Kegon school, is to dispel the

illusion of the separate ego and therefore to restore everyone's consciousness to fundamental communion with Buddha
and through him with all other beings.[1]   We might call this
religion a cosmotheism, and though it did not exercise much
practical influence, its graphic representation of the cosmic
life contributed much to the glorification of Buddha Lochana
as represented in the Central Cathedral, where the scripture
was repeatedly explained in lectures and sermons.

Besides the disciplinary school of Ritsu and the cosmotheism of the Kegon school, there were schools of analytical
study devoted to cosmological and psychological problems.
This branch of Buddhist learning originated in psychological
analysis for the sake of introspection in meditation and was
elaborated by the Hindu patriarch Vasubandhu in his
*Abhidharma-kosha*, the "Store of Analysis," and hence is
known as the *Kosha* (Jap. *Kusha*) school.  This school, with
its associate school the *Satyasiddhi* (Jap. *Jōjitsu*), came into
Japan as the scientific equipment of religion, and their
influence was limited to the sphere of science or philosophical
speculation.   Vasubandhu and his brother Asanga worked
out a system of mysticism on the basis of his psychological
and cosmological theories, the religion of mystic contemplation called *Yoga*, or Union (of the individual soul with the
cosmic).   Its philosophy was systematized into the *Dharma-
lakshana*, the Criteria of Laws and Truths, and found its
chief exponent in the great Chinese scholar Yuan-chang,
better known in the West as the author of the great memoirs
of the "Occidental Countries," *i.e.*, Central Asia and India.
When Dōshō, referred to above, studied in China under this
great master, the school was in its ascendancy, and hence
the majority of the Japanese Buddhists who went to China

---

[1] The philosophy of Kegon shows some similarities with Leibniz's monadology ;
its conception of mutual spiritual communion through Buddha was a sort of pre-
established harmony.

in the eighth century were trained in the philosophy and religion of that school. Thus this branch of Buddhism, known in Japan as *Hossō*, became the predominant teaching in this period, and its doctrines were accepted as standard dogma, the scholastic theology of Japanese Buddhism.

The religion of the Hossō school aims at discovering the ultimate entity of cosmic existence in contemplation, through investigation into the specific characteristics (the " marks " or " criteria ") of all existence, and through the realization of the fundamental nature of the soul in mystic illumination. Its philosophy starts with an analysis of the mind and pursues it through an examination of sensation and apperception to the ultimate soul-entity called the *Ālāya*, the " Store " of the unconscious, so to speak. An inexhaustible number of *Bīja* (" seeds ") are, it is taught, stored up in the Ālāya-soul ; they manifest themselves in innumerable varieties of existences, both physical and mental.[1] Thus, things (*dharmās*) exist by virtue of these primordial seeds and various combinations of their qualities and marks (*lakshana*) make up the whole cosmos. Though there are infinite varieties of distinct nature in the whole extent of individual existence, they all participate in the prime nature of the Ālāya and are pervaded by the universal foundation or entity (*Dharmatā*) of existence. Accordingly, the aim of Buddhist training consists in examining the deeper nature of things, especially of our own soul, and in finally realizing the prime essence and substance of the cosmos. This training of " going back to the source " is carried out by a gradual ascent of meditation to the height of an all-penetrating vision, in which all beings are seen in their respective natures as well as in their unity in the fundamental " Store." Thus, the philosophy of Hossō is a

---

[1] This conception of the " Store " of the soul may be associated with that of the " Unconscious " in modern psychology. Similarly the conception of the " Seeds " may be likened to the " primordium " in Driesch's biological theory.

peculiar combination of realism and idealism, and its religion a profoundly mystic one.

The analytical study of psychological problems is, according to the Hossō view, a necessary prerequisite and associate of contemplation, which is to be consummated in the full realization of the prime nature of the universe as manifested in the Buddha's soul. The special feature of the Hossō school is its elaboration of the gradual stages in mystic contemplation, which are classified into ten. The first stage is unspeakable Joy (*Pramuditā*) in facing the truths of existence. Thence the contemplation proceeds to conviction in the truth of Vacuity, or the stage of Purity (*Vimāla*), then to Illumination (*Prabhākāri* and *Archismati*), further to Penetration (*Durangamana*), Stability (*Achala*), and so upwards ultimately to the stage of the " Clouds of Truth " (*Dharma-megha*) wherein the innermost nature of all beings is realized face to face.[1] Those who are well qualified in the exercise of contemplation and have achieved spiritual progress are entitled to share the glories of *Tushitā* (Satiated), the celestial abode of the future Buddha Maitreya. Hence the aristocratic tendency of the Hossō school, the attainment of spiritual heights being the privilege of a select few. This trait of the Buddhism of the eighth century had a close connection with the aristocratic régime of the time, and the alliance between the Buddhist prelates and the court nobles bore lamentable fruits in the corruption of Buddhism as a result of meddling of religion with politics.

[1] This gradual ascent is also arranged in four stages : (1) Facing the Actualities (*Kritya-anushthāna*) ; (2) Penetrating Insight (*Pratyavekshana*) ; (3) Universal Vision (*Samanata*) ; and (4) Facing the Perfect Mirror (*Ādarsha*).

# THE CULMINATING PHASES OF THE CULTURE OF NARA

THE eighth century was a period of classical grandeur in
fine arts as well as in State and religious organization.
Architecture occupied naturally the foremost place in the
arts, as palaces and temples were the stages on which the
court life exhibited grandeur and religion ornate ceremonies.
Not only in the magnitude of the temple buildings but in
the configuration of the groups of edifices, the architecture
of the Tempyō era was a manifestation of majestic beauty,
the imposing grandeur of which has never been excelled since.

As architecture was an embodiment of the cosmotheistic
idea, so sculpture represented the profound inspiration of
mystic contemplation as well as the high flight of soaring
imagination.    In contrast to the naïve charm and serene
poise of the preceding centuries, the sculpture of the eighth
century was eminent for bold conceptions, vivid expressions,
dignified postures, all executed in strong relief and powerful
curves.   The commanding dignity of Buddha, the beauty of
celestial glories, the grace and power of the heavenly beings,[1]
and the awe-inspiring gestures of demonic beings, all found
masterful embodiment in wood, bronze, or plaster.   The art
of Tempyō was indeed a happy combination of idealistic
aspiration and realistic execution, and therein we see well
combined the deep inwardness of the old Indian art and the
vivid expressiveness of Greek genius, the latter as inherited
from the Gandhara art.   Although this high development of
sculpture was chiefly imported from China flourishing under

[1] See Plate V.

the glorious Tang Dynasty, Japan produced its own artists, who worked from their own inspiration.[1]

Besides the beauty of individual statues, we have to notice in the art of Tempyō an impressive feature in its grouping. The group was not like that in Greek art but consisted of different statues so arranged on a dais or platform that the central figure, usually a Buddha, was surrounded by various beings, celestial, human, or demonic—a group being intended to represent a paradise or cosmos.   In this the Tempyō sculpture was an embodiment of the Kegon cosmotheism as well as of the Hossō mysticism, and foreshadowed the representation of the cosmos in pictorial cycles which was to appear in the ninth century.   Another point to be noticed is the portrait statues, mostly of life-size, of the leaders of the age, whereby strong personalities were immortalized in art, and so inducing to meditation on their lives and characters. This aspect of Buddhist art is to be seen again in the thirteenth century, when strong men worked for reformation.[2]

Although Buddhism was the dominating force of the eighth century, the indigenous religion maintained its influence upon the people, and Confucianism played an important rôle in social and political institutions.   There were, naturally, important interactions between these forces : Shinto was primarily a tribal cult and comprised local worships, but the progress of political unity reacted upon it, while the inspiration of Buddhism tended to broaden its ideas and spiritual vision. The ancient belief in man-gods or god-men was elevated by the universal ideals of Buddhism ; similarly the reverence towards the Throne was confirmed both by Buddhism and by the raised level of Shinto worship.   Instead of reacting against

[1] No individual artists have attained eminence in this period, but the artists are recorded according to family groups.  This shows that they had a kind of guild organization, based on family heritage and under the protection of the Government.
[2] See Plate VI.  Cf. Anesaki, *Buddhist Art*, pp. 23-25.

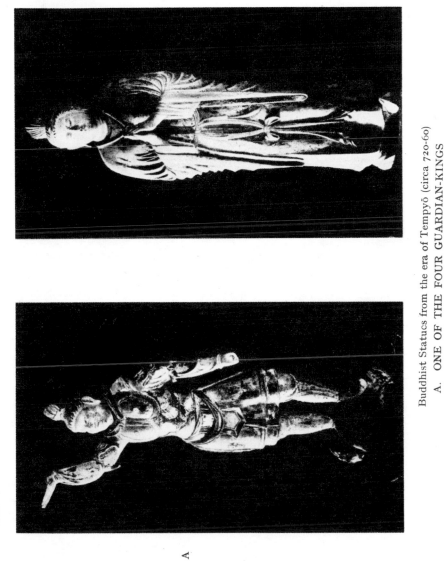

A

B

Buddhist Statues from the era of Tempyō (circa 720-60)

A.  ONE OF THE FOUR GUARDIAN-KINGS
(installed in the Initiation Hall of Tōdai-ji)

B.  BRAHMĀ, THE CHIEF DEITY OF BRAHMANISM, PAYING HOMAGE TO BUDDHA
(installed in the Hokke-dō Chapel)

PLATE VI

STATUE OF THE ABBOT RŌBEN
Installed in the Rōben Chapel of Tōdai-ji
(8th century)

Buddhism, Shinto raised its prestige by identifying itself more closely than ever with the interests of the central government, co-operating with Buddhism in that respect. The identity of the Sun-goddess with the Buddha Lochana was formally proclaimed in connection with the foundation of the Central Cathedral, when an oracle was secured from the Sun-goddess identifying herself with Buddha and giving sanction to the building of the cathedral. Another, more important, alliance was accomplished by means of an oracle ascribed to the Shinto god Hachiman, or the "God of Eight Banners," believed to symbolize the Eightfold Path of Buddhist morality. The oracle declared that the god desired to pay respect to the newly-founded cathedral in Nara and accordingly the divine cart of the god was brought from the west to the capital, and finally a shrine was erected for the god beside the cathedral, so that he might remain a guardian of the temple. Though at its original site his worship flourished none the less, he became a decidedly Buddhist-Shinto deity and played a great part in the later history of the nation, being regarded as next in importance to the Sun-goddess.[1]

The union of Confucianism with Buddhism was a more natural one, because the former was able to supply the latter with its practical ethical teachings, especially its inculcation of virtues. Filial piety was ever an integral part of the Hindu religion, as manifest in the practice of ancestor-worship called *Sraddhā*, the cardinal virtue in the religious life of the

---

[1] Later in the ninth century, when the capital was removed to Miyako, another temple dedicated to Hachiman was erected near the new capital, and this new site of worship played an important part throughout several centuries, even down to the nineteenth. Further, in the twelfth century, when the military government of the Minamoto was established at Kamakura, another sanctuary was erected there, because the Minamoto regarded Hachiman as the tutelary deity of their clan. Since then the deity has become the chief patron of military men. Hence the god is referred to as the "God of War," somewhat inaccurately, though it is not quite a mistake. Undoubtedly he played a very important part in Shinto religion. Further reference will be made in Book IV.

family.  Buddhist ethics perpetuated this sentiment and practice.  Though in theory it was not worship of the ancestors but an exercise of religious piety for the sake of the dead, in practice it corresponded to ancestor worship and filial piety as inculcated by Confucianism, and this consideration accelerated a union of the two systems.  Likewise the family and communal cults of the indigenous Shinto deities found in Buddhism a great spiritual support.  Thus, in the exercise of filial piety and the practice of ancestor worship the three systems joined hands in influencing the people at large, the Government was always anxious to encourage their teachings and officials were instructed to give distinction to persons eminent in filial virtue.

As an instance of the connection established between Buddhism and Confucianism, we may cite the case of Isonokami-no-Yakatsugu, a high official who died in 781. He dedicated his mansion to Buddhist worship, and in the precinct he established a library of Confucian books open to the public.  He stated the object of the establishment in the following words :

The two gateways (of spiritual life), the Inner and Outer (Buddhism and Confucianism), are one in the ultimate essentials.  Superficial thought would regard them as two different teachings, but there is indeed no gap between them.  Long since have I embraced the (Buddhist) faith, and now dedicate my whole mansion to the pious cause, and store the books of the Outer Way in order to supplement the Inner Way.  Since the precinct is a Buddhist sanctuary, Buddhist commandments should be strictly observed within it. . .  Let those who enter this place be finally released from the sorrows and worries of the present life and attain the highest perfection of Supreme Enlightenment.

This was typical not only of this period but of all the following ages, the results of the compromise being that Confucianism was regarded as the teaching for the present life and Buddhism the way to spiritual bliss in the future life.

The rise of a national literature was another remarkable

feature of the eighth century. Oral traditions had been written down by a curious adaptation of Chinese ideographs early in the century, and the stimulus given by that achievement encouraged the writing of poems and other works in Japanese. Lyric poems were composed not only by court nobles and ladies but by monks and peasants, by soldiers and their wives. In these poems were expressed naïve emotions and virile ideas as well as Buddhist or Taoist sentiments. Some poets expressed their adoration of the country or of the clan ; others gave free vent to love or to sentiments of nature, the changing seasons, flowers and birds, clouds and mists, the moon and stars. Buddhist and Taoist influence provided a pensive and melancholy tone, and the sense of the transiency of earthly existence was compensated by consolation derived from the belief in the continuity of life. But the idea of transmigration did not yet degenerate into the submissive resignation to fate, as shown in later literature. Refinement made a remarkable advance but did not result in effeminate sentimentalism, as was to be the case later.

These poems of the eighth century are preserved in abundance in the twenty fasciculi of the " Collection of Myriad Leaves " (*Mannyō-shū*) compiled towards the end of the century.[1] The collection represents the poetic genius of a people just emerging from a primitive outlook and aspiring towards deeper sentiments and higher ideals. To illustrate the religious and moral sentiments expressed in these poems a few specimens will suffice. Yakamochi, the great warrior poet, sings of the music of birds in a tone of melancholy :

> The myriad flowers, they lend their various beauty
> To every season, to every year-time give appropriate music,
> The birds of bush and forest,
> And eye and ear of man alike are charmed

---

[1] Longer poems of the Collection are translated in F. V. Dickins' *Primitive and Mediæval Japanese Texts*, vol. ii (Oxford, 1906). The following quotations are taken from it. Cf. K. A. Florenz, *Geschichte der japanischen Litteratur* (Leipzig, 1909), pp. 75-124.

By song of bird and form and hue of flower.
But mid the rivalry, while sad I feel and weary,
For all is fleeting, bird's music, flower's beauty.
As hare-month cometh
And lush the bushes show,
E'en night-imprison'd the bird he singeth ever,
Who, as our fathers have handed down to us
From time remotest, belike the offspring true of nightingale is.[1]

The sense of transitoriness is more directly expressed by Okura, the learned official :

In this our world the ills of life succeed,
As years and months slide, in sequence ever endless ;
Life's accidents uninterrupted follow
And life's evils must meet as they may.

.        .        .        .        .

Fair maiden ever the wont of maidens following,
Fine outland jewels upon their long sleeves broider,

.        .        .        .        .

Such time of blossom they fain would stay but may not,
For ne'er the days rest, but surely bring time's hoar-frost
.To whiten tresses erst black as pulp of sea-shell,
While wrinkles in rosy faces
Come why or whence one knoweth not.[2]

A soldier sent to the western front sings :

In dread obeisance to my high Lord and Sovran
On frontier service must I to furthest Westland
From home and kin fare.
Sad is my lady-mother,
Her robe's hem lifting her son she stroketh fondly.
My lord my father, he standeth by, and trickling
I see the tears adown his hoary beard fall.
I am but man and mortal,
The term unknowing of my days by the gods appointed,
And o'er sea faring across the fearful waters,
Still shipway making around the capes and islands,
On voyage perilous thus far I wander forth,
The god implore I, high god of Suminohe,
In weal and health keep my dear father ever,
My dear mother in happiness keep ever till I return
And once more see the homeplace.[3]

---

[1] Dickins' translation, p. 279.    [2] *Ibid.*, p. 92.
[3] *Ibid.*, pp. 300-301.

In the two hundred and fifty years since its introduction into Japan, Buddhism achieved great results, broadening the mental vista of the people and elevating their spiritual level, refining their æsthetic sense, promoting their love of nature, benefiting them by welfare work and relieving them from fear and distress. Confucianism played an important part in civic life, gave a system of moral ideas and legal institutions, and extended educational influence in the service of the government and in co-operation with Buddhism. National unity had gradually been achieved since the time of Prince Shōtoku, and governmental organization was firmly centralized in the permanent capital. Cultural work was conducted in the provinces and economic conditions were improved. Schools were established, sciences and arts were introduced and further cultivated. In short, out of a primitive state of tribal life Japan was speedily transformed into a civilized nation.

However, no sooner did those civilizing achievements reach a climax in the glories of the era of Tempyō as manifested in the grand dedication ceremonies of the Central Cathedral, than signs of corruption began to manifest themselves. The accumulation of wealth and power, both in the Government and in the Buddhist hierarchy, caused degeneracy to appear in every phase of their aristocratic life. As the nobles strove for oligarchic domination, the Buddhist prelates abused their privileges for further aggrandizement. In addition to the arable lands allotted equally among the free people, the lands newly open to cultivation were granted to the cultivators as their private properties. Much of this private land fell into the hands of Buddhist temples and monasteries through donation, or by virtue of their own enterprise, and even as mortgage forfeits. Thus not only was the principle of the nationalization of land gradually obliterated by the increase of these private properties, but the accumulation of wealth in

Buddhist institutions tempted the clergy to strive for worldly power.  Their ambition extended into politics, and one of the high priests is believed to have aimed at the throne.  Shinto priests became servile followers and servants of the Buddhist clergy and shared their privileges and wealth by flattering them.  A reformation, political and religious, was the need of the time, and vigorous spirits were arising in the last part of the eighth century, whose efforts bore fruit in the inauguration of a new era, which was to last for four centuries and to become the classical period of Japanese civilization.

# BOOK III

## THE PERIOD OF HEIAN
## AN AGE OF PEACE AND EASE
### (About 800–1200)

# THE NEW DEPARTURE AND
# GENERAL FEATURES

THE centralization of government, the codification of the
legal institutes, the organization of the ecclesiastical in
stitutions, and the final subjugation of the aborigines in the
north-east had been achieved step by step in the course of
the seventh and eighth centuries. Buddhism had attained
the dignity of a State religion, Confucianism had contributed
to legal and educational institutions, the amalgamation of
Shinto with Buddhism had made progress. But there was
something missing in the spiritual life of the nation—a basic
unity of ideas and beliefs and a deeper foundation of spiritual
and moral life. More unity was the need of the time, both
in the sphere of politics and of religion.

The tide turned in the removal of the capital, in 794, from
Nara to Miyako, modern Kyōto. This was a bold step on
the part of the political reformers, because it was bound to
encounter strong resistance from political conservatives as
well as from the ecclesiastical aristocracy who were in favour
of Nara as the time-honoured centre of national life. But
the step was taken in spite of the opposition, particularly
because freedom from the interference of the ecclesiastical
dignitaries was necessary for political regeneration. A parallel
reform in religion was carried out by the two great leaders
whose work we shall see below.

The new capital was eminent for the beauty of its environs
and it became the centre of culture, the stage of a brilliant
court life, remaining the imperial residence until the revolution

in 1868.[1]   It was in this capital of Japan that a highly-
organized bureaucracy centralized the power and wealth of
the country, and Buddhism instituted imposing hierarchies
monopolizing the mysteries of elaborate rituals.   The ruling
classes supported these religious institutions, the hierarchy
and aristocracy co-operated and vied with each other in
manifestations of pomp and splendour.   It was in this
beautiful Miyako that belles-lettres and fine arts secured
support and encouragement from the luxurious and sentimental life of the court nobles and ecclesiastical dignitaries.
Finally, in the course of time, abuses of religion, an extremely
emotional trend of life, neglect of administration and education, one-sided accumulation of wealth, these and other evils
became appalling, and the long reign of peace and pomp
succumbed of itself.   But the four centuries of " Peace and
Ease " (Heian, the poetical name of Miyako) are looked upon
as the classical age of Japanese art and literature as well as
of Buddhist mysteries.

In the course of the seventh and eighth centuries six
branches of Buddhism had been introduced.   They were
rather different forms or methods of learning and discipline
than churches or sects, and several of them were cultivated
even in one and the same college or monastery.   Yet the
divergence of the subjects pursued and of the training methods
could not fail to alienate them one from another and to produce men of different types and tendencies.   Moreover,
worldly interests and ambitions instigated competition between individuals as well as between ecclesiastical bodies.

---

[1] Besides the political reason, the Chinese theory of " Air and Waters," referred
to above, gave a strong impetus to the removal of the capital to Miyako, because
the topography of Miyako fulfilled the conditions of the three hills and two streams
far better than Nara.   It is also to be noted that the beauty of the place had much
to do with the sentimental life of the residents.   Not only did the gentle curves of
the surrounding hills tend to refine sentimental life, but the varieties and changes
produced by mists and showers due to the vaporous atmosphere contributed much
to the growth of tender emotion and finally of effeminate character.

In this way united effort was wanting more and more, and the influence of the religious bodies began to wane as a result of the removal of the Government from Nara. A new system of teaching and ideals, a higher synthesis, whether a reformation or a new departure, was demanded. Two prominent men appeared to achieve this task, each in his way, at the opening of the new era. They were men of very different types, but common to both were the aim of establishing a united centre of Japanese Buddhism, the policy of securing support from the Government, the means of deriving material from Chinese Buddhism, and the method of emphasizing ceremonies and mysteries. They were Saichō and Kūkai, and their teachings and organizations were to dominate the religious and social life of the coming centuries.

The ambitious scheme started by the two great leaders in conjunction with the new political era was to unite Japanese Buddhism in one centre and to embrace all social work under the control of one organized church. Neither of the leaders, however, fully attained this objective, because of the rivalry between the two branches of Buddhism which they established ; yet the idea proved to be the strongest force in social and religious control during the four centuries of the Heian. The aim, the organization, and the church polity inaugurated by these leaders well represented the ruling idea of the age, that State and Church ought to be in close co-ordination.[1] Indeed, the firm establishment of the central government in the eighth century had been made possible by the assistance, both moral and physical, of the Buddhist Church, while the latter's work was, in a way, a reflection of the political attainment of national unity. Each of the two centres of the Buddhist hierarchy organized at the beginning of the ninth century attempted to control all phases of social life. The

[1] It is interesting to note that the date of these Japanese reformers falls together with that of Charlemagne and Leo III in Europe. Another parallelism can be drawn between the East and the West in events of the thirteenth century.

Government found close associates in the Buddhist churches, and the oligarchy, into whose hands fell the rule of the country, derived satisfaction for their sentiments and temperament from the religion of those churches.  The aristocracy and the hierarchy shared a common fortune and fate, and all movements of the time were manifestations of the powerful political and ecclesiastical scheme of centralization.

# SAICHŌ AND HIS WORK

## Saichō's New Scheme

SAICHŌ,[1] who is better known by his posthumous name
Dengyō, was one of the silent monks who had been studying
Buddhism with a vision of a coming new era and seeking after
a new pathway for the future. The descendant of a Chinese
immigrant, he was born in 767 at the foot of Hiei, the mountain which later became through his effort the greatest centre
of Japanese Buddhism. In early childhood he entered
monastic life, and was ordained at Nara, in 785. Though
then a lad of eighteen years, he had been meditating on the
fate of Buddhism in Japan, and his dissatisfaction with the
bureaucratic rule of its organization impelled him to retire
from its centre and to live in solitude among the mountains
near his home. There he trained himself, forming a little
group of his fellows, and was able, in the course of three years,
to build a little monastery, which later developed into the
grand institution of Mount Hiei. His thought and effort
during about a decade of seclusion are little known, but the
outcome of his work is shown in his share in the removal of
the capital to Miyako, in the valley on the western side of
Saichō's mountain abode. This took place, as stated above,
in 794. Saichō had assisted this project in sympathy with the
ruler's idea of a political reform and also as it provided a great
opportunity for his own religious plan. The removal was
successful, and Saichō was rewarded by generous government

[1] This name means "Clarissimus," and his posthumous title *Dengyō Daishi*,
"The Propagator of the True Religion." The latter was given in 866 and was
the first instance of this kind of distinction, a sort of canonization.

donations to his institution, in defiance of the jealous prelates
of Nara.  Thus was inaugurated a new era in both the political
and ecclesiastical régimes.

In about twenty years after his retirement into the moun-
tains, Saichō achieved a great deal in developing his monastic
institutions and thereby in establishing a new centre of
Buddhism in co-ordination with the new political centre.
Numerous sanctuaries and colleges were built, then and later,
on the slopes and in the valleys of Mount Hiei, and the whole
institution was officially declared to be the " Chief Seat of the
Buddhist Religion for Ensuring the Security of the Country "
(*Chingo-kokka no Dōjō*), this implying, on the part of the
Government, the rejection of the old centre of Buddhism in
Nara as such.  In 804 Saichō was despatched to China, by
imperial decree, for the " search of truth."  He came back
to Japan in the following year, bringing with him the scriptures and treatises of the Tendai school of Chinese Buddhism,
together with material necessary for the performance of special
ceremonies.  All this secured for Saichō more independence
from the old ecclesiastical organization, and his institution
on Mount Hiei made such progress that it became the most
powerful centre of that Buddhist hierarchy and it later came
to control even State affairs.  This highly protected church
organization became the source of many evils, but it proved
also to be the fountain-head of Buddhist discipline and
learning from which flowed the streams of reformed Buddhism
in the course of the following five centuries.

Thus Saichō was a great organizer, but we must not fail
to note the ideals behind his work, the religious faith and
philosophical ideas which inspired him.  We have to consider,
first of all, the issue which made him an opponent of the
Hossō school and an advocate of the Tendai.  The former
emphasized, as pointed out above, hierarchic degrees of
spiritual attainment both in theory and practice, and the

result was a highly aristocratic religion in which only a few elect monopolized the privileges of spiritual illumination. In the doctrinal terms the Hossō school stood for excluding from the Buddhist perfection the type of mind which could be contented with mere contemplation—a tenet somewhat analogous to the Christian doctrine of predestination. On the other hand, the Tendai doctrine adopted by Saichō for his purpose of reformation emphasized the universality of salvation or the attainment of Buddhahood, embracing even the most vicious of existences, such as beasts and infernal beings. The philosophical background of this universalism was an idealism, which we shall try to elucidate, while that of the predestination theory was a realism of analytic tendency. Far-reaching indeed were the issues raised by these two tenets. Originating in India,[1] the division had been developed in China along theoretical lines, and now it was transplanted into Japan and resulted in more practical issues between the old aristocratic Buddhism and the new reformed type. Thus, for comprehending the point in question, it is essential to see what was the idealistic philosophy of the Tendai school, which became through the efforts of Saichō the leading force of religious faith and philosophical thought for several centuries.

*Philosophy and Religion of the Tendai School*

It was the Chinese philosopher monk Chih-i (531-97) who formulated a system of religious philosophy on the basis of the book *Hokke-kyō* or *Lotus ;* it is known as the school of Tendai (Chinese, *Tientai*), from the name of the mountain where he lived. The chief import of the book is to interpret the person of Buddha as a manifestation of eternal meta-

---

[1] The origin of the division in India may be traced back to the antithesis between the two thinkers, Nāgārjuna and Vasubandhu, who are regarded as respective representatives of the theory of " Non-being " and of " Being."

physical entity, and thus to synthesize the two aspects of his being, his actual manifestation or incarnation in human life, and the ontological foundation of his real entity. To cite an analogy from Christianity, the synthesis attempted by the Johannine Gospel between the human being Jesus and the divine Logos finds in this book a parallel in Buddhism. This conception of Buddha's being may, according to Tendai, be extended to other beings and applied to the relationship between the concrete, particular, and temporal aspect of existence on the one hand, and the metaphysical, universal, and eternal on the other. To say something exists, taking its actual, particular aspect alone, is one extreme ; it is the other extreme to say any particular thing does not exist, denying reality to anything but the universal entity. Things and persons exist and change perpetually, they appear and disappear ; but the world is an orderly existence maintaining its law (*dharma*) of being and change, as pre-eminently shown in the law of moral and physical causation. This reign of law or the endurance of the fundamental nature (*dharmatā*) is the truth of being ; the Truth is everlasting and universal, not to the exclusion of its particular manifestations in concrete beings. This co-ordination of the two aspects is, in the *Lotus*, illustrated by the instance of Buddha's person and is applied in the philosophy of Tendai to all other beings.[1]

Thus the philosophy of Tendai establishes a synthesis, called the Middle Way, between the two extremes of commonsense realism and transcendental idealism, in repudiating either the former position that a particular being is a reality in itself and by itself, and the latter conception of reality amounting to the denial of anything but the absolute and transcendental. The Middle Way is at the same time the all-embracing One Road (*Eka-yāna*), because it presupposes the basic unity of Buddha and all other beings, and emphasizes

[1] See Anesaki, *Nichiren, the Buddhist Prophet*, Appendix.

the possibility, nay necessity, of raising all beings to the dignity of Buddha himself. The historical Buddha was, according to this conception, a manifestation of the universal and primordial Buddha-nature for the sake of inducing all beings to the full realization of their own real nature or metaphysical entity identical with that of Buddha himself. Moreover, Buddha can and will appear, besides his historical appearance on earth, at any time and in any of the inferior existences for the sake of saving them. This is possible on account of the common basic principle pervading all existence, the same basic nature manifesting itself in numerous forms, qualities, tendencies, relations and so on.[1] Thus the whole realm of existence is nothing but a stage of " mutual participation " of beings and their conditions, a grand harmony of all possible instruments glorifying in unison the fundamental oneness of existence.

In the light of this world-view, the ideal aim of Buddhist perfection consists in the full realization, on the part of every one, of the Buddha-nature, or in the participation of our life in Buddha's purpose and work. For Buddha-nature is universally and primordially inherent even in existence of the utmost viciousness, and all of them can be elevated to Buddhahood. Indeed, mankind stands midway between Buddha, the Supreme Enlightened, and the most degraded infernal being, and, therefore, has the possibility of advancing further on the way to Buddhahood or of descending to the beasts or to the nethermost purgatories or hells. Hence the task of man consists in comprehending the truth of the all-pervading Buddha-nature and of mutual participation working throughout the realms of existence, especially the truth of the interaction and interdependence of different beings and their qualities, functions, and so on. This is first done in meditation,

---

[1] Ten of the categories are enumerated : substance, quality, appearance, potency, function, and so on. Ten kinds of existences are enumerated, from Buddha down to human beings, then beasts, and so on.

in which one's spiritual eyes are opened to the unity as well as the diversity of existence, and therefore vigilance is to be maintained towards the possibilities inherent in life of either advancing or retrograding on the path of moral and spiritual life.    In human life, even one single thought or one act has the power of stirring up a character or tendency destined to bring us to any of the diverse realms of being.

Ardour in putting faith in Buddha or vigilance in trying to follow his steps is the necessity of religious life.    Thus meditation is necessarily to be followed by constant effort in moral life.    The maxim is : Strive for attainment in Buddhist perfection by emulating the life of Buddha ; live a moral life ; save yourself by saving others and save others by saving yourself ; guard vigilantly against vice of any kind, because always at hand is the danger of becoming a beast or " furious spirit " even in this life.    Since all the virtues and vices manifest in the different kinds of existence are inherent in every one of us, since the splendour of celestial being as well as the torture of purgatory are nothing but manifestations of our own nature, all those conditions are to be visualized in meditation.    This means the Buddha-like enlightenment in the true nature of the cosmic existence ; it is the enlightened Buddha-soul that is fully alive to these realities and therefore compassionate towards all beings.    In short, religion and morality amount to one and the same thing, the realization of the Buddha-nature in ourselves.

Seen in this light, both the exercise of contemplation and a life of moral striving are vain unless founded on and aiming at full-hearted faith in Buddha, who is our leader on the way of salvation and the Lord of Truth.    Faith here means not only adoration of Buddha as our master and dependence on his teachings, but a state of the soul wherein we identify ourselves with the innermost secrets of the Buddha-soul.    This point brings us to consider the meaning of Buddha's personality.  According to the doctrine of the Tendai school, Buddha is really a man and yet the Truth itself.  As a man of historical reality, he attained the full truth of existence and lived accordingly ; he is the Tathāgata, the Truth-winner.  This aspect of his being is, however, but a manifestation of the *Dharmatā*, the fundamental nature of the universe, which consists in the correlated unity of all the varieties and variations of existence.  In other words, in Buddha we see the one who has come down from the height of enlightenment to live among us in order to reveal the real nature of our being.  He is the Tathāgata, the Truth-revealer, and he is the Way, the Truth and the Life.  This is the aspect of his personality expressed by the term *Dharma-kāya* (Jap. *Hosshin*), the " Truth-body." All and every one of us participate in this universal Buddha-soul ; it is in fact inherent in us, although we may be quite unaware of it.  Faith is nothing but a realization, a bringing to full consciousness, of the innermost identity of our own being with the Dharma-kāya.

However, this very fundamental nature of our life is too subtle and abstract for most of us ; and hence the Truth-revealer condescends for our sake ; he has appeared among us to arouse our soul to communion with him and to lead us on his path.[1]  The historical Buddha, Sākya-muni, is but one of those adaptive manifestations ; he is a Buddha in the *Nir-māna-kāya* (Jap. *Wō-jin*), the " Condescension-body," the concrete object of our faith.  Yet he is the Buddha *par excellence* for us living in this world and in this world-period, because of the moral and metaphysical bond connecting a being and the world he lives in.  Besides this condescending manifestation, Buddha reveals his wisdom and power, exhibiting them in the blissful glories of celestial existence.  This supernal revelation is, again, adapted to the respective heights of enlightenment on the part of those who have made

[1] Cf. The *Lotus*, *SBE*, vol. xxi. pp. 307-310 ; Anesaki, *Nichiren*, pp. 151-52.

a certain advance in moral purity and spiritual vision.   Hence the infinite varieties of Buddha's *Sambhoga-kāya* (Jap. *Hō-jin*), the " Bliss-body," and hence the varieties of celestial abodes for different blissful lives.   Among those abodes of bliss, however, Tendai Buddhism gives a special preference to the " Paradise of Vulture Peak " (Jap. *Ryōzen-Jōdo*), an idealization of the Vulture Peak where Buddha Sākya-muni is said to have revealed the truth of the *Lotus* based on the metaphysical conception of the connection between the world and the individual, already referred to.[1]

In sum, these three " bodies," or aspects of Buddha's being, make up the Buddhological Trinity, which is identical with the triune nature of our own life, the corporeal, the spiritual, and the metaphysical, so to speak.   Thus, faith means the communion of our soul with the Buddha-soul in its triune nature, our participation in his dignity and work. In other words, communion in faith presupposes a basic unity existing between the worshipper and the worshipped.   One who realizes this fundamental oneness of our being with that of Buddha cannot but proceed to save others by leading them along the same pathway of Buddhist enlightenment.   This exertion is moral life, the life of the Bodhisattva, the Buddha-to-be.   Faith is perfected by moral life, as morality is based on faith.

### Moral Life and the Mystery of Initiation

The fundamental maxim of Tendai ethics is " to put on the robes of the Tathāgata, to occupy the seat of the Tathāgata, and to enter the abode of the Tathāgata," in short, to live the life of the universal self.[2]   A special contention of

---

[1] See Anesaki, *Buddhist Art*, Plate VI.   The other paradises taught in Japanese Buddhism being the Tushitā-Heaven of the future Buddha Maitreya, referred to above, and the western paradise Sakhāvatī, or Land of Bliss, to be spoken of later.

[2] This maxim is based on a passage in the *Lotus* (see *SBE* vol. xxi, p. 222). Cf. Anesaki, *Ethics and Morality (Buddhist)*, in Hastings' *Encyclopædia of Religion and Ethics (ERE)*, vol. v. p. 452.

Tendai Buddhism, and more especially of Saichō, was that advance in moral life " in imitation of the Tathāgata " could be possible only on being initiated into the mystery of the fundamental oneness of life. The mystery consists in taking vows in the presence (though only ideal in the modern sense) of all the Buddhist saints, especially of Buddha as master of all. This was a modification of the old Buddhist ceremony of ordination (*Upasampadā*, Jap. *Jukai*), which consisted in expressing faith in the Three Treasures and taking the vow of observing the commandments. The specific point in Saichō's contention was that the confessions and vows were to be made not to human masters, as in other branches of Buddhism, but to Buddha himself, which meant to one's own innermost soul and entity. And therein lay the mystery, that by taking vows with these convictions and uttermost zeal, one could arouse the innermost good, including power and wisdom, which was inherent but otherwise dormant. Once aroused, this would insure for us an incorruptible firmness of moral and spiritual life and could last throughout any number of lives, in spite of obstacles, temptations, nay despite even casual guilt and the commission of sin. The initiation, therefore, was taught to secure the awakening and abiding of the fundamental Buddha-nature, the mystery of " securing the entity of moral life." [1]

With this doctrine of moral life and with faith in the mystery as the key to perfection, Saichō conceived a plan of organizing on Mount Hiei a special institution for the performance of the mystery. The scheme consisted in establishing an Initiation Hall (*Kaidan*) where ceremonies could be conducted to

---

[1] This entity is, of course, identified with the basic Buddha-nature and the awakening of it through the mystery is interpreted as even transforming the corporeal life. The ceremony of initiation, the acquisition, or rather restoration of the "entity," and the practice of Bodhisattva morality, these three make up the whole of the mystery. Cf. Hastings' *ERE.*, vol. v. p. 454.

carry out and amplify the teachings of Tendai, independently
of similar institutions established in the preceding century.
This plan of Saichō had an ideal and a practical bearing. It
was ideal in the sense that the proposed organization aimed
at carrying out the doctrine of the identity of all existences,
and therefore at leading all people to enlightenment in the
truth of the *Lotus*. Besides this ideal or doctrinal contention
directed against the Hossō doctrine of " exclusion," spoken
of above, the plan was meant, as a matter of practical importance, to be a declaration of full independence from the
authority of the ecclesiastical organization in the old capital.
For, unless an independent seat of ordination had been
organized, Saichō would continually have had to submit to
arrogant interference from the old orthodoxy, and could not
have ordained his disciples under his own direction and
authorization.

Thus, when Saichō in 818 asked the Government for an
authorization to institute an independent seat of ordination,
the prelates in Nara presented to the Government a joint
protest. Saichō tried to repudiate the arguments adduced
by his opponents, but the opposition only grew fiercer. This
problem of the Initiation Hall aroused much dispute on
side issues of doctrinal points, and the last few years of
Saichō's life were devoted to vehement polemics, which seem
to have injured his health, as he died in 822. But his
combat had not been in vain. When his death had put an
end to his strenuous efforts, the reverence towards him by
the emperor and people was so great that just a week
after his death the Government granted its consent to the
establishment he had planned. The opposition from
Nara never entirely ceased, but the life of the reformer
left a triumphant after-glow which, far from fading, grew in
brilliance.

In reviewing the work of Saichō we cannot but be impressed

by the broad foundation of his ideas and his far-reaching vision. Not only was the doctrine of his Buddhism a higher synthesis of the various branches of Buddhism preceding him, but he embraced in his institution of Mount Hiei various branches of Buddhist discipline and learning. The doctrine of Tendai based on the *Lotus* was the fundamental basis of all his ideas and work, but this did not mean that his work was mere philosophizing. For realizing or visualizing the teachings of the *Lotus*, he instituted various methods of mystic contemplation, which were destined later to diverge into different branches, such as meditation in pious devotion on the Buddha Amita's paradise, and a more Quaker-like method of spiritual exercise known as Zen. Besides the mystery of initiation, Saichō adopted various mysteries for invoking certain Buddhas and saints, ceremonies which attracted the aristocrats of his time and the following ages much more than the idealistic philosophy of Tendai. In this aspect of his Buddhism, which was called Shingon, Saichō found a great rival in the person of his younger contemporary, Kūkai. Saichō's successors met this rivalry by accommodating themselves too much to the rival's method of embracing promiscuous cults into Buddhism. This compromise gradually obliterated Saichō's fundamental tenet of converging all idea and practice to the faith in the Buddha Sākya-muni as is taught in the *Lotus*. This was one of the causes of degeneration creeping into Hiei, because the adaptation involved surrender to worldly motives and interests.

In establishing this great centre of a united Buddhist church, Saichō showed marked ability as an organizer besides being a thinker and mystic. The institution of Hiei came to comprise numerous establishments for cultivating the manifold branches of Buddhist training and soon developed into a vast number of sanctuaries, meditation halls, colleges, and monasteries. The slopes and valleys of the mountain were covered by thousands (three thousand, it is said) of such buildings.   Thus Hiei became the greatest seat of Japanese Buddhism and out of it different new branches of Buddhism were destined to blossom forth in the twelfth and thirteenth centuries, even after the degeneration of Hiei itself.[1]

[1] Cf. Plate XX.

# SHINGON BUDDHISM AND
KŪKAI'S WORK

*Kūkai, His Spiritual Struggle and Career*

KŪKAI (774-835)[1] was a man of keen insight, a worthy rival
of his elder contemporary Saichō, sharing with him the idea
of a higher synthesis and unified organization of Buddhism.
The son of a provincial noble, he was sent to the university
in the capital to prepare himself for an official career. There
he was instructed in Confucianism, but being dissatisfied
with its teachings he studied Taoism by himself. Not finding
entire satisfaction even in Taoism, in his search for truth he
left the capital and went to live in a Buddhist monastery.
Then he passed years in wandering among the mountains
and forests, training himself more in Taoist than in Buddhist
ideas, but the years of mental struggle came to an end
when he saw in vision a certain Buddhist saint, and he became
a Buddhist. This conversion is said to have taken place when
he was about twenty-two years old, and he wrote down the
process of his struggle and conversion in the twenty-fourth
year of his age, in 798. The confession is in the form of
dialogues between three men representing the three religions
respectively and is intended to be a comparative criticism of
them. Though written in the embellished rhetoric of the
time, the lines betray his earnest search for truth, his ability
in grasping the fundamental issues, and his future scheme of
a synthetic religion. His chief work written twenty years

---

[1] He is better known by his posthumous title *Kōbō Daishi*, which means " The
Propagator of the Law," as in the case of Saichō.

later (in 822) was the mature development of this youthful treatise.

Seeing Saichō go to China, the ambitious young monk Kūkai followed his example, and his study there in the years 804-6 made him a master in the then flourishing form of Buddhism known as Shingon, a combination of mysticism and occultism, with which he had had some contact in the years of his self-training.   After his return from China he organized Buddhist mysteries according to the new system and founded a monastery on Mount Kōya, about fifty miles south of Miyako.   There he trained a small group of his disciples, besides carrying out occasional tours.   The fifteen years of his life at Kōya were a period of preparation and training, and when his rival Saichō died, Kūkai was at once brought into prominence, in 823, by his appointment to the abbacy of a great State temple, Tōji, in Miyako.   Later he was made presiding priest of the Inner Sanctuary (*Nai-dōjō*) of the imperial court, and his influence extended from Miyako to the provinces.   He was at the zenith of his fame and popularity when he had himself buried alive, as it is said, in an attitude of deep contemplation (*samādhi*) at a secluded spot on his beloved Kōya, in 835.   His able disciples continued to propagate his doctrine and mysteries and his religion ruled the faith of the nobles and the people throughout the following centuries.   He is even to-day adored by many people as a saint of supernatural powers who could work miracles anywhere on emerging from his contemplation in the cave of Mount Kōya.[1]

### Shingon Buddhism, a Mystic Ritualism

The Buddhism advocated and propagated by Kūkai was an all-embracing syncretism of a highly mystic nature.   Its

[1] See, for stories of his miracles, Arthur Lloyd, *The Creed of Half Japan*, chapter xxi.

PLATE VII

A

B

BUDDHIST PAGODAS, MODIFIED FORM OF INDIAN STUPA AND SYMBOLIC OF THE " SIX ELEMENTS "

A.   Of Yakushi-ji, near Nara (early 7th century)
B.   Of Murofu-dera, in Yamato Province (early 13th century)

scheme extended the Buddhist communion to all kinds of existence, and therefore to all the pantheons of the different peoples
with which Buddhism had come into contact.  In embracing
the deities and demons, saints and goblins, Hindu, Persian,
Chinese and others, into the Buddhist pantheon, Shingon
Buddhism interpreted them to be but manifestations of one
and the same Buddha.  This Buddha, however, had little
to do with the historical Sākya-muni, and was called *Mahā-
Vairochana* (Jap. *Dainichi*), or Great Illuminator, a term
originally derived from the solar mythical epithet of Buddha.
His body, it is taught, comprises the whole cosmos, composed
of the six " elements " or components, earth, water, fire, air,
ether (or vital energy), and consciousness.[1]  Thus, Shingon
teaches that we can discern, when free from illusion, the body
and life of the Great Illuminator even in a grain of dust or
in a drop of water, or in a slight stir of our consciousness.
Moreover, any and every motion of matter or sound is his
utterance, while human speech and letters are a translation
of the cosmic language.  Similarly every law ruling the world,
every idea and thought occurring to the human mind, is but
a reflection, more or less faint, of the ideas stored up in the
cosmic soul.  The body, speech, and thought of the Great
Illuminator make up the life of the universe, whether as a
whole or in parts, and the aim of Shingon ritual amounts to
evoking the vitality of the " three mysteries " in the body,
speech, and thought of every one of us.[2]

The methods of evoking the cosmic mysteries in the

[1] The six elements are symbolized in a modified form of the pagoda, consisting
of five blocks of stone, square, circular, triangular, crescent, and spheroidal, respectively, which, together with infinite space, represent the six "elements."  The
same six are represented by various other symbols, such as letters, colours.  The
letters are *A, Va, Ra, Ka, Kha,* and *Hum.*  Arthur Lloyd's identification of these
letters with the Egyptian formula *Abraxas* is not well established.  For pagoda,
see Plate VII.

[2] This threefold category is common to all the systems of Hinduism and to
Manichæism.  Probably through the latter channel it influenced Augustine and
entered the West, in the phrase " thought, word, and deed."

individual life consist in various kinds of symbolism, which are taught to be adequate for the purpose, ranging from the highest of realizing a union with the Buddha to the lowest of praying for a little benefit.  Numerous deities or demons are interpreted as embodying this or that aspect of cosmic life, and every one of them is represented by definite conventions, usually in more than one form for one deity, either in a picture or in a statue or in a letter, while their functions are symbolized by their respective attires, the objects they hold, and other attributes.  In the ritual performed before these deities, the postures, movements, and utterances of the serving priests or worshippers are prescribed on the assumption that they will evoke the mysterious powers of the deities and thus answer the purposes of worship.  The contention of Shingon Buddhism amounts to " adequately " (in the mystic sense) representing cosmic mysteries in visible and tangible forms, in contradistinction to mere doctrine or meditation as advocated by other branches of Buddhism.  These symbols and rituals had been elaborated in the countries of the continent in the course of centuries, and it was the task of Kūkai to organize their intricacies into a system of doctrine and mystery.

Shingon Buddhism, as it was an attempt to unify the pantheons of various religions, proceeded from its mystic ritualism to a systematization of its world-view.  The result was a curious but ingenious device of graphically representing the cosmos in two pictures or diagrams, called *Mandala*. These diagrams symbolized two aspects of cosmic life, its being and vitality, in the ideal or potential entity and in the dynamic manifestations.[1]  The point emphasized was the harmony between unity and diversity.  The Great Illuminator was considered to be the all-comprehensive soul as well as the all-creating source of the universe, while all other exist-

[1] Cf. Anesaki, *Buddhist Art*, pp. 38-42 and Plate XVI.

ences, including deities, demons, men, beasts, and so on, were stated to be manifestations of his powers and intentions.

Now the ideal side of the world is called the " Realm of the Indestructibles " (Skt. *Vajra-dhātu*, Jap. *Kongō-kai*), in which the basic and indestructible Ideas are present in the all-comprehensive soul of the Great Illuminator. In the graphic representation of this realm, the centre is occupied by the Great Illuminator seated in deep, serene contemplation on a white lotus, all encircled by a pure white halo. He is surrounded by his emanations, various Buddhas and saints —each in a white halo—and by further emanations represented by figures and symbols arranged in the squares surrounding the central one. All of these indestructible potential Ideas are destined to manifest their activities, which make up the dynamic aspect of the universe.

The dynamic side of cosmic life is represented in the graphic scheme of the " Womb-store " (Skt. *Garbha-kukshi*, Jap. *Taizō*), wherein the manifold groups of deities and other beings are arrayed according to the kinds of the powers and intentions they embody. In the centre there is a red lotus flower, with its seed-pod and eight petals, which symbolizes the heart of the universe and corresponds to the nine squares of the Indestructible Cycle. The seed-pod of the lotus is the seat of the Great Illuminator and the petals are occupied by other Buddhas. They are all surrounded by a double halo of red discs, symbolic of activity. The further manifestations may be divided into two classes, representing the wisdom and the mercy of the central Buddha—the wisdom which illumines us in the truth of universal communion and represses folly and subjugates vice, and the mercy which includes all beings in the all-embracing love of the cosmic Lord.

The universe thus seen under its two aspects, the potential and the dynamic, is nothing but the life and being of the Great Illuminator himself, while the developments of the world embody the inexhaustible fullness of his wisdom and mercy. This graphic representation of the two cycles in the two *Mandalas* was partly an outcome of speculation but largely a modification of ritual performance, in which those figures and symbols were arrayed on the ceremonial dais and were used for the purpose of evoking the respective mysterious powers. Each figure and symbol is conceived to contain a certain power which is inherent in every one of us too, and worship means nothing but a realization by acts of ritual performance of the inherent unity.    Seen in this way, religion is enlightenment in the truth of essential unity, which means a harmonious union in faith with the " enfolding power " (Skt. *Adhishthāna* Jap. *Kaji*) of the universal Lord.

Consequent upon the realization of this union, all the manifestations emanating from the Great Illuminator can be evoked by our acts of worship.    The ways of worship in Shingon ritual are modelled on their standard representations in the two Mandalas.    Bodily postures of sitting in meditation, or of moving and joining hands in imitation of deities as depicted or symbolized in the Mandalas, are combined with the handling of symbols and objects such as lotus flowers, weapons, the symbolic thunderbolt (*vajra*), and so forth, all of which contribute to the efficacy of the performance by embodying cosmic activities in actual life : they are, essentially, the body, speech, or thought of the cosmic Lord.    All ritual utterances, repeating Buddha's names, mystic formulas, sacred texts, are a part of the cosmic speech which is being voiced perpetually and everywhere by the Great Illuminator.    A special significance is placed by Shingon Buddhism in the efficacy of mystic formulas in evoking divine power—a peculiar trait of this branch of Buddhism derived from the Hindu belief in the mysterious power of hymns and formulas.    Hence the name *Shingon*, which means the " true word," being the Chinese translation of the Sanskrit *mantra*, the word for

PLATE VIII

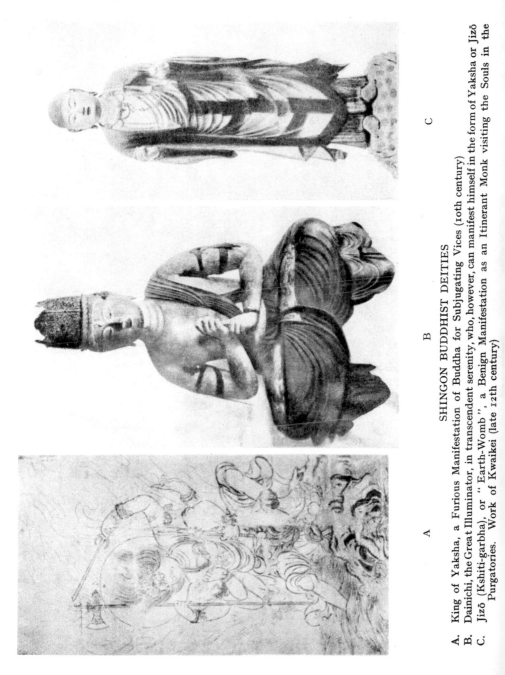

A          B          C

SHINGON BUDDHIST DEITIES

A.   King of Yaksha, a Furious Manifestation of Buddha for Subjugating Vices (10th century)

B.   Dainichi, the Great Illuminator, in transcendent serenity, who, however, can manifest himself in the form of Yaksha or Jizō

C.   Jizō (Kshiti-garbha), or " Earth-Womb ", a Benign Manifestation as an Itinerant Monk visiting the Souls in the Purgatories.   Work of Kwaikei (late 12th century)

hymn. The same thing is also called *Dhāranī*, that is, an enigmatic phrase or sentence expressing the mysteries of the universe, and hence another appellation of this type of Buddhism, the " Way of the Dhāranī."

Religious acts are but manifestations of the " Three Mysteries " of the Great Illuminator; and any act, speech, or thought may evoke the mysterious powers of the deity, when done in faith and in harmony with the cosmic life activities. Understood in this way, symbols and mysteries find hardly any limit in their varieties and in the spheres of their use and application. They may be used for any purpose, even for torturing a hated fellow-creature as well as for the salvation of all fellow beings. The mysterious efficacy can be secured by a movement of the fingers, or by the utterance of a single formula, whereas a ceremony of great pomp and grandeur may be organized for the same purpose of calling mysterious powers. Herein lay the secret of Shingon Buddhism, by which it attracted all kinds of people and influenced the ambitious nobles and the simple people alike, that it promised to fulfil any sort of religious or other desires. We have also to note that painting and sculpture, dance and music, and other arts were necessary associates of the Shingon mysteries, and that the influence of Shingon upon the court nobles depended very much upon its artistic display.[1]

### Kūkai's Work and His Theory of Spiritual Development

Kūkai's scheme was to build up an all-embracing system of idea and practice, a cosmotheism syncretic and somewhat promiscuous in character. His work was as broad as his system and embraced nearly all interests of human life, art and art crafts, philology and literature, education and social work, philosophy and religion. As the organizer of mystic ceremonies in which minute details of painting and sculpture

[1] Cf. Anesaki, *Buddhist Art*, chap. iii. See Plate VIII.

were essential, he trained himself as an artist and could himself execute his ideas and teachings in delicate lines and brilliant colours.  He understood how to attract people by the combined effect of form and colour, light and incense, music and movement.  His institution of popular education, his missionary journeys in the provinces, his writings in rhetorical style, all helped to propagate his mystic religion. He succeeded in overshadowing all other forms of Buddhism by his theory and practice, and his popularity gradually overshadowed Saichō's work, so that the latter's followers found it expedient to emphasize more and more the Shingon aspects of their master's religion.  The result was that the Buddhism of the Heian period became predominantly Shingon, and mystic ritual and artistic display came to rule the life and sentiment of the aristocracy.  Their emotionalism and loss of moral vigour were in mutual causal relation with the hedonistic traits of Shingon mysticism.  During the following four centuries elaborate rituals were the order of the day in palace and temple.  Litanies and incantations accompanied the ceremonies ; gorgeous decorations were illuminated by sacrificial fires ; the sanctuaries were filled with the perfume of sprinkled waters and the fragrance of incense.  The survival of Kūkai's influence upon the fine arts can be seen even in present-day Japan in that his mystic ideas lay behind music and the dance in particular.

As Kūkai was a genius of synthetic art so he was a philosopher of all-absorbing syncretism.  In him were combined the dialectic mind of a Hegel, the theosophic tendency of a Philo, the syncretic mind of a Mani.  Indeed, the affinity or connection of Shingon Buddhism with Manichæism or the Alexandrian theosophy is a question of great interest.[1]  How-

---

[1] Arthur Lloyd's contention, in his *Creed of Half Japan*, that Shingon Buddhism was greatly influenced by Manichæism is not conclusive ; his work is often marked by hasty conclusions ; yet his suggestions are valuable and await further investigation.

ever this may be, the syncretic character of Kūkai's mind and the pervading influence of his mysticism were remarkable. His intellect could not rest until his ideas were expressed in metaphysical terms ; moreover, as the founder or formulator of a specific branch of Buddhism, he thought it his duty to elucidate the superiority of his system in philosophical language, as had been done by all his predecessors. The result was an essay on " The Ten Stages of Spiritual Development," written in 822, which was later condensed and given the title of " The Jewel Key to the Store of Mysteries." [1] The two essays trace spiritual development from the lowest stage of blind instinct to the full realization of cosmic mysteries in the enlightened soul identical with that of the Great Illuminator, and all forms of Buddhism are interpreted to represent intermediate stages between the two.

In the Introduction to the " Jewel Key " Kūkai expresses his deep commiseration towards all beings immersed in the ocean of births and deaths, and his style, perhaps too rhetorical, shows the mystic flight of his imagination. He says in one place :

> " Vast, vast, extremely vast
> Are the scrolls of yellow silk,[2]
> Hundreds and thousands ' In ' and ' Out.' [3]
> Profound, profound, very profound
> Ways are marked and ways shown, hundreds of ways.
> What benefit in writing and reading, finally to die ?
> Unknown and unknowable, self never knows self ;
> Thinking, thinking, and thinking, yet no sign of wisdom !
>
> .    .    .    .    .
>
> Mad are beings in the three realms of existence,
> And none aware of his own madness !
> Blind are beings, four in the modes of their birth,
> Yet all unaware of their blindness !

---

[1] The titles in Japanese are respectively : *Jūjū-shin-ron* and *Hizō Hōyaku.*

[2] Buddhist manuscripts were written on scrolls of yellow silk or paper.

[3] The " In " means Buddhism and the " Out " Confucianism and Brahmanism. Cf. above, p. 100.

Born, born, and reborn without limit,
And still dark as to the origin of birth ;
Dying, dying, and dying without end,
Yet veiled is the ultimate goal of life."

This passionate expression may be regarded also as a reminiscence of the author's own spiritual trouble in his years of struggle, while its lofty conception shows the height of his vision which has overcome all the commotions of worldly existence.

The majority of beings are immersed in the depths of blindness, entangled in the instincts of food and sex (the first stage). When they rise out of the depths, they see the necessity of moral rules and observances, yet the rules serve merely as a moderation or restraint. This is the status of Confucianism which emphasizes moral life and yet is devoid of spiritual illumination (the second stage). Others, like Taoists and Brahmans, extend their spiritual vision somewhat beyond the present· world, yet being content in the attainment of supernormal powers they are living in a fool's paradise (the third stage). Higher than this, a school of Buddhism rises to a height of spiritual life and teaches the truth of non-ego but falls into the pit of nihilism (the fourth stage) ; while another is satisfied with exterminating the root of Karma and aspires to nothing higher, a self-conceited egoism (the fifth stage). In contrast to these stages of the Little Vehicle, the Great Vehicle makes an advance in discovering the source of all existence in the soul of the believer, but is deluded in denying reality to the objective world (the sixth stage). This denial of the world, however, leads to a vision of the prime entity, the Ālāya, which is unborn and undying—the teaching of the Hossō school (the seventh stage). This realization of the eternal reality convinces us of the original identity of all beings, which therefore are to be embraced into the Sole Road of salvation, the doctrine of the Tendai school (the eighth stage). Further upwards the mind of the Kegon Buddhist reaches the stage (the ninth) of realizing the vast communion of existence in this very life. But ideal vision is the chief trait of the Kegon religion, and we need, according to Kūkai, to proceed to a fuller realization of cosmic mysteries even within a particle of matter or in every single act of our own life.

The highest, the tenth stage is attained by Shingon Buddhism which is not a mere system of doctrine but the actual embodiment of the life and idea of the Great Illuminator, especially in the performance of mystic rites. Kūkai sums up his religion as follows :

> The healing power of the exoteric doctrine [1] has wiped away all dust ;
> Now opens the store of the True Word (Shingon),
> In which all hidden treasures are brought to light,
> And there embodied are all virtues and powers.

This condition of spiritual development is called " The Soul filled with the Glories of Mystery," which is further characterized thus :

> The Buddhas in the innumerable Buddha-lands
> Are naught but the Buddha within our own soul ;
> The Golden Lotus, as multitudinous as the drops
> Of ocean water, is living in our body.
> Myriads of figures are contained in every mystic letter ;
> Every piece of chiselled metal embodies a Deity,
> In whom are pregnantly present the real entities of Virtue and Merit.
> In realizing all this every one shall attain
> The glories of being, even in this corporeal life.

In sum, all the arguments and dialectics of Kūkai had as objective the justification and glorification of the mystic practices through which he influenced his age and posterity.

[1] Other branches of Buddhism besides Shingon are regarded as exoteric doctrines and as preliminary to Shingon esotericism.

# RELIGION AND SOCIAL LIFE

## *Two Centuries of Aristocratic Oligarchy*

THE new conditions in the beginning of the ninth century, especially concerning religion, marked the climax of Chinese influence. The establishment of a centralized government and the organization of a bureaucracy on Chinese models had been fully achieved ; Buddhism had imported innovations in abundance from the Asiatic continent ; in arts and literature Japan had learned much from the glorious culture of the Tang Dynasty. A tide of reaction was to be expected. In addition to this, China had passed the zenith of her civilization, and the decline of the Tang Dynasty became evident in the course of the ninth century. The Japanese court sensed the situation and put an end to the despatch of a regular envoy to China in 894. The codification of the Engi Institutes, comparatively free as they were from Chinese influence, signalized an independent development of Japanese culture. These Institutes were proclaimed in 901, just two centuries after the Taihō Institutes. Thus we may date from the beginning of the tenth century a period of seclusion, or severance from Chinese models in all aspects of social life. This made Japan's own development independent of the vicissitudes of her great neighbour, but it meant too the beginning of self-satisfaction, which lasted more than two hundred years until the middle of the twelfth century.

Growth and change gave place to rest and peace, vigour and aspiration to refinement and elaboration, and stagnation set in. In contrast to the frequent despatch of scholars and monks to China in the preceding centuries, we see only a few isolated cases of Japanese Buddhists going across the sea, and none of the officials went. Instead of importing new arts and literature, Japan produced her own, delicate and refined in style and sentiment, tending to become more and more effeminate and emotional. The central government in the hands of an oligarchic bureaucracy gradually lost its hold upon the provinces, as the aristocrats cared more for a life of ease and luxury than for administration or military organization. The term " court noble " became another name for emasculated men of refined taste and delicate sentiments, while the provincial governors and military men were children of the wilderness. Training was neglected and culture meant refinement in the arts of poetry and music, or even in the art of distinguishing different kinds of incense and perfume. The delicacy of all the products of this age is often attributed to the peculiar genius or fundamental character of the Japanese people. But this view overlooks the fact that the culture of this period did not pertain to the whole people : it was pre-eminently an aristocratic culture, that of a class which lived in self-content without incentive or competition except among its own members. All we are about to review can only be understood as phenomena peculiar to an age of aristocratic culture in a secluded nation.

What is to be noted in connection with the ethos of the aristocratic régime is the relation between the emotional trend of life and the prevailing ethical teaching, particularly as exhibited in a division between the head and heart. Viewed from the negative side, Confucianism was chiefly responsible for it, because its moral teachings were too formal or stoic to satisfy the demands of the heart and made little appeal to the tender side of human nature. Even avowed Confucianists felt this and called upon Buddhism to supply the deficiency. The aspect of Buddhism resorted to for this purpose was naturally not its metaphysics but its arts and mysteries, and in this respect Shingon Buddhism was peculiarly attractive, offering to the devotees its rich pantheon and gorgeous rituals suited to any need or desire. A minister of State handling government affairs with all the dignity and formality of an aristocrat, or a professor of Confucian ethics and politics in the university, would, upon returning to his home, become transformed into a devout Buddhist praying before the image of his patron deity. Women played an integral part in court life and in society under an aristocratic régime such as the one now being considered. They naturally represented the emotional side of human nature and induced men to share in the sentimentalism of their poetry as well as of their devotion to Shingon arts and mysteries. Thus ensued a dualism in life, the mind being occupied with civics and politics, while the heart was immersed in sentiment and mysteries. It was a dualism but its two constituents never faced each other in antagonism. They were juxtaposed and kept apart as if there were a partition between them, and yet were well reconciled. This dualism was visible in nearly every phase of social and spiritual life, in the compromise between secular life and religious aspiration, between Confucian ethics and Buddhist mysteries, between political effort and poetic sentiment. All this was played on the stage of an aristocratic culture with the figures of the Fujiwara nobles surrounded by Confucian savants and Buddhist prelates, the people at large remaining the spectators but being at the same time the financial supporters and subservient tools.

### The " Double Aspect " Shinto and a Dualism of Life Motives

In spite of the overwhelming influence of Buddhism, the worship of the national deities never lost its hold upon the

PLATE IX

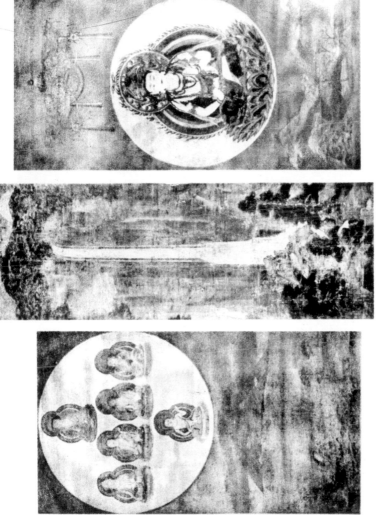

A                 B                 C

SYNCRETIC BUDDHICO-SHINTO PAINTINGS

A. The Deities and Hills of Kasuga, the Buddhist Noumena of the Shinto Deities of Kasuga appearing over the Hills

B. The Waterfall of Nachi adored as a manifestation of the Deity of Kumano, whose Noumenon is identified with the Buddha Amita—a survival of the original Nature-worship (late 12th century)

C. Kokūzō (Akāsa-garbha), or "Sky-Womb", the Noumenon of the Deity of Asama, appearing in the air above Mount Asama (late 14th century in the Museum of Fine Arts, Boston)

PLATE X

## A PORTABLE SHRINE OF A SYNCRETIC SHINTO DEITY
Belonging to, or for the use of, the Deity of Kumano
(early 13th century)

mind and life of the people.   This was not surprising, because
Buddhism always endeavoured to adapt itself to the national
traditions of Japan, and these were inseparably interwoven
with Shinto ideas and observances.   The connection and union
of the two religions had been inaugurated in the eighth
century, and now steps were taken to a more systematic
combination.   Kūkai's Shingon Buddhism was especially well
suited to this purpose.   His followers used their conception
of the two aspects of cosmic life to justify the union ;   the
Buddhist deities were assumed to be the real entities of the
Shinto deities.[1]

The Buddhist pantheon in general was thought to represent the Indestructibles, while the deities of the Shinto
pantheon were interpreted as their partial appearances.   The
real entity, or prime noumenon, was called the *Honji*, the
original, and the manifestation the *Suijaku*, the manifested
trace.   In carrying out this combination or parallelism, every
*kami* was regarded as a manifestation of a certain Buddhist
deity, and the majority of the Shinto sanctuaries were
furnished with an *Oku-no-in* (Inner Sanctuary), where a
Buddhist cult was observed, while the front sanctuary was
left comparatively intact.[2]   This syncretic religion is known
as *Ryōbu*, or " Double Aspect " Shinto ;   it was an extension
of the Buddhist communion to Shinto deities and at the same
time an adaptation of Buddhism to the native religion.

Now, this Double Aspect Shinto was an expression of the
compromising attitude so characteristic of the Japanese mind.
Shinto had always been a dual religion ;   of its two aspects,
one was chiefly concerned with ordinary everyday affairs,
and the other dealt with " hidden " or occult matters.   In its
mythology the opposition between these two aspects was

---

[1] See Plates IX and X.

[2] However, the Shinto shrine in the foreground was altered in the course of
time, and to-day, after the " purification " of Shinto, there is practically no Shinto
sanctuary in its original purity.

symbolized by the story of the subjugation of the descendants
of the Storm-god by the emissaries of the Sun-goddess.   The
rise of the Sun-goddess to supremacy, in the seventh and
eighth centuries, gradually obscured the occult aspect of
Shinto but this change of front was rather political or social
than religious, and the people in general still held to occultism,
chiefly in connection with the worship of some local deities,
especially those of the Izumo group.   To its aid came the
occultism of the Chinese Onyō-dō, the theory of the two
principles Yin and Yang, and its application to divination
and exorcism ; Shingon Buddhism, with its highly-wrought
mysticism, served to supplement and elaborate the current
occultism, so that it carried further the mixture of various
elements in popular faith and superstition.   As a modification
of Shingon Buddhism with an emphasis on the occult side
of religion, Ryōbu Shinto represented a revised form of the
old compromise between the Sun-goddess and the Storm-god,
lord of darkness and magic.   Thus the dual nature of the
Shinto religion was transferred to a compromising alliance
with the Shingon scheme of the universe represented in the
cycle of the two Mandalas.   This disposition to dual accommodation made a background to social life in general during
the period of Heian, and was manifest in the relationships
between religion and secular life, between intellectual and
sentimental life, and in many other respects.

First, we take the correlation between religion and secular
life.   Religion was always regarded as a matter of the beyond,
and yet secular life was never considered to be incompatible
with religious ideal as was the contention of Shingon Buddhism.   A man living the life of a householder may well practise
religious mysteries and may view even so-called secular acts
as essentially religious, since everyday life is a partial realization of cosmic life and every individual an embodiment of the
deepest reality.   Secular life, the life of the household, is a

stage for the practice of religion, when the spirit of the higher
ideal is kept in view; the religious ideal can and ought to have
its place in the family and the State. Such was, in general,
the contention of Mahāyāna ethics, but the idea was carried
out by Ryōbu Shinto and Shingon in a peculiar kind of
combination, that is, one person could live the two kinds of
life, religious and secular, in alternation or juxtaposition. H῾
might devote a certain portion of his time or a certain season
of the year to religious practice in a monastery or among the
mountains and pass through austere training. Or he might
become a regular monk on retirement from active life and
devote the last stage of life entirely to religion. Compromise
or the fusion of religion and life was the result. Life of this
kind was called *Ubasoku-dō*, or " the Way of the Upāsaka,"
the lay disciple of Buddha, a kind of " Tertiary Order," and
a man living in this way was called *Ubasoku* or *Nyūdō*, " One
who has entered the Way." Later we see instances of these
*nyūdō* who meddled with public affairs, even engaged in
warfare, or were addicted to sensual pleasure while wearing
monastic robes, and this degeneration of the Ubasoku-dō
caused many irregularities in social and political life.

One form of the Ubasoku-dō was the life of the mountaineer
priests known as *Yama-bushi*, " those who sleep among
mountains." They were, as a rule, men of lower caste
representing the crude side of religion, and they exercised a
great influence upon the people by appealing directly to
vulgar ideas and superstitions. Their ideal leader or patron
saint was En-no-Gyōja, spoken of above, with whom they
pretended to have communion and to share miraculous powers
by virtue of their austere training. These men were mostly
married and lived among the people, but they had to make
periodical disciplinary pilgrimages to the mountains where
the spirits of the great Gyōja or other leaders were believed
to abide and even to appear. Their work consisted chiefly

in exorcism and similar occult practices and they were revered
accordingly, or rather dreaded, by the people and even by the
nobles.  They also conducted young men at the time of adoles-
cence to sacred mountains and initiated them into mysteries
—a system of religious " Boy Scouts " of the olden times,
which continues even to-day to have some influence upon the
youth of country districts.  Their chief influence was in the
propagation of occultism among the people at large, and most
of the later Shinto sects can be traced back to the religion of
these mountaineer priests.  They increased in number and
influence to such a degree that the Buddhist reformers of the
thirteenth century encountered strong opposition from them,
because in trying to popularize Buddhism they encroached
upon the monopoly of the Yama-bushi.

### The Fujiwara Oligarchy in Control of Confucian Factions and Buddhist Hierarchy

In spite of its zeal for social work, Buddhism was a religion
peculiarly weak in political organization ; moreover, its social
activity had reached a zenith in the eighth century, the
Buddhism of the ninth century and later becoming sacra-
mental and ritualistic.  In contrast to Buddhism, and partly
supplementary to it, Confucianism was pre-eminently a
system of civic morality and political theory.  Its ethics
amounted to keeping the social order in accordance with, and
for the sake of, the established political régime.  Education
was considered to be an integral part of government, while
legal institutions were a kind of moral teaching inculcated
by the rulers.  We have seen in the Constitution of Prince
Shōtoku (604) some of those teachings, and proclamations
issued by the sovereigns and governments in the succeeding
centuries showed the same traits.  In the ethical system as
it appeared finally in the Engi Insititutes, the prominent

feature was, besides the importance given to the Shinto cult, an elaborate system of bureaucratic organizations together with an educational system. Thus was consummated the process of centralization with all its consequences—bureaucracy, formalism, formation of factions, and even luxury and hypocrisy. An oligarchy of Confucian literati vied with the Buddhist hierarchy in the consolidation of the aristocratic régime, for which, however, Confucianism was more responsible than Buddhism.

The chief instrument of the oligarchy was education. The provincial schools established in the eighth century were gradually neglected, and the university in the capital became the sole seat of higher education which supplied men to the bureaucratic system. Among its faculties, that of history and literature was the most important, because history was regarded as the foundation of government, while literature was necessarily an ornament of the governing class. In this way the University was the source of moral and professional education for officialdom and was chiefly responsible for the evils of the over-centralized bureaucracy. In the course of time, influential families established their own schools and vied with each other in attracting talented men and soliciting their adherence to clan interests. The Confucian literati made factions in entering into alliances with influential families contending for power and wealth. Each faction sought the patronage of a powerful man or family, while ambitious men knew how to make advantageous moves among the learned factions. In the course of the ninth and tenth centuries Confucianism degenerated into a tool of factious ambition and bureaucratic strife.

This combined strife naturally made victims, and the most prominent of them was Sugawara-no-Michizané (d. 903), who was typical of the age in his career and sentiments. He was born in a family of Chinese scholars and was himself a

great scholar.[1]  But like his parents, he was a devout Buddhist
and a pious worshipper of Kwannon, the deity of mercy.
His prayers to the deity are preserved in elegant Chinese
and testify to his religious piety as well as to his mastery of
classical Chinese.   He was a Confucianist in mind and a
Buddhist at heart, without being aware of any feeling of
inconsistency.   The emperor of his time, being anxious to
counteract the rising power of the Fujiwara, made Michizané
a minister of State.   But a savant, even under the patronage
of the sovereign, was powerless to combat the powerful clique,
and when his lord himself had been compelled to abdicate,
he was deprived of his position and exiled to a remote place.
During the years of exile he had no other consolation than
expressing his loneliness and mournful sentiments in poems
(both Japanese and Chinese), as well as in prayers to his
Buddhist deity of mercy.   Although he never professed to be
a Taoist, his poems betray a mood of Taoist quietism in
combination with the Buddhist temper of resignation.   Indeed,
it was a mystery of fate that Michizané, having passed through
the brilliant career of a scholar and a life of political struggle
peculiar to his age, was destined finally to develop his true
being in exile as a poetic genius.

Not only was .Michizané's case one of many but the instances of similar victims became more varied and numerous
in the course of time.   The vicissitudes of fortune among the
different families or members of a family contending for
domination, or among men and women striving for favour
and promotion, or interference of these rivalries with love
or family affairs, all the strifes and intrigues of court life,

[1] He is now revered as a patron deity of literature, but as a matter of fact the
origin of his worship was a superstitious belief that he had been so revengeful
towards his former political foes that he became the demon of thunder and killed
some of them by a thunderbolt.   His divine title, *Tenjin*, was originally intended
to signify thunder, and therefore he is identified by syncretic Shinto as the Hindu
Mahesvara.

tended to make men sensitive and emotional and not seldom pessimistic.  Envy or hatred, discontent or jealousy, agony or disillusion, as the case may be, aroused the sense of vanity and weariness of life.  Nor were the clergy free from similar distressing circumstances and the consequent emotions, but there were cases of the highest prelates giving up their ecclesiastical position and retiring to hermitages.  Thus, under the surface splendour of aristocratic life there flowed a stream of depressing sentiment, which drove not a few persons to the monasteries or mountians to live the life of an anchorite or to follow the Way of Ubasoku, referred to above.  There were not many cases of suicide from despair as in the later ages, yet extreme forms of renunciation verged on it, though there were also cases of those who had once run to an extreme but later returned to a life of pleasure-seeking in secret. Naturally people outside the powerful Fujiwara clan more readily fell victims to this mood of revolt or despondency and resorted to poetry or religion for consolation, not to speak of political plot or court intrigue.[1]

In considering the pessimistic undercurrent of the time, we have to take into account the influence of Taoist ideas. Taoism was, as Kūkai refuted it, a method of ascetic training living in the bosom of nature and aiming at supernormal attainments.  Indifference towards life necessarily meant aloofness from all changes and troubles, and this temperament

---

[1] Not only men but women were among the victims.  A typical example of the ethos of the time is furnished by the story of Ono-no-Komachi, who flourished at the turn of the ninth and tenth centuries.  Famous for her beauty and poetic genius, she had won the heart of the heir-apparent to the throne, when the Fujiwara expelled her from the court, because they saw in her a formidable obstacle to their plan of supplying the princess-consort from among their daughters.  Thenceforward she lived in retirement, resisting love suits and temptations and devoting herself to poetry.  Her story is also told as an illustration of the transitoriness of beauty and the vanity of pride, her sternness towards suitors being taken for mere pride. The following centuries are full of similar stories of men and women who fell victims to court intrigues.  At any rate, the history of Japanese poetry owes to these circumstances one of its best poetesses and one of similar romantic stories.

produced many hermits who ridiculed human life and took pride in their own freedom as emancipated men.  This had been the case in China with the men who took refuge among the mountains in an age of social disorganization in the fourth and fifth centuries.  It survived more or less the changes brought about by the establishment of the powerful dynasty of the Tang, and the signs of decadence in the ninth century were synchronous with a revival of the Taoist ideal of emancipation.  The Chinese poet who represented this ethos was Haku Rakuten,[1] and when his poems were introduced into Japan he was welcomed by nobles and men of letters and became a beloved poet in this country even in his lifetime. The pessimistic mood of the time had not only prepared the soil for his poetry but was accelerated by its influence. Though later, in speaking of the sentimental life, we shall refer chiefly to Buddhist influence, we must bear in mind that Buddhist and Taoist influences worked together.

The Fujiwara family, the authors of the oligarchic régime, had shared their glory with the royal family at the beginning, but when they advanced in power they treated the sovereigns as mere puppets.  The real rise of their power may be dated from the last part of the ninth century, but for a time the rivalry among the various branches of the family prevented the sole supremacy of any.  But the end of the tenth century beheld a decisive step towards the consummation of their rule, when Fujiwara-no-Michinaga took the regency of state.

The reign of Michinaga as the regent of state and patri‑arch of the family lasted over thirty years (995-1027) and is

---

[1] His Chinese name is Pai Chu-i (773-847).  Rakuten or Lotien is his *nom-de-plume* and means " Enjoying Nature."  Accidentally, in modern Japanese the same word is used for optimism.  Though not an optimist exactly, he was not a bitter pessimist, because " enjoying nature " meant taking delight in the tranquil aspects of nature and identifying oneself with the eternal serenity of nature— a misanthropic optimism, or quietism.

marked by the outward splendour of court life.   Wealth, talent, power, and institutions, long since accumulated and established, all contributed to the one cause, the satisfaction of the ambitions and sentiment of this patriarch and his clientele.   The talent and power of the brilliant court ladies worked together with the romantic sentimentality of the nobles to produce the utmost refinement of æsthetic sense emancipated from ethical considerations and Confucian conventions.   Brilliancy of costumes matched the splendid decoration of palaces ; frequent banquets and concerts were accompanied by free exchange of love poems ;   picnics, rhyming competitions, meetings for art criticism, musical concerts, and similar pastimes became the order of the day. Magnificent temples and elaborate chapels were built for the sake of piety as well as of enjoyment ;   statues and altars were decorated with gold and jewels ;   artists and artisans were employed to an incredible number.   Buddhist ceremonies were as frequent as pastimes, in the court and in the temples. Sermons and sacraments were attended by throngs, both men and women, nobles and commoners.   Monasteries and temples were endowed in abundance, in recompense for services done by the monks and priests in ceremonies held on occasions of births . or deaths, or at the celebration of various jubilees. Bishops and abbots shared the brilliant life of the court nobles.

There was another circumstance that contributed to the pomp of the Buddhist church.   The Fujiwara bureaucracy monopolized high positions of State and excluded able men of other families from promotion, while a way was open in the Church to all according to ability and talent.   The consequence was that the Buddhist hierarchies attracted men of ability and ambition from all quarters, and the prelates were men well trained not only in religion but in politics.   Often their talent was used more for secular affairs than for piety or learning, and their religion and church were used as tools for worldly ambition.   Moreover, the mystic Buddhism of Shingon was well suited to covetous demands, as it supplied worship and mysteries for the benefit of selfish interests, and the court nobles were easily controlled by ecclesiastical nobles. In this respect the followers of Kūkai vied with the prelates of Hiei in compromising themselves to the aristocrats and in making them in turn the tools of their own ambition.   The doctrine of Tendai Buddhism, the proper tenet of Hiei, was obscured by Shingon mysteries, and some of the Hiei prelates publicly declared their own scripture, the " Lotus of Truth," to be equal in theory but inferior in practice to Shingon mysteries.   The result was an indiscriminate worship of deities according to convenience.[1]  The high ideals of Saichō's foundation were thus degraded by superstitious performances and his philosophy was abused in justifying the degeneration.

Thus, under the external splendour there was pronounced corruption, ready to disclose itself as occasion offered.   The temples and their rich properties became a prey to avaricious priests, and the relaxation of the official registration of the clergy from the last part of the ninth century aggravated the evil.   The corruption of the hierarchy vied with the irregularities of the priesthood in the provinces.   The great Buddhist centres increased their influence in proportion with the exercise of occult ceremonies, and the power thus acquired became the weapon of ambitious prelates and villainous priests.   The

[1] The most noted of those who accelerated the degeneration of the institutions of Hiei was Ennin (794-864), the third patriarch of the institution.   He modified the religion of Hiei into the occult mysticism of Shingon, though maintaining other branches of learning and discipline.   Annen, who flourished in the last decades of the ninth century, was another pronounced factor in the degeneration.   Enchin (814-891) founded another seat of mystic Buddhism at Mii, as a result of his dissension from Hiei, and this temple, Mii-dera, was destined to become a formidable rival of Hiei, both in ecclesiastical and military contentions.   The division of these branches has interesting bearings upon the history of dogma in Tendai Buddhism in Japan, but the subtle points disputed had little significance for the people's beliefs.

increase of their land and other properties gradually induced them to organize armed defence, and the monk-soldiers (*sōhei*) proceeded from defensive to offensive acts in asserting their rights or claims, attacking their rivals, and even intimidating the Government. The power and outrages of the monk-soldiers grew so alarming in the course of the eleventh century that the Fujiwara, who were the creators of this force, finding themselves impotent to control the monks, had to resort to the help of military men from the provinces for suppressing their riots. This point had a significant bearing upon the political and social changes which were to take place in the latter half of the twelfth century, because when those military men who had their strongholds in the provinces were called to the capital to combat the monk-soldiers they began to realize their own power. From this time on their self-assertion grew, until they controlled the whole situation and supplanted the Fujiwara oligarchy. In short, the mutual acceleration in corruption of the court nobles and the ecclesiastical prelates was the chief feature of the time, though at first hidden under the parade of pomp and glory.

## Gradual Rise of Buddhist Pietism

Notwithstanding the corruption in the hierarchy of Hiei, there were always men of sincerity and pious souls among the monks and laymen. They resisted on their part the degeneracy of the time but none of them seriously attempted to turn the current and achieve a reformation. Most of them were trained in the philosophy of Tendai but practised their religious devotion in worshipping the Buddha Amita (or Amida) with his abode in the Land of Purity.[1]

---

[1] The Japanese name for this paradise is *Jōdo*, and hence this branch of Buddhism is better known by the name of Jōdo Buddhism. Its Sanskrit original is Sukhāvatī, the Land of Bliss, Japanese *Gokuraku*. Buddhism teaches the existence of innumerable paradises corresponding to the infinite abundance of Buddhas

Now, apart from the question of its origin, this worship of the Buddha Amita, the Lord of Infinite Light, set a stream of pious contemplation flowing in Buddhism through its history in India and China.   The belief was that he had once been a royal prince and then a monk, who, out of compassion for his fellow beings, took a vow to dedicate all the merits of his long, strenuous self-training to their spiritual benefit. By the mysterious virtue of his meritorious work, he finally accomplished the task of establishing a paradise, the Land of Purity, located " far beyond millions and billions of leagues in the west," where he could embrace the pious souls who would call upon his name.   He is believed to be residing there even now and working perpetually for saving even those who are not capable of learning and discipline.

There were in India and China some recluse monks devoted to meditation on the Buddha Amita and to invoking his name for being received by him to his paradise.   In the earlier stage of this form of Buddhism in Japan, Amita was worshipped as one of those innumerable deities in the Shingon pantheon, and pious thinking of him was associated with visualizing the splendour of his paradise, especially in gazing intently upon the glories of the setting sun.   Though only one of the many deities in the grand pantheon, Amita was regarded as one of

But the principal ones are : the Paradise of the Vulture Peak, of the Buddha Sākya-muni. which is in this world ; the Heaven Tushitā, or " Contentment," of the future Buddha Maitreya, located above us ;, the Paradise of Crystal Light, of the Buddha Bhaishajya-guru, which is located in the east ; and the fourth the Sukhāvatī.  It is to be noted that the Buddha Bhaishajya-guru was mostly worshipped for the benefit of the present, while Amita for future life.

The Sanskrit original of the name Amita is *Amitābha*, " Infinite Light," or else *Amitāyus*, " Infinite Life."   There are two principal texts in Sanskrit, the larger and smaller *Sukhāvatī-vyūhā*, the descriptions of the paradise, how it was founded by the Buddha Amita, how the pious will be taken in there, and so on.   Both are translated into English and found in vol. 49 of the *SBE*, together with another text translated from Chinese describing the methods of contemplation on the Buddha and his paradise.

Cf. Arthur Lloyd, *The Creed of Half Japan*, pp. 160-67, 208-24 ; Hans Haas, *Amida unsere Zuflucht.*  Lloyd's arguments that this faith in Amita was derived from Christianity are not well-founded.

the most powerful deities, especially as the one who cared for the life beyond, in contradistinction to many other deities of Shingon invoked for present benefits. Thus there were not a few Shingon prelates or Tendai philosophers who invoked Amita's name as a pious practice and ended their life in gazing towards the west, the location of the Land of Purity. Little breach or antagonism was felt between this pious meditation and Shingon mysteries or Tendai theology. Yet the devotion to the Lord of Infinite Life, the saviour of all, whether in intent contemplation or in simply calling his name, was destined to achieve a development of its own as a simple religion of pious devotion, especially because the vow taken by Amita was believed to have the power to save those unable to undergo hard training in spiritual exercise or disciplinary life. This became more and more evident in the course of the eleventh and twelfth centuries, when mystic ritualism had become too irksome and very few indeed had proved themselves capable of high attainments in mystic or philosophical religion. Then the devotees of Amita-Buddhism began to alienate themselves from the complicated teaching and practice of the prevailing forms of Buddhism, and came finally to declare independence and to achieve thereby a religious reformation. This movement was favoured by the currents of the time, especially by the widespread belief in the imminence of the Millennium.

This belief in the Millennium was based on a group of predictions presenting a pessimistic view of the fate of Buddhism which was long current among Buddhists. An old Buddhist legend distinguished three periods in the fortunes of the Buddhist religion after Buddha's death. The first thousand years was the period of the " Perfect Law," in which monastic discipline was perfectly observed. The second thousand was that of the " Copied Law," in which true faith declined but piety was shown in the foundation of numerous temples and monu-

ments.    The third period of the " Latter Law," to last a
further ten thousand years, was the age of degeneration, full
of vice and strife.[1]    This apocalyptic legend was almost
universal in the Buddhist countries, and since Chinese and
Japanese Buddhists usually put Buddha's death in 949 B.C.,
they believed, whether in apprehension or in hope, that the
last period was to start in the year A.D. 1052.    Indeed, the
actual conditions of that time exhibited many signs of degeneration or change ;   and men in the eleventh century
thought that the prophecy was being fulfilled.[2]

Moreover, this prediction was believed in not merely by
isolated individuals ;   the idea was embodied in the intention
and organization of the grand institutions on Mount Hiei.
For Saichō's foundation of Hiei was intended to be a preparation for the coming age of degeneration.    He expressed his
idea thus :   " Approaching is the end of the Copied Law and
nigh is that of the Latter Law, and this is the time ripe for
the propagation of the unique truth of the ' Lotus of Truth '."
He had not stated exactly how the scripture should furnish
the religion of the latter days, but his followers interpreted
this to mean the necessity of accommodating the truths
revealed in the *Lotus* to the character and needs of the people
of the latter days.    No wonder, then, that those living in these
centuries regarded the grand institution of Hiei as a pre-
monitory provision for the coming changes, though not
necessarily catastrophic.    This sense of an anticipation was
later to take the form of aggressive propaganda, particularly
in the person of Nichiren, the reformer of the thirteenth

---

[1] The name for the three periods are : *Sad-dharma* (Jap. *Shō-bō*), *Pratirūpa-
dharma* (Jap *Zō-bō*), and *Paschima-dharma* (Jap. *Map-pō*) respectively. Cf.
Anesaki, *Nichiren*, pp. 4-5.

[2] Many of the numerous temples built in and near Miyako in the course of the
ninth and tenth centuries were burnt down in the eleventh, but this is no wonder
because such wooden structures easily succumb to fire. Another point in the
prevailing sentiment of that time was the death of Michinaga in 1027, with whose
reign the Fujiwara oligarchy had reached its zenith of splendour.

century. In these earlier centuries, however, it was manifested for the most part in a rather pessimistic mood of
resignation and in quiet contemplation ; the faith in Amita
Buddha seemed to answer exactly the demands of the age.[1]

The faith in Amita gradually took hold of pious souls
even under the prevailing ritualism and in the midst of the
splendours of aristocratic life. It found a great exponent in
the person of Genshin (942-1017), better known by the name of
Eshin Sōzu, "the Abbot of Eshin-in," who witnessed the
zenith of the Heian culture in the court life of Michinaga and
yet felt keenly the need of a deep inspiration in religious life.
He was a profound thinker and the leader of a school of
philosophy which asserted the Buddha-nature to be inherent
in every one and its attainment to mean the restoration of
our own original possession or the awakening to our prime
nature. And this could be done, according to him, by examining the innermost depths of our soul in contemplation and
realizing there a manifestation of Buddha's wisdom and
power. Thus he emphasized the idealistic tenet of Tendai
philosophy and aspired to purify the religious life of Hiei by
excluding abuses of mystic ritualism. He lived in Yokawa,
a spot on Mount Hiei secluded from its hierarchic centre, and
trained himself and his sincere-minded disciples. He was,
however, not content with mere philosophy and meditation
but aspired to a faith which should bring immediate peace.
His contemplative temper gradually took definite shape in

[1] The beginning of the faith in Amita in Japan can be traced back to the eighth
century, but here we mention a few later votaries. The ex-Emperor Uda (d. 931),
a monk of the Shingon branch, expired facing West, towards the Land of Purity.
Another royal personage, Kūya (903-72), born a prince and a beggar monk in life,
promulgated that religion by chanting Buddha's name to the melody of popular
songs. He is known as the "Saint of the Market" because he worked as an
itinerant and induced men in the street to believe in Amita and to chant his name.
Another instance was that of Kakuban (1095-1143) who was an abbot and learned
man of the Shingon branch and combined the invocation of Amita's name with
his Shingon mysticism. Here in this case, the mystery of "Calling the Name"
was identified with the mystery of the "Word," as stated above in considering
the three mysteries taught by Shingon Buddhism.

the concentration of the mind on the Lord of the Western Paradise, and his visions were written down in a treatise on " Birth in the Land of Purity." [1]   This was done when he was forty-two years old, in 984, and the book was destined to command the pious faith of the following centuries.

In this book he gives vivid descriptions of the various resorts of transmigration, their causes and miseries, and of the holy paths culminating in the eternal bliss of the Western Paradise, prepared by Amita Buddha for the sake of people in the Latter Days, the age of degeneracy.   There he depicts the glorious manifestation of the Lord, accompanied by his saints and angels, for receiving the souls of those who invoke his name :

When a pious person dies, the Buddha appears before him.   The Lord of Compassion (Kwannon), one of his great Bodhisattvas, brings a lotus flower to carry the pious soul, and the Lord of Might (Seishi) reaches him welcoming hands, while other saints and angels innumerable in number sing hymns in praise and welcome of the pious.   Born in the Land of Purity, the pious man is like a blind man who suddenly recovers his sight, and finds himself surrounded by radiant beams and brilliant jewels of untold price.   In every direction the air resounds with harmonious tunes, the sky is full of radiance, large heavenly birds and birds of paradise are flying to and fro.   Some of the beings in Paradise are singing in adoration of Buddha, some passing to and from other Buddha-lands, while others are poised in the air in serene meditation.   Amita Buddha sits on a lotus seat like a golden mountain in the midst of all glories, surrounded by his saints.   The Lords of Compassion and of Might lead the newly born before the Buddha's seat. [2]

The pious philosopher depicted the glories of Paradise also in paintings, in which we see his visions reproduced in graceful lines and harmonious colours. [3]   In this respect he made a new departure in Buddhist painting, liberating it from the rigid

[1] The Japanese title is *Wōjō Yōshū*, a *vade mecum* of the resorts of transmigration and of the way to paradise, in six fasciculi.

[2] Many of these passages are adapted from Buddhist scriptures and not original of the writer.   Yet in his words and style we can discern the expression of his pious visions, which are testified by his paintings too.

[3] For his art see Anesaki, *Buddhist Art*, chap. ii, Plates I and XI.   He is believed to have instructed his contemporary Hirotaka to paint the scenes of the ten resorts of transmigration, and the work is preserved to this day as an object of religious reverence and æsthetic admiration.   Comp. Plate XI.

PLATE XI

THE BUDDHA AMITA WITH HIS ATTENDANTS APPEARING
OVER THE HILLS

Attributed to Genshin (11th century).    Thirteenth century

conventions of Shingon iconography and inspiring it with fresh vitality emanating from his own piety. He was also a poet combining imagination with mystic vision. As writer on the vices and miseries of life, on the varieties of existence and on the states of perdition or spiritual beatitude, he may be compared to Dante[1]; while as a painter of paradise and saints he may be called the Fra Angelico of Japanese Buddhism. Though he was never engaged in active propaganda, he exerted considerable influence upon his contemporaries and the following generations, chiefly through his writings and paintings. We must not fail, on the other hand, to see that his words and pictures could hardly have been inspiring unless his personality, eminent in virtue and piety, had represented the faith he himself embraced and transmitted to others. Another point to be remembered is that he did not remain a mere mystic but gave emphasis to the moral bearings of religious faith, which amounted to trying to induce others to the same faith.

### Arts and Literature of the Fujiwara Period

The régime of the Fujiwara oligarchy had its seat in the aristocratic life of the court, where grace and refinement set the prevailing tone. In spite of the inner decay which had manifested itself long before, the eleventh century was indeed an age of " Pomp and Splendour,"[2] as it was named, and the luxurious life of the nobles bore fruit in refined manners, delicate sentiment, and in finesse in art and literature. The stage was " Flowery Miyako surrounded by the ninefold circles of the cloud of flowers "; the actors were the " Cloud-

---

[1] A. K. Reischauer has an article on *Genshin, the Dante of Japan*, to be published in the *TASJ*. The influence of Genshin's visions is reflected, among many, in the story of a princess who passed through vicissitudes of fortune and thus realized in her life experiences the miseries and fortunes of all the six resorts. This story is told in the *Heike Monogatari*, for which see *TASJ*, vol. xlix. part I.

[2] This is a translation of Japanese " *eigwa*," and the romantic history of the period, *Eigwa-monogatari*, well describes the life and temper of the age.

gallants " and " Flower-maidens," as the noblemen and court
ladies were called ; and the scenes were flower fêtes, poetic
contests, pleasure trips, love stories, court plots, romantic
adventures, religious ceremonies, mysticism often culminating in recluse life.   Even religion was transformed into
play ; prelates and monks appeared on the stage in brilliant
colours.   Every aristocrat was a poet ; not only court nobles
but bishops and priests exchanged poems, not seldom love
poems, with the court ladies.   There was striking freedom of
expression, in which romantic motives played a great part.
A good many men and women were painters and musicians,
and they frequently met for pleasure or inspiration, when
they would devise various arts, even such as competing in
distinguishing different kinds of incense.[1]   No wonder, then,
that the period is regarded as the classical age of refinement,
grace, and brilliancy.

Buddhist art had once been eminent in vigour and
grandeur, especially in the eighth century, and these traits
had been preserved more or less in Shingon art, in spite of
its rigid iconographic rules.   But now in the course of the
tenth and eleventh centuries the change of ethos brought
about by the Fujiwara aristocracy replaced vigour by elegance,
expressiveness by finesse.   Iconographic convention was less
strictly observed and there was more freedom of composition ;
gentle outlines, fine touch, graceful attire, less brilliant but
harmonious colouring, these characterized the arts of the
eleventh century.   Temple architecture had lost grandeur
and approached that of the noble's mansions, decoration
became richer by the addition of more painting on pillars,

[1] This contest later developed into an art, where five different kinds of incense
were combined in various ways and the assembled ones competed in distinguishing
them.   The results of the contests were written down in conventionalized designs
amounting to fifty-four in number, named after the titles of the fifty-four chapters
of the *Genji Monogatari*, to be spoken of below, p. 157.   These patterns are used
to-day for decorative purposes.

friezes, and door wings, and also by inlaid work of metal and
mother-of-pearl.   In painting there was more imagination
than inspiration ;  statues were elaborated in soft curves and
tender expressions, models being often taken from living men
or women of eminent beauty.[1]   The deities, especially the
Bodhisattva, both in painting and sculpture, were represented
like women in expression and posture.   In these works of art,
heavenly beings were brought nearer to human beings, but
fancy played a great part in enhancing æsthetic sentiments
by depicting the bliss and glory of the heavenly worlds.   Art
and religion, and life too, were brought closer to each other ;
life was a display of art, as art was an integral part of life.

Parallel with the development of a refined style in the
plastic arts, the native, or *Yamato*, style of literature began
to flourish.   From the eighth century the national literature
had made steady progress, and the cessation of communications with China further favoured its growth.   But the more
important factor in the formation of a characteristically
Japanese literature regarded as classical was the influence of
women.   Under the aristocratic régime of the Fujiwara,
women played an integral part, not seldom even in politics,
and her influence naturally made itself felt in the sphere of
sentimental life, particularly in literature.   Her taste and
ability were shown in the use of soft and liquid Japanese, in
which every syllable ended with a vowel, while she shunned
the terse expressions of monosyllabic Chinese, which was
rich in compound consonants.   Moreover, the delicate sentiment and refined taste of the court life could never be masculine, but found its best exponents in the women of high
training and refinement.   Naturally, the life of the " cloud-
gallants " and " flower-maidens " supplied rich material for

---

[1] The artist who perfected these devices was Jōchō (*d.* 1057) who served
Michinaga and was revered as the brightest star of the time.  A long stream of
artistic tradition flowed from his art and ruled the art movement until the fourteenth
century, or later.  See Plate IVв.

romantic stories, while the nature and atmosphere of Miyako were peculiarly suited to quicken the romantic temperament of the age. The chief forms of expression were romance or improvised poems, but similar styles and sentiments were applied to religious literature, mostly lyrics and hymns.[1]

It is possible to express in one word the sentiment permeating all this literature, and that was *awaré*, which meant pity and sympathy. The poets refined in æsthetic sense and tempered by the sentiment of *awaré* saw in things of nature images and movements responding to their own emotions and passions and were deeply moved by the various changes and aspects of nature. They heard in the rustling of reeds in the darkness voices yearning for the moonlight. They saw the evanescence of human life in the stream perpetually flowing and never returning. The cherry blossoms just beginning to scatter themselves, as well as the crimson leaves of maple saturated with the autumnal rain, appealed to their sensitive state of *awaré*. The writers of romantic stories expressed their sympathy towards amorous adventurers, who knew how to win the hearts of others, or towards those lovers who were tormented by unrequited love, or those who abandoned the world because of despair in love. And the incidents of love stories were always conceived and depicted in association with nature's changing aspects as symbolic of the lover's passionate emotion. What gave this sentiment a tender touch and a sense of mysterious depth was the belief in *karma*— that every relation of love, whether sexual or filial or otherwise, was a result of a remote connection established between the lovers in some past life, an invisible nexus of karma. This nexus might have lasted through many lives and might further continue to link the lovers through coming lives, whether in human form or in heavenly bliss. This link was

---

[1] The favourite form of poem was the *imayō*, a stanza of forty-eight syllables, or the *tanka*, which allows only thirty-one syllables. All classes, even to-day, take delight in improvising *tanka*.

called *sukusé* and the belief in it gave a strong impetus to the free play of romantic sentiment and to the depth of passionate affection.

In this reign of romantic sentiment every one was a poet —court noble or lady, prelate or anchorite, endowed with the gift of tears which were shed on changes of physical surroundings and on incidents of human life. The pathos of life was usually associated with the varying aspects of nature, at the same time the mind yearned for something beyond the actual, often tending to an aspiration for spiritual communion. The poets perceived that this world was not the only reality, yet they were not courageous enough entirely to give up worldly attachments. They wavered between the two worlds and moved back and forth in their emotion. Melancholy, not quite pessimistic, aspiring for beyond yet not ready to resign this life, they moved and lived and played in the sentiment of *awaré*. The literature of the period was preeminently an expression of *awaré*, which was developed in romantic love stories, sung in lyric poems, and even in Buddhist hymns.[1] The romantic sentiment of *awaré* was in close touch with a close observation of nature and life, which is testified also by the painting of this period, in its delicate colouring, the finesse of line, and the dreamy expressions of figures.

As the religious background of this sentiment we have to note the influence exercised by the *Hokke-kyō*, the Lotus of

---

[1] The most important of the stories is the *Genji Monogatari*, a long series of love stories written by a court lady, Murasaki Shikibu (Lady Violet). An English translation of the first part made by K. Suyematsu is incorporated in *Persian and Japanese Literature* (Colonial Press, New York). A new translation produced by Arthur Waley bears the title, *The Tale of Genji* (the first volume) to be completed in seven volumes.

For love poems of the period see Clay MacCauley's translation (*TASJ.*, vol. 27, 1899); B. H. Chamberlain, *Japanese Poetry*, pp. 89-105.

See also *Diaries of Court Ladies of Old Japan*, translated by A. S. Omori and K. Doi (Houghton Mifflin, 1920), and an introduction to it by A. Lowell; another by Sei-Shonagon is translated into French: *Les notes de l'oreiller* (Paris, 1928); the same into English by A. Waley: *The Pillow-book of Sei Shonagon* (Allen and Unwin, 1928).

Truth.   We have spoken several times of the rôle played by
this book in the propagation of Buddhism in Japan.   In the
Heian period its influence permeated the hearts of many
through frequent lectures on it, as well as by private readings,
public recitations, and the making of copies.   From 796 a
ceremony had been observed in the imperial court at which
were held dialogues on this scripture, and it was recited at
nearly every religious meeting.   To be well acquainted with
the important passages of the book was regarded as an indispensable condition of accomplishment, and to be able to
compose poems on its sermons, parables, and visions, was an
essential requisite of a poet.

Besides its characteristic as a source of religious inspiration, the Hokke-kyō was rich in literary qualities.   It contained
an abundance of materials appealing to the fancy and imagination.   The transfiguration of the Vulture Peak and the manifestation of supernal glories set forth in the opening scene ;
the resplendency of the heavenly worlds in response to the
spiritual illumination of a king who, having left his royal
dignity, has attained supreme enlightenment ; the heavenly
shrine (*stūpa*) appearing in the sky, from which Buddha
proclaims and gives assurance of the further propagation of
his religion in the Latter Days ; the myriads of mysterious
beings issuing out of the earth and taking vows before Buddha
to work strenuously for religion, these are depicted in a highly
imaginative style and with the vividness of apocalyptic vision.
The prodigal son who is welcomed home by his noble father
and educated to be his worthy heir ; the scene of a thunderstorm and heavy rainfall after which plants and flowers grow
luxuriantly ; the burning house from which a thoughtful
father, by means of a special device, takes out his children,
these parables are intended to elucidate the all-embracing
tact of the educative methods adopted by Buddha.   The
showers of heavenly flowers scattered upon the spot of

Buddha's sermon ; the illumination of all beings by the rays of Buddha's spiritual illumination ; and finally the revelation of the eternal entity of Buddha's person, these were told and heard in pious devotion. The guarantee given by Buddha to his disciples of their future destiny as Buddhas ; the instantaneous enlightenment of a girl Nāga (serpent) on hearing Buddha's sermon, these inspiring stories in assuring salvation for all beings were received with tears of hope and gratitude. In addition to these stimulating stories and good tidings contained in the book, the supreme beauty of the Chinese translation played a great part in deepening and extending its inspiration. It is, then, no wonder that the *Hokke-kyō* played in Japanese literature a rôle nearly akin to that of the Bible in English literature.

The ethos and temperament of the age produced by this book and other circumstances can be summed up as a reign of sentimentalism. Its sway had much to do with the social conditions and moral life of the times. In ancient Japan, before the prevalence of Confucian ethics, there had been little restraint in manifestations of love, and it was freely expressed in poems exchanged between lovers. After the ninth century, Chinese influence had changed this, and the freedom was much restricted ; now came a reaction and life was dominated by emotion and passion. Young nobles and ladies lived under the sway of romantic fancy, paying little heed to moral obligations. Living in ease and luxury they were addicted to beautiful emotions and dreamy sentiments. They found pleasure even in trouble and despair, if these could be idealized in sentiment and poetry. Æstheticism, effeminacy, sentimentalism, any of these epithets may be applied to the temper of the times. But the mirage of sentiment was destined to be dissipated soon by a fierce storm of battle, and the dreamers or their descendants had to undergo retribution in agony and remorse.

*The End of Peace and Splendour*

In the last half of the eleventh century a political change took place, by which the power was transferred largely from the hands of the Fujiwara to those of the emperors in monastic robes.[1]    This change, however important politically, brought little change in the atmosphere of the age ; the sway of luxury, sentimental æstheticism, and religious ritualism, survived the vicissitudes of the time.    The reign of the monk-emperor Shirakawa during the years 1073-1129 was especially remarkable for the erection of numerous temples,[2] and also for the frequent riots of the monk-soldiers. This abnormal régime culminated in the civil wars, which broke out in the capital in 1156 and 1159, and which signalized the passing of the old régime.    These wars exposed mercilessly the moral degeneration of the age.    The members of the royal family, the court nobles, the military men, and even some monks, all were involved in combat, in which fathers and sons, brothers and cousins, uncles and nephews, fought one another.    Hatred, intrigue, murder, were mutual. The sites of luxurious life were reduced to ashes, and the " cloud-gallants " and " flower-maidens " were thrown into the hellish fire and carnage.[3]    Mystic rituals did not avail and Buddhism served only in giving a message of consolation to dying men, persuading them to forget hatred and to invoke the name of Amita Buddha at the moment of death.

[1] They had nominally retired from the throne and therefore wore monastic robes but were still the actual rulers, at first from behind the scenes but later in public.

[2] Within a single century from 1075, six gigantic temples were built in Miyako, together with numerous chapels and nine-storied pagodas.    All of these were burnt down one after another, as if to testify to the transitoriness of life and to herald a profound change in the times.    Another one built in 1164 known as the San-jusangen-dō, in Miyako, remains to-day, eloquent of past glories.

[3] A scene from these battles is vividly depicted in a famous scroll painting in the Boston Museum of Fine Arts.

Cf. the *Hogen Monogatari* translated into English by E. R. Kellog, in *TASJ*, vol. 45, part I.  (1917.)

These battles and their results brought to light the power of the provincial soldiers. Their leaders were either provincial governors, first appointed by the central government but later fixed to the soil, or local chieftains who had started their life as custodians of landed properties in the provinces owned by the court nobles or Buddhist temples. In the course of centuries these properties gradually became extra-territorial counties disregarding the central government, and their custodians became chiefs of the counties, keeping and training retainers. The chief and the retainers lived in close association through generations, sharing the toil of expeditions and the pleasures of robust country life, greatly in contrast to the emasculated life of the court nobles. Away from the degenerating influence of court life, they cultivated military discipline and the virtues of fidelity and valour. Thus they represented the native spirit of provincial life, the old clan spirit, which had survived the apparent centralization of government and had ever maintained its vitality in the provinces.

The power of these provincial chiefs had been shown in the suppression of riots and rebellions, which were frequent after the eleventh century, but so far this had been regarded as a merely local matter. Now, in the middle of the twelfth century, they came to the front in the polity of the capital, and began to realize the real strength of their position, of which they themselves almost had been unaware. They were no longer content with being tools of the Fujiwara oligarchy but aspired to become themselves masters of the situation. Their ambition was finally attained, and their domination meant the rise of feudalism. For they had strong footholds in the provinces and their fiefs were virtually feudal territories. This change had tremendous significance for the social and moral history of the nation, and was consummated, in the course of several centuries, in the full establishment of a feudal régime and in the elaboration of the morality peculiar to the warrior class, now known as *Bushidō*, the Way of the Warrior.

The military clans which came to the front in the twelfth century were the two renowned family groups, Taira and Minamoto, known also as Heike and Genji respectively.[1]  The contest between these two had once brought a temporary subjugation of the Minamoto by the Taira, and the latter became for a while the sole masters of the capital and of the whole country.  But the victors, having settled down in Miyako, soon came under the sway of the luxurious and enervating life of the court nobles, while the rival clan Minamoto was preparing for another reversal.  The reign of the Taira ended in 1185, when the Minamoto gave the *coup-de-grâce* to the former victors, and thereby to the religious and literary sentimentalism of the Heian period.  The change of régime impressed the people with a sense of utmost bewilderment and brought with it far-reaching changes in all phases of social life.  The régime under the military dictatorship of the Minamoto was eminent in the simplicity of its administration, in contrast to the bureaucratic rule of the Fujiwara : its effect will be seen presently.

The glories of the " Peace and Ease " were merely superficial, especially in the last stage, concealing a decadent tendency in all phases of social and moral life.  The weakening of intellectual insight was proportional to the growth of morbid sentimentalism and superstitious mysticism.  Piety in contemplation degenerated into a mere routine of repeating Buddha's name.  Almost aimless itineracy, religious pilgrimages, and training in the mountains, came into vogue, serving

---

[1] *Hei* is the Sino-Japanese reading of the Chinese ideogram adapted to designate the name Taira, and similarly *Gen* that of Minamoto.  *Ke* and *ji* both meant clan or family, and hence the names *Heike* and *Genji*.  The epic *Heike Monogatari* and another version *Gem-Pei Seisui-ki*, tell the pathetic stories of the successive rise and fall of these two clans.  The former is translated into English by A. L. Sadler (*TASJ.*, vols. 48-49).  Attention must be drawn to the fact that the *Genji Monogatari*, referred to above, has nothing to do with this military clan Genji.

as consolation for minds in trouble and agony.  Essays on doctrine and inspiring books of exhortation gave place to *acta sanctorum* of over-sensitive piety and hymns of effeminate style.  Spiritual unrest was universal, but it did not end in despondency.  New forces had been preparing.  The change of régime brought fresh vigour to life and belief, and the new era opened with a remarkable rise of religious aspiration and moral energy, culminating in the appearance of strong personalities.

# BOOK IV

# THE AGE OF FEUDAL STRIFE AND RELIGIOUS STRUGGLE

## (ABOUT 1200-1600)

# GENERAL FEATURES OF THE KAMAKURA PERIOD (1186–1333)

THE establishment of the new military government under the dictatorship of the Minamoto in 1186 marked an epoch-making change in the history of Japan. Their firm military rule extending over the whole country from their head-quarters in the east, at Kamakura, was in strong contrast to the luxurious life and lax administration of the court nobles in Miyako. This momentous change, though not unprepared for, startled the people, at least in the western half of Japan. The cherry blossoms in full bloom had been suddenly dispersed by a frosty storm. So did the poets feel and sing, and the people saw the change actually take place ·before their eyes. It was not a mere political revolution, but social, moral, and religious at the same time. The Buddhist hierarchies lost their prestige to a large extent, together with their political supporters at court ; ceremonies and mysteries were much discredited, while undercurrents of unrest and aspiration manifested themselves in various ways.

The change was, in one of its aspects, a revival of the indigenous spirit, a revolt of the crude ideas and chivalric temper of the warriors and peasants living in the eastern provinces against the over-refinement of the aristocrats of Miyako. The Minamoto gave their clan cult a higher position and the people followed, which meant a renewal of the communal Shinto worship. But a total break with either Confucian ethics or Buddhism was impossible, and combinations of various ideas and practices began to appear in religious beliefs and moral teaching.

The moral principles adopted by the military leaders and inculcated on their retainers consisted in the worship of clan deities, the Confucian ethics of fidelity and submission, and an aspiration for the transcendental ideals of Buddhism. Yet the combination was not an artificial eclecticism nor a product of chance, but more or less a necessary result of the changed social structure, based on clan relationships and nurtured by the spiritual heritage handed down from the preceding ages.   Confucian morality as applied to the life of the warrior inculcated fidelity to the chief of the clan, which, together with the circumstances of the time, engendered an acute sense of honour, both individual and tribal.   This system of ethics was supported religiously by the cult of the clan deity, adherence to family tradition, and obedience to the will of the superior.   In addition to these, the spiritual ideals of Buddhism furnished the fighters with training in self-control and fortitude.   This combination constituted the foundation of the class morality of the warriors, which was destined to rule their mind and conduct during the coming six hundred years, throughout its evolution and modifications. The Buddhist religion of the new age was not one of ceremonies and mysteries but a religion of simple piety or of spiritual exercise.   Dogma gave way to personal experience, ritual and sacerdotalism to piety and intuition, and this new type of religion exerted its influence beyond class limits, exhibiting many democratic features.

Another important feature of this period was the appearance of strong personalities, both among the warriors and the religious leaders.   Under the bureaucratic régime, institutions held sway over individuals, the social structure was heavy at the top, though the masses were not as yet painfully conscious of pressure.   Now the scale was turned to a certain degree, the leaders of the age arose from among the obscure or oppressed.   Yoritomo, the founder of the dictatorial government at Kamakura, was the son of a military captain who had been vanquished by his opponents ; though his power rested upon the clan spirit of the warrior class—their fidelity to the son of a slain chief—his success depended much upon his astute statesmanship, partly the result of his training in hardship as an orphan and exile. In religion, the new era opened with the diminution of the prestige of the aristocratic hierarchy ; the reformers appeared among those monks who had kept themselves outside ecclesiastical polity. The influence of those religious leaders was therefore not so much the effect of their doctrine as of their strong personality. A militant spirit crept into religious circles, and religious fervour inspired military men ; there were religious leaders of commanding power, just as some warriors abandoning arms showed ardour in religious activity.

We may distinguish three forms of Buddhism which signalized the change and then ruled the people's faith during the warlike ages between the thirteenth and sixteenth centuries. The first was the pietist faith of Amita-Buddhism. Its leader was Hōnen, a remarkable representative of pious devotion. The second was the intuitionism of Zen, a new form of Buddhism introduced from China by the puritanical mystic, Dōgen. The third was the revivalism of Hokké Buddhism propounded by Nichiren, a militant propagandist of prophetic ardour.

# AMITA-BUDDHISM OR JŌDO PIETISM

*The " Easy Method " of Salvation and Hōnen, its promulgator*

WE have seen how, since the tenth century, faith in the
Lord of the Western Paradise had been gaining a foothold in
the hearts of some people, and how the belief in the approach
of a world change accelerated spiritual agitation. Now many
people saw in the political catastrophe of the twelfth century
a sign of the arrival of the " Latter Days," while the weakness
of the bureaucracy and the corruption of the ecclesiastical
institutions were mercilessly exposed.

" The fateful days have arrived ; we, the weak and
vicious people of the ' Latter Days,' could not be saved but
by invoking the name of the Lord Amita." The idea expressed in this saying of Genshin found response in nearly
every heart and gave a great incentive to simple faith in
the grace of Amita-Buddha, who had opened the gateway
of his paradise to all without distinction of training or knowledge. The worship of Amita was released from its association
with intricate ritualism or methodic contemplation and
became a religion of pious devotion. An antithesis was thus
drawn between the " Way for the Wise," the wise who could
go through severe training, and the " Way to the Land of
Purity " through simple faith in the Buddha's grace. The
one was the regular religion of Buddhism, hardly within the
reach of people of the latter days, while the other was
the way specially provided for by the Buddha for the sake
of sinful and depraved beings. The one was a method of
hardship for perfection, the other an " easy way " of salvation ;

and the " easy way " of simple devotion was not salvation
by " one's own power " but " by another's," which meant
the Buddha's. The time was now ripe for the rise of this
new gospel of salvation ; the sentiment and aspiration of the
age demanded a leader of the new religion, a personal
embodiment of piety, pure and simple.

The man who consummated this development of devotional
piety was Genkū (1133-1212), better known by his other
name Hōnen, whose treatise written in 1175 signalized the
independence of Amita-Buddhism, or Jōdo pietism, Jōdo
being the Japanese name for the Land of Purity. The essay
bore the title of *Senchaku-shū*, which meant " Selection,"
namely, selection of the faith for all, implying the abandonment of the high and unattainable ideal of Buddhist perfection.
The gist of the whole work is given in one passage, which
reads :

There may be millions of people who would practise (Buddhist) discipline
and train themselves in the way of perfection, and yet in these latter days of
the Law there will be none who will attain the ideal perfection. Consider
that it is now an age full of depravities. The only way available is the
Gateway to the Land of Purity.

Hōnen was a man of meek temper and responsive heart,
and in this respect he represented the heritage from the
culture of the preceding age, while he was a typical pioneer
of the new age in his aspiration for the salvation of all. In
fact he demonstrated his zeal by abandoning all his former
attainments and devoting himself exclusively to faith in the
grace of the Buddha.

Hōnen was born in 1133, in a province far from Miyako,
as the only son of a local chief. When he was eight years
old a sad fate befell his family. Bandits raided his home
and the father died from a wound inflicted by them. The
dying father asked, as his last request, that the son should
never think of revenge, as was usual at that time among

warriors, but should endeavour to become a virtuous monk. The idea was that revenge would bring forth another act of revenge on the part of the enemy, simply perpetuating reciprocal hatred and murder throughout many lives to come ; that, therefore, the son should devote his life to religion and pray for the salvation of his father as well as of the assailants. This shows that the father was a deeply religious man. The mother demonstrated her faithfulness to the husband by at once parting from her only child and sending him to a monastery near home.

The impressions left upon Hōnen's mind in his early boyhood remained as a perpetual guide in his spiritual life. The pious desire of the father moved the boy's heart to its depths ; he saw the misery of human life in the sad fate of his family, of which he shared the sorrows and afflictions so common to that age of disturbance. And indeed, we are told that some of the assailants and their children were later converted to a religious life by Hōnen's inspiration. Some of such and other details may be partly legendary ; at any rate the once pitiful fatherless boy became the saviour of many people, and brought his father's will to an unforeseen fulfilment.

After five years Hōnen was sent to Mount Hiei to be trained for an ecclesiastical career. An obedient novice and thereafter a studious monk, he passed nearly thirty years on Hiei and went through all the branches of learning and disciplinary training taught and practised there. He became renowned for his learning and virtue, and could have aimed at a high position in the hierarchic organization, but his soul sought after something more than erudition or fame. He had studied, meditated, and prayed in search of repose of the soul, until he was finally converted to a whole-hearted belief in Amita's grace. He had tasted, as he later stated, several rich and delicious foods, philosophical wisdom, moral discipline, mystic ceremonies ; but his soul hungered until he

found an everlasting satisfaction through the daily fare of
rice which he secured in the all-saving grace of the Buddha
Amita. During these years of spiritual struggle he felt deep
dissatisfaction with the existing forms of Buddhism and
disgust at the corruption of Hiei, yet he never manifested
any sign of a rebellious spirit, persevering in pursuit of a
new life and light. When, however, he had attained the final
stage of his conversion, at about forty years of age, his
conviction was so firm that he bade farewell to Hiei for ever.
Thereafter he lived in a hermitage alone for a while but in
spiritual communion with his saviour, and two years later he
wrote the essay spoken of above. His life was passed in
piously repeating the name of the Buddha and in rather
confessing than preaching his piety to any who might come
and see him in his retired abode.

Simple indeed was the fundamental tenet of Hōnen's
religion : it was nothing but to put absolute faith in the
redeeming power of the all-compassionate Buddha embodied
in the person of Amita, the Lord of the Western Land of
Purity. There the Buddha has completed his scheme of
salvation, by virtue of his long training and accumulation
of merit. The vows he took in a remote past are fulfilled in
the establishment of the paradise where he will take any and
every person who will trust in him and invoke his name,
the " Name " being the mysterious embodiment of his saving
power. The formula provided for the purpose of this name
calling is *Namu Amida Butsu*, that is, " Adoration to the
Buddha of Infinite Life and Light." [1] Faith is of course the
fundamental requisite on the part of those to be saved, in
repeating his holy name ; what is required in this faith is
nothing but childlike trust in Buddha's fatherly love and

---

[1] *Namu* is a corruption of Sanskrit *Namah*. The formula had been in use before
Hōnen, especially among the votaries of Amita, as Shingon mystics too when they
turned their worship to him. But it was Hōnen who exhorted an exclusive use
of the formula as an expression of devotion and gratitude.

compassion.  No sin, no weakness, on our part, can be an
obstacle to our devotion to him, because his saving power is
unconditional, his grace being extended freely to all believers.
Says Hōnen :

> There shall be no distinction, no regard to male or female, good or bad,
> exalted or lowly ; none shall fail to be in His Land of Purity after having called,
> with complete desire, on Amita.   Just as a bulky boulder may pass over the
> sea, if loaded on a ship, and accomplish a voyage of myriads of leagues without
> sinking ; so we, though our sin be heavy as stone, are borne on the ship of
> Amita's primeval vow and cross to the other shore without sinking in the sea
> of repeated births and deaths.[1]

Thus Hōnen's religion was a simplified form of Amita-
Buddhism, purged of mystic elements and tempered to a
pious devotion.   Though Hōnen betrayed, in his emphasis on
the redeeming power of the Buddha's " Name," something
of his heritage from Shingon Buddhism, the practice of
repeating the Name was transformed by him into a childlike
expression of his spirit of prayer, or rather of trustful self-
abandonment.   On the other hand, he was not quite free from
doctrinal ideas in discussing the antithesis between his pietism
and other forms of Buddhism ; yet his own personal faith
was rather the result of his aversion to dogma and dialectic
than a fruit of them.   The kernel of Hōnen's religion was a
simple faith in Buddha's grace and accordingly a life of piety
and gratitude.   Everything in the world suggested to him the
presence of the all-embracing love of the saviour, and his
sentiment in perpetual devotion was often improvised in
verses with touches of pious mysticism.   To cite two of
his poems :

> In all lands no tiniest hamlet lies,
> Howe'er remote, but that the silver Moon
> Touches it with its rays.   But when a man
> Opens his windows wide and gazes long,
> Heaven's Truth will enter in and dwell with him.

·                  ·                  ·

---

[1] Cited from Hōnen's *Catechism in Twelve Articles.*

The morning haze, in springtime, veils the light
Of nascent day, and grudgingly transmits
A few pale strokes of yellow light, as though
Pure light were not ; and yet, behind the veil,
Lo ! the bright Sun floods all the world in white.[1]

.            .            .

Hōnen well represented the ethos of his age in being sincerely disgusted with the present world and the sinfulness of human life ; he embodied likewise the yearning spirit of his contemporaries in trusting himself to the mysterious power of salvation extended by the free gift of the Lord of the Western Paradise. As his monastic life before conversion was not rich in incidents, so his life after the firm establishment of his faith moved over the smooth sea of devotion. He lived in the bright sunshine of present peace and in the serene atmosphere of a firm belief in future bliss, piously repeating the Buddha's name and exhorting his disciples and admirers to the same practice. Though he lived in seclusion, in Yoshimizu (the " Fountain of Joy "), his fame attracted all classes of men and women to his hermitage. The saint of Yoshimizu was looked upon as a source of religious inspiration, a real Fountain of Joy. Many people came to see him and were soon converted to his faith. Among the converts there were monks who had been repelled by the scholastic philosophy or ritualism of orthodox Buddhism ; nobles and ladies who had been afflicted by the sudden collapse of the pompous court life and aspired after eternal bliss beyond this world ; military men who had become disgusted with their warlike pursuits and sought after spiritual refuge ; common people who had long been denied the blessings of deeper spiritual

---

[1] The translations are from Arthur Lloyd's pen. Though the translator has lost somewhat the simple purity of the original, the author keeps his wording here in memory of his lamented friend. In the first poem the word rendered by " dwell " is *sumu* in the original and the word may mean both " to abide " and " to shine in purity."

satisfaction and found Hōnen's gospel a new gateway wide open to all.

In addition to his power of religious inspiration, Hōnen had a remarkable degree of personal charm, which was a reflection of his broad sympathy and pure faith. His kind heart was but another aspect of his own devotion to the grace of Buddha. He says in a letter :

> Think in love and sympathy of any beings who have an earnest desire to be born in the Land of Purity ; repeat Buddha's name for their sake, as if they were your parents or children, though they may dwell at any distance, even outside the cosmic system. Help those who are in need of material help in this world. Endeavour to quicken faith in anybody in whom a germ of it may be found. Deem all these deeds to be services done to Amita Buddha.[1]

Such was his conviction which he always put into practice in his life. It was this spirit of charity that bore witness to his teaching and secured so many converts, even among men and women of the utmost vice or in the lowliest positions.

The life of Hōnen, peaceful as it was, had borne fruit in inspiring many hearts and giving consolation to afflicted, bewildered souls. Many of his disciples worked in propagating his gospel among the people, and his religion penetrated into remote corners of the country. Among his numerous followers arose, inevitably, those who ran to extremes and took pride in neglecting the duties of life in the contention that morality had no meaning in face of religious faith. Moreover, the fame of the apostle of the new gospel rose so high that the ecclesiastical authorities regarded him with jealousy or un-easiness. Persecution was started against him in 1204, when the monks of the old centres of orthodox Buddhism made an appeal to suppress the new propaganda and to punish its

---

[1] This is a passage from a letter sent to the widow of Yoritomo. She asked in her letter various questions especially concerning the relationship between faith and work, because some teachers of Jōdo pietism taught that " work " was useless, nay injurious, to an exclusive faith in Buddha's grace. The passage clearly shows the attitude of Hōnen towards this question—to which we shall return. *Cf.* Coates and Ishizuka, *Hōnen*, p. 461.

agents. Hōnen endeavoured to warn his followers against any excess of zeal and against trespassing the moral codes of human life, and this submissive attitude more or less appeased the persecutors, but they kept watch for an opportunity to renew the attack and suppression. This arose when two court ladies, upon being converted by Hōnen's disciples, became nuns. The case was charged as an act of seduction, and the Government executed the " seducers," while the master and his leading disciples were sentenced to banishment. This took place in 1207, when Hōnen was seventy-four years old. Touching stories are told of his departure from Miyako and of his farewell words to his disciples. Suffice it here to quote a poem left to them :

> What though our bodies, fragile as the dews,
> Melt here and there, resolved to nothingness?
> Our souls shall meet again, some happier day,
> In this same lotus-bed where now they grow.

On his journey [1] to the place of exile, and while there, he converted those who came into touch with him.

After one year of banishment in a desolate island in the Inland Sea, the sentence was mitigated, allowing him to live nearer to Miyako, in a monastery among the mountains, because his opponents still insisted on keeping him away from Miyako. Whether close to the sea or amid wild hills he lived in peace, the joyous peace in Buddha's grace. One of his poems written down at his mountain abode gives us a picture of the exile's hut in an evening calm :

> A hermit's cell, and by its lowly door
> A formless mist, but, by and by, the mist
> Transforms itself into a purple cloud
> That forms the vestibule of Paradise. [2]

His exile lasted more than four years. When he was released and welcomed by his disciples in Miyako, towards the end of

---

[1] Plate XIIA represents him as preaching to the villagers at the port of embarkation for the island of exile. It is one of the many illustrations in his great biography.

[2] Arthur Lloyd's translation.

1211, his health was failing and he was glad if only to die among his old friends and followers.

Hōnen's last days were worthy of his saintly life. Early in 1212 he lay down on a sick-bed. As days passed, his sight became clearer than before and his hearing sharper, so we are told. His whole time was devoted to uttering Buddha's name and to giving instructions to his disciples. The last of his instructions is called " The Testament in One Piece of Paper," the briefest confession of a pietist saint :

Our practice of devotion does not consist in that of meditation as recommended and practised by sages of the past. Nor is our "Calling the Name" (*Nembutsu*) uttered in consequence of enlightenment in truths attained through learning and wisdom. When we invoke Buddha and say "Namu Amida Butsu," with the firm belief that we shall be born in Buddha's paradise, we shall surely be born there. There is no other mystery here than uttering His Name in this faith. Although the three kinds of thought and the four methods of training [1] are recommended, all these are surely implicit in the faith that our birth in Buddha's Land is certain. If I knew anything more profound than this, I should be forsaken by the two Lords (the Buddhas Sākya-muni and Amita) and be cast outside the embracing vow (of Amita).

However extensively one may have comprehended the teachings propounded during the lifetime of Sākya-muni, he should, as soon as he has put faith in salvation, regard himself as an equal of the most ignorant, and thus should whole-heartedly practise *Nembutsu* in company with any simple folk, entirely giving up the demeanour of a wise man.

After he had finished writing this, the last moment seemed to approach. His voice became sweeter as he continued to utter Buddha's name until the noon of the following day.[2] His last utterance was to recite the famous lines in praise of Buddha :

> His light pervades the worlds in all the ten directions,
> His grace never forsakes any one who invokes His Name.

---

[1] The "three kinds of thought" are : sincere thought, that there is nothing more important than birth in Buddha's land ; the profound thought and belief, that all-embracing is the vow taken by Buddha to save all, even the sinful and depraved ; the earnest desire to dedicate everything to the cause of faith. Cf. *SBE.*, vol 49, Part II, p 188.

The "four methods" are : expression of reverence towards Buddha ; exclusive faith in Him ; uninterrupted repetition of his name ; untiring devotion to Buddha throughout life.

[2] The 25th day of the first moon (Feb. 29th in Julian calendar), 1212.

Surrounded by his devoted disciples, the saint ended his life of eighty years, a life which had been eventless in appearance but profoundly significant for his age and the ages to follow.[1]

### Hōnen's Disciples and other Pietists

Hōnen's gospel was soon promulgated by his devout disciples and found its way to palaces and cottages. We find his influence so overwhelming that the ecclesiastical authorities persecuted his followers from time to time. The persecutors' hatred of him even after his death ran so high that his buried body only narrowly escaped the outrage of being exhumed and carried off by Hiei's monk-soldiers. The warriors, the new aristocrats of the new era, in the eastern provinces were also brought under the influence of the new gospel, and forty years later, when Nichiren started his new propaganda as we shall presently see, he found his most formidable opponents in the followers of Jōdo Buddhism.

Hōnen's religion, as we have tried to show, was a very simple gospel of salvation by faith, but dissension on doctrinal points soon ensued among his disciples. Some of them who had been trained in the old schools of Buddhist philosophy imported their ideas into the new gospel. One of them taught that our thought directed to Buddha's grace was once for all sufficient for salvation. This doctrine of " One Thought " (*Ichinen-gi*) was based on the metaphysical conception of the identity of our soul with Buddha's as taught in Tendai philosophy. Being adapted to the inclination of

[1] His biography was written by one of his disciples five years after his death, and his writings and sayings were collected gradually later on. A second, more voluminous biography, was compiled eighty years later; this is regarded as the standard one. It has been translated into English by H. C. Coates and R. Ishizuka—*Hōnen, the Buddhist Saint* (published by Chion-in, Kyoto, 1925). This biography is full of details of Hōnen's life, various cases of conversion, instructions given by him on various occasions, letters sent to his followers, and so on. Stories of a transfiguration of Hōnen's body, of a marvellous illumination of his abode, his preaching to a serpent, several visions, and the like, are included. These stories and anecdotes may be regarded as a parallel to the *Fioretti* of St. Francis of Assisi.

easy-going believers it found a number of advocates and
grew in influence, joining hands with neglect of moral discipline.
Another, on the other hand, imported scrupulous formalism
into the religion of piety and insisted on the necessity of
" many," *i.e.*, constant, thoughts on Buddha.  This doctrine,
the *Tanen-gi*, found some followers also and was identified
with the prevalent method of mechanically repeating Buddha's
name, especially in company with many fellows.

Another division took place as regards the question
whether moral work was necessary or allowable besides pious
devotion, or injurious to it, and similarly how much morality
was needed besides faith pure and simple.  Herein we see a
division of opinion similar to that which divided Christian
thinkers from time to time as to the relation between faith
and work.  Further, it was disputed whether the faith on our
part, the counterpart of Buddha's grace, was to be ascribed,
in its origin, to our own will and capacity or solely to Buddha's
free gift.  This last question involved a deep-lying difference
of the temperamental background of faith between those
eager to discard all effort of human life in face of the entire
dependence on Buddha's redeeming power and those still
holding the sense of responsibility in life.

These differences are too subtle to be treated here in
detail but we have to note that they were due not merely
to doctrinal interest but much to differences in the training
and temperament of the leaders and advocates.  The important
point in the dispute was the different degree of emphasis laid
on the meaning of the " saving power of the vows " (*Hongwan-
riki*), the vows taken by the Buddha Amita.  The new gospel
consisted in a whole-hearted trust in that mysterious power,
but there was room for dissension as to the rôle of the
believer's faith in salvation.  Buddha's grace and our faith,
both were recognized as essential, in conjunction or co-
operation, but question was raised as to whether even our

faith itself was a free gift of grace having nothing to do with our capacity or intention.[1]  In the technical terms of Jōdo doctrine, what rôle is played by our own faith, " one's own power," in contradistinction to " another's power," Buddha's grace ?  Perhaps an emphasis on this distinction betrayed in itself lack of absolute confidence in Buddha's saving power ;  yet the distinction had been made by the master himself, in order to give prominence to the characteristic feature of his gospel in contrast to other forms of Buddhism, which he judged as depending too much on one's own power, the method common to all the Buddhist teachers who founded a new branch within Buddhism, of making a sharp distinction, not seldom far-fetched, between the new form and the others. At any rate some interpretation was to be made, within Jōdo Buddhism itself, as of the relationship between the two categories of the saving power.  Some naturally gave more or less recognition to the rôle of faith, or will to believe, on the part of those to be saved ;  while others deemed it necessary to put the whole weight on Buddha's grace, to the denial of any part taken by our own capacity in salvation.  This latter interpretation was that even faith is not our own act or possession but exclusively the gift of grace.  The most conspicuous representative of this latter was Shinran, the founder of an independent branch of Jōdo Buddhism now known as *Shinshū*, the " True Doctrine."

Shinran (1173-1263)[2] was one of those young monks of

---

[1] Here the point somewhat reminds us of the Christian doctrine of predestination.  This is especially the case with a section of Jōdo Buddhists who teach that our salvation has become a fixed destination when the Buddha Amita accomplished his task of establishing his paradise, in the past of ten world-periods ago, as the result of his vows and work.  Thus here we have a Buddhist doctrine of predestination, though without those to be doomed to hell.

[2] Further on Shinran, see Arthur Lloyd, *The Creed of Half Japan*, pp. 268-73 ; by the same author, *Shinran and His Work* (Tokyo, 1913): A. K. Reischauer, *A Catechism of the Shin Sect* (*TASJ.*, vol. 37, 1912).

There are many obscure points in Shinran's life-stories, and some critics have doubted even his historical reality.  But some of his autographic writings have recently been identified, and a number of his preserved letters seem to be genuine.

Mount Hiei who were dissatisfied with current Buddhism and struggling for a new path of freedom.  As a young man he had been troubled by the problem of sex also ; he was twenty-eight years old when he was converted to Hōnen's religion in 1201.  His personal contact with the master lasted only six years, as we are told ;  after the latter's exile Shinran lived in remote provinces and worked as a popular preacher among the countryfolk.  He discarded his monastic robes and the regular habit of shaving the head.  There are obscurities as regards his " marriage " but at any rate he lived an ordinary family life and was the father of several children.  This he did in order to " give a living testimony," as his followers say, that the secular life of common people was no obstacle to salvation.  Though married life for a priest was scarcely exceptional, it had never been justified by doctrine or faith but was regarded as a mere concession.  Shinran, on the contrary, regarded celibacy rather as a sign of lack of absolute trust in Buddha's grace, because no sin was an obstacle to salvation through grace.  Shinran never publicly protested against the idea of purifying oneself from sin, yet strongly denounced it as an impediment to real faith.  Any scruple about sins or depravities was, in Shinran's faith, reliance on " one's own power " and therefore a menace to the absolute faith in " another's power," in Buddha's grace.  This step taken by him was a very significant one in the history of Buddhism, and was one of the reasons why his religion exerted so wide an influence through coming centuries, even up to the present.

Thus Shinran carried the idea of Buddha's grace to extreme conclusions.  A saying of Hōnen runs—" Even a bad man will be received in Buddha's Land, how much more a good man ! "  Shinran turned this to—" Even a good man will be received in Buddha's Land, how much more a bad man ! " [1]  In short " neither virtue nor wisdom but faith " was his fundamental tenet, and faith itself has nothing to do with our own intention or attainment but is solely Buddha's free gift. He says :

Whether sage or fool, whether good or bad, we have simply to give up the idea of estimating our own qualities or of depending upon self. Though entangled in sin and depravity, even in living the life of the most despised outcast, we are embraced by the all-pervading light of grace ; indefatigable faith in salvation itself is a manifestation of Buddha's act of embracing us into His grace, because nothing can impede the working of His grace.

(Our salvation is) " natural, as it is," in the sense that it is not due to our own device or intention but provided for by Buddha Himself. It is "natural," because we need not think of our own good or bad ; everything has been arranged by Buddha to receive us into His Paradise. It is " natural," because His grace is intangible and invisible and yet works by " naturalness" to induce us to the highest attainment. [2]

Shinran's religion may be called a kind of naturalism, in the sense that nothing is required on our part, whether effort or training or transformation, as the salvation as provided for us by Buddha is simply to be accepted and relied upon without questioning or conditions.

The foundation of salvation has been laid down in the vows or " primeval vows " (*Hongwan*) taken by the Buddha Amita, and the mystery of his " Name " is the sole key to salvation. Our destiny is entirely in Buddha's hands, is encompassed within his plan of saving all as expressed in his vows ; nay, our salvation is predestined and well-nigh

[1] Here good and bad, of course, are understood in the ordinary moral sense but also associated with the idea of conforming to the standards of Buddhist discipline including rules of conduct and mental training. This striking saying of Shinran is usually interpreted in a sense similar to the parable of the prodigal son and his elder brothers, as stated in Luke, or to the simile of the one of a hundred sheep gone astray. But some followers of Shinran, particularly his modern worshippers, would contend that it means negation of morality.

[2] Taken from his utterances recorded by his disciples. The idea of " natural, as it is " may be traced back to the ancient Buddhist conception of *Tathatā* (" Thatness "), a highly abstract metaphysical idea ; but we have it here in a very different sense and application. It is in Japanese *Hōni jinen*, of which the name Hōnen is a condensed appellation. Another point to be noted is that this naturalism is shifted by Shinran's modern followers to an emphasis on the instinctive nature of man.

accomplished, because Buddha has already, millions of æons ago, perfected his scheme of taking all to his Realm of Bliss. "Calling Buddha's Name" in pious devotion and absolute trust in him, Shinran taught, is the way thereto, but no idea whatever of invocation or supplication is to be cherished; it should be uttered as the expression of trust and gratitude towards his grace. Further, even this gratitude is rather reminding ourselves of Buddha's "primeval vows" already completed, than thanking him in anticipation of the bliss to be attained. As a corollary to this idea, Shinran strongly denounced the idea of estimating the amount of faith by the frequency of repeating Buddha's name, as was done by most other Amita-Buddhists. Similarly he disregarded such signs of grace as vision and illumination, and particularly the apparition of Buddha and his saints at the moment of death of a pious person, which were deemed essential to salvation, such as were recorded in Hōnen's life. Thus, Shinran purged, much further than his master had done, Jōdo Buddhism from its association with traditional mysteries and methods of spiritual exercise, and brought religion into much closer contact with the daily life of the people at large. His teachings left room for an indulgent tendency to creep into religion, and so vulgar forms of his religion arose from time to time and often encouraged and justified indulgence in desires and passions.[1]

Shinran worked as a preacher, never regarding himself as a teacher or superior but as a simple member of the fellowship in the faith in Buddha's grace. He wrote some essays, more or less learned, but more letters of intimate instructions. The writings through which he exercised the greatest influence were hymns in Japanese. These hymns are known as *Wasan*,

---

[1] For the sub-sects of Shinran's followers, see below, p. 232. A combination of his teaching with modern naturalism is well illustrated by a modern drama which was once very popular—*The Priest and His Disciples* by Hyakuzo Kurata —and translated into English by G. W. Shaw.

or " Colloquial Hymns," but in reality they are not quite in popular language. Let us cite a few of them : [1]

> Vows are accomplished, forty-eight in number,[2]
> He has attained His aim, the Buddha of Infinite Light ;
> Assured are we now of birth in His Land,
> To us who trust in Him and utter His Name.

> Virtues and merits accumulated through countless æons
> Are embodied in the sole Name of Amita consummately.
> The Sacred Name, the outcome of His long meditation,
> Is now given us, even though immersed in sin and depravity.

> In the worlds beings are as numerous as fine sands in the basin of the
>     Ganges;
> They are all embraced by Amita's grace and never forsaken,
> Only if they would call His Name,
> Our Lord is, therefore, called Amita, the Infinite.

> Without end is the dreary ocean of births and deaths,
> Immersed in it are we since eternity ;
> We can in no way be carried across (to the other shore),
> But by being loaded on the ship of Amita's vow to take all.

> No choice is given to the learned or the pure in conduct,
> No one is rejected, not even sinful ones utterly devoid of merit ;
> Call on His Name, put faith in Him sincerely,
> Then pebbles will soon be transformed into gold.

> Lo ! A torch illumines the ever-dark night of illusion !
> Never regret that your eyes of wisdom are troubled.
> There is here a ship on the ocean of births and deaths,
> Grieve no more over heavy sins and obstacles !

Shinran attempted to annul the distinction between religious and secular, both in teaching and practice. He lived in obscurity among the countryfolk, seeking scarcely

---

[1] These translations are not intended to be verse but divided into lines for keeping the original lines. A group of the *Wasan* has an English translation from U. Oshima's pen, published under the title *Hymns of the Pure Land* (Kyoto, West Hongwan-ji, 1923).

[2] This number is sacred to Jōdo Buddhists, since the vows taken by Amita, while a plain monk still, are counted in that number, as preserved in a Chinese translation of the *Sukhāvatī-vyūhā*. Cf. *SBE*, vol. 49, Part ii, pp. 11-22.

any publicity ; in that respect, as in his married life, he was one of the many popular teachers working in the provinces. Even when he had returned to Miyako, his native place, and passed several years until his death there, he made no public appearance but remained an obscure man. Yet the seeds sown during the decades of his preaching bore fruit in due time, first in the east and later in the capital. His disciples and his children worked as his apostles, and we see his influence increasing more and more in the course of a century, until the body of his followers became a powerful church organization in the fifteenth century. It was an irony of fate that Shinran's descendants organized a formidable system verging on a popedom, in which they played the rôle of vicar of the founder and even of Buddha.[1]

·       ·       ·       ·       ·       ·

The main stream of Amita-Buddhism was the pietism of Hōnen, but there were other currents of the same faith, pursuing more or less the old course, either the contemplative method or the practice of mechanically chanting Buddha's name. The religion of meditation on Amita and his Land of Bliss was later formulated anew by Shinsei (1443-95), but this little concerns us here. The practice of repeating Buddha's name was propagated by Ippen (1239-89), known as the " Itinerant Sage," because he preached and encouraged the practice of chanting by going around far and wide. He adopted a method of propaganda somewhat after the model of the " Saint of the Market," spoken of above, that of registering the names of those who confessed devotion to the grace of Buddha and chanted Buddha's name in assembly. It is said that the persons registered during the itinerancy of

---

[1] One of his grandsons, Nyoshin (1239-1300), was a man eminent for piety, but the main line of the family was carried on by his great-grandson, the grandson of his daughter, Kakunyo (1270-1351), and the latter's son Zonkaku (1290-1373). These two were the chief systematizers of Shinran's religion and organizers of its church. Some of the writings ascribed to Shinran come down from these two successors.

Ippen amounted to more than two millions and a half. His missionary journeys, with which he combined relief work of various kinds, covered nearly the whole of Japan, and in this respect he revived the method of eighth century Buddhism in Japan—a feature of his religious activity differing from Hōnen's quietism and representing the new ethos of the Kamakura period.[1] Another peculiarity in the teaching of Ippen was the exhortation that every utterance of Buddha's name be accompanied by the idea of the last moment of life close at hand and that therefore the act of devotion be a preparation for death at any moment. His followers formed a separate body called *Jishū*, namely the " Time Doctrine," because it inculcated pious thought at every moment, and also because the service to be held regularly six times a day was considered to be essential to salvation. This school continues to exist and has a certain amount of influence among the lower classes, though it is slowly declining.

### Art and Literature of the Early Kamakura Period

The rise of Amita-Buddhism was an assertion of piety as against the doctrinalism and ritualism of the orthodox church. But in its sentiment the new religion of piety inherited much of the sentiment of the preceding age, and this temper expressed itself in the religious art of the thirteenth century, namely of the early Kamakura period. Imageries in pious thought, visions of superhuman existences, of the blissful realms, of celestial hosts playing heavenly music among the variegated clouds, these gave a new impetus to religious painting and sculpture.[2] The works of art produced in this atmosphere were delicate in tone and elaborate in execution,

[1] See Plate XIIв, where Ippen's disciples are represented relieving distress from famine.

[2] Cf. Anesaki, *Buddhist Art*, Plates I, XI, XII ; pp. 27-30. Comp. Plates IVв, XI, XII, and XIII in this book.

brilliant in colour and rich in composition.  Golden lines were laid on in fine gold leaf, instead of being drawn with the brush, and the whole effect was highly delicate.  Jewels and stones were inlaid for eyeballs in statues, to give a more realistic effect.

Although no clear demarcation can be drawn between the art of the later Fujiwara period and that of the Kamakura, the latter can be distinguished from the former by the soft tone of the outlines, as well as by a higher degree of brilliancy, besides the richness of imagination.  All this represented breadth of vision and depth of faith.  But, on the other hand, the eclectic tendency of the age can be seen in the prevalence of combinations of figures, Buddhist and Shinto, Japanese and Chinese, arranged generally in groups.[1]

Another class of painting which marks this period is the semi-religious painting executed on long scrolls.  The representation of various scenes one after another in horizontal series had been a fashion in the preceding centuries, the subjects being mostly *genre* pictures of court life, often with landscapes in the background.  This scheme and technique were now applied to the representation of religious themes, such as the lives of saintly men, miracles worked by Buddha and other deities, especially those miracles which were supposed to have led to the foundation of the temples dedicated to those deities.[2]  These paintings were religious in motive, and yet serving as narratives they depicted in a more or less realistic style various scenes from life, often humorous and amusing.[3]

[1] Cf. Anesaki, *Buddhist Art*, Plate XXVIII.   Comp. Plate IX in this book.

[2] The scroll is called *e-maki-mono*, the stories of the saints *e-den*, and the stories of the temples *engi*.  See Plate XII A-B.

[3] It is in this respect that the *genre* paintings of this period do great service to historical investigations, and also show us the close relation between life and religion.

Among the painters of this period we might mention Takuma Jōga and Tosa Yoshimitsu, the latter of whom executed most of the scenes from Hōnen's life illustrating his great biography.  Among the sculptors the most famous were Unkei and his son Tankei.

A. A Scene from the Life of Hōnen, His Preaching to the Villagers at the Port of Embarkation for Exile. By Tosa Yoshimitsu (or his fellow) (early 14th century)

B. A Scene from the Life of Ippen, the Itinerant Sage, at a Famine Relief. By En-i (dated 1299)

PLATE XIII

THE "DAIBUTSU" OR THE GIANT STATUE AT KAMAKURA,
REPRESENTING AMITA

(Erected 1252)

The great cataclysm had wrought a powerful change in sentiment, dispelling the emotionalism of the court nobles. The vigorous spirit of the provincial warriors became the predominant tone of the age, manifesting itself in stern serenity, meditation, inwardness. Literature soon seized the new spirit of the age, and epics came to the foreground. The new style was characterized by free use of Chinese and Buddhist expressions, serving to add brevity and force to Japanese. Rhapsodists recited the rise and fall of the contending clans with touching or thrilling episodes. In these stories figured the men and women who were afflicted by the vicissitudes of fortune and by the miseries of life, or those who were saved from tribulation and agony by faith in Buddha's grace.

Underlying all these stories were grave sentiments, the sense of the evanescence of human life, the deep sense of sin accumulated in former lives, and yet calm resignation in the face of fate and misery. Against the background of this mournful sentiment cases of sudden conversion to faith were exalted, pictures were drawn of future bliss longed for, or of beatific visions realized in this life, and stories told · of childlike devotion to the holy teachers.

Literature more properly religious underwent a similar change. Buddhist teachers wrote essays and epistles in simple yet powerfully appealing vernacular, in contrast to the dogmatic treatises of the preceding ages, which had been written in scholastic Chinese. Hymns and litanies were composed in a new style, terse and expressive ; they were chanted sometimes in the mournful tone of an elegy, sometimes with a jubilant air as of an angelic chorus.[1] Biographies of holy men were compiled and circulated with illustrations. Stories were told of journeys in other worlds, whether blissful

---

[1] Some of the hymns are cited above, in connection with Shinran. Cf. Anesaki's article in *ERE*, on " *Hymn (Japanese)*."

heavens or woeful existences.  Visions and apparitions, of deities and angels, of devils and monsters, were told and graphically represented, sometimes in earnest and sometimes humorously.  In short, the consternation resultant from the great social catastrophe, together with the high spiritual aspiration of the new age, worked to produce a highly spirited type of art and literature, characterized by breadth of vision, height of aspiration, sincerity of sentiment, and vigour of expression.

# NICHIREN AND HIS PROPHETIC RELIGION [1]

*Nichiren, His Struggle and Life of Combat*

THE Buddhism of Hōnen was representative of the new age
in its simple and pure piety, but it shared much of the
sentimentalism prevalent in Miyako. There now appeared a
man who represented the vigorous spirit of eastern Japan,
combining with it the profound idealism of Buddhism, and
from whom Amita-Buddhism encountered the most formidable
attacks. This man was Nichiren, and his name meant
" Sun-lotus," which symbolized a combination of Shinto
and Buddhist ideals, the Sun embodying light and life, and
the lotus purity and perfection. His character and career
were unique in the religious history of Japan. In him were
harmonized the fervour of a prophet and the sweetness of a
saint, the wisdom of a learned doctor and the enthusiasm of
an ardent reformer. In contrast to Hōnen's life, Nichiren's
was full of perils and adventures. In his numerous essays
and epistles we find expressions of deep thought, sharp
dialectic, cries of warning, persuasive admonition, animating
encouragement, and his own touching confessions as well.
Authentic material for drawing a vivid picture of his life
can be secured from his own professions of belief and from
the narratives of his career and adventures, all handed down
in his own writings.

Nichiren was born in 1222, the son of a fisherman in the
south-eastern corner of Japan, a fact which Nichiren himself
interpreted in his later years to have special significance

[1] Cf. Anesaki, *Nichiren, the Buddhist Prophet* (Harvard University Press, 1916).

for him as the representative of Japanese Buddhism, because
he deemed his native place to be nearest the place of sunrise.
Early in his boyhood he was sent to a monastery on a hill
near his home and passed there several years of novitiate.
As he grew older he was tormented by the question of what,
among the various branches of Buddhism then prevailing,
was the true doctrine of Buddha himself.  An earnest desire
for the solution of this problem led him to Kamakura, and
then to Hiei, in 1243.  He remained in that great seat of
Buddhism for about ten years and visited other centres of
Buddhist learning as well, endeavouring to exhaust the
depths of Buddhist truth.

At last, when he was about thirty years old, he attained
the conviction that the true Buddhism was nothing but the
doctrine of the *Lotus of Truth* as expounded by Saichō, the
founder of Hiei, and that all other branches were false and
corrupt.  At the same time he became convinced that the
whole teaching of the scripture Lotus as well as Saichō's
tenets should be interpreted and carried out in practice by
adjusting them to the needs of the time, the age of the
" Latter Law."  These points of his conviction had a complicated background of doctrinal speculation, in accordance
with the general trend of Buddhist thought and as a result
of Nichiren's erudition.  But all these doctrines and speculations were fused by the white-heat of his faith and zeal, and
he reduced the whole of his religion to a simple method, that
of uttering the " Sacred Title " of the scripture, in the
fórmula *Namu Myō-Hōrenge-kyō*, which meant " Adoration
to the Lotus of Perfect Truth." [1]  It was for him not a mere
oral utterance but a real embodiment of the truths revealed
in that book, because the " Title " was representative of the

---

[1] *Namu* is a corruption of the Sanskrit *Namah*, "Adoration," and *Myō-
Hōrenge-kyō* is the Sino-Japanese form of *Sad-Dharma-pundarīka-Sūtra*.  This was
calling on the name of the Scripture instead of calling on the name of Buddha.

whole revelation, which was to be realized in the spirit and embodied in the life of all who adored Buddha and his revelation.  To utter the " Sacred Title " was, according to Nichiren, the method of at once elevating oneself to the highest enlightenment of Buddhahood and of identifying self with the cosmic soul.  This method he deemed to be the only adequate way available for the degenerate men of the latter days.

With the fire of these earnest convictions, he went back to his old monastery which he had left nearly fifteen years before.  Early on a summer morning in 1253, he climbed the summit of the hill and " announced the Sacred Title to the universe " taking as witness the sun as it was rising from the horizon of the Pacific Ocean.  At noon of the same day he propounded his new thesis to his former abbot and fellow monks, breaking into bitter protest against the prevailing Buddhism.  They were shocked by the audacity of his contentions, and the pretentious young prophet was driven out of his native province.

He spent most of the following seven years in Kamakura, the seat of the dictatorial government.  During this time, the city of Kamakura was the scene of many frightful events ; ominous rumours were current of plots against the Hōjō, who were divided in family strife, and in addition there was a series of disasters, storms, inundations, earthquakes, famines, pestilence, appearance of comets.  The people were panic-stricken, and the Government resorted to offerings at Shinto sanctuaries and occult rites conducted in Buddhist temples. Nichiren regarded not only the disasters themselves, but the spiritual bewilderment caused by them, as results of the false religions prevailing ;  his conclusion was that Buddha and his angels had withdrawn their protection from the country.  In demonstration of his contention he wrote an essay entitled *Risshō-Ankoku-Ron*, " The Establishment of

Righteousness and the Security of the Country," as a remonstrance for presentation to the Government.

In this essay Nichiren pointed out relentlessly what he deemed to be the evils of the time, and laid the heaviest responsibility for the calamities upon Jōdo Buddhism, denouncing Hōnen as a spirit of hell. Later he proceeded to attack other branches of Buddhism. Shingon Buddhism was, according to him, the greatest evil threatening the life of the nation, while Amita-Buddhists were doomed to hell. Besides these chief menaces, Nichiren attacked the conservative formalism of the disciplinary school called Ritsu, and also the newly-introduced method of meditation, Zen, of which we shall speak presently. In short, all Buddhist leaders of the time were traitors and hypocrites, by whom the nation was being led astray and doomed to ruin. Disasters could not be averted unless the Government were ready at once to suppress all those false religions and the nation were to be converted to the unique truth of the Lotus. Otherwise, he warned the Government, the nation would, in addition to the existing miseries, be ruined by internecine strifes and suffer foreign invasion. In conclusion he said :

> Ye men of little faith, turn your minds and trust yourselves at once to the unique Truth of the Righteous Way ! Then ye shall see that the three realms of existence are (in reality) the Kingdom of Buddha, which is in no way subject to decay ; and that the worlds in the ten quarters are all Lands of Treasures, which are never to be destroyed. The Kingdom is changeless and the Lands eternal. Then how shall your life be otherwise than secure and your mind serene in enlightenment?

The document, filled with fierce remonstrance concluding with these fervent words, was sent to the government authorities. The latter made no response, but a mob attacked the prophet, probably with the tacit permission of the authorities. His hermitage was burnt down and he had a narrow escape through the darkness of the night.

When Nichiren had returned to Kamakura, after several

months of missionary journey in the adjacent provinces, he renewed his cries of warning in the streets and parks. The Government saw in him a disturber of the peace, and he was arrested and banished to the wild coasts of the peninsula of Izu. Abandoned and alone in his place of exile and surrounded by dangers, Nichiren reviewed his past life, and found in the scripture more encouraging assurance of his own mission and deeper inspiration. The result of this calm reflection and ardent aspiration he formulated in the " five theses " of his mission. They were :

First, as to the doctrine promulgated, his religion was based upon the unique authority of the Lotus, the consummation of all teachings of Buddha. Second, as to the capacity of those to be taught, mankind of that degenerate age of the Latter Days could be trained only by Buddha's teaching in its simplest expression, not by any complicated system. Third, as to the time, his time was the age of the Latter Law, in which the Lotus alone would remain efficient for the salvation of all. Fourth, as to the country of its promulgation, Japan was the land where true Buddhism was destined to prevail ; whence it should be propagated throughout the world. Fifth, as to the successive rise and fall of systems, other forms of Buddhism had done their missions and the way had been prepared by the old masters for the acceptance of the Perfect Truth.[1]

All these five conditions seemed to Nichiren to be in process of fulfilment by his activity, and the dangers he was encountering assured him more and more of his high mission. Thus three years' life in exile only added fire to his ardour.

After his return from exile in 1263, Nichiren found himself surrounded by ardent followers more numerous than before,

[1] The sixth thesis, the person who was to accomplish the mission, was declared later ; we may assume that in this essay Nichiren implicitly asserted himself to be the man. But a clearer conviction was to be reached later, when he was exiled to Sado, for which see below, pp. 197-198.

and he worked with enthusiasm and in more uncompromising attitude. He then went on missionary journeys, during which he was nearly killed by a local chieftain, who as an ardent Amita-Buddhist had ever been Nichiren's mortal opponent and attempted to assault him by surprise. But this peril was to be followed by more serious and persistent persecution. At this time, Kublai Khan, the Mongol conqueror of China and Korea, was planning an expedition to Japan. Rumours of this increased the apprehension of the people, and finally a Mongol envoy demanding tribute of Japan came *via* Korea. Nichiren seized the opportunity and renewed his remonstrance to the Government, reminding them of his prophecy of a foreign invasion published eight years before. He challenged the prelates of the temples and monasteries endowed by the government to organize a public debate with him. The authorities simply ignored Nichiren's propositions. He was confident, however, that when the Mongol crisis became more serious, the eyes of the authorities and of the people would be opened to the truth of his religion.

Three years passed in combat and struggle, in which Nichiren persistently urged conversion upon the nation. Finally the Government saw in this insolent monk a conspirator against the nation and sentenced him to banishment. The real intention of the authorities, particularly of the chief of police who was Nichiren's bitterest opponent, was to deprive him of his life on the way to exile; and Nichiren himself was well aware of it and prepared for the last moment, thinking that death should bear best testimony to his mission. It was past midnight (in the autumn of 1271) that he arrived at the place of execution, and there everything was ready for his last moment. Suddenly—and miraculously, as he himself and many others too believed—the sky seemed ablaze. " A bright object," as his own account says, " like a ball of fire flew from the south-east to the north-west, and every one's face was visible in the light." The officials and soldiers were panic-stricken and the sword fell from the executioner's hands. Execution had become impossible, and the hated monk was again sentenced to banishment.

This narrow escape from death, the third and most perilous, impressed him so deeply that he regarded his life thereafter as a second life, life after a resurrection. The fifty years he had lived seemed now to have been merely introductory to his great mission, and he submitted himself to the sentence of banishment in hopeful delight, with a firm conviction that the proper part of his life, the revelation of his true destiny and ideal, was to begin.

The place of his exile was the desolate island of Sado in the Sea of Japan. When he arrived at the port to embark for Sado, the winter gale was raging on the northern sea, a new experience to him who had known only the southern sea-coasts. He had passed, he writes, " mountains beyond mountains " on the way thereto, and " waves upon waves " were whirling before him, as if symbolic of his life full of perils. This was a supreme moment, in which he found further confirmation of his faith in his mission, the perils working only to strengthen his trust in Buddha and in the prophecies contained in the scripture. A letter he wrote at this time marked a significant step in the consummation of his confidence in the mysterious connection existing between himself and the saints predicted in the scripture to appear for the salvation of all in the Latter Days.

Nichiren passed a winter amid snow and hoar-frost in an abandoned cottage, suffering extreme cold and hunger. His thoughts naturally turned more intensely than before to the fate of those Buddhists who would work in the days of degeneration and suffer persecution for the sake of the true Buddhism. In these thoughts about his missions he always interwove his idea about his country, which had given birth to

him and therefore was destined to become the centre of the
Buddhist Church of the world.   In brief, his exile of three
years in Sado was the climax of his life, and during this
time he achieved what he deemed to be the pivot of his
work, a graphic representation of the " Supreme Being."

Before considering this point, let us note a fiery expression
of Nichiren's conviction of his mission.   We cite from the
*Kaimoku-shō*, or " Opening the Eyes," an essay written
early in 1272, when the first winter in Sado was nearly over,
a comparative and critical review of various religious and
moral systems and on the consummation of all those in the
true Buddhism.   He says in conclusion :

> Finally, let the celestial beings withdraw their protection, let all perils
> come upon me ; even so, shall I dedicate my life to this cause. . .   Be it in
> weal, be it in woe, to desert the Lotus of Truth means to fall to the hells.   I
> will be firm in my great vow.   Let me face all manner of threats and
> temptations.   Should one say to me, ' Thou mightest ascend the throne
> of Japan, if thou would'st abandon the Scripture and expect future bliss
> through belief in the *Meditation on Amita*;[1] or thy parents shall suffer
> capital punishment, unless thou utterest the name of the Buddha Amita !'
> Such temptations I shall meet unshaken, and shall never be allured by them,
> unless my principles be shattered by a sage's refutation.   Any other perils
> shall be dust before a storm.   I will be the Pillar of Japan ; I will be the
> Eyes of Japan ; I will be the Great Vessel of Japan.[2]   Inviolable shall
> remain these oaths !

Here we see Nichiren's conviction of the truth of his
teaching expressed in fusion with his belief in his own mission,
both of which were more firmly implanted in his mind by his
experiences at the execution ground and in the ice and snow
of Sado.

### Climax of Nichiren's Life and His Retirement

As the first winter passed and the spring breeze began to
melt the snow and ice, sunlight came to the prophet's sur-

---

[1] One of the three fundamental texts of Amita-Buddhism.

[2] Nichiren's religion emphasized the adoration of Buddha as the lord, the
teacher, and the father of all beings.   Here the " Pillar " meant the supporter,
and therefore lord ; the " Eyes " the function and dignity of the teacher, the
revealer of truth ; and the " Vessel " the source of life, saviour, therefore fatherhood.

roundings. Some inhabitants of the island were converted, and not a little consolation reached him from his followers in the main island. In the following year (1273) he wrote another important treatise, " The Spiritual Introspection of the Supreme Being." Then he proceeded to make a graphic representation of the " Supreme Being " as the visible standard of meditation and worship.

The " Supreme Being ", according to Nichiren, is Buddha in his metaphysical entity, the enlightened soul in full grasp of the whole truth of existence. This entity, the Buddha-nature, is inherent in every being, whether human or celestial, or even bestial and infernal, and can be, ought to be, realized in every soul when it enters into full communion with Buddha. This truth was embodied in the person of the historical Buddha and his eternal life revealed in the *Lotus of Truth*. In fact, Nichiren regarded himself as the man destined to perpetuate Buddha's saving work for the sake of depraved beings in the latter ages of the world, and therefore authorized to furnish the unique standard of faith for them. The Sacred Title of the Lotus had established this standard for oral utterance, and now he proposed to furnish the same for spiritual introspection through visualization, because the vast universe, with all its beings, was nothing but an extension, an outward manifestation of every one's Buddha-nature. The visualized standard was made for the purpose of impressing one's soul with the true and everlasting nature of its own identity with the eternal Buddha and that of every other existence. The Supreme Being meant a perfect union of the individual and the world, the oneness of the Buddha-nature and its inexhaustible manifestations.

The graphic scheme was, accordingly, intended to be a miniature of the cosmos, including all kinds of beings arranged about the cosmic Lotus of Truth, in adoration of it, and illuminated by the wisdom and mercy of Buddha.[1] The representation was, however, neither a picture of those beings nor a mere symbolic diagram, but an arrangement in titles, of all classes of existence according to their respective grades of spiritual ascent around the primordial Buddhahood, which was represented by the Sacred Title.[2] Nichiren regarded this representation of the Supreme Being as the chief work entrusted to him by Buddha for the salvation of mankind in the latter days, a predestined mission to be achieved by the "Messenger of Buddha."

After two years and a half, Nichiren was released from exile and went back to Kamakura. This was a sign that the Government was then willing to arrange a compromise with him, and this change of attitude towards him was chiefly due to the anticipation of a Mongol invasion, which soon became a reality. The Government wished to give the prophet official sanction for his propaganda, on condition that he abstain from his fierce attacks upon other Buddhists. But Nichiren did not like to see his teaching granted as one among others. He would accept no compromise but forced his demands as vigorously as before. One month passed in these negotiations, and then we see him in secluded retirement among the mountains of Minobu, on the western side of Mount Fuji (1274).

The clamorous prophet was now suddenly changed to a silent recluse. This sudden change was interpreted in various ways by Nichiren's later followers, but he himself gave a clear account of his motive. He had given his warning to the nation and to the Government persistently and forcibly enough, yet they could not realize the true significance of his

---

[1] Cf. Anesaki, *Nichiren*, chapter vii.

[2] In all these conceptions and schemes Nichiren betrays his indebtedness to Shingon mysticism ; but in substituting the names and titles for the images and diagrams used in the Shingon Cycles, he was a follower of Tendai, who emphasized the importance of the "title."

mission. On his part he had done the utmost in fulfilling the " five theses " of his propaganda and accomplished two, out of three, plans of his religious scheme, that is, the proclamation of the Sacred Title and the revelation of the Supreme Being. Now there remained the third, namely preparation for the establishment of the central seat of the Buddhist Catholic Church, which, as he conceived, was to rule the world throughout the ensuing ages of the Latter Law. Though he firmly believed in the realization of this ecclesiastical scheme, he put the actual establishment of the *Kaidan*, the Holy Centre, in an indefinite future. The conviction of his great mission, and also the sense of his own sinfulness and his idea of expiation, were closely allied with this ideal scheme. This idea of expiation requires a little further elucidation.

By sin Nichiren understood nothing else than estrangement from the truth and the teaching of the *Lotus*, the falling away of individuals from the primordial oneness of the universal life. But sin was not merely a matter of the individual person, it was a common heritage of all beings, for all had estranged themselves from the unique truth of the Scripture. Nichiren deemed that the dangers and persecutions he had been suffering were means of expiating this sin, both his personal sinfulness and the common share. Now he had done something towards expiation by enduring the perils of his life and by standing indefatigably for the cause of the Truth. But his individual expiation was but a small fraction of the ultimate and universal expiation, although his own part in it was the key to universal salvation. And since the salvation of all was possible only through its essential organ, the Catholic Church, its establishment was to be the final consummation of his mission, which presupposed an entire transformation of the world and of the whole of mankind. Hence, expiation in the full sense, even on the part of

Nichiren alone, was incomplete until the central seat of the Church should be established, and all mankind be united in the same faith of the true Buddhism. Expiation, the chief reason for his retirement, was therefore only another aspect of his efforts for the establishment of the Holy See. The prophet who had done his part in the past had now to work for the future.

Thus the chief occupation of his mind and life in retirement was to pray and prepare for the grand scheme of the future, and it is said that he despatched one of his elder disciples to the foot of Mount Fuji to select the spot for the Holy Centre.[1] Japan, for Nichiren, was the country where the Universal Buddhist Church was to have its central seat ; but Japan in an ideal sense meant the whole world—transformed in the light of the Scripture.[2] Nichiren deemed himself to be the man sent by Buddha to open the way for the transformed world, the messenger of Buddha, an incarnation of the Truth. Why then should he cherish any doubt as to the ideal destiny of his country and the fulfilment of his world-wide scheme ?

With these thoughts, and in earnest prayer for their fulfilment, the recluse passed his days in peace and diligence among the peaks of Minobu, which he deemed to be an earthly paradise because of his abode there. Indeed, Nichiren's conception of the Buddhist Church was an extension of his idea of the paradise inherent in every soul and to be realized in the life of each enlightened soul as well as in the universal communion of such souls. He considered the spread of his gospel the necessary condition for the transformation of the

[1] Several temples have since then been established there, where even to-day some bigoted Nichirenites pray, with an admixture of superstitious ideas, for the realization of Nichiren's ideal scheme.

[2] This idea of the present world as paradise was emphasized by Nichiren especially in contradistinction to the paradise of the Buddha Amita in the west, far away, millions of leagues beyond.

world, perhaps through a catastrophe. And the catastrophe seemed to him to be heralded by the rise of the Mongols proceeding to a world war. Thus with firm trust in the ideal destiny of his religion and country, Nichiren watched the repeated invasions of the Mongols (1274 and 1281), their devastation of the western islands, and their final defeat effected by a storm. A hermit in appearance, yet a prophet and reformer, he was, as he thought, preparing for the fulfilment of his prophecies.

The prophet had now attained the sixty-first year of his life, and his health had been impaired for some time, but this was not surprising in a man who had exhausted his energy in encountering perils and dangers. "Our Lord Sākya-muni revealed," thought Nichiren, "during the last eight years of his earthly life, the Lotus of Truth on Vulture Peak; then he left the Peak and went north-eastward to Kusināgara, there to enter the Great Decease. Now that I have spent eight years amid the peaks of Minobu, time has come to me to prepare for the end of life." With this thought he left his beloved retreat at Minobu. Taking a route to the north-east, he arrived at Ikegami, near modern Tōkyō. There he was prostrated with sickness. During nearly a month of his illness he gave lectures anew on his old *Risshō-Ankoku-Ron* and entrusted to his disciples the work to be carried out after his death. On the 13th day of the 10th moon of 1282, the prophet expired, surrounded by his devout disciples.

Nichiren's prophetic zeal and his perseverance in hardships were emulated by many of his monk-disciples and lay followers. Even during the years of his retired life their activity covered nearly all the eastern provinces. This missionary activity was extended later to the north and to the west. In 1294, the youngest of his disciples, Nichizō, started propaganda in Miyako, making a direct appeal to the Throne. The activity

of the Nichirenites in western Japan dated from this time
and was destined to have important bearings upon the
promulgation of the faith.   In 1295 another apostle, Nichiji,
started for the north and is believed to have worked among
the Ainus and gone over to the continent.

Nichiren's religion represented in many respects the robust
spirit of eastern Japan which had always been in revolt
against the ritualism and sentimentalism of the aristocratic
Buddhists of Miyako.   It is no wonder that his appeal found
an easy acceptance among the virile warrior classes and the
earnest peasants of the eastern provinces.   Thus we find
amongst his adherents many warriors, and among his monk-
disciples the sons of warriors.   There were also women of
strong character among them, and his instructions given to
them are full of tender sentiments and stimulating admonitions.
These men and women found in their master's personality
and teachings satisfaction for their vigorous spirit and a
religious support for their patriotism, as well as fulfilment of
their universal and spiritual ideals.

We have seen in Nichiren's combative propaganda a
vigour almost unprecedented in the whole history of Buddhism.
This was chiefly due to the power of his original personality,
but we must note that methods of propaganda had been
undergoing remarkable changes during these two centuries.
There were itinerant teachers, popular sermons, prayer
meetings, all in contrast to the ritual performances and
dogmatic discussions of the Heian period.   Monastery and
cottage, hermitage and mansion came into closer touch ;
religious teachers gave counsel and rendered services in the
daily life of the people.   Popular propaganda was further
carried out by Nichiren and his followers.   The method first
adopted by Nichiren was preaching in streets and parks.
Wherever he could get an audience he mounted a platform
and preached.   His disciples went into temples and monasteries

where their adversaries were preaching or giving lectures and entered into hot debates with them, crying : " Be converted to the right faith, or convince me and I will surrender to your standpoint." In this respect the Nichirenites revived the method of the Indian fighter Ārya-deva, and like him offered even their own lives if defeated in the debate. This fierce side of the " repressive propaganda " was, however, supplemented by the " persuasive way " of meek admonition and kind counsel. But the " repressive " method was not limited to his attitude towards his adversaries, because Nichiren regarded it as a necessity for the sake of all people in the degenerate ages of the Latter Law. As he never showed leniency towards his disciples, especially as regards matters of discipline, so he was very exacting towards himself and, as said above, regarded all his sufferings, both voluntary and involuntary, as a life of penitence. Thus Nichiren's method opened a new era in the propaganda of Japanese Buddhism, and his followers who kept to his method later became famous for their aggressive attitude, especially against the Amita-Buddhists. This induced the latter in reaction to become more and more combative, and of this we shall speak later.

# ZEN BUDDHISM

*Introduction of Zen, its Aim and Method*

To the reformatory activity in religion a new feature was
added by the introduction of Zen Buddhism, an intuitive
school of Buddhist meditation then prevailing in China.[1]
Originally meditation was one of the three branches of
Buddhist training—moral discipline, spiritual exercise, and
wisdom—but a school of Buddhism in India laid special
emphasis upon meditation and developed it into a systematic
practice. This method had been introduced into China in
the sixth century, and later it secured a firm foothold in the
south of that country. There it was amalgamated with the
tranquil temper of Taoist quietism and absorbed into itself
the poetic genius of the Chinese in the valley of the Yangtzu.
This was introduced into Japan in the last part of the twelfth
century, when renewed communication with the continent
and the interest of the Japanese in Chinese art and literature
favoured the acceptance of this new form of Buddhism
together with its arts and poetry.

The person chiefly instrumental in introducing Zen was
Yeisai (1141-1215), who had been a monk in Hiei, but being
dissatisfied with the scholastic doctrinalism of that institution,
made two journeys in China. Having mastered the new
method of spiritual exercise, he brought it to Japan in 1191,
and founded monasteries in Kyūshū and Miyako to train

[1] The Sung dynasty in China was then declining, holding only the southern
half of that country. The establishment of the Yuan, the Mongol, dynasty changed
the prevailing form of Buddhism from Zen Buddhism. Later we shall refer to this
point again.

disciples in the method of Zen. His influence was limited to monks and nobles, but his example was followed by other leaders who were seeking some kind of reform in Buddhism. The propaganda was reinforced by Chinese refugees who had been driven from their country as a result of the dynastic change then taking place.

Another leader and organizer of Zen Buddhism in Japan was Dōgen (1200-1253) who had also been at Hiei and had been initiated into Zen by a disciple of Yeisai. After his return from China in 1228, Dōgen lived mostly in seclusion and endeavoured to organize small convents and carry out strict monastic discipline as he had learned it in China, and as he deemed it to be the genuine method of Buddha himself. He found that Miyako was not the place for real monastic discipline and therefore retired to a secluded spot in a northern province, where he instructed warriors as well as his monastic disciples. The further extension of his influence and of his Zen method was almost entirely due to the efforts of his able disciples. He never worked for propaganda, yet his personality was the fountain-head from which flowed the wide-spreading stream of Zen. He well represented the lofty purity and serene composure of Zen training, the essential aim of which consisted in overcoming the worries of the world and in thereby attaining poise of mind and strength of character. Dōgen made every effort to avoid contact with men of high rank, and herein we see his difference from Yeisai, although the essential principles of the practice did not differ much in the branches of Zen they represented and introduced.

Dōgen certainly inspired Japanese Buddhism with a new spirit, but none of his teachings originated with him. This was no wonder, because it was the claim of Zen Buddhism in general that no teaching was adequate to express the spirit of Buddhism, and that the deepest truth had been transmitted from Buddha himself to his genuine disciples, not in words but from soul to soul. Thus the written documents left by Dōgen were either exhortations or expressions of his own sentiments. We might best illustrate his personality and temperament by some of his improvised verses :

> Only a few moments will last
> The dew-drops on the edges of the blades of grass,
> Until the morning sun rises to dry them up.
> Blow gently and soft, O Breeze of autumn,
> Sweeping over the wild prairies !

> Calm and serene in the midnight,
> Lo ! a deserted boat on the water,
> Not tossed by the waves nor drawn by the breeze,
> Braced in the pale light of the moon !

> O poor scarecrow standing alone
> In the rice-field among the mountains !
> Thou art thyself unaware of thy watch,
> Yet thy standing is not in vain.[1]

Thus serenity, purity, or simplicity was Dōgen's ideal and his life was a living example of that ideal.

### The Aim and Inspiration of Zen Meditation

Zen is an intuitive method of spiritual training, the aim of which consists in attaining a lofty transcendence over worldly care. The Zennist is proud to see in his method an unwritten tradition directly transmitted from Buddha to his great disciple, Mahā-Kāsyapa, and then successively to the masters of Zen. Not only does the Zennist defy reasoning and logic, he takes pride in transcending the usual channels of thinking. He denounces any idea to formulate tenets, for any formulation deadens the soul and life. Zen aims at giving an intuitive assurance of having discovered in the

---

[1] " Without thought yet doing something " was an ideal of the Zennist's life.

PLATE XIV

PORTRAIT OF A *ZEN* ABBOT, ENNI OR SHŌICHI-KOKUSHI
By Chō-Densu or Minchō

(Early 15th century)
(note the facial expression)

innermost recess of one's soul an ultimate reality which transcends all individual differences and temporary mutations. This reality is called the mind or soul, or the fundamental nature, or the primeval feature (of the world and the soul).[1] It means the fundamental unity of existence underlying and pervading all particular beings and changes, which is, however, not to be sought in the external world but directly and most clearly in one's own inner heart. Like the Ātman of the Upanishad, it is the ego, not individual but cosmic, which at the same time is to be realized in every soul. When one realizes this through training in Zen, he has absorbed the universe into himself, which amounts to identifying himself with the cosmos.[2]

Formulated in this way the philosophy of Zen is an idealism, though the best Zennist is pragmatic enough not to lose himself in barren abstractions, but to test his spiritual attainment in life activity and to express it in art and poetry. The moral ideal of Zen is " beyond good and bad " but the test of the attainment lies in moral life, especially in straightforward action and daring conduct not bewildered by circumstances, whether in weal or in woe. The soul which has attained this eminence of spiritual illumination identifies itself with the whole cosmos, and is therefore no more troubled by particular incidents or vicissitudes : not disturbed, therefore neither caring for gains and pleasures, nor afraid of encountering calamities and adversities. The life of an ideal Zennist may be compared, as the Zennist is

---

[1] " Mind " or " Soul " (Sanskrit *chitta* and Japanese *shin*) has in Buddhist terminology always a twofold meaning, phenomenal and metaphysical, individual and universal. In Zen the metaphysical side is emphasized, like Hegel's *Geist* or the Stoic *Nous*, but at the same time the other aspect is never neglected. The prime nature of the soul is called *honrai no memmoku*, to which a reference is made by Luis Frois in connection with a Zen monk converted by him to Christianity.— Delplace, i. 149 : *Fourai nome mogui*.

[2] See further, Anesaki, *Buddhist Art*, chap. iv. Comp. Plate XIV. in this book where the strong personality of a Zen abbot is represented.

proud to say, to a solid rock standing in the midst of a raging
sea and defying the surging billows. He can jump into the
whirlpool of life and not be overwhelmed. His calm resolution
has something like resignation, but all is the result of tranquil
self-possession and so there is always firm fearlessness in his
action. Morality or life activity is for the Zennist not an
end in itself, but a test of his spiritual attainment, a natural
expression of the noble loftiness of his mind. Reflections of
moonlight in the waters may be agitated but the moon itself
always remains serene and pure ; so the moon of the Zen
spirit is undisturbed in spite of its reflections in the waters
of human life.

Zen was introduced just at the time when the military
men were rising to the position of rulers and administrators.
There was need of a religion which could fulfil the task of
training the ruling class in mental firmness and resolute
action and of satisfying their spiritual aspirations. For this
purpose the old religions did not answer ; the traditional
Buddhism was too sentimental and effeminate, or too intricate
and mysterious for the simple and sturdy minds of the
warriors ; Shinto was too naïve and primitive, and Confucianism too formal to appeal to minds which had passed
the crisis of imminent death more than once. The method
of Zen was simple enough to be practised even in camp life,
and yet profound enough to inspire and invigorate the mind
or to calm it amidst agitation, and to show it the right way
through the perplexities of life.[1] In these circumstances,
Zen was welcomed by the military men and through them
exercised influence upon the people at large.

Under the reign of the court oligarchy, the virtue of
military men had consisted solely in fidelity to the clan

---

[1] The situation can perhaps be realized by taking the analogy of the Stoic soldier-
emperor Marcus Aurelius. Though there is no writing corresponding to his
*Meditations* left by Japanese warriors, the family instructions left by military chiefs,
to which we shall refer later, are somewhat similar in spirit.

and in submission to its chief. Now times changed, and those who had been serving the oligarchy only in military tasks had to rule the country and to administer justice. Their field of action extended far beyond the battle-fields and something more and higher was required than valour to fight and die. Therefore they found in Zen a great source of inspiration and edification.

The Hōjō statesmen were foremost in recognizing the need of religious training and in appreciating the merits of spiritual exercise in Zen. They were eminent for their administration of justice and also for the purity and simplicity of their private life. Instructions given to Hōjō Yasutoki by the famous monk Myōye (1173-1232) are remarkable for an exhortation to virtue in the tone of a Taoist transcendentalist and with the care of a Confucian moralist.[1] Though Myōye was not a Zennist, his influence upon the Hōjō statesmen is one of the instances which give evidence of the openness of the minds of the warriors to higher teachings. From the middle of the thirteenth century, training in Zen came more and more into vogue, and bore fruits in the high spiritual attainment of the warrior statesmen so trained. Among many others, the Hōjō Commissioners Tokiyori (ruled 1246-56) and Tokimuné (ruled 1268-84) are the best examples. Various anecdotes are told which illustrate the height of their spiritual attainment and those stories supplied modes of spiritual training for many military men in following ages.[2]

---

[1] Yasutoki ruled as Commissioner in 1224-42, and was the author of the Jōei Institutes, the fundamental code of the Hōjō government, for which see J. C. Hall, *Japanese Feudal Law* (*TASJ*, vol. 34, part I.). Yasutoki's brother Shigetoki was a pious Amita-Buddhist and one of those who were instrumental in persecuting Nichiren. Yasutoki's son, Tokiyori, was the first statesman trained in Zen, but he was an Amita-Buddhist too. He was Commissioner when Nichiren first appeared in public.

[2] Some of those stories are much idealized, yet were none the less inspiring to those endeavouring to attain spiritual serenity.

Tokiyori sought training in Zen under various teachers and took the monastic habit, *i.e.*, became a nyūdo, in 1256, although he continued to work in the govern-

In brief, spiritual exercise in Zen worked in a peculiar way to inspire the warriors and to give them guidance for harmonizing their spiritual aspirations with their practical training in war craft and rulership.   The sense of honour was given a spiritual basis, identifying the value of personality with the dignity of Buddha-to-be ; the virtue of courage was elevated by lofty ideals which transcended vicissitudes of fortune, even life and death.

Spiritual attainment in Zen training served also to foster a peculiar sense of the affinity of man's soul with nature, not her active and agitated aspects but the purity and serenity pervading the universe and absorbed into the heart of the Zennist.   This mood or " air-rhythm " (fūin), as it was called, namely the sentiment and temper of transcendental calmness, found its expressions primarily in poetry and then in painting, which was but a graphic representation of poetic inspiration.   The mind enlarged, illuminated, liberated and

ment until his death in 1263.   When he perceived the approach of death, he wore the monastic robes, sat in the regular Zen position, and expired after having recited the following stanza :

> " High hangs the mirror of Karma
> For thirty-seven years ;
> One hammer stroke breaks (it to) pieces.
> Now opens smooth the Great Road ! "

This translation is only to give a literal wording.   The terse simplicity of the original Chinese in sixteen ideograms, without distinctions of person or tense, without conjunctions and prepositions, gives the verse the tone of a riddle.   This kind of utterance as well as the presence of mind in face of death were regarded as a testimony to the high attainment in Zen.   The practice of writing in this way a " farewell to life " (jisei) was later extended more widely, even among the common people.   Such poems were spiritual legacies left to posterity as well as confessions of faith.

Tokimuné, high-handed diplomat and stern ruler, visited his instructor in Zen, when about to send out his army against the Mongol invaders.   In full armour he stood before the master and said :   " Master, the great thing has arrived ! "   The master asked him :   " How shalt thou go forth ? "   Tokimuné, not giving any verbal answer, made a loud cry, usual with a Zennist, and made a jump.   The instructor said in approval :   " Truly a lion !   Good, thy lion roar !   Go straight on !   Never turn thy face ! "   This is a specimen of Zennist instruction or examination.

See further :   K. Nukariya, *The Religion of the Samurai* (London, 1919).

elevated through Zen contemplation, looks upon the world and human life with penetrating insight in perfect composure. The soul is withdrawn from emotion and passion ; individuality vanishes in the vast recess of eternity ; natural surroundings are faced in abstraction, deprived of dazzling colours and vivid motions. This abstraction is neither a mere logical generalization nor a state of indifference in torpor, but penetration into the heart of nature which is at bottom pervaded with the same vitality as the human soul. Being imbued with this sense of affinity, the Zennist is fond of speaking of human life in terms of nature, such as a mind clear as moonlight, a person free as clouds and waters, the soul itself enigmatic as the dragon in thick clouds, and so on. This mood or " air-rhythm," an all-pervading serenity embraced in the heart, is expressed in riddle-like poems, terse in expression and full of suggestion, as well as in landscape paintings without colour or shading. This peculiar sense of æsthetic enjoyment is applied to the house, the garden, and all the surroundings of an abode, and alike to the manner of sitting, the way of sipping from tea-cups or of using fans, in short to nearly every detail of life.

In fine, Zen was a striking combination of paradoxical tendencies or temperaments, idealism and pragmatism, impersonalism and individualism, transcendentalism and naturalism, all in their peculiarly Zennist sense. It was the result of an adaptation of Hindu idealism to Chinese quietism, and then to the intuitive insight and practical nature of the Japanese people. Therein were united harmoniously the soaring flights of the Hindu intellect, the profundity of Buddhist meditation, the serene pose of the poetic genius of the southern Chinese, and the vigour and versatility of the Japanese character. Especially adapted to the training of the warrior class, Zen gave a firm basis and broad vision to the mental life of the fighter and ruler. In this spiritual training, ethical principle was always associated with æsthetic refinement, since the sense of the unity of all existences as realized in the enlightened soul made the basis of all idea and action, vision and effort. The ideal of Zen was to overcome the idea of weal or woe, and its ethics amounted to making man live and act untrammelled, in simply listening to the inner voice of the pure soul. Thus even in intense action calm aloofness was essential, and æsthetic refinement was regarded not only as a means for the composure of mind but a natural expression of the soul deriving its poise and peace from the bosom of the universe. The Zennist's love of nature was nothing but a discovery of her beauty identical with his own soul, and likewise his moral action a projection of his spiritual illumination into the wide world. This combination of moral life with the sense of beauty was the basis of *Bushidō*, the " Way of the Warrior," serenity and simplicity, calm resignation and bold idealism, these permeated more or less the life of the people through the influence of the warrior class.

# SOCIAL DISINTEGRATION AFTER THE FOURTEENTH CENTURY

## An Age of Melancholy

THE firm and high-handed rule of the Hōjō dictator gradually succumbed to inner decay, through moral corruption and financial stress. The royalist party took the opportunity and gave the final blow to the Hōjō, in 1333. However, the restored imperial régime lasted only three years and was followed by political and social disintegration. The dynasty was divided into two. One branch and its supporters stood for the direct rule of the Throne and against military dictatorship ; the head of the other was a puppet of military leaders who asserted their feudal prerogatives, at the head of whom stood the Ashikaga generalissimo. The division and struggle for principles and interests lasted for fifty-six years (1336-1392), until a nominal dynastic unity was restored under the hegemony of the Ashikaga. The victors in power were the military party, but the moral lessons left by the royalists were to have enduring effects upon the ethics of patriotism.

Peace reigned for a short while after the union, but as a result of the weakness of the dictator (*Shōgun*) selfish motives and relentless strife were rampant. The Emperor was treated as a puppet by the Shōgun, the latter in turn by his Commissioners (*Shikken*), who were again abused by their *major-domos* (*Shitsuji*) and lower retainers. The reign of disorder is well designated by the current phrase of the time *ge-koku-jō*, which meant " the stricture of the superior by the inferior." Herein we see the worst effects of the extreme individualism

of Zen Buddhism combined with the clannish spirit and
feudal interests of the military men.   The Zen ideal of
" beyond good and bad " was abused to an extreme of
" nothing good or bad."

The social atmosphere under these circumstances could be
nothing but melancholic.   The free rein given to selfish
motives and human passions was necessarily accompanied by
arrogance and despair.   No one was secure in his position or
wealth, many passed through bewildering changes of fortune.
Even the virile spirit of the military men was dismayed ;
not a few of them took the monastic habit, having become
weary of warfare and of the struggle of life.   The romantic
history of the dynastic division, the *Taihei-ki*,[1] is said to
have been composed by a monk who had once been a fighter
for the royal cause, and the book gives vivid descriptions of
passion and struggle, of the sudden rise and fall of fortune.
The dismal atmosphere of the time as depicted therein was
similar to that of the epic *Heike Monogatari*, but there was
in the *Taihei-ki* little consolation of faith or refinement of
artistic sense as found in the other.   There lingered still some
reminiscences of the Heian culture, which tended, however,
only to aggravate the melancholy sentiment, for the present
unrest was brought into sharp contrast with the idealized
glories of the past.   The strengthening effect of Zen training
was there, but it gave no clue to the practical solution of
social and moral problems.   The ruler was powerless, even
exposed to threats, whilst the people were always subject to
oppression and never safe ;  every one tried to promote his
own interests but many fell victims to a calamitous fate.
Human life had lost light and hope, yet entire resignation
was not possible.   The atmosphere was something like that

---

[1] The title means " Record of the Great Peace," surely an irony on the reality.
Though an epic narrative for entertainment, the book inspired many minds with
enthusiasm for the imperial cause and contributed to the restoration of the imperial
régime in the nineteenth century.

of the last phases of Greek civilization; Epicureanism was combined with Cynicism, and people drank wine in tears.

A typical representative of the time was Kenkō (1288-1350). In his *Tsuré-zuré-gusa*, or the "Stray Notes of Leisure Hours,"[1] he seemed to hold himself aloof from life, pretending to be emancipated from human passions and worldly troubles; yet he was still a man of the world even in his hermitage and sighed over or laughed at human incidents. He spoke much of the evanescence of life; yet being still attached to it, he could not refrain from looking at life with longing attachment or sarcastic cynicism. In his life he was a recluse, but he could not restrain himself from occasionally meddling with plots of human passion. Yet he was not strong or malicious enough to be a Mephistopheles but remained a cynic of the Jean Paul type. This "erotic hermit," as he was called, was not the only man of his kind; not a few shared a similar combination of conflicting mental dispositions and their lives were often a series of tragicomedies.

Even in the dismal dusk of social life, there was some light lingering or in sight. Moral examples given by the courageous royalists of the Southern Dynasty, the influence of Zen in refining the artistic sense and the daily life of the people, the rise of individual genius in arts and learning— these will presently be mentioned. Even apart from these, the fourteenth century beheld a great advance in the propaganda carried on by ardent followers of the Buddhist reformers of the preceding century. Some of these missionaries concentrated their efforts on Miyako, while many others worked in the provinces and diffused their edifying influence

---

[1] An English translation of this book was made by G. B. Sansom, with the title *Idle Jottings*, *TASJ*, vol. 39 (1913). A man of similar type was Kamo no Chōmei (1153-1213) who left diaries of his hermit life, translated by J. M. Dixon, in *TASJ*, vol. 20.

among the people at large.[1]  Centres of religion and education
were founded in the country districts, and their work filled
in some of the gaps left by over-centralization during the
Heian period.  It was these establishments scattered over the
country that saved letters and culture from the destruction
which threatened the capital as well as many of the feudal
states.  The wide distribution of these centres worked together
with the division of sects to create manifold types of culture,
giving the people opportunities of developing individuality.
The rise of democratic forces fostered in this way by Buddhist
foundations was a new factor in the civilization of Japan,
and its significance for the coming centuries should be
noticed.

### The Dynastic Division and Its Moral Lessons

The dynastic division referred to above was but a revival
of the perennial conflict between the royalist cause and the
clan spirit.  The conflict had once seemed to have been ended
by the firm establishment of the central government in the
eighth century, but the old clan spirit had never died out.
This evinced vitality in the rise of the military men whose
strongholds were the fiefs in the provinces, and the consolidation of a feudal régime under the dictatorial government
at Kamakura was a consummate expression of the clan
spirit.  The temporary restoration of the imperial régime in
1333 was only to be followed by a graver division of the
nation into two parties, royalists and feudalists, the latter
representing the clan spirit and interests.  The Emperor and

---

[1] Among the Nichirenites we may mention : Nikkō (1245-1333) who worked
in Suruga ; Temmoku (1258-1337) who worked in the eastern provinces ; Nichizō
(1269-1342) in the capital ; Nichijū (1314-1392) in the capital and the north-east.
Among the followers of Shinran : Ryōgen (1294-1335) in the capital and the central
provinces ; Zonkaku (1290-1373) in the capital and the central provinces.  Among
those of Dōgen : Eisan (1268-1325), who founded a great centre, Sōji-ji, in Noto ;
Gazan (1275-1365), a disciple of Eisan, who worked extensively in the east and
north.

his court were too weak to resist the claims of the feudalists, and after several battles the royalists were driven out of time-honoured Miyako. They took refuge in the mountains in the south and established a temporary court there, while the opposing party raised a counter-dynasty in the capital under the leadership of the Ashikaga, the descendants of the Minamoto. Hence the appellations of Southern and Northern dynasties. The Southern dynasty held possession of the three Insignia of the Throne which were respected with religious reverence by all and which therefore proved a great moral strength to the royalists. In force the Ashikaga party could have crushed their opponents at one stroke but they did not dare. We shall see presently how this moral strength inspired both fighters and thinkers standing for the royal cause.

The royalists resisted in vain the overwhelming power of the feudalists, and many of the royalist generals perished soon after the outbreak of hostilities. These warriors fought almost hopeless battles with determined resolution and met their inevitable fate in calm resignation. Their spirit of undaunted courage and unfailing allegiance to their cause, even to death, were emulated by their sons and retainers, who sought to follow their examples both in life and death. Even their opponents were moved and awakened to the necessity of moral lessons even in fighting battles and struggling for interests. This inspiration survived the age of war and manifested its power later in the restoration of the imperial régime in the nineteenth century. The name of Masashigé, foremost of these loyal heroes, exercised an enormous influence upon posterity. His perseverance in defence against a formidable siege, his faithfulness to the sovereign throughout calamity and adversity, his resolve to die in the last struggle, these are told and re-told in every household and school. He and his sons are the greatest of national heroes and are almost deified.

Another representative of the royalist party was Chikafusa (1292-1354), the pillar of the Southern Dynasty. He wrote books in the midst of war and even during a desperate siege. In these works written in tears and blood he endeavoured to show that the imperial dynasty was of divine origin. He enunciated the theory that the Insignia of the Throne, a mirror, a bead, and a sword, symbolized the virtues of veracity, mercy, and discrimination (or justice) respectively.[1] According to Chikafusa, these virtues are a national inheritance embodied in the reign of the imperial family and in the life of loyal subjects ; this morality is not a mere theory or teaching but a living fact of national life ; Buddhism has supplied a metaphysical basis to this life, while Confucianism has achieved the task of systematizing the teaching of these virtues and inculcating them among the people. Chikafusa, in supporting his ideas of national life by Buddhist idealism and Confucian ethics, aimed at bringing all religious and moral forces to a focus in faith in the holiness of the Throne. His writings contain political ideas and moral lessons to be derived from the history of the nation, all backed by religious and metaphysical considerations. As a thinker he was an eclectic, as was usual with most theorists of his age ; but his ideas and teachings, from whatever source they were derived, were fused into the white-heat of his patriotic religion. He was a fighter and thinker, and his life of effort and endurance was a living testimony to his faith. Thus this patriotic creed became a model for many Shintoists in the following centuries.

Besides the patriotic creed of these leaders, we have to note the significance of the family idea in the moral life of the warriors. As mentioned above, the feudal régime, embodying the selfish interests of the contending clans, exhibited

---

[1] For the origin of the three see above p. 11. The bead is, more exactly, a crooked bead, one of a series of pierced stones for decorative purpose. It is a Chinese theory that a stone or jewel symbolizes the virtue of clemency.

its evils in the disorder of the time ; but at the same time
the clan spirit displayed its vitality in maintaining the moral
integrity of the warriors and in perpetuating their spiritual
legacy in the family. This legacy contained moral and
religious instructions and was in fact a modified application
of the Buddhist idea of the vows taken by a Bodhisattva
for the furtherance of his moral training and for perpetuating
his ideal aims. The legislative documents and family instructions formulated by some members of the Hōjō had evinced
this desire of perpetuating their spiritual legacy ; and now
solicitude for the spiritual life of posterity became an urgent
matter for the head of a family in an age so upset by struggle
and vicissitude. This was particularly the case with the
leaders of the royalist party ; their indefatigable spirit of
loyalty was not to end with the death of the leader—that
might happen at any moment—but it was to be perpetuated
by their posterity. Zeal for the perpetuity of ideals increased
as the times became more adverse, and developed into religious
ardour with visions beyond the present. " To persist in one's
ideal aim through seven lives to follow," this Buddhist
conception was applied to the case of fighting for a principle
nearly lost for the present. So that many a leader standing
for the royalist cause left behind him moral instruction and
spiritual inspiration to his children and retainers—the *Yuikai*
(" teachings left " or spiritual legacy) or *Kakun* (family
instructions).

These instructions were confessions of faith on the part of
the writer, as well as rules of conduct and principles of life
for himself and his kinsmen. Naturally these documents
were held in reverence by descendants and retainers as
sacred embodiments of family ideals. The faith expressed
therein was mostly Buddhistic, amounting to confession of
faith in Buddha as the protector of the righteous. Another
important point in this faith was the belief that any thought

or ardent desire could produce its effects not only upon the life of the individual but upon the processes of the universe, and thus work, somewhat mysteriously, for the final attainment of the aim. More immediate help was asked for and expected from Shinto deities, especially the ancestral or tutelary deities of the respective clans. Loyalty to the sovereign and fidelity to family traditions were strongly admonished, and the virtues of charity, justice, honesty, modesty, valour were also inculcated. Advice was given to the heirs of military leaders as to the administration of feudal territories, treatment of the soldiers, care of provisions, and as to codes of honour in peace and war. In short, religious beliefs and worldly wisdom, spiritual training and military discipline, moral ideals and practical counsels, these were fused into the one principle of the warrior's honour. The principle and practice of Bushidō, the " Way of the Warrior," found here definite formulation, and these teachings were destined to sway the ruling classes throughout coming centuries. Some of these documents exercised an influence beyond the limits of the clans and families and became in some respects a national heritage.[1]

The captains and soldiers who flocked to the banner of the Ashikaga, ostensibly supporting the Northern Dynasty, were mostly those who cared more for their own interests than for justice and ideals. There were among them detestable villains, yet others decided their partisanship not simply for selfish interests but out of consideration for the honour and possessions of the family. In the course of time it became evident to the leaders of the feudal party that the clan or the family could never attain real prosperity unless founded upon moral principles and spiritual faith. This idea induced the third Shōgun of the Ashikaga, Yoshimitsu (ruled 1368-94, died 1408), to commission his advisers and scholars to

[1] Cf. the author's article, *The Idea of Moral Heritage in the Japanese Family*, in the *Open Court*, April 1917; also the author's article on *Vow (Buddhist)*, in Hastings' *ERE.*

formulate codes of honour and rules of etiquette. The moral principles therein propounded were naturally nearly the same as set forth in the instructions described above ; and in this respect the Ashikaga surrendered themselves to the ideal of their opponents whom they were overpowering by arms. Yoshimitsu also succeeded, through his wisdom and moderation, in restoring unity in 1392, and was able to rule the whole country in comparative peace and order for some time.

The rules of conduct formulated by Yoshimitsu's advisers laid special emphasis upon the observance of decorum and based the standards of life on firmness of will and the maintenance of spiritual tranquillity. The chief aim was to control the crude mind and life of the warriors by propriety of behaviour and observance, thence to open a way to higher spiritual training. The rules of monastic life as practised by the Zen monks were taken as models, the ideal of calmness and the principles of spiritual exercise being applied to the arts of fencing, archery, and even to dancing. Through these codes of honour, the ideal of serenity and composure permeated the life of the warriors, and later, during the reign of peace, penetrated into the life of the common people through the example of the upper classes.

Not only did the spiritual influence of Buddhism lie at the back of these seemingly secular matters of life, but Buddhist teachers tried to mitigate the brutality of the struggle and cared for the spiritual consolation of the people in the midst of war. Besides those Buddhist workers of the fourteenth century mentioned above, there were Zen masters who instructed the warriors, cultivated literature, and cared for the people. Musō (1271-1346), the adviser to the Ashikaga, was the greatest of the teachers who made an effort to check the moral degeneration of the time. Another point to be noted in this connection was the introduction of a new school of Confucianism by Zen monks. It was the system of Shushi

(Chinese Chu-hi), a Chinese philosopher of the twelfth century, who combined Buddhist metaphysics and psychology with Confucian ethics and inaugurated a system of rigorous moral discipline. This system was destined to become an integral factor in the moral life of the warrior class after the seventeenth century, and thereby to exert a great influence upon the life of the nation. Thus, even the period of social disintegration and war did not fail to accomplish something in the religious and moral development of the nation, but laid some foundation for the culture and refinement to be manifested in the long peace which was to commence two hundred years later. In fact, the period of Yoshimitsu was like an Indian summer before the coming of the wintry dark age of the fifteenth century. Yet the seeds sown were to endure during the winter and to put forth shoots and bloom in the culture of the Tokugawa period, in the seventeenth century.

### Art Movements in the Ashikaga Period

The rule of the Shōgun Ashikaga Yoshimitsu assisted by his wise minister Hosokawa attained a comparative peace, and his life during his reign (1368-94) and retirement down to his death in 1408 is known as the flourishing period of Muromachi, Muromachi being the name of a street in Miyako where his palace stood. The life of the warrior was permeated with the spiritual training of Zen, while the morals of fidelity and honour were supported by artistic refinement and embodied in the rules of propriety of life and manners. In all this there was a peculiar combination of contemplative serenity and elaborate taste, inspired by the personal example of Yoshimitsu himself and supported by the wisdom of his advisers. He lived in pomp in the Flowery Palace of Muromachi, but often retired to the Zen meditation hall. The Golden Pavilion (*Kinkaku*) built at the foot of a gentle hill for his temporary retirement was a secluded recess in the bosom of nature. Brilliantly decorated in gold, this pavilion was certainly a spectacle, but its splendour was quite different in tone from the pompous style of Louis XIV. Its gold glittered in the midst of green hills and forests, the whole garden was constructed after the model of nature, with a lake, islets, rocks, and promontories. Pretentious gorgeousness was carefully avoided, all was arranged as if moulded by the hands of Nature ; structure and decorations in nowise vied with nature but kept harmony with or made a part of it.[1] Beside the Gold Pavilion there was a hut-like tea-room among the trees, built of wood with the bark on. The nobles and prelates assembled there in tranquil sitting, exchanged poems or talked on matters " outside the world," in which sipping tea always filled the rôle of holy communion, so to speak. There was luxury in the aristocratic life of this period, but it was subdued in tone and peculiarly sober and chaste in expression.[2] This renaissance of art due to Yoshimitsu's inspiration is called that of the North Hill, the site of the Golden Pavilion.

The spiritual mood and the artistic refinement of this epoch was a product of Zen, but two points are specially to be noted : the inspiration of Chinese culture and the influence of tea. It was in 1368 that the new native dynasty in China, the Ming, finally supplanted the Mongol Dynasty, and a revival of the native spirit reawakened the arts and culture of the old Sung Dynasty, which had influenced Japan in the thirteenth century. While in China the rule of the

[1] See Plate XVA.

[2] The influence of Nature upon the life and art of the Ashikaga is well characterized, perhaps a little too much idealized, by Okakura (*The Ideals of the East*, pp. 178-81) as follows :

" It required the artists of the Ashikaga, representing the Indian trend of the Japanese mind released from Confucian formalism, to absorb the Zen idea in all its intensity and purity. They were all Zen priests, or laymen who lived almost like monks. The natural tendency of artistic form under this influence was pure, solemn, and all of simplicity."

Mongol conquerors had almost deadened the pure poetic genius of the Chinese,[1] Japan retained its training in Zen even during the turmoil of the dynastic strife ; now, in the peaceful reign of Yoshimitsu, intercourse with regenerated China was renewed, and the consequence was an overwhelming importation of Chinese art and poetry. Not only did Chinese learning recover its vigour, but many Chinese monks came over to reveal their culture, and Japanese monks received anew from them instructions in Zen and its arts. The influence of this renaissance was shown in another flourishing period of Zen art in the following century.

This latter is known as the art of the East Hill, where the Shōgun Yoshimasa (reigned 1449-73, died in 1490) built the Silver Pavilion (*Ginkaku*). Grandson and imitator of Yoshimitsu, he was absorbed in æsthetic pursuits, even in the midst of war and financial stress. His pavilion and its garden, though on a smaller scale than his grandfather's, represented the artistic refinement of the time and a further permeation of the Zen spirit.[2] Yoshimasa shared the taste and fate of the Sung Emperor [3] who had sacrificed his throne for his æstheticism ; and after Yoshimasa there ensued a period of incessant wars, both in the capital and in the provinces. Indeed, the epoch of the East Hill consummated the moral degeneration and social disintegration, for which Zen individualism and its associate æstheticism were greatly responsible. But on the other hand, the arts of this period were the source from which the renaissance of the

[1] The Mongol Emperors advocated a form of Buddhism inspired by Lamaism, an occultism in contrast to the intuitionism of Zen.

[2] The names of the artists connected with this epoch are Sesshū (1420-1506), the greatest of the Zen monk-painters, Sesson, the former's disciple, Kano Masanobu (1452-1490) and his son Motonobu (1475-1559), the founders of the long line of the Kano school, a branch of Japanese Zen painting infused with secular motives.

[3] Emperor Hui-tsung (reigned 1101-1125) lost his throne on being captured by the Mongol invaders. A great patron of fine arts and himself an artist of genius, he inspired art movements in China and Japan. Ma-yuan, Hsia-kuei, Mu-hsi, these are some names of Chinese painters held in great reverence by Japanese artists.

sixteenth century derived its heritage and inspiration. Whatever might be the merits or demerits of these artistic movements in their bearings upon the moral and social life of the ages, these two epochs marked significant manifestations of Zen culture, so potent in moulding the life and artistic sentiment of the nation.

Among the means by which Zen culture influenced the Japanese, tea played a prominent part as hinted at above. Tea had been imported in the twelfth century by Yeisai, the Zen teacher, and its use produced gradually growing effects by being made the centre of a peculiar cult of simple beauty. Tea was believed to be a calming beverage and used by the Zennists for preventing commotion or sleepiness during the meditative session. Through the wide spread of the Zen practice, tea became an indispensable drink in daily life, special tea-gatherings were organized by men trained in Zen for exchanging free talks and enjoying the quiet surroundings of the tea-room, which was built especially for the purpose. It was tiny like a primitive hut and as simple as the wild forest, yet was designed in a tasteful style in accordance with the serene mood of Zen quietism—a little chapel dedicated to the cult of serenity and simple beauty. The tea-gathering, often called ceremony, held in this chapel has left its traces in every phase of Japanese life, from mansion and palace to cottage and hermitage, in the habit of taking tea at any moment, the love of flowers and their presence in every household, the habit of frequently cleansing the hands, and so on.

We shall not enter here into the details of this cult of tea, or *Tea-ism*, but may say that the tea cult was preeminently a democratic practice based on the Zen ideal of equality. Anyone participating in the gathering had not only to free himself from worldly cares but to disregard all social distinctions. A dictator or a feudal lord sat on the same matting with others.   There the host and the guests talked on things outside the world, the " air and the moon," the " wind and stream," or anything else which could help to tranquillize the mind.   Thus the tea-room was an oasis in the desert of war and intrigue, where the weak were consoled and the strong pacified.   It is said that even an assassin delayed until the close of a tea-gathering his attempt on the life of one of those present.   The artistic and moral phases of Zen individualism and naturalism, together with its democratic ideas, found here a striking expression.[1]

[1] See further : Anesaki, *Buddhist Art,* chap. iv ; K. Okakura, *The Book of Tea.*   For a tea-room, see Plate XVb.

PLATE XV

A

B

A. Kinkaku or the Gold Pavilion, with its Garden (14th century)
B. A Tea-Room Rokusō-an, or the "Six Windows" (late 16th century)

# RELIGIOUS STRIFE

### The Militant Religions and Sectarian Strife

WAR and strife ravaged the whole country during the last half of the fifteenth century and the larger part of the sixteenth. Religious leaders shared the warlike spirit and practice of the age and combined their religious ambition with the contest for power. The Nichirenites concentrated their propaganda in the capital and succeeded in founding centres of missionary work there. The followers of Shinran, now called the *Ikkō* men, namely the " One-direction " or " Whole-hearted," deserved the name by manifesting zeal in battle, and established several strongholds in the central and north-central provinces. The contest for the metropolis was a feature of the age common to religious leaders and military captains, and the rivalry between the two militant churches in and near Miyako was marked by bloodshed, so that the enmity between them became proverbial. While the larger religious bodies were engaged in the occupation, partly religious and partly military, of the capital, minor sects arose abundantly in the provinces, within and outside the various branches of Buddhism and of Shinto; this again parallel with the rise and fall of many minor feudal states. In short the sectarian strife was a part of the feudal division and a reflection of the age of political agitation, while religious persecution was frequent in these years, an almost exceptional feature in the religious history of Japan.

In the course of the fourteenth century, the Nichirenite zealots worked steadily in the eastern provinces. The " Earthly

Paradise " of Minobu, the place sacred to them in memory of their prophet, grew to be a great seat of learning and missionary enterprise. Its temple buildings were enormously extended by Nitchō (1422-1500), a learned prelate and able organizer of the Nichirenite movement. Many others concentrated their efforts on Miyako and tried to convert the royal family and high nobles. Their aggressive propaganda encountered everywhere fierce resistance from other Buddhists, and their offensive remonstrance directed against men in high positions so enraged them that they persecuted the offenders. Many stories are told of cruel cases of torture, the most terrible one being that inflicted upon Nisshin (1407-88), known as the " Pan-crowned," because a burning iron pan was placed upon his head, which became simply a mass of horrible scars. Nisshin endured repeated tortures and long imprisonment and yet survived his persecutor, the Dictator Yoshinori.

The efforts of these zealots bore fruit in the foundation of many centres of propaganda, which are said to have numbered eighty thousands throughout the country. The last and bitterest of the combats was fought in Miyako in 1536, when the soldier-monks of Hiei in alliance with the Ikkō fanatics attacked the Nichirenites and burnt down twenty-one of their great temples in the capital and drove them out of the city. Shouts of " Namu Myō-Hōrenge-kyō," the slogan of the Nichirenites, vied with " Namu Amida-butsu ", the prayer of the Ikkō men ; many died on either side, each believing that the fight was fought for the glory of Buddha and that death secured his birth in paradise. The Nichirenites later recovered their influence in Miyako but dissension among themselves weakened their cause. In addition to this defeat the Nichirenites encountered persecution and malicious measures of suppression at the hands of the military dictators, who became actual rulers of the country in place of the

Ashikaga and who would not tolerate any signs of resistance or disobedience.   The repeated blows inflicted upon the Nichirenites by those tyrants were fatal to their activity and they gradually lost their vigour.[1]

The Ikkō men, on the other hand, were united under their leader, whom they revered as the descendant of Shinran and the vicar of Buddha.   Well organized under this leadership they waged war, offensive or defensive, against their opponents as well as against the feudal lords, especially in the central provinces.   The Ikkō vicar of Buddha was called *Hosshu*, the Lord of Religion, and he was indeed the pope of Ikkō Buddhism.   The ablest of the Hosshu was Rennyo (1415-99) who well understood how to concentrate the faith and allegiance of his adherents upon his own person.   Through his ability and efforts, the reverence paid to the descendants of the founder became a characteristic feature of the Ikkō religion.   This was a combination of religious faith and the feudal morality of allegiance, and is well recorded in the creed formulated by Rennyo and recited at every meeting of his followers.   It says :

We have now entirely given up any thought of relying upon our own capacity (for attaining the final bliss) through various practices and manifold training ; and we trust ourselves whole-heartedly to (the compassionate hand of salvation extended by) Buddha Amita, believing that He will surely save us and bring about the great consummation for our future life.   We are convinced that our birth in His Land of Purity is assured and His saving act established, at the moment when our minds are centred upon Him, and that we have henceforth only to repeat His Name, as expression of gratitude. That we have been able to hear this gospel and to believe in it, is solely due to the gracious advent of the Saint, the founder of our religion, and to the precious instructions given by the patriarchs who have descended from him— this indebtedness is deeply impressed upon our minds.   As this is so, we shall henceforth faithfully observe the prescriptions laid down by them all.[2]

---

[1] Persecution by Nobunaga in 1579, by Hideyoshi in 1586, and by Iyeyasu in 1608.   We shall see more of these three dictators.

[2] This is called *Gaike-mon* or *Ryōge-mon*, " Confession," and is one of Rennyo's *Go-bunshō*, " August Epistles."   For other Gobunshō, see C. Troupe, *The Gobunshō* (*TASJ*, vol. 17, part I).

Indeed, this creed was used as an expression of faith and at the same time as an oath of allegiance through fire and blood, and the Ikkō fanatics recited this before going to battle in the name of their religion.  This simple yet powerful document worked well to inspire the believers with fanatic zeal for their religion, in peace and in war, and served the purpose of Rennyo for concentrating adherencc to the person of the pope.  Thus he was an organizer of militant fanatics, and established several centres of his religion which served also as military strongholds.  One of these places in a northern province was once burnt down by foes but was soon restored. Another centre erected near Miyako was also attacked and burnt down by the Nichirenites (in 1532).  A stronghold established at Osaka (in 1496) occupied a strategical spot which later proved to be invulnerable, resisting a siege by the overwhelming forces of the military dictator Nobunaga. Rennyo's descendants extended their influence in the western provinces, and there they made alliance with certain feudal lords in warfare.  After the fall of the opposing dictator, the abbacy of the Ikkō men was transferred to Miyako and continues to this day the greatest centre of Buddhism in Japan.[1]  Thus the descendants of the humble preacher, the modest reformer of the thirteenth century, were infected with the militant spirit of the sixteenth century in fortifying their positions by military force combined with religious fervour, and organized a hereditary popedom after the model of the royal family.  As natural reaction to this formidable organization (and by an irony of fate) a considerable section of the Ikkō men organized a secret society called *Hiji Monto*,[2] or " Advocates of Secret Practice," claiming their genuine

[1] That is Hongwan-ji in Kyōto, which was later divided into two branches. West and East.   Their temple buildings imposingly command the valley of Miyako, Plate XIXв.

[2] The extent of their influence is attested in the reports of the Jesuit missionaries in the sixteenth century.  See Léon Pagès, *Histoire de la religion chrétienne au Japon*, p. 126.

descent from Rennyo and defying the authority of the Ikkō pope. Their origin is obscure and their practice kept in strict secrecy, but they thrive even to-day in many provinces.

As we have seen, the great Buddhist centres became dens of fighting monks and vagabonds, almost perpetually engaged in bloody combats between themselves or against military chieftains. Their power and arrogance went so far, in the sixteenth century, that the military leader Nobunaga, who was extending his power over the whole country, found a serious menace in such Buddhist strongholds and reduced the establishments on Mount Hiei to ashes (1571) and also forced Mount Kōya to submission (1581). These centres were not without virtuous or learned monks, but these men were overshadowed by the arrogant bonzes, and any attempt at reform was thwarted; the final result was their submission to the forces of the military men. The degeneracy and disintegration of those great centres caused the rise of schismatics and heretics, who organized themselves within the churches or formed secret societies and disseminated absurd doctrines and questionable practices.

Minor sects arose with a great variety of tenets and practices. Most of them derived their material from Shingon mysteries, and some of them debased the Shingon theory of the double aspects of the cosmos to an obscene cult of sex. The chief agents in sustaining these questionable religions were the Yama-bushi, the mountaineer priests, of whom we have spoken before. They organized orders and extended their evil influence in various ways. Some of these or other ambitious priests organized their own doctrines and methods and endeavoured to attract the reverence of the masses. They pretended to have discovered a new mystery or to represent forms of cult handed down to them in secret or directly from the gods. These rites were generally a combination of Shingon occultism and Shinto mysteries, while the Chinese theory of the cosmic principles, *yin* and *yang*, played a great part, especially in connection with allusions to sex.   Magic, sorcery, exorcism, divination, these practices swept the whole of society.   Priests and sorcerers practising these arts were so numerous in this period that many Buddhist leaders and reformers encountered opposition from them and not a few died at their hands.   None of these sorcerers attained personal distinction, yet their ideas and practices still continue to rule popular superstition and to exert influence upon the religious life even to-day.[1]

The uncertainty and misery of life in this period produced an atmosphere of moral depression.   Spiritual unrest and unsatisfied yearning manifested themselves in the art and literature of the time.   Ghastly stories were circulated, visions of ghosts and devils teriorized the people, commonplace ideas and things were recounted in exaggerated ways ; even fairy-tales were absurdly comic, and equally extravagant were the stories of heroes.   In painting, misery and horror were depicted and curious deformities represented in glaring contrast or combinations of crude colours.[2]   Besides these gloomy aspects, humour played a part in the popular art and literature of the age and heralded the rise of a democratic mood in the last part of the sixteenth century.

### The Work of Zen Monks and the Idea of Equality

Even in the midst of unrest and confusion civilizing work more or less prevailed, being carried on chiefly by Zen monks. As the holders of land property, libraries, collections of art, belonging to their monasteries, and as the men most advanced in culture, the Zen monks were not only able to maintain their own culture but worked to educate others.   Since their

[1] Cf. Percival Lowell, *Occult Japan* (Boston and New York, 1895).
[2] See Plate XVI.

PLATE XVI

THE *GAKI-ZÔSHI*, OR THE SCROLL OF THE HUNGRY GHOSTS

A part representing a street scene, where the Hungry Ghosts are mingling with the people (13th century)

leaders were instructors and advisers to the military captains, and their counsel and help were indispensable to the rulers, the Zen institutions were highly patronized by the dictatorial and feudal governments and virtually entrusted with the work of educating the people and cultivating learning.

Moreover, their indifference to creed enabled the Zennists to stand aloof from the religious strife raging around them, and to carry on their work, religious, literary, and educational. Thus we owe to these Zen monks not only the preservation of letters and the maintenance of popular education, but culture in poetry and painting and the further elaboration of the tea-cult. They were also largely instrumental in keeping up communications with China, which brought over to Japan the products of continental civilization and resulted in some commercial profit.

What the Zennists achieved in popular education was perhaps greater than the work done by Buddhists in any of the preceding periods. In addition to reading and writing, practical moral lessons were given ; thanks to the wide distribution of the monasteries, the Zen monks diffused the benefits of their instruction among the people at large. Collections of moral maxims and didactic poems were compiled by these monks, and these manuals of moral lessons were used until quite recent times as they exercised great influence upon the moral life of the lower classes.[1]

The social disintegration of the fifteenth century was not without some beneficial effects. The rise of a democratic spirit was one of them, the result of the ideal of equality and the propagation of popular education. In an age of warfare, hereditary rank lost much of its prestige, while

---

[1] Among the most widely circulated of these collections were : the *Dōji-kyō*, or " Instructions to the Infants " ; the *Teikin-wōrai*, or " Home Instructions " ; the *Jitsugo-kyō*, or the " Maxims of Truth." The moral principles therein taught are mostly Confucian, together with the Buddhist idea of indebtedness. Cf. *TASJ*, vol. 9, part III.

power and ability came to rule. Centres of culture were established in the provinces, mostly under the patronage of the divided feudal states, and these establishments gave impetus to individual accomplishments and ambitions.

Signs of democratic upheaval were visible late in the fifteenth century, in the prevalence of popular literature and art, among other things. Besides tales of adventurers and popular heroes, we find a series of comic dramas, called *Kyōgen* or farce, which were full of humour and sarcasm directed against feudal magnates and ecclesiastical prelates. Offering free expression to popular sentiment and to the people's keen interest in current events, the comic drama of the age took material from social life at large, in contrast to the court literature or war stories. Another sign of the age may be seen in a popularization, and often vulgarization, of poetry, consisting in witty versification made jointly by more than one person, which was destined to become the poetry of the people in succeeding centuries.[1] Games and pastimes also became more popular than in any of the preceding ages, and nobles often mingled with the people in various amusements. Even the originally aristocratic tea-meeting was practised by the people in general, and many rich merchants took part in a large tea-party organized by Hideyoshi in 1588. The further development of such tendencies will be treated in connection with the renaissance at the end of the seventeenth century.

### Shinto, its Revival and Theorists

We have seen an upheaval of Shinto ideas in the fourteenth century ; now in the fifteenth, an age of confusion and combat, further progress was made in the systematization of Shinto theology. This meant an assertion of national ideas

---

[1] Its name was *renga* or *haikai*, which later became *hokku*, of which we shall speak again. Cf. p. 291.

amounting to adoration of the Throne as against the feudal division and the reign of selfish interests, but all this was propounded as ideals and scarcely took practical form in social agitation or religious reformation. The name of Ichijō Kanera (or Kaneyoshi, 1402-81) stands foremost in this respect. He was a noble of high rank, for a time the premier in the imperial court, and a poet and man of wide learning. His efforts in the domain of religious thought were directed towards harmonizing Buddhist philosophy and Confucian ethics with national tradition represented by Shinto.

His philosophy was an idealistic monism, amounting to an identification of the cosmic soul with the individual, while his ethics aimed at elucidating how the individual soul could realize this fundamental, metaphysical identity in actual life. Shinto, according to Kanera, teaches the existence of many deities, but metaphysically speaking they are one, because each deity is but a manifestation of the universal soul in a particular aspect of its activity and all gods are one in spirit and entity, especially in the virtue of veracity. Veracity manifests itself in its practical application as the virtues of charity and justice, and these three make up the triad of divine virtues.

The national embodiment of the divine virtues, Kanera taught, is shown in the three Insignia of the Throne, the mirror for veracity, the bead for charity, and the sword for justice. The final aim of the Japanese nation, therefore, consists in practising these virtues in their national life. In this Kanera only followed the theory propounded by Chikafusa, the loyal warrior of the Southern Dynasty, but went a step further as a theorist and combined it with Buddhist metaphysics and Chinese cosmology. The same triad, realized in spiritual enlightenment, as he thought, makes up the threefold aspects of Buddhahood, Wisdom (*Prajñā*), Emancipation (*Moksha*), and Truth (*Dharma*). Further, the cosmic manifestations of the triad are seen in the three kinds of universal illumination, the sun, moon, and stars. The destiny and duty of mankind amounts to substantiating the triad in the personal life of the individual and in the corporate life of the nation. This, according to Kanera, is the essence of Shinto, which is not a mere nationalism and yet is most conspicuously and palpably represented by the sovereign and people of Japan.

Thus Kanera was a syncretic theorist who tried to show the philosophical foundation of the Shinto religion by the help of Buddhism and Confucianism. It is also important to note that Kanera and Chikafusa, the Shinto revivalists, belonged to the class of court nobles who resisted more or less the rule of the military men ; and that these Shinto ideas were a great source of inspiration to those who fought for the restoration of the imperial régime in the nineteenth century.

Another branch of Shinto revival was represented by the Urabé, a family of diviners who served as priests in the Shinto sanctuary of the court. The most prominent of the Urabé organizers was Kanetomo (1435-1511). He based his theories on a group of books pretending to transmit direct revelations from the gods, some dating probably from the fourteenth century and others of his own compilation. Kanetomo called his Shinto the " Fundamental " (*Sōgen*) or the " Unique " (*Yui-tsu*) Shinto, but in reality he was an eclectic, taking much in theory and practice from Shingon mysticism, Tendai philosophy, Chinese cosmology and methods of divination.[1]    His division of Shinto into esoteric and

---

[1] Those books bear titles such as " The Book of Mysteries of Heaven," " Of Earth," " Of Man." The centuries between the fourteenth and the sixteenth were an age of " pious frauds " and produced many books claiming divine origin. One of them, *Wa-Rongo*, containing oracles and poems attributed to the gods, was translated into English by G. Kato, *TASJ*, vol. 45, part II. Kanetomo explains *Sō* to mean the source or matrix of entity, and *Gen* the beginning of manifestation— simply a new version of the double aspects of existence as taught by Shingon Buddhism.

exoteric was entirely Buddhistic, and also his theory of the three metaphysical categories, substance, appearance, and function. Likewise, he made much of the analogies between human nature, physical and mental, and the five elements taught in Chinese cosmology, drawing close parallels between the viscera and the emotions, between the sense-organs and the elements, besides the analogies between the twofold division of the soul and the two celestial bodies, and the like. The characteristic feature of the Urabé Shinto was its practice of sorcery and divination, and in this respect it represented the popular side of that religion in contrast to the more ethical teachings of Shinto nationalists. Yet the ambition of Kanetomo was to unify all Shintoists under his authority and to make his family the head of a national Shinto church. He succeeded more or less in attaining his aim, took the court sanctuary under his charge, established a centre of Shinto worship at his own residence ; and later on his family monopolized the right of authorizing the ordination of priests and the establishment of sanctuaries. Their success in this domain was chiefly due to their influence upon the court circles, and thus some Shintoists with political aspirations worked under the protection of the Urabé, each assisting the other in promoting their prestige and interests.

In addition to these public manifestations of Shinto revival, Shinto methods of purification and exorcism were practised by many eclectics who belonged both to Shinto and Buddhism and worked to disseminate superstition—a trait of the Shinto religion still playing a part in the social life of the present-day Japan. Yet there were some enthusiasts of sincere conviction and more or less original religious experience. These popular teachers propagated their beliefs, from which sprang various branches of popular Shinto, to be mentioned later on.

# KIRISHITAN MISSIONS [1]

## JAPAN'S FIRST CONTACT WITH EUROPE AND CHRISTIANITY

### Beginning and Progress of the Missionary Work

WHEN Japan was engaged in fierce internecine strife and her religious bodies involved therein, the tidal wave of European aggression was marching to the Far East. We have seen how much foreign influences had controlled most phases of Japanese civilization; the age of social disintegration was no exception to that. Yet the impacts of arts, religions, and institutions had come mostly from or through China; the Japanese people had hardly dreamt of anything beyond India or on the other side of the Pacific Ocean. Meanwhile, the wide world was changing; Columbus aiming at the fabulous Zipangu or Japan had discovered America; Vasco da Gama had circumnavigated Africa; Portuguese pirates and merchants occupied a part of India and reached Malacca. On the other hand, a restless section of Japanese crossed the seas as pirates or adventurers to the coasts of China and further to Malay. These outward flows were made possible partly by the internal conditions of unrest and division, because Japanese piracy was chiefly undertaken by the semi-independent clans of western Japan followed by individual

---

[1] "*Kirishitan*" is the Japanese corruption of Portuguese *Christan* and used here to designate the Catholics and their religion in Japan in the sixteenth and seventeenth centuries. The appellation was indeed used in pride by Kirishitans themselves, but the name was used in later years by all Japanese with its sinister associations of an evil religion using magic, attempting to occupy Japan and to make her a territory of Spain, and so forth.

adventurers, vagabonds, fugitives. In fact the first Japanese with whom Francis Xavier, the great Jesuit missionary, came into contact at Goa and through whose counsel he decided to come to Japan, was a fugitive who had left his home on account of a crime, Paul Yajiro (or Hanshiro), of Satsuma. Thus the first important contact of Japan with Europe was opened by this meeting of an apostle of the Christian gospel and a criminal fugitive converted in a foreign land.

It was in 1549 that Xavier arrived at Satsuma, with his guide Paul and other missionary companions. They were received, if not quite welcomed, as men from India preaching a *Tenjiku-shū*, the religion of India. At first no Japanese could have suspected that these apparently innocent preachers of the Tenjiku-shū had behind them the tremendous forces called Christianity and European civilization, while their activity was destined to produce a profound consternation, which finally caused the rulers to persecute the followers of the new religion and to stop foreign intercourse eighty years later. At any rate, the new missionaries were first an object of curiosity, then welcomed as people whose countrymen and associates would supply new commodities, particularly fire-arms, and finally revered or hated as the propagators of a religion which was entirely different from any of the religions existing in Japan.

In these changes of attitude and in all the reactions towards the new missions were involved many non-religious motives—childlike curiosity towards strangers and novelties, greed for commercial profit, idealized visions of the far-distant countries of the west, rivalry between the feudal states, intrigues in the families and governments of the feudal lords. But religious motives played no less a part. Yearning for something authoritative and unifying instead of divided Buddhist and other sects, demand for palpable evidences of salvation in contrast to the somewhat vague idealism of Zen, admiration for the self-sacrificing lives of the missionaries in contrast to the corruption of the priesthood in general, these induced many people to accept the new religion.   On the other hand, the tenacious hold which the indigenous deities had upon the people's mind in conjunction with patriotic motives caused many to take a stand against the exclusive and jealous deity of Christianity.   The doctrine of original sin with all that it implied was no less repulsive to some, particularly Confucian rationalists and Shinto optimists. Besides these and similar doctrinal issues, semi-religious, moral, and liturgical matters played no less determining parts, such as the questions of monogamy and chastity, of ecclesiastical administration, of works of charity, or the impressions of litany, music, images, decorations, sacraments. A full account of all these factors would make a highly interesting chapter in the religious history of Japan as well as in the history of missions and contacts, but suffice it to say that nearly all possible motives and circumstances operated in this first contact of the Far East with Europe.

When Xavier arrived in 1549, Japan was divided into many contending powers, and each feudal state was ruled entirely by the will of its lord.   Thus, while Xavier's idea of winning the central government, whether Dairi or Shōgun, to his side, had proved entirely a disillusionment, he succeeded in securing the favour of two " Kings," those of Yamaguchi and of Bungo.   Though the Church foundation in the former was of only short duration, the latter became the first stronghold of the missions.   During a stay of twenty-seven months the great apostle not only visited Miyako and other places, but won several converts among the Samurai, Buddhist priests, and common people, and left behind him an able worker, Cosme de Torres.

Soon there were new arrivals of missionaries and more

neophytes ; the preaching and education were reinforced by works of charity ; churches, colleges, hospitals, leproseries were established. There were vicissitudes in the fate of the missions in different places according to the changes of feudal lords or of their caprice. But the general progress of the propaganda was quite steady, despite the opposition of Buddhist priests and minor local persecutions, and in the course of ten years several thousands were baptized, mostly in west Japan. From 1560 the missionary fields were extended to Miyako and the central provinces, where resistance was no less fierce than in the west, but the mission was rewarded by the conversion of some nobles. Among these were the Takayama family, who later proved instrumental in inducing a number of powerful supporters, and they themselves remained faithful to the new faith throughout half a century of hardships and vicissitudes, up to their banishment to Manila in 1614.[1]

When Vilela started his mission in Miyako, the conditions in the capital were at their worst. The city had been devastated repeatedly by wars, fires, and floods, and the people were suffering from famine, pestilence, and brigandage. The missionaries suffered similarly, in addition to obstructions and persecutions. But these ills gave opportunities for winning converts, in giving peace to the bewildered souls through preaching or in obliging the distressed through charitable reliefs. When, in 1569, a powerful captain, Nobunaga, entered Miyako with his strong army to put a check to the anarchic confusion, he brought a great relief to the people and also to the Kirishitan Church, because he thenceforward favoured the missionaries and protected the

[1] The stories of Justo Takayama Ukon's life illustrate a happy union of the valour of a Japanese warrior and the fidelity of an ardent Catholic. His brilliant military achievements, his moral integrity and deliberateness in critical moments, his dauntless spirit combined with meek soul, his earnest zeal in piety expressed in his generosity and charity, all this should be noted as a fruit of Kirishitan missions.

Church.  Four years later he supplanted the old régime of the Ashikaga and established his firm rule in the central provinces.  This was a blessing to the Church, and nearly ten years of his rule brought a thriving period of Kirishitan propaganda, when Jesuit missionaries numbered 80 in 20 stations and several educational centres, with 200 churches and 150,000 converts.[1]

The motives that instigated Nobunaga to patronize the missions and missionaries are obscure, because he never expressed any inclination to be counted as a Kirishitan. Certainly curiosity towards new importations and the vain-glory of attracting foreigners to his court played a part therein, though his career was too short to establish any commercial relations with the Portuguese.  But the chief motive seems to have been his anti-Buddhist prejudice and policy, because he saw in the fighting monks and militant centres of Buddhism a great menace to his ambition and always worked to suppress them.  Whatever may have been the motive of his welcoming the Jesuit fathers, the people in central Japan saw in his patronage a great assurance of the value of the new religion.  In fact the seminary in his castle of Azuchi educated a number of young nobles in European fashion, and some of them were finally baptized, among whom were sons of Nobunaga himself.

The death of this patron in 1582 was a great blow to the Church but its prosperity continued so long as Hideyoshi, known as Taiko-sama in the missionary records, successor to Nobunaga in power, seemed to favour the missions.  But

---

[1] That is, about one per cent of the whole population but nearly two of the population of the western half of Japan, because the extension of the missions to the eastern half dated much later.  The greatest number of Kirishitan converts attained was in the first years of the seventeenth century, and it is estimated at 750,000 (in 1605), i.e., four per cent. of the whole population, though the north-east was still entirely untouched at that time.  Contrast this with the present number of Christians, including all the Catholic and Protestant Churches, which amounts to less than one-third of one per cent.  Cf. Delplace, i. 201.

this did not last long. The ambitious tyrant began to feel a menace in the allegiance of his Kirishitan vassals to a certain foreign power, the popedom whose real nature was inscrutable to him. This " patriotic " motive was involved in some private irritations on his part, and in 1587 he suddenly issued the famous edict prohibiting Kirishitan propaganda, and ordered all the foreign missionaries to withdraw at once.[1] This was an entirely unexpected blow to the missionaries, especially because it took place when Coelho, the provincial, was being cordially received by him at his camp. But the missionaries managed more or less to evade the order, while several Kirishitan Daimyos and others protected the fathers, who stayed, from pursuit. The missionary work continued nearly unmolested but only in private. The edict of 1587 thus proved but a nominal prohibition, yet it was the first proclamation against Kirishitan propaganda and was later to be executed more thoroughly by Taiko's successors and to be consummated in its extermination. Another grave substantial blow at that time was the high-handed transfer to the direct rule of the dictatorial government of Nagasaki, the " little Rome " of Japan, the port opened and administered by the Jesuits and Portuguese dating from 1569. But some time had to pass before a real check of the missions was to be carried out by fierce persecution.

### An Intermediate Stage in the Fate of Kirishitan Propaganda

An intermediate stage lasting about thirty years, from 1587 to 1614, was a period of the further progress of Kirishitan missions, which, however, began to suffer by internal dissension between the Jesuits and the other missionary bodies appearing on the stage. It was a period of wavering, on the

---

[1] One year before, Hideyoshi persecuted disobedient Nichirenite Buddhists who had refused to take part in a festival organized by him.

part of the government, between a policy of promoting
foreign trade and another of suppressing foreigners' religious
missions.  Speaking in general, the issues of the missionary
movements and reactions were gradually divided into two
fields, one of political and commercial considerations on the
part of the government, and the other of more purely
religious motives on the part of the missionaries and converts.
In other words, the rulers following Taiko's steps tried to
keep apart commerce and religion, favouring the former and
discouraging the latter.  But when this discrimination proved
futile they were compelled more and more to restrict foreign
trade on account of religion, and finally to put an end to
both, which culminated in the purely political, or " patriotic,"
measures of national seclusion.  On the other hand, the
missionary bodies had desired to secure ecclesiastical advan-
tages by winning the ruling classes who were desirous of
promoting political and commercial connections with Portugal
or Spain.  When this had failed and the consolidated government of Hideyoshi and then of the Tokugawa had become
hostile to the foreign religion, its missionaries began to
concentrate their efforts on the common people.  After 1587
they could not work so much in public as before, but among
the people only, and finally after 1614, in secret from house
to house, even only in the night.

Let us now consider some salient points.  After 1587 the
Jesuit fathers behaved very cautiously in order not to provoke
the suspicion or anger of Taiko, yet held their sway over the
converts, including a number of great Daimyo under Taiko.[1]
The Jesuits advanced their work, particularly in the provinces
under the rule of Kirishitan Daimyo.  They could have

---

[1] Among these the most conspicuous was Konishi, known as the "Great Admiral,"
who protected his fellow-converts, patronized the missionary works of charity,
and firmly held his faith even until death.  It is to be noted that Konishi and
some other nobles were induced to faith through the example and admonition of
Justo Takayama.

achieved more even under Taiko's rule, had not a force appeared to disturb the steady advance. This was the coming of the Franciscan missionaries in 1592, involving in their missions a diplomatic message from the governor of the Philippines. Taiko, ever directing his covetous eyes to the south apart from his Korean expedition, received the envoy well, but tried to keep out religious propaganda. In defiance or ignorance of the temperament of the tyrant, the newcomers worked with the utmost zeal in religious propaganda, and soon their churches and hospitals began to attract public attention. When the differentiation of religion and trade was thus proving hardly feasible, an unfortunate incident took place in 1596, known as the affair of the *San Felipe*. - This was the name of a Spanish merchant ship stranded at Tosa. When the local authorities of that province badly treated the crew of the ship, one of them tried to intimidate them by boastfully recounting the power and territorial extension of Spain. It is believed, quite naturally, that this report was sufficient in convincing Taiko and some of his ministers of the ulterior purpose of Kirishitan missions, that they were nothing but a tool of territorial aggrandizement already partially achieved elsewhere by Spain. It is questionable whether this case alone or some Portuguese endorsement of the evil report was instrumental in causing the tyrant to make up his mind, but the result was the capture and crucifixion of twenty-six missionaries and converts, most of whom were Franciscans. This martyrdom took place early in 1597 and signalized the coming of a long series of persecutions and martyrdoms.

After this blow, however, there was a period of temporary relief, chiefly due to the death of the tyrant-persecutor in 1598. Two years later a decisive battle determined the fate of the supporters of Taiko's infant son and transferred the dictatorial power to the hands of Iyeyasu, the founder of the Tokugawa Shogunate. The political change brought about some changes of feudal territories.   This evoked a few local cases of persecution, but the general situation was not unfavourable to Kirishitan propaganda, because the new holder of power, being desirous of securing the commercial profits of foreign trade to himself, was trying to use the Franciscans from Manila as tools.   Other religious orders, Dominicans and Augustinians, followed and opened their missions in 1602.   Not only the meddling of some Franciscan missionaries in politics but the suspicion directed towards all the missionaries made the situation worse, which was aggravated by the coming of the Dutch and English, who endeavoured to supply evil informations about Spain and Portugal.   These circumstances gradually convinced the new ruler of the evils of the new religion, chiefly from political considerations.   When the Franciscan missionaries were being proud of having established stations at Yedo, the capital of the new government, by 1608, the latter was taking steps to suppress them.

Thus the coming of new missionary bodies not only worked to arouse suspicion on the part of the rulers and to cause them to persecute, but also did harm to the missionary cause by producing dissension between the Jesuits and the newcomers.   The issues involved were the questions of the united control of the whole missions, of episcopal authority, and so on, culminating in an ugly contest for episcopal succession.   Sectarianism, which had ever been regarded by the Jesuits as the weakness of their opponents, the Buddhists, crept into the field of their own propaganda.   Even baptized names were differentiated, Diogo and Diego, Joan and Juan, as if essential to salvation.   The fraternities (Jap. *kumi*) constituted for piety by different orders were a factor in maintaining the integrity and solidarity of the converts, especially when persecuted, but they often tended to alienate the respective members.   Not unnaturally both the converts and the persecutors called the different orders by the word

PLATE XVII

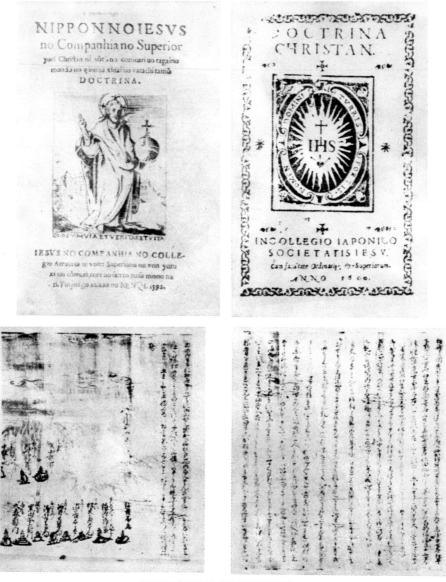

**KIRISHITAN DOCUMENTS**

A. Title-page of the Doctrina Christiana in Romanized Japanese. Two editions, 1592 and 1600

B. A Part of the Letter addressed to the Pope Urban VIII by the Kirishitan Leaders in the North-east, dated Sept. 29, 1621. The original in the Barberini Archives, Rome

KIRISHITAN RELICS

A.  A KIRISHITAN TOMB-STONE, bearing the name of Maria Tominaga (dated August 21st, 1622). Recently unearthed near Ōmura

B.  A STATUETTE OF MARIA, unearthed from the old Castle grounds of Akita

*mompa*, signifying sect. On the other hand, it should be noticed that the missionary zeal of all the four orders with the reinforcement of new arrivals reaped fruit in different provinces, even in the extreme north-east, and the piety of the converts was much enhanced by the organization of fraternities, especially the Jesuit Annunciation, the Dominican Rosario, and the Franciscan Cordon. But all this meant a lowering of the propaganda from the upper strata of society to the lower, from the towns to the villages, from the plains to the mountains, finally into the mines, the preliminary steps to the rage of persecution, which terminated in the final extinction of Kirishitan propaganda.

Before closing the review of this intermediate stage, we must mention the difficult rôle played by Bishop Cerqueira (1598-1614 in Japan). It was he who steered between difficulties in the years of hardship, handling the delicate question of the slave trade, trying to keep in check the over-zeal of the newly-arrived missionaries, defending the persecuted by all his means, and all this under the stress of penury. He witnessed great changes in Japan, passed through many vicissitudes of fate, and died at Nagasaki in 1614, when hundreds of Kirishitans were being deported and exiled from that port which was then no more the " little Rome " of Japan but was becoming a scene of tortures and martyrdoms by fire and sword.

After this comes the last phase of Kirishitan religion, its persecution and extermination. Though this falls in the seventeenth century and belongs to the following period, we shall speak of it in continuation of the history given above.[1]

### The Persecution and Extermination of Kirishitans

The policy of unity and order established by Iyeyasu early in the seventeenth century implied that every phase of

[1] For relics of Kirishitan missions, see Plates XVII and XVIII.

national life was to be controlled by the will of the ruler. Iyeyasu was a persistent statesman, who knew well how to tighten the grip of his will upon everything, but at the same time prudent enough not to arouse animosity on the part of his subordinates, and also of wide view and wise enough not to trespass the limits of reason. The whole policy of his government was, therefore, to maintain the existing status of everything under his control. Apparently a policy of toleration was his attitude towards religion, but any sect asserting itself beyond the assigned limit would never be tolerated. He made a kind of established church of Buddhism, but an intractable section of Nichirenites was severely suppressed; similarly the Kirishitan Church was intolerable to him, because of its allegiance to or connection with a foreign power, no matter whether Rome or Manila or Macao. The extension of Iyeyasu's power inevitably led to increasing pressure upon the followers of the foreign religion, first upon his vassals and then slowly but more extensively upon the people at large.

The demonstration of a decided step in this policy was the great banishment of 1614, mentioned above, which reduced the young Church to an orphan and put a check upon any support from the outside. The Mother Church tried everything to come to help, and a number of missionaries were smuggled into Japan in spite of strict vigilance.[1] Yet they were sooner or later arrested and executed together with the hosts who had harboured them. The years after 1615 were a period of smuggling and concealment for the missionaries, who hid themselves in every possible way, even between concealing walls or in subterranean cells. The converts

---

[1] Besides a good number of individual smugglers there were smugglings in groups on systematic plans. Between 1614 and 1643 we can count thirteen of these planned penetrations. At least 79 European and Japanese missionaries set foot on Japanese soil as smugglers, of whom 36 were Jesuits, 18 Franciscans, 16 Dominicans, and 9 Augustinians, while 66 were martyrs and 4 apostates. The way of executing them before 1633 was burning alive, but after that mostly by suspending in a pit.

suffered similarly, and all kinds of torture were devised, even dipping into the boiling mud of a crater, or scratching necks or bodies with bamboo saws. The cruelty of torture and the rigour of persecution were unparalleled in Japan.

Equally without parallel was the fervour with which hundreds and thousands of Kirishitan people, mostly from the lower strata of society, withstood temptations, threats, terrors, tortures, and finally died as martyrs, though there were many apostates too. Their faith was simple and sincere, they believed in the future destinies, Paraiso or Inferno, just as taught by the Church, as if all these were tangible realities at hand. Some of them saw in vision God's Mother with her Child inviting them to heaven, while they were hung on the cross soon to be consumed by surrounding flames ; others lost any sense of distress or pain in the near prospect of reaching the heavenly realm on being beheaded ; others heard voices encouraging them to stand the agony with the promise of celestial bliss. The governors, who had always regarded the common people as easy victims to threats and intimidations, were surprised at the audacity and tenacity of these martyrs, which were beyond conception and imagination. Some of the persecuting officers were nearly converted out of admiration for the martyrs, while others became more firmly convinced of the mysterious evil nature of the foreign religion and treated Kirishitans in more vehement hatred or dread. Missionary reports rightly compared the suffering Church of Japan with the primitive Church before Constantine's time.

Under these circumstances the final extermination of Kirishitans was an inevitable fate, but there was a factor which accelerated this fate. That was the personal temperament of the third Shōgun Iyemitsu, grandson of Iyeyasu, who ruled from 1623. His father was a man of narrow vision and a statesman as cautious as Iyeyasu, but the young Shōgun was a wanton child of the aristocracy, who had no other standard of conduct than his own capricious will.  Any one who would not blindly submit to his command was a traitor, and Kirishitans who obstinately resisted the commands from on high were the worst rebels against him and the State.  Whenever a foreign missionary was discovered, the nervous tyrant gave the order to burn him alive.  Every Daimyo was compelled to search for converts in every corner of his territory, or he had to fear a thunderbolt from the tyrant.  The suppression of Kirishitans was no more a religious or political issue but simply the will of the ruler who identified himself with the State.

Thus the rule of Iyemitsu was a reign of terror which carried out its policy everywhere at any price.  All feudal governments had to obey his command and the worst were the Daimyo who had apostatized and their descendants, because they became most violent persecutors for the purpose of dispelling the suspicion hanging over themselves.  The persecuted endured the oppression and torture in a mood of suffering in joy, taking as model the Lord's own passions,[1] nor had they any hope of attempting active resistance.  Yet when the pressure became too heavy and persecuting devices too cruel, in addition to the strictures of taxation and corrupt administration in the territory of Arima, the desperate people, chiefly Kirishitans but others too, finally rose in arms, in 1637-38.  They not only defeated the troops of the local government but stood wonderfully well the siege of their fortified stronghold by the central government with the best forces of western Japan.  The commander of the government forces was killed, their several assaults failed, the Dutch navy helped in the bombardment.  The insurgents were crushed

[1] There is a Japanese document from this period which the present writer calls "Cautions on Martyrdom."  A paragraph of it says : "When one is persecuted on account of being Kirishitan, it is forbidden to fight in defence.  In the case when one fights in defence and is killed in it, he is not a martyr, because he did not die voluntarily for the sake of Deus."  Another treatise, "An Epitome of the August Passions," was handed down among the surviving Kirishitans.

only after a siege of several months by the loss of several
thousand officers and soldiers. One can imagine how the
tyrant Iyemitsu was irritated and enraged. Over thirty
thousands of the insurgents, including women and children,
were massacred. The surviving inhabitants were forced to
evacuate the coasts up to three miles from the sea. Search
for Kirishitans was conducted anew throughout Japan ; those
found were killed or forced to apostasy under pain of heavy
penalties. All possible measures of insuring against smuggling
of foreigners, of keeping strict vigilance against any survival,
of testing every inhabitant of the empire as to his religious
allegiance, were inaugurated or carried out with increasing
rigour. The organization of the Inquisition Office endowed
with a tremendous authority over the local governments was
the consummation of these measures, and the first head of
the office was an apostate, Inouye Chikugo.

This was practically an end of the Kirishitan religion and
the consequence was the entire isolation of Japan from the
world ; only a few Dutch merchants and a number of Chinese
being allowed to come to Japan, while any Japanese attempting to go abroad was put to death. The high patronage of
Buddhism and the privileges given to its priests were, as we shall
see, another sequel. Thus was established a reign of national
seclusion lasting over two centuries, certainly due to the "evils"
of Kirishitan but more to the caprice or cowardice of a tyrant.

In spite of all this, however, there were surviving Kirishitans
and cases of martyrdom even to the last years of the seventeenth century. Moreover, they survived in western Japan
throughout the two centuries of isolation and strict inquisition.
They were discovered by the French missionaries who came
to Japan after the reopening of the country in 1859. The
survivors had indeed tenaciously held to their faith in a
prophecy that they would meet *Padres* wearing black robes
coming from Rome after seven generations.

# END OF CONFUSION AND DAWN OF PEACE

THE period we are now about to close exhibited most varied social and religious movements. It had started with a general awakening of religious spirit and produced the most significant personalities in the religious history of Japan; but it came to a miserable end in strife and confusion, which weakened social ties and edifying influences. Nevertheless, the forces fostered in the Middle Ages left behind them a precious heritage. Zen Buddhism lost much of its invigorating power among the warriors, yet the school of Confucian ethics it had introduced was destined to exhibit its full power in the following period. The code of honour and the training in etiquette among the warriors, which had been started in the fourteenth century, supplied a basis for the moral life of the warrior class who became the rulers as times changed. Another point to be noted as an inheritance from the Middle Ages, especially from the latter part, was an artistic expression of national genius, of which we shall treat here in brief.

The art of the Muromachi renaissance was primarily a result of the inspiration given by Chinese art introduced by Zen monks. Under the patronage of Yoshimasa some indigenous characteristics were given to it, but it was after all a manifestation of æstheticism monopolized by the nobility and *literati*. Now the art of the sixteenth century exhibited its vitality not only in a further refinement of technique but in the expression of fresh vigour aroused by the hopeful outlook of the times. The triumphant entry of Nobunaga into Miyako had heralded a new era, giving promise of the advent of spring after a long winter. The real bloom of culture came in the reign of Hideyoshi, who unified the nation under his military power.

The reign of Hideyoshi as ruler of the whole country (1586-98), short though it was, marked an epoch significant in many respects. His extremely humble origin and marvellous career of rapid promotion and successful achievements impressed the minds of many with stirring hopes ; his reign saw considerable changes in the social fabric, and nearly all of his captains, the new nobility, were men of humble origin. Moreover, the expeditions sent to Korea by Hideyoshi, a military movement of great injustice though it was, aroused feelings of national pride and stirred an air of glorification. The works of art produced under this influence were grand castle architecture, palace buildings decorated with carvings, gorgeous screen paintings in gold and brilliant colours, all serving to glorify the pride of the hero and to express the exalting mood of the new age. Japanese art freed itself, for the first time in its history, from religious motives and foreign influence, and was thoroughly secularized and partially popularized. A point to be noted, however, is that even this secular art was impossible apart from the models of Zen art. The art movement under Hideyoshi's inspiration is known as the renaissance of Momo-yama (Peach Hill). An age full of hope and aspiration, it was a consummation of the artistic development of Japan, in which all former achievements were fused. Its inspiration surged like the rise of the tide after a low ebb—an age of national resurrection.

The turn of the sixteenth and seventeenth centuries may well be compared, in the greatness of its significance, to the turn of the twelfth and thirteenth. There were some similarities between these two periods in their social and political aspects, but a remarkable difference is to be noted—the new vigour in social life here manifested itself first in art and then in a revival of learning, while in the thirteenth century the new spirit found its chief expression in religion. That the later age was not indifferent to religion, however, may easily be seen from the fact that there were many Christian martyrs and not a few ardent Buddhists among the military leaders and the people. The apparent decline of religious influence may partly be due to the circumstance that Zen Buddhism was widely diffused and lost its specific religious influence through the permeation of its artistic sense into secular life. But perhaps a graver cause lay herein, that the arrogance of the ecclesiastical authorities and the degeneration of many Buddhist centres had positively repelled the best characters from those religious bodies. Moreover, warlike pursuits had attracted talented men to military activity, while the religious bodies themselves were entangled in warfare or intrigue. Various incidents vividly record how those who dared to resist the corruption of their fellow-priests fell victims to their atrocities. The great centre of Hiei, which had supplied the religious reformers of the thirteenth century, had long since become a stronghold of bandits and was finally exterminated by Nobunaga. A similar fate befell many other Buddhist centres, which otherwise might have produced leaders and reformers. Thus, spiritual leadership nearly died out, and the age naturally exhibited irreligious traits. Yet the religious inheritance from preceding ages was not entirely exhausted, but was destined to manifest itself in another form, in the rise of Confucian ethics of a highly religious character, an important feature of the coming centuries.

# BOOK V

# THE TOKUGAWA REGIME OF
# PEACE AND ORDER
## (1600-1868)

# THE ESTABLISHMENT OF A FIRM RULE

*The Religious and Educational Policies of the New Era*

THE restoration of peace and the establishment of order, for which the way had been prepared in the sixteenth century, was consummated at the beginning of the seventeenth, when Tokugawa Iyeyasu gave the final blow to his opponents and became Shōgun, dictatorial ruler over the feudal states. He soon inaugurated a revival of culture and learning to supplement his military and political achievements. The seeds of art, literature, moral culture, and religious training, scattered since the fourteenth century, had yet existed through confusion and neglect. The reign of Nobunaga in the second half of the sixteenth century and the further two decades of Hideyoshi's reign had evinced the vigour of a new growth. Now under the high patronage of the Tokugawa, arts and learning were revived and soon began to flourish ; religions ceased to fight and worked to give peace to mind and life. As the new government in all phases of its administration sought to keep peace and order, so the people, weary of a long reign of turbulence, were quite satisfied with following the initiative taken by the rulers. There was a new vitality on all sides, but it was more spent in reviving and elaborating old legacies, than in achieving new developments. Thus ensued a peaceful era of national seclusion which was destined to last nearly two centuries and a half.

One of the first needs of the new Government was to put a check to religious strife. The most important policy was the prohibition of Christianity at any price as stated above.

Its counterpart, the protection of Buddhist Churches, was carried out not so much on account of a real faith in that religion but rather because it was a useful tool against Kirishitans or a respect paid towards ancient heritage. Hence any intractable propagandists were severely punished, no matter what creeds they represented, simply because of their disobedience or aggressive propaganda. All the Buddhist sects had to keep within their respective spheres of influence, according to the *status quo* or to the assignment of the Government. Vigilance against Kirishitans was maintained both by the officials and the Buddhist clergy, who were entrusted with the right and responsibility of conducting a religious census within their respective jurisdictions. Every family was required to belong to a definite Buddhist establishment, and the clergy in charge had the right to examine the people's life and ideas. Thus Buddhism became the established religion of the State, though divided into sects and sub-sects within itself; its clergy lived and moved under the protection and supervision of the Government authorities. The Commissioner for Ecclesiastical Affairs (*Ji-sha Bugyō*) occupied an important place in the Government, while rich endowments were granted to Buddhist temples, monasteries, and colleges.[1] The majority of the Buddhist clergy were obedient servants of the Government, and in the long period of peace they gradually became lazy, or else effeminate intriguers. For the people at large religion was rather a matter of family heritage and formal observance than a question of personal faith.

Another important measure taken by Iyeyasu was the adoption of the Shushi school of Confucianism as the orthodox

[1] The greatest Buddhist centres inaugurated and patronized by the Tokugawa were Eastern Hiei (at Ueno) and Zōjō-ji (at Shiba) in the new capital Yedo (modern Tōkyō), corresponding to Hiei and Tōji in the old capital, Miyako. The latter became a great centre of Buddhist learning, having at one time more than ten thousand monks and novices within its boundaries, and to it is largely due the preservation of books and traditions.

PLATE XIX

BUDDHIST TEMPLES IN MIYAKO

A

B

A. CHION-IN TEMPLE, dedicated to Hōnen, erected near his hermitage
(Completed in 1639)

B. HIGASHI-HONGWAN-JI TEMPLE, dedicated to Shinran (Completed in 1895)

system of morality. This system, since its introduction in the fourteenth century, had been cultivated by the Zen monks, and the seeds sown by them began to grow and achieve an independent development. It well suited the purpose of the new government in encouraging learning as well as in establishing a standard of ethical teaching for the *Samurai* class, who had been fighters and now were entrusted with administration in the feudal state. The standard system of ethics thus established was destined to rule the life and ideas of the Samurai throughout the coming centuries.

The Shushi system was the Stoicism of the Orient, and was eminent not only in its disciplinary rigour but in its conception of human life as consisting in the realization of the Way or Reason of Heaven in human life, social and individual. It presupposed the heavenly sanction of the social order as conceived by the communal ethics of China. As benevolence and justice were the virtues of the superior, so obedience and observance of propriety were the duties of the subordinate. The co-ordination of these two sides of life was the whole of moral life. Expressed in social terms, moral life was nothing but the subordination of the ruled to the ruler, of children to parents, of wife to husband, of younger brothers and sisters to the elder, and lastly, mutual confidence between friends.[1]

Speaking in general, the Confucian conception of life was static, and Shushi ethics were pre-eminently disciplinary in their view of social life and in their training of the individual. For the faithful observance of those human relationships in social life was based on a severe training in self-control. This latter aspect harmonized well with Zen Buddhism, and since the Confucian teachers in the early seventeenth century had once been Buddhists, they inherited much rigorous training, together with the metaphysical theory of the ultimate identity

[1] This was called the "Five Relationships" (*Go-rin*) of human life, to which the "Five Norms" (*Go-jō*) were supplementary, namely, Benevolence, Justice, Propriety, Wisdom, and Honesty.

of the self with the Way of Heaven. Since the Way was taught to be something pre-established and ordained, the duty of the individual was understood to consist in conforming to it, and the static and conservative nature of this ethical system found a congenial soil of growth and nurture in the feudal régime which was aiming at the stabilization of social order. Emphasis was laid on the gradation of classes and on the subordination of the individual to the social order imposed from on high. A breach between this ethic of subordination and the individualism of Zen culture was inevitable and most of the orthodox Confucianists, deserters from Buddhism, sharply attacked their former religion. Buddhism now encountered public opposition for the first time since its introduction into Japan. One of the consequences was, as we shall see presently, a division of creeds and ideals according to the classes, the creed of the Samurai being Confucianism and that of the people Buddhism.

### Bushidō, its Modification and Development

The ethics of order and stability exerted their influence not so much on account of their intrinsic value as by virtue of the feudal régime under a strong military rule. The Shōgun, the military dictator, was the supreme autocrat, but he was surrounded by his ministers and advisers ; the feudal lord was a similar autocrat within his dominion, but he ruled through his Samurai ministers.[1] Thus, the actual rulership was more and more transferred to the class of the Samurai as such, while the nation at large had no share either in government or in education. The Samurai were trained in civic arts and political sciences as well as in self-culture and personal

---

[1] Especially because the feudal lords were required to spend half of the year in Yedo.

morality. The feudal régime was strongly supported by the class discipline of the Samurai, and thanks to this the Tokugawa régime exhibited the rare instance of a long peace lasting more than two centuries, interrupted only by a few cases of riot or insurrection. Though the peace was partly due to the seclusion of the nation, it was also to be credited to Confucianism.

This whole scheme of training of the ruling class was called *Bushidō*, the Way of the Samurai, but here we have to note a significant transformation of that discipline, for the Samurai, the warrior of the preceding ages, now became the preserver of peace, although girt with two swords. He had little prospect of fighting, and yet had always to be ready to die for his lord. As a ruler he had to be well versed in the theory and arts of administration, but no less essential was military discipline. These combined requirements produced some happy results but also some abnormal convention, which we shall see presently

In the rigidly stratified society and the reign of enduring peace little room was left to individual valour or personal distinction, as every man was required to conform himself to his social status and to fulfil his assigned duties. Special emphasis was laid on propriety of behaviour according to prescribed standards. The expression of obedience, or rather the absence of self-assertion before a superior, was the most important of all rules of conduct, and minute details of the rules accumulated year by year, even the relation between husband and wife being standardized. Obedience and reverence on the part of the inferior had its counterpart in the proper maintenance of dignity on the part of the superior, all of which required calmness of manner, subdued tone of speech, gentleness of expression.

There were rules for every act, in salutation, in conversation, in fencing practice, in handing over a sword, and even in committing suicide.[1]   These rules may be compared to the manners of the mediæval knights of Europe, but the main difference between European knighthood and Japanese Bushidō as regards decorum lay in the great quietness and sternness of manner in the latter, which was an inheritance from Zen training, in contrast to the gallantry of European chivalry.   All these regulations were understood to be not only necessary for the ordering of social life but equally important for self-training.   We shall here not enter upon the politcial and military aspects of Bushidō, but suffice it to say that it became under the firmly established feudalism a Stoic system of ethics, a social code of class morality.

Thus Bushidō was a moral discipline controlling the life and death of the ruling class, a religion of self-renunciation, a perfection of self in accordance with the cosmic and social orders, especially shown in the fidelity to the lord served and in the devotion to parents and teacher.   In this morality of devotion and reverence, Buddhist and Confucian influences were the integral factors, but now Shinto contributed greatly to the inculcation of loyalty, as a consequence of the firm establishment of the feudal states, and further in association with the revival of ancient learning.   The close bond between the lord and the retainers lasting through generations in an age of peace, the continuity of families long settled in their estates, the increasing authority of the village community, these gave renewed energy and solidarity to the clan and communal life.   This was always backed by the Shinto cult amounting to the adoration of ancestors and the veneration of communal sanctuaries.   Bushidō was not a religion in itself but it had its cult, mostly family worship and observ-

---

[1] This, which was called *seppuku*, is usually known in the West by the name *harakiri*, but this was a vulgar expression which a Samurai would have been ashamed to utter.   The idea underlying this practice was that a Samurai ought to dispose of his own life voluntarily in the case when death alone could save his honour.   See Nitobe, *Bushidō*, pp. 116, 122 ;   Brinkley, *Japan*, vol. ii, pp. 185-192.

ance, in which joyous festivals were celebrated in the Shinto manner while all matters pertaining to the worlds beyond were dealt with in Buddhist rituals.

### Social Stability and the Rise of Learning

The transformation of Bushidō was concomitant with a change in the warrior's life—the phase of the transition from camp life to civic order. All the measures adopted by the Tokugawa Government aimed at stabilizing peace and order, implying more centralization and encroachment upon divided powers. An ingenious scheme was made for keeping the court nobles at Miyako quiet and contented by assigning to them certain branches of learning as their privileges. The Emperor, living in an atmosphere of sanctity in the time-honoured capital, was always likely to be made a weapon against the Tokugawa régime, and it had always been to his court nobles that ambitious feudal lords had looked for accomplices in setting up a new rule. Iyeyasu's device was to give each of those ancient families the privilege of being the head of a certain branch of art or learning, so that they should devote their time to the culture of their respective arts, their pride thereby being satisfied and their revenue secured. Every prominent family was given the honour of being the *Iyemoto* ("fountain-head") of a certain art or learning with the privilege of granting to qualified persons a title showing proficiency in that art. Thus, poetry, calligraphy, music, astrology, archery, a kind of football, the tea ceremony, and the like had each its "fountain-head" in a noble family monopolizing its culture. This system of art tradition, which had originated in the reform measures and social conditions of the fourteenth century, was now adopted by the Tokugawa for taming the court nobles. Though this grant of monopolies caused stagnancy in arts and learning, it had the merit of perpetuating and elaborating traditions. This culture of monopolized traditions had important bearings upon the conservative temperament of this period, and its influence still lingers in New Japan.

Buddhist bodies now ceased to be militant churches and eagerly worked for helping the Government in their peaceful policies. They produced no more originators and propagandists but elaborators and systematizers. Monasteries richly endowed became centres of learning, and each sect organized a hierarchy of ecclesiastical ranks sharing in the stratified structure of society. Some of the learned monks extended their study not only to Confucianism but to literature and philology, while many others were preachers or popular educators, all contributing to the revival of learning and to the establishment of social order as conceived and enforced by the Government.[1]

The majority of the orthodox Confucianists of the early seventeenth century had once been Buddhists, and even after their desertion of Buddhism they wore quasi-Buddhist robes, which remained a custom among the Confucianists for a while. In fact, these teachers derived their knowledge first from the Zen monasteries, where Confucian ethics were re-

[1] To mention some of the Buddhist workers in the seventeenth century : Tenkai (1536-1643) and Sūden (1569-1633), advisers to Iyeyasu on political and ecclesiastical matters ; Genyo (1541-1620), the great organizer of Zōjō-ji and other colleges and systematizer of the Jōdo dogma ; Nichijū (1549-1623), Nichiken (1560-1635), and Nichion (1572-1642). the systematizers of the Nichirenite dogmas ; Taku-an (1573-1645) and Ingen (1592-1673), Zen teachers of great influence upon the nobles and people ; Gensei (1623-68), a virtuous hermit and poet of the Nichiren sect ; Tetsugen (1630-82), the editor of the Buddhist Tripitaka and organizer of famine relief ; Keichū (1640-1701), the Japanese philologist who opened the way to the study of the ancient *Collection of Myriad Leaves* and further of the ancient history of Japan. The reader may gather from this list the kinds of work carried out by able Buddhists at the turn of the régime. One monk deserves a special mention. He was Tōsui (d. 1683) who had been the abbot of a large monastery but left the post and lived among beggars and worked for them as a protest against the growing easy life of other Buddhists. Tōsui found admirers in recent times. Concerning Buddhism in relatively modern times, see Plates XIX and XX.

PLATE XX

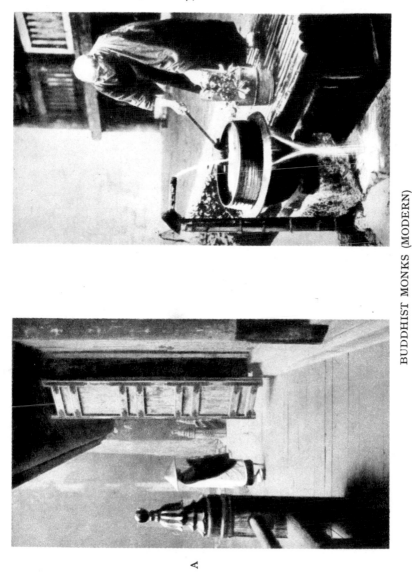

BUDDHIST MONKS (MODERN)

A. An itinerant Monk praying at the Kodō Hall of Mt. Hiei
B. A Monk going to offer Flowers to Buddha. Side of the Chūdō Hall of Mt. Hiei

garded as supplementary to Buddhism. In contrast to the Confucian antagonism to Buddhism, the Buddhists held an attitude of tolerance or aloofness towards Confucianism. There was arranged a division of labour in which Confucianism took the chief responsibility of training the Samurai class, while the people at large were left to the care of Buddhism ; and the attitude of the Confucianists towards Buddhists implied a certain contempt of the common people.

Although the Confucianists declared their independence of Buddhism, they were aware of a defect of their own system in its lack of religious sentiment, and some of them took refuge in Shinto. Similarly, the Shintoists were anxious to add a tinge of philosophical depth to their teaching, and yet being too proud to take from Buddhism, their religious rival, imported cosmological ideas from Confucianism. An implicit alliance of the two systems was thus established, in which the negative cause was the opposition to Buddhism and the positive link was the desire to justify the existing régime and to emphasize the importance of national and communal cults.

The pioneer of the Confucianists who advocated Shinto was Hayashi Razan (1583-1657), the great leader of the Shushi school and organizer of a Government college for Chinese culture. Not only a man of erudition but of statesmanlike ability, he served Iyeyasu in advising him to authorize the orthodox ethical system, and advocated Shinto as the foundation of national life, emphasizing the significance of the communal cult as the basis of social order. Razan's influence as a Shintoist, however, was very limited and was not to be compared to his leadership in Confucianism. A more abiding impression on Shinto and national ideas was left by a younger contemporary of Razan, Yamazaki Ansai (1619-82). Having been trained both in Confucianism and Shinto quite independently from other leaders, Ansai arrived at a similar conclusion as Razan and further organized a Confucian-Shinto cult, chiefly ancestor-worship. He thought the fundamental principle common to the two systems to lie in the training of self in accordance with the way of heaven and in the practice of social virtues. " Rectify the inner (soul) by devotion (to the cosmic reason) and thereby regulate the outer (order) by righteousness." This saying of the Chinese philosopher Cheng, a comrade of Shushi, was the cardinal maxim of Ansai's teaching. With this he identified the opening words of the Shinto " Pentateuch " [1] which said : " Divine revelation is invoked by prayer, and divine providence is secured through honesty." Yet Ansai was a positivist when he interpreted devotion and honesty to consist solely in the practice of virtues in accordance with the social status of every person. He was not satisfied until his ideas were organized into a religious cult, in which he acted as the high priest. As a Shintoist he was also a nationalist, and his school produced not a few enthusiasts who later worked for the restoration of the imperial régime.

A parallel alliance sought from the Shinto side was represented by Deguchi Nobuyoshi (1615-90), a priest serving at the Geku (" Outer Temple ") of Isé, where existed a tradition of combining Shinto with Chinese cosmology and whence the Shinto " Pentateuch " (claiming divine origin) was handed. The combination worked out by Nobuyoshi was very similar to that of Ansai, the specific point being an attempt to establish a religion verging on monotheism, in which the ancient " Heavenly Central Lord " was regarded as the supreme deity. Another exponent of Confucian Shinto was Kikkawa Koretaru (1616-94). Though he had been trained in the Urabé school of eclectic Shinto, he discarded the occult phase

---

[1] *Gobusho,* the " Five Books," dating probably from the fourteenth century. Cf. above p. 238. Ansai's school is also called the *Sui-ga,* a term made from the two words meaning " revelation " and " providence."

of his school and emphasized its ethical teachings.  These Shinto theorists, like their Confucianist comrades, rarely worked for popular education but exerted their influence through the nobility, taking pride in being advisers or teachers to the ruling class.

# CONFUCIANISM AND ITS SCHOOLS[1]

## *The Orthodox School and Its Teachers*

CONFUCIANISM, now the orthodox teaching of the State, attracted men of sober temper and conservative tendency, while men of originality and energy were arising outside. The greatest educator in orthodox ethics was Kinoshita Jun-an (1621-98) who served as an instructor to the Shōgun and trained many able disciples. His influence upon the Shōgun induced many feudal states to employ Jun-an's disciples as instructors to their Samurai retainers, and in those days the ethical education of the whole territory depended upon the teaching of the chief instructor. Thus these disciples of Jun-an were the chief factors in moulding the education of the Samurai class according to the principles of the Shushi School. One of them, Arai Hakuseki (1657-1725), a man of broad interests and liberal views, was more of an historian than a moralist, and in spite of his training in the conservative orthodoxy worked as a progressive adviser to the Government. His ability lay rather in the sphere of state affairs than in philosophy or ethics, and he represented the Confucian influence upon the politics of the day.[2]

Another, a genuine Shushist, was Muro Kyūsō (1658-

[1] On the schools of Confucianism in this period see R. C. Armstrong, *Light from the East* (Toronto, 1914). The book is to be used with caution. Cf. Anesaki's review on it in *Harvard Theological Review*, 1916.

[2] Arai had some knowledge of the Occidental countries through Dutch sources. He was also the man to whom was entrusted the examination of the Jesuit Father Sidotti, who was smuggled into the country in 1709. In the report presented to the Government by Arai on Sidotti and on Christianity in general, he says, though not quite explicitly, that the Christian religion is not so injurious to the country as considered by the authorities.

1734) who succeeded in overturning Arai's liberal policy and in consolidating the rule of rigid orthodoxy. He was a man of rigorous self-training and a severe teacher, and his doctrine was significant as a reflection of the time when personal initiative and individual freedom were deemed incompatible with the firm establishment of social order. He emphasized the necessity of self-vigilance in personal life and the practice of benevolence in social life. Vigilance in self-introspection, according to him, is the sole means of preserving and fostering the prime nature of man, the inalienable human nature identical with the cosmic soul. But he conceives this participation in the cosmic life to consist solely in training oneself in accordance with one's social status and duties. Virtue is nothing but a realization of the heavenly reason or order in human life, and just as there is an unchangeable orderliness in the movements of the heavenly bodies, there are order and gradation in human society. The cardinal virtues are filial piety, loyalty, and obedience, because every individual is bound by gratitude towards his father (the mother is not mentioned), the lord, and the sage or teacher (meaning chiefly Confucius). The sense of indebtedness is the source of benevolence, while justice means the practice of good-will in human relationships according to social grades. Protection and obedience, benefaction and gratitude, benevolence and fidelity, each of these combinations represents the fundamental nature of our life, the foundation of human life based on the heavenly reason. Thus Kyūsō's ethics were a static view of life, and he sought to base them on the training of the individual under the guidance of Heaven.[1]

---

[1] See further : G. W. Knox, *A Japanese Philosopher, TASJ*, vol. xx ; his *The Development of Religion in Japan*, Lecture vi. Kyūsō also believed in the omnipresence of Divinity, or rather deities, who were, according to him, omniscient and ideally virtuous. This belief in the deities was a feature of its philosophy which induced some of his disciples to make alliance with Shinto, as was the case with Razan and Ansai.

Most of the Confucianists of this period were government teachers, but we have one significant instance of a popular teacher.   This was Kaibara Ekken (1630-1714), a physician by profession and the author of many manuals of practical morals and hygiene.   He had been a follower of Shushi but gradually deviated from orthodoxy, because he laid emphasis on the dynamic aspects of cosmic life and morality.   His insistence on " cosmic vitality " implied an ethical view of regarding the whole cosmic process as a continuous life and therefore of emphasizing the virtue of filial piety towards both actual parents and the source of cosmic life.   Thus, according to Ekken, moral life was nothing but service rendered to the cosmic father, not only in observing his will but in participating in his love.   And Ekken applied this theory of love and piety to all human relationships.   He was a metaphysician, but descending from the height of speculation to the practical realm of life, he worked as a popular teacher of ethics.   His idea of the love-relation between the universe and the individual verged on religious piety, and yet he was never immersed in mystic contemplation but devoted himself to educational work, taking a keen interest in the daily life of the people in general.   His instructions covered all matters pertaining to human life, and his books were widely read among the people throughout the Tokugawa period.   He was exceptionally liberal-minded for a Confucianist, yet quite a conservative after our modern standard ; in many points of his teachings he only justified the conditions prevailing at the time.

### The Mito School of Confucianism

Besides its influence upon Samurai discipline and its service to the existing régime, orthodox Confucianism worked in a subtle and unexpected way in the direction of finally undermining feudalism and restoring national unity under the imperial rule.   One of the schools representing this tendency was a group of thinkers and historians gathered under the banner of the lord of Mito, Tokugawa Mitsukuni (1628-1700). In spite of his family connection with the Shōgun, he was a royalist and nationalist in principle, and he started the compilation of a large history of Japan.   His idea was that the permanent security of the country depended upon the sanctity of the Throne, and that the ethical principle of loyalty was ultimately to be directed towards that highest authority of the national life.   Mitsukuni considered an appropriate compilation of national history to be an essential task for elucidating moral principles embodied in the nation's long life. For this purpose he summoned Confucian scholars and Japanese philologists, and these men formulated their ideas, besides collecting historical materials and collating old books. Admirable, indeed, were Mitsukuni's earnest zeal in his work and the pious assiduity of his successors, as can be seen from the fact that the complete work, amounting to 226 volumes, was not completed until 1906.   An historical compilation continuously and persistently worked at and finished in the course of two centuries and a half (it was started in 1657) is creditable to Mitsukuni's spiritual legacy and the fidelity of his descendants.   This work of historical compilation brought about the formation of a special school of Confucian ethics known as the Mito school.

This work started by Mitsukuni was a perpetuation of the legacy left by Chikafusa, the champion of the Southern Dynasty in the fourteenth century, and the ethical basis of the historical compilation was laid on the Confucian conception of righteousness.   This implied that history should be an ethical criticism of the past for the sake of the present and future, ethics and politics being inseparable in Confucianism. Mitsukuni and his collaborators applied this idea of historical study to the national life of the Japanese, which they conceived to centre around the sanctity of the Throne. They endeavoured to explain the permanent relationship established between the ruler and the people in this way, and they therefore exhorted an almost religious adoration of the sovereign. Though Mitsukuni and his advisers never protested against the existing régime, but emphasized the virtue of loyalty to the feudal lord or the Shōgun as an integral part of Samurai morality, their idea implied that true loyalty was to be directed ultimately to the imperial family. Some new conceptions crystallized out of these ethico-historical considerations, the most significant being *Koku-tai* and *Tai-gi meibun*. The former meant literally the " Substance of the State," and was used to designate the fundamental structure of national life, and therefore the highest principle of all human relationships within national life to be centred in the adoration of the Throne. *Tai-gi meibun*, literally " Major Righteousness and Status-order," designated the supremacy of the " major " loyalty to the Throne over every other minor relationship, including even allegiance to the feudal lord.

Thus the ethical principle of the Mito school was a nationalism. Its principle implied, too, that all private considerations were to be sacrificed to the national cause of " major righteousness," a teaching of patriotism demanding the suppression of individual claims and personal sentiments. Though rather contrary to the ethics of the feudal régime in its emphasis on national principles, this ethic reflected the ethos of the time in emphasizing the formal principle of " righteousness " (*giri* or *tai-gi*) to the suppression of human instincts or sentiments. Herein we can discern a division between the head and the heart, and Mitsukuni himself exemplified it to a certain degree. Though himself a devout Buddhist, especially in remembrance of his mother's piety, Mitsukuni considered his religious faith as his personal matter, and stood publicly for Confucian ethics with a strong leaning to

Shinto ideas. Similarly, he pronounced himself to be ready to sacrifice his close family tie with the Shōgun in favour of the "major righteousness," should his loyalty to the Emperor be at stake. These national ideas inherited in his family and fostered by the thinkers of the Mito school were destined to inspire many nationalists with a semi-religious adoration of the Throne. It was largely due to this influence that later in the nineteenth century the last Shōgun of Tokugawa submitted himself to the Throne in loyal obedience and restored the government to the Emperor. This prince was born in the Mito family and was educated in the legacy of Mitsukuni.[1]

### Division of Schools among Confucian Teachers

Thus we see seeds sown which were destined later to produce a grave split among the Confucianists, between the supporters of feudalism and the advocates of nationalism. Indeed, division into schools or factions had always been a prominent feature among Confucian scholars, and it was natural to those who monopolized the orthodox teaching under the protection of the government to look with suspicion at any who dissented from orthodoxy. This antagonism implied pressure exerted by the government upon the heterodox; it developed almost into persecution, when the authority of the Shōgunate Government began to wane and the orthodox teachers began to be nervous about their prestige, early in the nineteenth century. The dissension, however, was an academic one in its early stage in the seventeenth century. When the orthodox system had been established under government patronage and its burden began to press upon the free and energetic thinkers, these sought new ways outside orthodox Shushism. Just as most of the first orthodox

---

[1] As a matter of fact, various political circumstances compelled his abdication, but the decisive step taken by him, in spite of the possibilities of much more resistance, was a result of his ethical conviction of the sanctity of the Throne.

Confucianists had once been Buddhist monks, so nearly all the supporters of the heterodox schools had been trained in orthodox Shushism and then went over to different camps. One of the two principal heterodox schools was represented by the scholars who discovered and advocated the teaching of Wang Yang-ming (1472-1528), a Chinese soldier-philosopher ; the other comprised those who inaugurated new interpretations of Confucian ethics, with the claim of restoring them to original purity. The former is known by the Japanese pronunciation of Yangming as the *Yōmei* school, and the latter is called the " Ancient Learning " (*Ko-gaku*) school.

The pioneer of the Yōmei school was Nakaye Tōju (1608-48), known as the " Sage of Ōmi," Ōmi being his native province, where he lived in retirement and instructed his fellow-villagers. Being dissatisfied with the formalism of the orthodox school, he discovered on his spiritual journey in search of truth a new path in Yōmei's teaching of the " Prime Conscience " (*Ryōchi*). His conversion took place when Tōju was thirty-two years old, and thenceforward he devoted his efforts to training himself and instructing others in the method of spiritual culture after Yōmei's theory and practice. The " Prime Conscience," according to Yōmei and Tōju, is the universal soul, the soul of the cosmic Ruler (Chinese, *Ti*), while man is his image, though often obscured and distorted, a microcosmos, a concrete manifestation of the universal will to love.[1] Thus the relation of the individual to the cosmic

---

[1] Tōju had once lived in Iyo, in Shikoku, where he is said to have had contact with a Kirishitan, who gave him a special medicine for chilblains. It is possible that the Confucianist of Shikoku mentioned in Pagès (p. 637) under the head of 1626, was Tōju—he left Iyo for Ōmi in 1634. In fact, Tōju's doctrine is redolent of monotheistic piety, as will be seen further.

For Yōmei himself, see F. G. Henke, *The Philosophy of Wang Yang-ming* (Chicago, 1916), a translation of his works and life. The translator's rendering of *Ryōchi* (Chinese, *Liang-chih*) is " intuitive knowledge," " intuitive faculty of good." The book should be used with great caution, especially because the translator has interpreted Wang's technical terms much in the connotations of the Shushi school, as if interpreting and translating Schopenhauer in the sense of Hegelian terminology.

Lord is filial, and moral life amounts to practising filial piety towards the Lord. This is the cardinal virtue, while all other virtues are various aspects of this as applied to the circumstances of life. This emphasis laid by Tōju on filial virtue was not a mere theory but the result of his intimate experience as a son profoundly devoted to his mother. This trait runs through all his ideas and modes of life, a characteristic trait of his personality enhanced by the intuitive tendency of Yōmei's system in general.

Though Tōju never neglected practical virtues, he thought that they were worthless unless derived from the deeper source of the Prime Conscience embedded in the innermost recess of our soul as endowed by the Lord, and this was to be realized through spiritual exercise in devotion to the father and lord of the universe. Here was the chief point at which Tōju deviated from the orthodox Confucianists, in laying special stress upon spiritual exercise and in putting less importance on knowledge and civic virtues. Tōju, when he expressed his devotion to the cosmic soul, was evincing a religious spirit verging on Buddhist piety, or not seldom on Christian monotheism. Yet he condemned Buddhism because of the ascetic nature of its ethics, and this in spite of the fact that he, like his master Yōmei, was an idealistic thinker and was compelled to borrow Buddhist terms in expressing his ideas. On the other hand, he found in Shinto a religion of childlike piety and simplicity, and explained the Shinto virtues of veracity (or honesty), sympathy, and endurance as identical with his ideals.

Though Tōju's direct influence was limited to the narrow circle of his few disciples, mostly his fellow-villagers, his inspiration was extended to a wider circle and produced many able men active in the fields of education, administration, and economy. These indirect disciples of Tōju trained in the culture of the Prime Conscience plunged into the activity of life and were eminent for their resolute action. These men differed in their spheres of activity and methods of work, but there was one common trait among them, a democratic attitude. They believed in the equality of mankind as children of the cosmic Lord, and consequently they always stood for giving all men full opportunities for the realization of the true self in communion with the universal conscience. Thus, in spite of their compromise with actual social conditions, they taught that every one ought to be a conscious and pious son of Heaven. When, later, social and political conditions seemed to have reached a breaking-point, some of these democratic-minded moralists attempted a revolution. One of them died a martyr's death, while some others helped to overthrow feudalism and contributed to establishing a new régime in the middle of the nineteenth century.

The school of " Ancient Learning " wished to restore Confucianism to its original purity by purging it from the mixture of Buddhist transcendentalism. For the thinkers of this school considered the Shushist theories of the soul or of the reason and the associated practice of self-examination to be a deviation from genuine Confucianism. These men were more or less pragmatists, in the sense that they emphasized the practical value of ethical teachings and rejected all subtle arguments about metaphysical principles. As such they had no desire to found a group or school, but each of them developed independently a common tendency, which may be characterized as a dynamic view of the world and its direct application to human life. Though pragmatists, most of them believed in an all-permeating vitality in physical occurrences as well as in human acts. The destiny of mankind was, according to them, to apply the fundamental living force to various aspects of human life, to education, government, economics, and even to military science. Thus the school produced a good number of educators and administrators. The rise of the Ancient Learning was not so much a scholarly attempt at a revival of ancient Confucianism as a protest against the methodic formality of the orthodox. It was also a manifestation of individual genius revolting against the subserviency of ethical teaching to political control and social conventions.

The Ancient Learning was represented by men of various types,[1] but the most characteristic of them was Yamaga Sokō (1622-85), who systematized the ethics of Bushidō by applying Confucianism to the principles of military science and the life of the warrior. He considered the whole universe to be a stage of moral order and human life as an embodiment of cosmic life in social order. The basis of moral life is, according to him, mental training aiming at serenity, sincerity, and magnanimity on one side, and courage, discernment, and firmness on the other. All other virtues are applications of the fundamental training, and the discipline of the Samurai is nothing but realization of these virtues in his life as fighter and ruler. He should always be ready to sacrifice his life for the sake of righteousness, and the several branches of military science and training are nothing but practical applications of this spirit With this view, Sokō himself underwent a rigorous training and instructed others both in ethics and military science. As a private master of military science, he was suspected and persecuted by the authorities, but his influence was not thereby checked.[2]

---

[1] Among them we mention: Itō Jinsai (1627-1705), the moral theorist and educator; Ogiu Sorai (1666-1728), the political philosopher and adviser to the Government; Dazai Shundai (1680-1747), the economist. For Dazai, see R. J. Kirby's articles and translations in *TASJ*, vols. 28, 32, 34, 36, 41, etc.

[2] A record of Sokō's lectures on the subject is handed down with the title *Shidō*, i.e., the "Way of the Warrior." Its contents may serve to show the nature and extent of his teachings; we give them here in bare outline.
I. The fundamental principles: Fidelity to vocation; an earnest desire to carry out the Way; efforts devoted to its practice.
II. Training of the mind: Composure of mind; Magnanimity; Purity of sentiment; Gentleness; Refinement, etc.
III. Training in virtues and the perfection of ability.
IV. Self-introspection and self-restraint.

*The Story of the Forty-seven Rōnin*

The effect of Sokō's moral instruction and military discipline was soon exhibited in the thrilling event of the " Forty-seven *Rōnin*," who avenged their feudal lord and were sentenced to death. Whatever we moderns may say of the ethical meaning or value of revenge, we must view the event against the background of the time, and thus estimate its significance as well as Sokō's moral influence. It was a time when vengeance was regarded as a duty of the children or retainers of a father or lord who had unjustly been put to death. The lord of the forty-seven *rōnin* (feudal retainers deprived of their fiefs), or *gishi* (righteous men), as they were called, was sentenced to death because of his attack on one of his colleagues who had insulted him. The death of the lord was followed by confiscation of his feudal tenure, while the opponent was treated leniently by the government and was allowed to live an easy life in retirement. When every petition to restore the feudal estate of the dead lord had proved fruitless, the bitter resentment of his faithful retainers was only to be appeased by revenge inflicted upon the person of the one who had abused their ill-fated lord and caused his death in disgrace. Many of the former retainers soon deserted the cause of vengeance, but some of them, under the leadership of one Ōishi, remained faithful to the avowed cause. When finally their long-sought opportunity arrived, there were forty-seven who successfully made an organized attack upon the enemy. The government sentenced them to death not by execution but by *seppuku* (or *harakiri*, in the vulgar term), a special concession to their honour.

The leader in the plot, Ōishi, was a disciple of Sokō and

V   Mindfulness of dignity and propriety : Self-respect and gravity ; Vigilance in seeing and hearing, etc.
VI. Vigilance in daily life : Daily life and its surroundings ; the use of wealth and its significance in life, etc.

conducted his plan at all points according to his master's instructions in morals and military arts. The moral inspiration of the case was enormous, and the leader and his fellows were regarded by his contemporaries as model Samurai. Indeed, we find in the conduct of these men an actual embodiment of the Samurai spirit of that time, while any age would but admire the leadership of Ōishi, the loyal spirit of his fellows, their touching confidence in their leader. They saw many of the original supporters of the cause falling off in the course of the two years which elapsed before their final stroke was attained ; they were betrayed by some of their former companions and constantly spied upon by their enemy. Yet they persevered through hardships and trials, poverty, betrayal, persecution, hope deferred, temptations — and nothing shook their resolution nor their fellowship. On entering the last stage of the plot, they kept a perfect discipline and achieved their aim with splendid strategy. Then they presented the case to the government and waited in noble calm the decision of the authorities. When the sentence was pronounced they accepted it with the serene consolation that their cause had been achieved, and they ended their lives with becoming dignity by their own hands. Thus, they lived and died as " righteous men," piously devoted to their dead lord and unalterably faithful to their common aim.

When, on a winter morning near the end of the year 1702,[1] the news of their success spread throughout the city of Yedo, the populace was swayed by enthusiasm over the " righteous men," and soon the story of their deed found its way to every corner of the city. When, nearly two months later, the heroes had been buried close to the tomb of their lord, the people poured into the graveyard in an inspired enthusiasm, mingled with deep sympathy, offering flowers and incense to them. Relics and writings of the heroes were collected, all the material

[1] The 15th day of the 12th lunar month, in fact January 3rd, 1703.

relating to their doings was eagerly compiled; the whole story as well as episodes in their lives were written down, and these publications were circulated widely and swiftly.[1]  The stories, as a whole or in parts, were soon dramatized and produced on the stage, attracting large crowds.  The influence of these more or less romanticized stories spread over the whole country during the following two centuries, and in recent years we have seen a certain revival of the adoration for these men and the literature concerning them.

In considering the great influence of the heroes, we have to take into account three points : (1) The moral lessons of the story as shown in the fidelity of these men to their avowed cause and their mutual confidence in fellowship ; (2) The spirit of Bushidō more or less permeating the people at large, and the eager aspiration on their part to see its moral ideas realized in life and acts ; (3) A dissatisfaction of the people with the corruption of the government circles and a protest against the suppression of freedom.  We shall presently see how these two last features of the age expressed themselves in other directions.  The story of the forty-seven *gishi* was a flash of Bushidō morality reacting upon effeminate tendencies engendered by the peace.  The whole story worked as a strong stimulant to the virile spirit of the nation during the long reign of peace and as material for an idealized reminiscence of the past ages of the heroes.  The same idea of loyalty was later transferred to the national cause, and the spirit of revenge was transformed into patriotic ardour in the Restoration of the nineteenth century.  And in fact, Sokō, the systematizer of Bushidō, did not limit his teaching of loyalty to the feudal lord, but taught the ethics of patriotism in a fuller sense of the word, as he expounded his ideas of national life in a

---

[1] For the story see : A. B. Mitford, *Tales of Old Japan* (London, 1871, 1928) ; F. V. Dickins, *Chiushin-gura, or the Loyal League* (London and Yokohama, 1880) ; J. Inouye, *Chiushin-gura, or the Loyal Retainers of Akao* (Tokio, 1895).

historical essay exalting the sanctity of the Throne.  In this respect he was an independent collaborator of the principles formulated by the Mito school, and his influence was recently revived by General Nogi's admiration of him—Nogi, the hero who voluntarily followed his sovereign in death in 1912.

# THE BLOOMING OF CULTURE AND THE RISE OF THE BOURGEOISIE

*The Era of Genroku and Its Ethos*

THE turn of the seventeenth and eighteenth centuries marked the end of warlike temper and the bloom of a new culture, and is noted for its brilliant manifestations. The epoch is known as the era of Genroku (1688-1704) and the ethos of the time marks a significant feature of the Tokugawa régime. A century had passed since the time of Hideyoshi and eight decades since the establishment of peace. Arts and learning revived and flourished, commerce regained its full volume, the people enjoyed peace and prosperity. Yedo, the new capital, was being transformed from a large military camp into a commercial centre; there still lingered, however, the temper of military men, while, at the same time, it was the centre of State orthodoxy in religion and ethics. On the other hand, Ōsaka, the greatest commercial centre in central Japan, was a city of guilds and merchants, full of independent enterprising spirit. The new growth of culture appeared first in this metropolis of the bourgeoisie and was gradually transplanted to Yedo. Thus there were two centres in the renaissance of Genroku; it was in Ōsaka that the refinement of the merchant class predominated, while in Yedo the heritage of the old militarism was being transferred to a certain class of citizens eminent for their dauntless spirit, whose influence was growing, especially in protest against the caprices of the ruling class. Together with the manifestations of the new culture, there were arising conflicts between bureaucratic formalism and democratic aspirations. The enthusiasm of the people for the forty-seven *Rōnin* was one of the signs, and we shall see more of them later.

One of the features of the age was a deepening gulf between the Samurai and the common people. For this were responsible both Confucian teaching and the class morality of Bushidō, which worked jointly in confirming the prerogatives and biases of the Samurai class, in antagonism to the free activity and aspiration of the people. Orthodox Confucianism served the rulers' purpose of keeping the people within fixed social restrictions, using them as tools of the governors. Husbandry was valued as the source of the nation's wealth, but the peasants were considered to be mere producers of rice and clothing materials. They were an integral factor of economic life, but only as tax-payers and providers for the Samurai, who thought it their right to be fed by the tillers of the soil. Trade was thought to be a form of mere cunning, and the merchant was treated as a base and mean seeker of profit. Bushidō became rather a code of class morality and education than the personal religion of the warrior it had been, and its discipline was naturally limited to that privileged class. Not only was the moral teaching of Bushidō inapplicable to the common people, but any attempt of the people to imitate or emulate the ruling class, whether in life or in education, was regarded as a transgression. Thus, the demarcation between classes was growing more and more rigid, yet the peace and prosperity accelerated the rise and ambition of the people, especially the merchant class. The culture of Genroku was in part a demonstration of this new force and aspiration.

The people, being weary of confusion and war, had gladly accepted the peace established by the military dictatorship; the government policies and official ethics had largely succeeded in enforcing rigid order; the result was a social structure of stratified classes, the Samurai rulers on top. The established régime of feudalism involved a sharp division between the feudal states, and within the feudal state the commune was an essential organization for maintaining peace and integrity. Migration was made extremely difficult, partly by the jealous guard of the feudal government and partly by the interference of the religious census. The people were allowed little choice, being bound to their hereditary estates and occupations. The family meant not only a continuity of lineage but an unchangeable means of obtaining a livelihood on the hereditary soil and in solidarity with other families settled in the same commune. Just as hereditary rank and estate assured the stability of a Samurai family and bound its members to its traditions, so the native soil and the hereditary occupation established for generations put restrictions upon, as well as gave safety to, the life of a merchant or peasant. Any ambition for personal advancement or any aspiration for individual freedom on the part of anyone was regarded as a menace both to society and to his own family. Everyone enjoyed the security of his family life and the protection of the commune at the price of individuality. Morality under these conditions simply meant conforming to the social conventions and traditions of the commune. This social stability ensured peace and order, but it was also the cause of various troubles now to be considered.

The burden of the rigid social rules fell most severely upon the woman, and the consequences were manifested in the problems of sexual morality. In a conspicuous contrast to the height of her influence in the reign of Buddhist sentimentalism, a characteristic feature of Bushidō was the debasement of woman and the consequent contempt for love and affection in general. The rise of the military men, together with Confucian ethics, led to the degradation of the position and dignity of woman in social life. Her sole virtue consisted in submission, the famous threefold submission towards parents, husband, and sons, according to the stages of her life. Her activity was almost confined to the household ; any show of ability or initiative on her part was regarded as a transgression. Any sign of undue respect towards her on the part of a man was denounced as disgraceful to him, especially to a Samurai. Love affairs were nothing but wantonness, and the word for sexual love, *koi*, was associated with degeneracy.[1] Marriage was contracted and arranged by the parents, who did not pay as much attention to the inclination or desire of the persons concerned as to the ranks or properties of the families to be linked by the tie of marriage or the choice of the parents themselves.

Quite naturally, under these circumstances, the sexual instinct often sought irregular outlets, that was partly an inheritance from the age of war and confusion but largely a product of the new age. Houses of ill-fame were established by government licence in segregated settlements, which were regarded as outside the regular standards of morality. Both the Samurai and the bourgeoisie discovered or rather created there a "paradise of gaiety," where freedom and equality prevailed in many respects. In spite of the many undesirable aspects of these resorts, they gave an opportunity for the display of defiance of conventional fetters and free play to the spirit of revolt cherished by the citizens against the ruling class. Wealth and rank often yielded there to gallantry ; the women, too, exhibited *otoko-gi*, an unyielding spirit of manliness. Some of these, courtesans though they were, became strong heroines, who asserted freedom and strength in repelling powerful lords or wealthy magnates, often sacrificing themselves for the sake of humbler lovers. Conflicts

[1] Herein was a reaction of the military men and orthodox Confucianists against the sentimental romanticism of the court nobles who had ruled in Miyako centuries before, together with its literature, the Yamato poetry full of poems and stories of love. Chinese poetry was considered to be nobler, more masculine, than Japanese.

between convention and freedom, wealth and love, scrupulousness and dauntlessness, were the subjects of many tragedies or tragi-comedies enacted in these places.[1]

The conflict between convention and instinct occurred in many quarters, among the Samurai and the people alike. Not only love affairs between young people, but even the relations between husband and wife suffered from the intervention of parents and relatives, even of neighbours. The interference was based on considerations or pretexts of family honour or the public opinion of the commune, either of which might be sufficient to divorce a loving couple. This external sanction was summed up in the word *giri*, which meant literally " duty and reason," and was understood in a narrow conventional sense. In contrast to *giri*, human instincts, lower and higher, were summarized in one word *ninjō ;* conflict between *giri* and *ninjō* became the order of the day in the family and social life. There were many cases of outbreaks of revolt and desperate fights on the part of the strong or passionate, but more numerous were the cases of weaker characters yielding to the pressure of the intervention but becoming debauched out of despair. Another way of solution often resorted to was the joint death of the loving couple, and this was called *shinju*, literally " whole-hearted fidelity." Many Romeos and Juliets, deriving consolation from the Buddhist promise of repeated rebirths, died in the hope that they might be joined in love in future existences, escaping the fetters of the present.

These tragedies, sacrifices to the conventional morality of the age, furnished much material for the novels and dramas

[1] In the majority of the stories, the heroine was a courtesan eminent for beauty and courage. Her lover was usually a refined but poor Samurai or merchant. The opponent of their love was a Samurai of higher rank but unworthy character. Usually the solution was the triumph of courage and fidelity over power or wealth. This outcome was rejoiced at by the audience, when the story was acted on the stage. Cf. Brinkley, *Japan*, vol. iv, pp. 145-47. This category of plays is still played on the stage even to-day.

of the Genroku era and following centuries.[1]  The sentimental reaction of literature of this kind was naturally great and extensive.  Readers and spectators, young and old, and even those who were acting the rôle of the oppressors in actual life, shed profuse tears of sympathy with the unfortunate lovers and applauded their fidelity.  One case of the *shinju* suicide would inspire others and cause them to take the same step, because unhappy love was pretty wide-spread in those times and the case was usually represented in an idealized way. This sympathy implied also a discontent against the fetters of social conventions, yet no one was strong enough to raise a public protest against the prevailing custom.  The sufferers sacrificed themselves in silence, while those who had passed that stage often became oppressors themselves, the cruelty of mothers-in-law towards daughters-in-law becoming proverbial.

### *The Culture and Art of Genroku*

In spite of the increasing pressure of the class rule, the spirit of daring was still alive among the people, especially the wardsmen of Yedo known as *Otoko-date*, the " Gallant Fellows " [2] ; love of valour and hatred of cowardice played a great part in their life.  A combination of the love of adventure, a survival from the age of war, and the proclivity to sensuousness, a sign of the new age, marked the era of Genroku.  This combination was exhibited in a pompous manner of life, in gay robes of striking colours and bold designs, as

[1] Chikamatsu (1653-1724), sometime called the "Shakespeare of Japan," was a great writer of these tragedies, besides his historical plays.  His material was taken from the occurrences of his day.
Cf. Aston, *Japanese Literature*, pp. 273-80 ; Florenz, *Geschichte der japanischen Litteratur*, pp. 592-95 ; Miyamori, *Masterpieces of Chikamatsu* (London, 1926), in which some of his love-tragedies are told.  In recent days a similar tragedy of an unhappy couple had a wide circulation ; its English translation—*Namiko*.

[2] Cf. Mitford (Lord Redesdale), *Tales of Old Japan*, a chapter on the stories of the Otoko-date.

well as stories of adventure or triumph of the valiant over the wicked. There was an air of freedom, seeking vents for self-assertion even under the oppression of social conventions ; there was a force of aspiration, though vague in aim and incapable of taking a free course. The culture of Genroku shows in many respects a continuation of the exhilarating spirit of the sixteenth century but at the same time its struggle with the heavy pressure accumulating from above.[1] A negative manifestation of this struggle was the love tragedies spoken of above, but a positive expression was shown more and more in the pretentious life of the rich bourgeoisie, with its accompanying manifestations in art.

The art of Genroku marked a change of temper on the part of its patrons, a turn from the exotic art of Zen to an enjoyment of beauty in life. The orthodox Kano Academy patronized by the government and aristocrats represented the old idealistic painting in form but was losing its spirit and vitality, while the new school of decorative art and *genre* painting grew out of the life and temper of the rising bourgeoisie. The greatest representative of the decorative art of this period was Kōrin (1658-1716), a rich merchant and artist. His art was partly a development of the renaissance of the Peach Hill, but his original genius was representative of the ethos of his time and signalized the coming reign of beauty. The *Ukiyo-ye*, the painting of life, followed the decorative school and further exalted daily life and its pleasures. The artists of these new schools arose among the people, worked for them, and became champions of democratic art, in contrast to the old school patronized by

---

[1] This accumulation of pressure is visible in the architecture of Nikkō, as for example, which was executed in the middle of the seventeenth century. The ill-proportioned heavy roofing and the sheer splendour of overcrowded decoration on pillars and friezes are emblematic of the social convention beginning to be burdensome upon the aspiring spirit, which struggled to express itself in the lavish use of engravings.

the aristocracy. Even the masters of the old school were induced to take up the new style, but kept it entirely apart from their own tradition, working on the new in disguise or anonymously. This meant a partial yielding of the old art to the new, and the aristocracy itself did not refrain from enjoying the *genre* in private. The term *ukiyo* which meant literally the " floating world " had suggested melancholy, the transitoriness of life, but now it was modified to a designation of the worldly life full of pleasure and enjoyment. The decorative school degenerated later to mannerisms, but the *genre* painting achieved a comparatively healthy development and continued to be the ruling force of popular art throughout the Tokugawa régime.[1]

The general tendency of the new era ran counter to the contemplative mood of the past centuries as shown in the exotic art of Zen. Yet the spiritual influence of Buddhism did not die out but found a fresh expression in a style of popular poetry. This is known by the name *Haikai* or *Hokku*, a line of verse complete in seventeen syllables.[2] Its great master was Bashō (1642-94) who lived nearly his whole life in close contact with nature, improvising on his journeys, thus evidently emulating the spirit and life of Saigyō, the monk-poet of the twelfth century. While Saigyō was purely a poet of nature, Bashō never lost contact with life, connecting various phases of human life with the changing aspects of

---

[1] It is a curious fortune of Japanese art that it became known to the Occident first through the *Ukiyo-ye*, not highly respected by the Japanese themselves. But the appreciation of it in the West has reacted upon them and it is now finding a proper place in art. Anyway we note that the poor appreciation of the *genre* was due to the aristocratic bias of the Tokugawa period.

[2] *Haikai* meant originally an amusement in versifying the first and last parts of a *tanka* of thirty-one syllables done by two or more persons. It involved a witty task of completing a verse as a joint work. *Hokku* was the first half of the improvised poem but it developed into an independent art of composing something humorous. Bashō gave quite a different tone to both *haikai* and *hokku*. Cf. p. 236

Cf. B. H. Chamberlain, *Ancient Japanese Poetry*; P. L. Couchoud, *Poètes d'Asie*, chapter on *Les epigrammes lyriques*.

nature.   Bashō was eminent for his fresh, joyous mood and democratic sentiment, in contrast to the mournful temperament of the wandering monk.[1]   He kept himself aloof from the commotion of the world but the phases of life which touched his sentiment gave joy to his serene and pure mind, making him a poet of wit and humour too.   Any trifle with which Bashō came into touch, a frog jumping into the water or a dragon-fly on a grass blade, stars twinkling between the leaves of mimosa, or peasant women cleaning potatoes in a rivulet, these and other scenes might be caught up by his poetic genius and wrought into a *hokku* poem, with subtle, often witty, touches of sentiment.

Bashō warned his disciples never to regard this art of rhyming as a mere amusement but to refine its taste and sense as a Way, namely, a way of spiritual training and purification, which could be realized only by a high flight of idealism and in sympathetic unison with human life and incidents of nature.   Thus his poetry was not mere literary art, but an expression of a contemplative mood and of serene composure of mind.   He tried to formulate his religion of nature or of beauty in more or less philosophic terms :

The secret of poetry lies in treading the middle path between the 'reality' and 'vacuity' of the world and in living a life unfettered and soaring, never bewildered by vicissitudes of life, never disturbed by gain or loss.   Grace of expression and delicacy of sentiment can be secured only through this spiritual training.   'Grace' (*sugata* or *omomuki*), 'Delicacy' (*hosomi*), and 'Serenity' (*sabi*), these are the three requisites for realizing the middle path between reality and vacuity.

In short Bashō's poetry in its religious background was a union of Tendai philosophy with the naturalism and quietism of Zen and Taoism.

---

[1] Bashō seldom stuck to one dwelling yet he loved his little hut in a quiet district of Yedo which was surrounded by *bashō* (banana plants), hence his name—*bashō* being a regular symbol of evanescence in Buddhist poetry.   The leaves of the banana plants are easily broken by the wind, therefore the symbolism.   His hut was in Fukagawa, now a district of factories and slums.

It was the Haikai poetry that transformed the antiquated poetry into a vernacular of light touch and yet often of profound sentiment. It is no wonder that this popular art aroused and trained the poetic taste of the masses, inviting them to a calm enjoyment or humorous observation of life and nature even in the midst of a busy life. It perpetuated the spirit of Zen culture in this modified form, and associated itself with the tea ceremony, flower arrangement, the gardening of miniature landscapes, pilgrimages to famous places, pleasure trips amid hills and waters, and similar tranquillizing pastimes so dear to the hearts of the Japanese people. The pursuit of those pastimes, an easy-going combination of contemplation and enjoyment, is called the " Way of Air and Stream " (*Fūryū no Michi*), *i.e.*, living and enjoying life with the mind free and transparent like air, fresh and abounding like streams.

# PEACE, REFINEMENT, AND DEGENERATION

THE most brilliant period of the Tokugawa culture was the eighteenth century. The consolidation of power had been achieved and the Shōgun ruled supreme. Yoshimune (Shōgun, 1716-45) mitigated the ban upon foreign culture and opened a way to the further introduction of Occidental science, which stimulated the intellectual life of the nation in various ways. The reign of Iyenari (1787-1837) marked the climax of the glories of the régime, but his luxurious life from the later part of his reign down to his death in 1841 bore witness to the degenerate tendency of the time in general. In spite of the rigid social structure established and of the Government's efforts for maintaining the status of the Samurai class, new tendencies and the demands for freedom manifested themselves in various ways. The first part of the century was marked by the rise of the common people, especially the merchant class, and by the renewed introduction of Western culture through Dutch sources. But towards its close signs became visible of the decline of the Tokugawa régime.

The solid rule of the Tokugawa was based upon a rigid stratification of classes. The Samurai class made up a hierarchy of positions and emoluments; similarly the people were divided into classes and their status was hereditary and almost unchangeable. The details of abode, food, and dress were fixed according to the classes and occupations; the manners of speech, salutation, walking and sitting, and many other things were rigidly prescribed. In short, every detail of life was assigned to each class and individual by laws and customs.

Despite these strict measures, the growth of the merchant class in wealth gave impetus to their ambition, while the Samurai, in spite of their rank, were often obliged to bow before wealth.  The Samurai were compelled to live a life of frugality, partly due to their ethical teaching and in consideration of others' opinions, but largely to their fixed income in emolument.  On the other hand, the merchants were able to raise their standard of living, in some cases to an excess of luxury.  Such were punished by confiscation of their property, as their pretentious life was judged to be " beyond the proper limit of their status."  The measures against luxury and the sumptuary laws issued repeatedly proved to be ineffective before the rising tide of the people's claims.  Officially, the Samurai stood higher but the merchants were really better off ;  the maintenance of the dignity of the Samurai became more and more difficult as the stress of their domestic finance increased, while their inclination to imitate the merchants' way of living made their morale and finances worse.  The social strata were now being remoulded.   The situation was aggravated when the Shōgun Iyenari departed from the strict policy of his earlier years and became himself extravagant and debauched.  The Shōgun's example was imitated by the feudal lords and the higher Samurai ;  fiscal deficiency was frequently covered by loans raised almost by force from the rich people.  Thus towards the end of the eighteenth century, the rise of the people and the degradation of the Samurai were reducing the established social distinctions to mere form and empty titles, and this was one of the causes which led to the fall of the Tokugawa régime.

The strict measures carried out in the first years of Iyenari's reign by the advice of his minister Sadanobu (1787-93) pursued the principles of the Tokugawa Government to their logical consequences, aiming at unity of ideas, uniformity of moral standards, gradation of classes, and so on.

He issued sumptuary regulations and enforced them with renewed vigour ;[1] even the court ladies of the Shōgun, always difficult to manage, were put under the strict rule laid down by the laws. The training of the Samurai in literary and military arts was systematically encouraged and super-intended. Every book or picture of an indecent nature was suppressed and its author and publisher mercilessly punished, some imprisoned and some exiled. Any idea or proposition deviating from orthodox Confucianism, except Buddhism, was forbidden expression and circulation, and in 1790 the famous prohibition of all the heterodox schools of Confucian-ism was proclaimed. These measures seemed for a while to work towards restoring sobriety of mind and uniformity of life and manners. But such artificial means of restraint merely imposed from above could not last long. The reform, moreover, was largely nullified by the Shōgun himself in his reactionary indulgence, and the same reaction took hold of all classes. Still worse, the severe rules remained officially on paper and were repeatedly but inconsistently enforced. The result was the prevalence of hypocrisy on the part of the comparatively submissive, or sarcastic ridicule of the reign on the part of the stronger. Bold thinkers expressed them-selves in some way, but always in disguise ; some Confucian-ists gave up their philosophical thinking and devoted them-selves to versifying, accompanied by drinking. Men of letters wrote jests under a disguise of sobriety or uttered serious things in joke.

As a result of the strict censorship, didactic romances came into vogue, in which figured incarnations of virtues or vices and their fate always demonstrated the triumph of virtue. Even the writers of obscene literature published their writings with the excuse of being didactic, merely by concluding the stories with some moralizations on the final

[1] Cf Hearn, *Japan*, pp. 182-86, 188-90 ; Brinkley, *Japan*, vol. iv, pp. 157-73

fate of the lewd persons therein depicted. These moral lessons in novels and romances were chiefly based on the fatalistic theory of an unfailing law of retribution, whether in the fate of an individual or in the fortune of a family. Herein were combined the Buddhist doctrine of Karma and the Confucian teaching of moral retribution. Since this combination was a reflection of the authoritative ethics and social conventions, these stories represented mere submission, not strong moral conviction, on the part of the author or readers. All contained moral lessons and there was no tragedy of character. Thus the censorship seemed successful, but the tranquillity was only superficial, being peace and order in the iron fetters of oppression. The people lived in apparent contentment, like " frogs in a deep well " ; yet human nature could never remain altogether passive ; it sought some vent for its active expression.

The exhilarating spirit of the Genroku renaissance had long before passed away, and the Epicureanism of the peaceful reign had further been modified by the interferences of the sumptuary laws. The enjoyment of life was veiled by apparent sobriety, and æsthetic refinement was exhibited in perverted ways of over-refinement. Every activity was narrowed down to circumscribed limits, and within the limits tempered, re-tempered, and over-wrought to extremes. The individual mind had either to submit itself blindly to the prescription, or to cherish revolt in silence and to become cynical. Even a didactic writer like Bakin (1767-1848) tried to find an outlet for his active mind in ideal stories of adventure outside Japan or in fantastic descriptions of imaginary lands and peoples.[1]

Buddhist preachers endeavoured only to attract the fancy of the hearers by extravagant narrations of paradises and

[1] Cf. Aston, *Japanese Literature*, pp. 359-360 ; Anesaki, *Japanese Mythology*, chapter X ; B. H. Chamberlain, *The Japanese Gulliver*, in *TASJ*, vol. 7, part III.

hells, or by romantic stories of ancient religious leaders. Painting became in general stylized and conventional, while some bold artists found their own satisfaction in monstrosities. Dwarf trees, miniature landscapes, minute carvings called *netsuke*, generally of ivory—these things were the outcome of the temper and current of the age. Men of letters wrote affected poems over their *saké* cups, and this was their desperate consolation, Some met for competition in drinking and gluttony, an extravagant indulgence and at the same time a curious self-torture. Sarcastic humour was heaped upon the Samurai, who knew only how to talk about " *bum-bu*," *i.e.*, accomplishments in literary (*bun*) and military (*bu*) arts. " Ah! bum-bu! bum-bu! " said a cynic writer, himself a Samurai, " they are like buzzing mosquitoes disturbing my sleep! "

# POPULAR TEACHERS IN RELIGION
# AND ETHICS

## *Popular Education and the Shingaku Movement*

THE establishment of the orthodox system of ethics had
another consequence, the neglect of educational influence
upon the common people. There was no system of public
education, instruction being left in the hands of poor schoolmasters who taught in wretched private schools only element-
ary lessons in reading, writing, and counting.[1] Moral instruction was given at home, having regard mostly to the sense of
shame[2] or sensitiveness towards the views of the community.
Buddhist priests had also great influence in this respect,
since they were moral overseers of the parish, exercising their
influence upon the life of the people mainly through the
religious census. These forms of moral influence were useful
and effective in the village districts where the commune
played a great part in life and the parish priests were highly
respected, but in the town the communal bond was weaker
and the parish priest was less intimate with the parishioners.
There the merchant class was growing in power and wealth,
and with luxury corruption crept in. The clerks in the
business houses were exposed to temptations, yet there was
no provision for their moral training.

To fill this gap, an ethical movement arose in the middle
of the eighteenth century, which was humanitarian in prin-
cir'e and popular in method. The movement was called

---

[1] Cf. Brinkley, *Japan,* vol. iv, pp. 136-41.

[2] Japanese, *hazukashii,* which stood for " voice of conscience " or moral sanction
in general.

*Shingaku,* or " Mental Learning," which meant the culture of conscience.   Its originator, Ishida Baigan (1685-1744), born of a peasant family, passed his early years as a clerk in a mercantile house in Miyako until the forty-second year of his age.   During this period of his life, he made good use of his leisure hours in studying Confucian writings and training himself in Zen meditation.   Not being content with his own attainment, he retired from business and devoted his whole time to study and spiritual culture.   Finally, being convinced of the soundness of his principle, and seeing the necessity of moral influence among the young employees of the business houses, this self-made teacher appeared in public, when he was forty-five years old (in 1729), as a popular lecturer on practical morality, and succeeded in attracting many hearers and adherents among the merchant classes.   His work was continued by Teshima To-an (1718-86) who carried out his master's plan more extensively and systematic-ally in Miyako and its vicinity.   The movement was trans-ferred to Yedo, in 1791, by the retired head of a rich firm, of the name of Nakazawa Dōji (1725-1803).   The governor of Yedo, aware of the needs of the time, patronized the pro-paganda, though not publicly.   The movement was extended to some other commercial centres and continued to exist until quite recent times in Tōkyō.

Shingaku as a doctrine was an eclecticism, aiming at uniting the moral teachings of all the religions and ethical systems prevailing in Japan, tempering them with the general principles of humanitarian ethics and mental culture.   The soul, it was taught, is the reflex of the heavenly reason in the individual, an idea common to Buddhism and Confucian-ism.   As a mirror, when perfectly smooth and clean, reflects every object faithfully and clearly, so our soul gives unerring guidance to our life, when it thinks and wills in accordance with the voice of the innermost conscience.   The training in listening to this voice is true Mental Culture ; benevolence, patience, faithfulness, and vigilance are the cardinal virtues, the means as well as the aim of spiritual exercise and moral life. " Flowers bloom pink, willow leaves are green, each according to its nature ; the crow caws and the sparrow twitters, each lives and moves by its nature. Why could not mankind alone among creatures behave similarly (according to nature) ? " Thus preached the Shingaku masters. Man's true and original nature, they explained, consists in living a virtuous life, virtue being his nature, yet he does otherwise, simply because he is misguided by selfishness, the root of all vices and ills. Thus the Shingaku teachers identify human nature with natural order and the latter with moral order, because all the three amount to the life of the cosmic soul. In this respect Shingaku was in sympathy with Zen Buddhism. Its teachers inherited a great deal from the Yōmei teaching of the " Prime Conscience " in emphasizing the necessity of cultivating the original purity of the soul, though applying it in a submissive attitude towards the existing order of social life. The ethics of Shingaku emphasized the importance of moral order, which amounted to assigning to everyone his duty and destiny in accordance with his social position and vocation. In this respect Shingaku was a product of the age and paid great respect to social traditions and communal laws and also encouraged the Shinto communal cult and ancestor worship.[1]

Shingaku teachers tried to mitigate the hostility between Buddhism and Confucianism, an antagonism which was puzzling the people as to the authoritative standard of their moral life. This negative task was supplemented by showing the fundamental identity of all religions and exhorting the people to the practice of the ethical truths underlying de-

[1] Some Shingaku sermons are reproduced in Mitford (Lord Redesdale), *Tales of Old Japan.*

nominational differences.   This insistence was natural in a movement which had in view the practical morality of the people at large, who little cared for the subtle polemics directed by the Confucianists against Buddhism, much less for doctrinal disputes among the Buddhists.   These popular teachers worked among the merchants and instructed them by lectures and writings, persuasive in tone and easy and intelligible to all men and women.   The movement flourished with great success until the end of the Tokugawa régime, but gradually dwindled into insignificance under the régime of Meiji, when the conservative character of its teaching no longer answered the demands of the new era.

### Sontoku and His Hōtoku Movement

While the Shingaku teaching was flourishing among the prosperous merchants, there arose in the first part of the nineteenth century another movement among the peasants, who were suffering from heavy taxation and frequent failure of crops.   The originator of this movement was Ninomiya Sontoku (1787-1856), often called the " Peasant Sage." [1] His teaching was called *Hōtoku,* or the doctrine of " Recompense " (or indebtedness), because it emphasized the indebtedness of mankind to nature and to fellowship among themselves.[2]   Man's true nature, Sontoku taught, consists in pious devotion to the order of nature, which manifests itself in the moral order of human life, especially in the relation between the lord and his subjects, parents and children, benefactor and recipient in general, expressed in grace and gratitude.   Nature evolves and changes by itself, but man has

---

[1] Cf. R. C. Armstrong, *Ninomiya Sontoku, the Peasant Sage* (*TASJ*, vol. 38, part II, 1910) ;   T. Yoshimoto, *A Peasant Sage of Japan* (London, 1912).

[2] *Toku* meant virtue, order, benefit, and *hōtoku* recompense of indebtedness identified with virtue and benefit, on the part both of benefactor and benefited. This identification of virtue and benefit marks the utilitarian trait of Sontoku's ethics.

to conquer his instinctive selfishness and endeavour to conform to the moral order of life. Similarly, our life is sustained
largely by the bounties of nature towards which we ought to
be grateful, but the gifts of nature cannot be benefits without
our own effort. Essential to this effort are moral sincerity
and economical frugality. Sincerity is nothing but conforming
one's life to the cosmic order ; effort means a certain control
of nature, shown most clearly in agriculture, while frugality
is an outcome of the sense of indebtedness, gratitude for the
benefit bestowed.

This teaching of morality was combined by Sontoku with
economic measures, such as a scheme for the rotation of crops,
an organization for the circulation of capital, accumulation
of funds for famine relief, and so on. Thus Sontoku viewed
human life as a stage of co-operation and mutual helpfulness,
and in practice combined moral ideas with economic measures.
His influence bore practical effects among the peasants, and
a number of impoverished villages were restored to prosperity.

In comparing Hōtoku with Shingaku, we see interesting
similarities and differences. Both were neither sectarian nor
doctrinal but entirely practical. They were more or less
eclectic and attempted to extract from various religions what
was beneficial to practical ethics and popular instruction.
In this respect they were useful supplements to official ethics
and they achieved much good among the people. As their
teaching was adapted to the needs of the respective spheres
of their activity, so their later development was differentiated
according to the circumstances of the peasants and merchants.
The Hōtoku teaching emphasized energy and work for the
agricultural population, while the Shingaku movement was
eminent in inculcating peace and submission, as the merchant
class had to live an orderly life within prescribed limits.
Shingaku ended its task with the fall of the Tokugawa régime
in consequence of the change in the merchant class brought

forth by the new spirit and methods of commercial enterprise. On the other hand, the Hōtoku movement continues to this day and still exercises some influence in the country districts, so far as the life of the farmer class has undergone comparatively little change. Yet this will not last long now since the farmer class too are undergoing deep changes due to the rising conflict between landowners and tenants. At any rate, these two movements for the people were significant phenomena in the age when Confucian ethics held sway over the upper classes and the people were neglected.

### The Work of Buddhists

The activity of Buddhists in this long reign of peace was of two kinds, one the learned work of elaborating doctrinal systems, and the other the practical work of popular preaching. In the course of the seventeenth century and early in the eighteenth most of the Buddhist scriptures and writings were collected and printed, and the learned monks proceeded to systematize their respective doctrines.[1] This learned work furnished each Buddhist Church with a system of orthodox dogmas, which implied necessarily the suppression of dissension; and the dispute between the orthodox teachers and the heretics went sometimes so far that appeal for a decision was made to the government authorities. The meddling of the officials with the subtle dogmatic discussions brought about some tragi-comic situations — the heretics being imprisoned for a long period awaiting a decision, but the decision whether

---

[1] To mention some of the eminent names in this connection: Ninchō (1645-1711), a Jōdo monk, made a careful collation of the whole Buddhist scriptures; Eku (1644-1721) and Jinrei (1749-1817) systematized the doctrine of the Shinshū Church and left many writings and disciples; Hōtan (1657-1738) revived the ancient school of Kegon philosophy and wrote over forty works, systematic and polemic; Fujaku (1707-1781) and Jiun (1718-1804) were strict observers of monastic discipline and also writers of many books on discipline and morality. Of Jiun we shall speak below.

they were orthodox or heretic was subject to the arbitrary judgment of the officials. Much energy was spent in the fight against heretics within a Church, partly due to the zeal on the part of the ecclesiastical authorities to enforce the standard teaching of the organized Church, but partly due to the general tendency of human nature to find some vent for the energy suppressed under the prohibition of aggressive propaganda outside. In spite of this, however, interdenominational polemics raged also, but they took more the form of academic discussion than religious proselytizing. Curiously enough, the Jōdo men, the followers of the pietist Hōnen, were foremost in the erudite elaboration of dogma ; and the Shinshū men were most ardent in fighting heresy among themselves.[1] These two bodies were engaged in disputes not only on doctrinal matters but over the title Shinshū, namely, on the question whether the Shinshū men were entitled to call themselves the followers of the " True Doctrine." It goes without saying that behind these disputes lay motives connected with interests and privileges.

On the other hand, the practical work of Buddhists was almost limited to preaching, except for some cases of relief work, because extensive religious activity could not be carried on without overstepping denominational lines which was forbidden as menacing the *status quo*. A Zen monk Hakuin (1685-1768) was a witty preacher and a great master of Zen training.[2] His pamphlets on Buddhist morality are incisive and entertaining and are enjoyed even to-day by many people. Ji-un (1718-1804) was a disciplinarian but at the

[1] In spite of this the *Hiji-monto*, or " Secret followers," the Shinshū heresy referred to before, p. 232, remained untouched. It is very striking that the high-handed authorities left them unmolested although their existence was well known.

[2] An anecdote told about Hakuin, a case of calumny invented by a pregnant girl, has so much similarity to the story of St. Mariane, that we may suspect an influence of the Catholic legend. The story of St. Mariane was circulated among the Japanese Catholics of the seventeenth century, and we have a written record of it among the objects confiscated from them.

same time a popular preacher and his sermons on the Buddhist Ten Commandments were widely circulated.[1]  But preaching became in general an art of specialists ; most of the learned monks kept themselves aloof from it as if it were disgraceful. The result was an over-refinement of preaching as an art, and degenerate mannerism crept into it, such as a peculiarly affected voice and articulation in utterance or the use of bluish powder on the shaven head of the preacher, or even to the extreme of suddenly changing dress during the preaching.  This degeneration of preaching made deeper the gap existing between the men of learning and the preaching priests, and the division worked to accelerate the further corruption of preachers and preaching.  In short, Buddhist activity shared the fate of every other social movement, being allowed only within narrowly prescribed limits and tending naturally to over-refinement and degeneracy.

[1] The sermons have been translated into English by J. L. Atkinson and G. W. Bouldin, though their rendering leaves much to be desired.  Cf. *TASJ*, vols. 33, 35, 36. 41.

# REVIVAL OF SHINTO

*Philological Study and National Ideas*

WE have mentioned a revival of Shinto in alliance with Confucianism in the beginning of the seventeenth century. In the course of the eighteenth century, Shinto entered a new path and prepared for another revival to follow. All the earlier Shinto theorists had depended much upon either Buddhism or Confucianism in interpreting Shinto ideas ; now the time became ripe for purging away the alien elements to a certain degree and restoring by means of scholarship the primitive religion of Japan. This was made possible by the philological studies of the ancient records compiled in the eighth century. Keichū (1640-1701), a Buddhist monk, was a pioneer in this work, having succeeded in deciphering the curious orthography of the *Mannyō-shū*, the Anthology of Myriad Leaves, which was almost illegible and had remained neglected for a long time. His work was carried further by Mabuchi (1697-1769), who was induced by his love of archaic poetry to the advocacy of Japanese ideas as they were supposed to have been before the introduction of foreign civilization. The movement along this line was associated with the royalist conceptions advocated by the Mito school of Confucianism ; moreover, the long peace strengthened the belief in the divine dignity of the throne,[1] which stimulated the rise of Shinto ideas and in turn was reinforced by them.

[1] The imperial court in Miyako was compelled to keep itself aloof from politics, but this seclusion " within the ninefold rings of clouds " was favourable to its dignity verging on sanctity. The foreign representatives who came to Japan in the middle of the nineteenth century were puzzled as to the real political constitution of Japan. But they were not entirely mistaken when they assigned to the *Tycoon* (Shōgun) the actual sovereignty and to the *Micado* a sort of popedom.

The greatest of the philologists and the pioneer of " Pure Shinto " [1] was Moto-ori Norinaga (1730-1801). Having succeeded in annotating the ancient writings, particularly the *Kojiki* which he interpreted as a faithful record of primitive Japan, he proceeded to an attempt at restoring pure Shinto, as he conceived it. A conscientious philologist yet a patriotic theorist, he explained the original life of the Japanese as representing the primitive purity of mankind, and rejected all teachings of metaphysics and ethics as a sign of degeneracy. His ideal world was the abode of the gods, the Japanese garden of Eden, so to speak, and in this respect he was sympathetic to the Taoist denunciation of all system and artifice in human life. In short, his contention was that the Japanese and their Shinto, when purged of all foreign accretions and influences, represented the pure, and therefore the best, inheritance of humanity from the divine ages.

Moto-ori's work was continued by Hirata Atsutané (1776-1843), a man of great ability but a bigot of doubtful character. He had never met Moto-ori but deemed himself to be his disciple and apostle, and pursued the contentions of the master to their consequences. Through the zeal of this man the Shinto revival took a definite form in vigorous propaganda, and his disciples tried to carry its chauvinistic ideas into practice in the anti-foreign movement in the nineteenth century.

The chief contention of Hirata was essentially the same as Moto-ori's and he directed vehement attacks upon Buddhism and Confucianism. Yet, on the other hand, he was acquainted with Western science and some elements of Christianity, probably through Chinese sources, and we can discern their influence in some points of his teaching. In his zeal to construct a system of cosmology and theology he went a step

---

[1] Called *Fukko* or *Ko*, *i.e.*, "restored to antiquity." For this movement see . M. Satow, *The Revival of Pure Shinto*, in *TASJ*, vol. 3, part I, Appendix.

beyond the traditional idea of the supremacy of the Sun-goddess, giving preference to the much disputed deity Ame-no-minaka-nushi (the Heavenly-Central-Lord), and taught a doctrine of creation. The Creator, according to Hirata, ruled the universe, residing in the region of the Polar Star ;[1] and the heavenly deities worked under the Creator for the good of mankind, especially of the Japanese who were their direct descendants. Hirata taught that Japan among the nations of the world was nearest the Polar Star ; that the earth was globular with a gourd-like appendage, the Land of Gloom, and so on. Moreover, according to him, Japan, the land of the gods, had no need of formulating moral teachings or of codifying laws ; the pure hearts of the people always retained the divine purity. This purity was, however, much contamin-ated by foreign teachings, which were distortions from the original divine teaching, the Way of the Gods. Thus the first need of the nation was to expurgate all the contaminations and to restore her life to its original purity. This proposition is subject to various interpretations and applications ; and, in fact, the followers of Hirata to-day are attempting to apply his chauvinistic ideas to the present situation.

Hirata's contention of the divine character of the Japanese nation was interwoven with the conception of the divine origin of the throne, and his followers made some contribution to the restoration of the imperial régime. Their influence upon the religious policy of the new government will be dealt with later.

## The Rise of Popular Theism

There was another aspect to the revival of Shinto, namely, the appearance of popular teachers in the first half of the nine-teenth century. Most of them are known as Shintoists and their followers to-day make up the so-called Shinto sects ;

---

[1] It was a popular Taoist doctrine that the Supreme Ruler dwelt in that region of heaven. Hirata shared his master's sympathy with Taoist naturalism.

but in reality most of them derived their inspiration from occult practices prevalent among the mountaineer priests, whose formal affiliation to either Shinto or Buddhism was only a matter of convention. The only loophole for them, under the strict rules of ecclesiastical administration, was to organize mountaineer pilgrims into a kind of fraternity called *kōsha*, though the membership was not necessarily permanent. Within the fraternity and specially during the mountaineer period, the leader exercised spiritual sway over the members ; the leadership was perpetuated by the leader's son or ablest disciple, while the followers often continued allegiance for generations ; thus in some cases the fraternity became a kind of religious order, despite the official allegiance of each member to a Buddhist Church. These teachers and their followers cherished certain kinds of faith peculiar to themselves, and some of them were men of intense religious experiences. They represented the crude, but comparatively pure, religious spirit buried in the heart of the people ; their religion had remained beneath the surface during the reign of perfect stability, when the government and Buddhist authorities kept strict vigilance over religion and made any new move wellnigh impossible. Now, when the Tokugawa régime began to give way to various agitations, these popular religions proceeded to appear in public and finally to achieve an independent growth. Some of these popular religious leaders organized their followers by more or less formulating their teachings, affiliating themselves to Shinto.

Besides religious fraternities for mountaineering pilgrimages, there appeared from time to time teachers of popular religion who inspired their followers by their own faith independent of any official religion. They worked among the people without any formal ordination or authorization and often were persecuted on that account by the Buddhist priests as their illicit rivals. These teachers appeared mostly in localities where the Buddhist priesthood was indolent.

A noteworthy fact in this movement is that chronologically the first and last of these popular teachers were women and that both of them taught a strongly theistic doctrine with prophetic utterances, warning people of the approach of a great world change to be brought about by their religion. Another remarkable point is that the first one and her religion remained entirely unknown until quite recently, in spite of a fairly large following, while the last attained a great fame even in her lifetime and her followers make up the largest Shinto body to-day. This latter is now known by the name of Tenri-kyō, or religion of " Heavenly Reason," and though its ascendancy belongs to the next period, we shall speak of its founder together with the other.

The first woman teacher was Kino (1756-1826), a peasant woman in Owari. Her religion had no name until its " discovery " by a scholar in 1927, and even now, when the followers begin to feel the need of a title, its official title is simply *Konotabi, i.e.,* "This Time," while the discoverer calls it the religion of *Nyorai,* or of *Isson,* " The Unique Reverend." An explanation of these titles will cover the essential points of this religion. Kino, the woman founder, had been an orphan and her married life ended in divorce. Her single life thenceforward was that of a servant until the forty-sixth year of her age, when she was suddenly called to her great mission through an inspiration. Her proclamation was that all the existing religions were incapable to save mankind whose life was immersed in sins, and that " this time " she was called to reveal the truth and to save the whole of humanity. Thus she deemed herself the saviour, the " Unique Reverend," transmitting the real and final message of God, whom she called *Nyorai,* the Japanese equivalent of Buddhist Tathāgata. This borrowing of a Buddhist term may suggest a certain amount of Buddhist heritage, yet her teaching had almost nothing to do with Buddhism but was entirely original, although it may be suspected of some contact with the Kirishitan creed. She taught the creation of the world by God, all Buddhas and deities being subordinate to him. God, the creator, she taught, is omnipotent, his sole motive is love, and his aim the salvation of mankind. The creation of the first man and then of his fellows, their fall ; the evils and sins of human life ; the dependence of all, including salvation, on the creator ; the commission given to Kino to save mankind, the first and last chance for men to believe in her and to be saved ; her great agony before her death ; the statement she suffered not on her own account but on account of her fellow beings ; these and similar points of her teaching make us strongly suspect it of Kirishitan influence.[1] But here we are not so much concerned with the derivation, if it could be ascertained, as with the import of her theistic teaching.

When she died in 1826, after nearly twenty-five years of her religious activity, she had secured a fairly large following, consisting mostly of simple peasant folk who were organized in almost monastic discipline and concentrated their faith in the person of the leader. They kept a record of all her utterances faithfully and minutely and their religious service consisted of reciting them and of a Quaker-like meeting in prayerful meditation. They were persecuted, but they withstood it and later were better organized under the leadership of an ex-Zen monk into a group of three orders; the monks, nuns, and tertiaries. They never professed communism but

[1] Another point of suspicion is her name. Her own name was Kino, but she called herself *Rusen* as a kind of religious title designating her saviourship. This name reminds us of Lucena or Lucia. In fact something like these is occasionally found as a female name in the official registers of the descendants of Kirishitan martyrs and apostates—*Rusu* or *Rutsu* being not at all Japanese but certainly corruptions of Lucia or Lucena. Moreover, the appellation *Nyorai* applied to the deity of this religion may not suggest a Buddhist heritage, as stated above, but rather a Kirishitan influence, because the God of the Kirishitans was popularly called *Deus-Nyorai*.

the life of the monks and nuns is entirely communistic, all
their clothing being supplied by the whole group and every
one of them possessing nothing beyond a few necessaries
which they carry from place to place.   Their dwellings are
the meeting houses, simple cottages built and furnished by
themselves and their followers.   There are now more than
sixty of these houses, while the original house where the
founder lived is regarded as the centre, and the followers
meet there twice a year.   Thus this religion of the " Unique
Reverend " is a remarkable original product representing the
simple religious spirit of the people which manifested its
vitality under a régime of strict religious census and extreme
formalism in official religions.

Now we come to the chronologically last of the women
teachers, Miki (1798-1887), of Yamato, who being possessed
of a god announced the arrival of the " important moment "
(Shun kokugen) when she was forty years old, i.e., in 1838.
She had passed her childhood in pious devotion to the Buddha
Amita, had lived her married life as a submissive wife but
showing much charity to outsiders.   In the year given above
she was possessed by a god who called himself the Lord of
Heaven and commanded her whole family to dedicate everything to his cause for the sake of mankind.   From that time
her free giving became so extravagant that her husband and
relatives regarded her as having gone mad.   In poverty and
struggles she persisted in her faith in her god and her mission.
Fifteen years had passed in the struggle and when her husband
had died her family had almost nothing left of its properties
and her only sympathizer was her daughter.   The mother,
having forsaken everything of the world, now appeared as
the apostle of the new religion which amounted to the belief
in the God of Heaven and to the admonition to purify oneself.   The human being, she taught, is the abode of divine
charity, and the only obstacle is the greed together with all

that it implies.  Get rid of every stain of the soul, restore its original purity, everything will follow and end in happiness—union with the divine spirit.  The mother and daughter effected mental cures in the firm belief that all ills and maladies were simply due to illusion caused by greed and associate vices.  This teaching gradually attracted believers and in the course of further fifteen years the mother was regarded by her followers as the saviour of the world, which was to undergo a remarkable transformation because of her appearance.  They were persecuted, but the following grew, so that she was a very prominent religious leader in her province at the time when the Tokugawa fell and the new government was inaugurated.  Thenceforward the last twenty years of her life were a period of the rapid growth of her religion, in spite of persecution renewed under the new régime.

During this period she started writing down the divine messages in verses of thirty-one syllables and she also organized a method of worship with dances and movements of the hands.  Besides the simple teaching of the purity of heart and the practice of healing, she amplified her idea of the arrival of the " moment " by teaching that there was a spot near her home where the divinity would come down and consummate the transformation of the world.  The place was called *Kanro-dai*, the " Terrace of Nectar," but there was nothing installed, the spot being now covered by a gigantic temple.  By consecrating this spot she believed she had prepared for the coming of a new world, a restoration of the age of the gods, of which she was the prophetess, to be realized in the future.

A more definite organization of this religion belongs to the next period, and here we shall close the part treating of the two woman teachers by pointing out two features of these movements.  One is the idea of a transformed world in which a vague consciousness of the falling régime is combined with an ideal aspiration for a better world, a human world saturated with divine spirit. The other point is the strong tendency to discard all doctrinal subtleties and to establish a religion of the simple pure heart. These tendencies were shared by other teachers and those who were more decidedly Shintoists emphasized the expected change of régime with patriotic ardour combined with articulate protests against the Tokugawa Government, and insomuch were political rather than religious.

However, Kurozumi Munetada (1779-1849), one of the Shinto teachers, was purely religious. He was a simple pious peasant who served a village shrine in Bizen. His deity was the Sun-goddess but he cared not so much for the traditional aspect as the purely religious aspect of her worship. He often called the deity simply *Oh-mi-Kami* (Great August Deity), though not neglecting its official name. The deity was for him the source of light and life, with whom we should be in perpetual spiritual communion through prayer and devotion. Human life, according to him, amounted to nothing but a realization of our intrinsic connection with the cosmic vitality. This communion he called *iki-tōshi, i.e.* " penetrating into life " or " pervaded by vitality." The chief way of realizing this penetration was " inhaling " the divine vitality by facing the sun in the morning and praying to the Sun-goddess. Kurozumi applied this and similar methods to therapeutic purposes, attributing his healing power to the divine vitality with which he was inspired and endowed by the Great Deity. This attracted to him many followers ; but his moral influence cannot be neglected. He regarded the utmost purity and a life of diligence and honesty as the first condition of securing the divine grace. Indeed, his faith in his Great Deity was so personal and intense that his religion verged on monotheism pure and simple.

To sum up, we see interesting progress in the independence

of Shinto. It had once been almost absorbed into Buddhism and persisted for centuries in the form of Ryōbu Shinto. This combination was modified, after the fourteenth century to a Shinto supplemented by Buddhist and Confucian theories of cosmology and ethics. Further, the Shinto advocated by the Confucianists of the seventeenth century severed itself from Buddhism, resulting in an alliance of Shinto and Confucianism. The " pure " Shintoists now claimed to have excluded all foreign elements and to have restored their religion to its original purity. However, they were in sympathy with, or under the influence of, either Taoism or Christianity. On the other hand, the popular teachers of religion, not necessarily regarding themselves as Shintoists, turned to the deep abyss of the human heart and there found the prime religious instinct—a simple heart and natural impulse—which had always been the soil of the Shinto religion.

A noteworthy point common to all these Shintoists or teachers of popular religion was a sense of discontent, whether articulate or not, in fact in many cases almost unconscious, against the existing régime, social and political. Those who gave utterance to that discontent thought more in political terms than religious and finally worked for political revolution. On the other hand, those more religiously minded emphasized piety and purity of heart, yet with a sense of some approaching world change, mostly expressed as the coming of a new kingdom of god or gods. In this way the social atmosphere in the first half of the nineteenth century was redolent with something verging on the Messianic conception of the Jews in the first century before Christ. It is, then, no wonder that a simple peasant woman like Kino or Miki preached a gospel not without resemblance to Christianity, even if the suspected influence of the ancient Kirishitan religion counted for nothing.

# THE LAST STAGE OF THE
# TOKUGAWA RÉGIME

WE now come to the end of the long reign of peace and order. The grand structure of the Tokugawa Government was firm and strong in external appearance but there was decay within, and a violent storm was brewing that was to overthrow it. Both internal conditions and external circumstances were making for a radical change, a change which finally compelled the Shōgun to resign and made possible the restoration of the Imperial régime—the fall of feudalism and the achievement of a complete national unity.

The negative motive common to all these revolutionary forces was the discontent with the existing régime, which expressed itself in various ways, such as protest against the curtailing of individual freedom and against the heavy pressure of orthodox Confucianism and communal ethics. We have seen one of these manifestations in the revolt of instinctive impulse against convention, even as early as the seventeenth century. In the eighteenth century, there was a decided rise of curiosity for new knowledge, which was partially satisfied by knowledge derived from Dutch sources through the tiny settlement of Dutch merchants at Deshima in Nagasaki. Some scholars acquired a knowledge of European sciences, especially medicine and natural history, combating the prejudice and ignorance of their people.[1] Some artists studied oil painting or etching and started sketching from

[1] The study of the human body by dissection was first undertaken by Sugita Gempaku, in 1771, an almost revolutionary novelty in medical science. Cf. K. Mitsukuri, *The Early Study of Dutch in Japan* (*TASJ*, vol. 5, part I).

life, a method long neglected in Japanese art.   Later, early in the nineteenth century, some Samurai turned from the study of military sciences to that of the contemporary history of the world and sacrificed their lives on that account, because the warning they had given concerning the world-wide movement of international commerce was regarded by the authorities as disturbing to the peace.   Thus the eager search after new knowledge which arose with a new vigour in the eighteenth century began in the following century to assume social and political significance, and was destined to put an end to the tranquil seclusion of the nation.   Indeed, without these preparatory steps the introduction of Occidental civilization in the era of Meiji, to be spoken of below, would not have been so rapid and smooth.

Even during the preceding centuries, protest had occasionally been raised against oppression and heavy taxation as demonstrated in several cases of riot in the feudal states,[1] besides the self-assertion of the bourgeoisie of Yedo described above.   Still, there had never occurred an organized rising in arms.   But the peace was at last broken.   In 1837, just two hundred years after the Christian insurrection at Shimabara, Ōshiwo, a renowned Samurai in the service of the Shōgun's prefect at Osaka, organized an insurrection.   He was a scholar trained in the spiritual culture of the Yōmei school, and was, therefore, a heretic in the eyes of the orthodox.   He had long resented the corruption of officialdom.   When a famine raged in the central provinces and the government neglected relief, Ōshiwo could no longer remain patient.   His organized men seized the stores of rich citizens and distributed money and rice therefrom.   But the insurrection was soon suppressed, and Ōshiwo together with his son and disciples ended their lives by their own hands

[1] One of these cases, that of the martyr peasant Sakura Sōgoro, in 1645, is told in Mitford (Lord Redesdale), *Tales of Old Japan*.

In fact, Ōshiwo had been well aware of his inevitable fate, yet he rose in arms in order to give vent to the unexpressed discontent of his contemporaries.[1]  Though somewhat impulsive, he also exemplified the courageous temperament of a Confucianist of the Yōmei school.  In learning, honesty, and the spirit of revolt, he well represented the leaning of his school, and his tragic death heralded the outbreak of a similar spirit which had been cherished in various quarters. His desperate step brought to light the tension between the rigid rule of the feudal government and orthodox ethics on the one side, and the rising aspiration of the people and the free tendency of the heterodox schools on the other.  Thus, when the time arrived in the latter half of the nineteenth century, the men of daring spirit arose to express themselves against the oppressive burdens of all the systems that had made for peace.  On the other hand, the impotence of the bureaucracy and the degeneracy of the higher Samurai were becoming appalling, as shown in the financial difficulties of the government, both central and feudal, and in the arbitrary and inconsistent measures adopted one after another.  Democratic aspirations, if not quite in the modern sense, were rising like a surging tide, especially among the lower Samurai and unemployed scholars.

Political ideas had much to do with the social agitation. Though the Shogunate Government ruled the country *de facto* the sovereign power *de jure* rested always with the Imperial family ;  and all distinctions of honour and rank emanated from the court in Miyako, including the formal appointment of the Shōgun himself.  The anomalous division of sovereignty remained unquestioned, so long as the power of the Shōgun's Government was strong enough to keep the feudal states in

---

[1] There were, in the same year, cases of similar insurrections in various places. One of them was organized by the Shintoist Ikuta, a disciple of Hirata, and the insurrection met the same fate as that of Ōshiwo.

perfect control.  But when doubt as to its ability arose, its authority was destined to decline, while the prestige of the Throne was to gain in proportion.  The occasion for challenging the authority of the Shōgun was given by the question of foreign intercourse, due to the repeated demands of the Western powers to open Japan to trade and commerce. Various forces arose first to question and finally to undermine the Shōgun's power.

As we have said, the Confucian historians of the Mito school had formulated the principle of the " Major Righteousness " and advocated the ancient constitution of Imperial rule.  Their propositions remained mere ideals, while the actualities of the feudal régime were tolerated.  The Ansai school of Shintoist Confucianism contended for similar ideas but its members were chiefly content in preaching and discussing.  Now, at the turn of the eighteenth and the nineteenth centuries, the weak points of feudalism in general and of the Shōgun in particular were gradually exposed.  The men standing for the royal cause realized, though but slowly, that their time was arriving.  Concomitant with this tendency, the three successive long reigns of strong personalities in the Imperial family worked to revive the reverence towards the Throne, though at first only among a minority.  The violent patriots of the Ansai school tried to agitate the court nobles surrounding the Throne, as they had lived long under the strictures of the Shōgun ; the followers of Hirata aroused enthusiasm among the people towards the divine dignity of the Throne by appealing to their religious sentiments.  A Confucianist, Rai Sanyō (1780-1832), giving up ethical theorizing, worked for the royal cause by propagating his historical writings hinting, more or less under disguise, at the illegitimacy of the Tokugawa's hegemony.  All these forces were waiting for a signal for their joint rising.

At this critical juncture the cabinet of the Shōgun had to

face the grave problems brought forth by the knocking of foreign nations at Japan's door. A Russian envoy demanding trade (in 1804) was followed by an invasion of the northern islands (in 1806), and finally by the occupation by force of a part of Tsushima (in 1861), an important island in the Straits of Korea. England and America repeatedly sent demands to open the country ; and upon the arrival of the American " black ships " commanded by Commodore Perry (in 1853), the Shōgunate Government realized that they were facing a formidable power. The vicious effects of the policy of seclusion were fully disclosed. The Government who had expelled the " black robes " in the seventeenth century was now at a loss how to face the sudden appearance of the " black ships." After much wavering and hesitancy, they finally agreed to open the country. The result was the treaties with five powers of Europe and America (1854-58).

The awkward position in which the Shōgunate Government was placed by this step was due to the fact that the official title of the Shōgun was " Generalissimo for Expelling Foreign Barbarians " (Sei-i Dai-Shōgun), and his authority rested ostensibly upon this commission from the Throne. Moreover, it was the Tokugawa themselves who had inaugurated and carried out the policy of excluding foreigners and had observed it for more than two centuries as a sanctified tradition handed down from Iyeyasu, the " divine " founder of the dynasty. Thus the prestige of the Shōgun was greatly impaired when he had yielded to the demands of the foreign powers. No sooner were the treaties discussed, than the question arose of the capacity of the Shōgunate Government to enter into such relations without sanction from the Throne. The theories of the " Major Righteousness " and " Status Order " were the moral reinforcement of the anti-Tokugawa movement ; the status order of the Shōgun was understood to forbid the steps taken by his government, while the " Major

Righteousness" demanded imperial authorization for any extraordinary step in national policy.

Attacks began to be made upon the cabinet of the Shōgun who had signed foreign treaties. Political and social discontent against the existing régime, enthusiasm aroused by the propagators of nationalist ethics, the semi-religious reverence towards the Imperial Throne, the hereditary hatred and dread of foreigners implanted by the alleged evils of Kirishitan missions—all these forces converged in vehement attacks upon the government. The leadership in this agitation was undertaken by the lord of Mito, a descendant of Mitsukuni, and the agitators looked upon him not only as a political leader but also as a moral inspirer. The high-handed measures taken by the government against the leader and his followers not only proved futile but stirred up more vehement indignation among the agitators. The outcome was the assassination by fanatics of the highest minister of the Shōgun (in 1860).

The assassinated minister was Lord Ii, who was chiefly responsible for all the measures taken by his government. His position was a pathetic one and his death a real tragedy. He was a man of high attainment in Buddhist training and as such he was firm and resolute in action. A statesman of wide vision put in a very awkward position and yet determined in his measures, he had always been prepared for the worst, having beforehand performed a Buddhist mystery corresponding to the Catholic sacrament of the last unction, even while he stood at the zenith of his power. With this resolute valour he dared to carry out his policy of opening the country, despite the violent oppositions and although he was aware of the weakness of the Shōgunate. His methods of suppressing the opposition may have been too drastic but they were perhaps inevitable under the circumstances. At any rate, his daring act, for which he sacrificed his life, saved Japan from a humiliation such as suffered by China some time

before.  Apart from the political significance of his career, we
have to note that his personality and life showed the last
flash of Zen training among the Samurai class, which had long
been overshadowed by orthodox Confucianism.  But no less
credit is due to his opponents, especially the lord of Mito, for
their integrity and patriotic ardour ; and it is interesting to
see that their spiritual training rested upon Confucian Shinto.
In short, the contrast of different trainings and principles
resulted in a tragic clash in connection with the problems in
the last days of the Tokugawa.

After the death of the strong minister, the decline of the
Shōgunate was a rapid process.  The Government was, of
course, unable to withdraw from the foreign treaties and
continued their course of opening the country to foreign
trade, while trying all means of reconciling the court in
Miyako and the opposing Daimyō.  Temporizing measures
only made the situation worse, and the agitators gained
rapidly in number and organization, under the watchword
" Adore the Throne and Expel the Barbarians " (Son-ō jō-i).
Patriotic poems of vehement tone were widely circulated,
violent propaganda and plots were organized, and on both
sides assassins threatened the lives of their opponents.

The fervour of the anti-foreign movement at one time
reached such a pitch that some of the strong feudal states
tried to give examples of expelling the " barbarians " by
bombarding their fleets.  Neither the semi-religious zeal for
the " sanctity " of the country nor the military training of
the Samurai proved efficacious against the cannonade by the
" black ships."  When the frenzied agitators realized the
situation, they were quick in changing their mind and
turned to a more concentrated effort to supplant the Tokugawa régime.  Their watchword was modified from Jō-i to
Tō-baku, i.e., from " Expel the Barbarians " to " Supplant
the Shōgunate," Son-ō remaining the same.  This was

only natural, since the trouble brought by the question of foreign trade was infinitely complicated by the anomalous division of the titular sovereignty and the actual power of government; the only way for its solution was to be sought in real national unity, whereby the nation in unity could take the situation in hand and face the pressure of foreign powers. The semi-religious agitation against the " barbarian " invasion gave way to a more definite practical political movement for the restoration of the imperial authority. Though this turn of the tide showed at first little likelihood of opening the country, the movement was destined to become an ardent welcome extended to the Occidentals and their civilization.

The changes now proceeded with amazing rapidity. The Shōgun " gave back " his title and power to the Throne in 1867. As said before, this step taken by the Shōgun was motivated not merely by political considerations but by a moral idea. Thus the spiritual legacy of the Mito school found realization in the decision of the last Shōgun, a descendant of Mitsukuni. The exclusionists were compelled to retire or modify their attitude; more liberal and far-sighted reformers quick to see the trend of events came to the front. Some of them had been preparing for the inevitable change by their study of Dutch or French books, and their motto was now " Open the Country and Achieve Progress " (*Kaikoku Shinshu*).[1] In sum, we discern three steps in the agitation: " Adore the Throne and Expel the Barbarians "; " Adore the Throne and Supplant the Shōgun "; and lastly, " Open the Country." And this progress was made possible by the restoration of national unity which caused the vehement

---

[1] Among those progressive leaders we count: Yokoi Shōnan (assassinated in 1869), the adviser to the lord of Echizen whom the American William Elliot Griffis served; Sakuma Shōzan (assassinated in 1864) who was a master in Dutch military science.

French was introduced by French officers sent by Napoleon III. to train officers belonging to the Shōgun.

sentiments of agitation to subside in the course of a few years and to take a more rational channel. The change was a " Restoration " and at the same time a " Renovation," of which we shall see more presently. Thus the long era of peace in seclusion was at an end. The new era of progress and struggle opened with a solemn declaration of the Emperor, now in full grip of the situation.

# BOOK VI

# THE ERA OF MEIJI AND THE PRESENT
# AN AGE OF PROGRESS AND PROBLEMS

## (1868-1929)

# THE NEW ERA, ITS START AND CHARACTERISTICS

THE great national movement had succeeded in overthrowing the old régime and in establishing a new, the era of Meiji.[1] The nation now faced a twofold task, the consolidation of national unity under the new régime and the advancement of civilization in accord with the general trend of the world. The one was the Restoration (*Fukko*) of the unified nation out of feudal division, the restoration of the imperial government which was thought to be possible only by organizing a government after the model of the pre-feudal régime. This movement was necessarily conservative and nationalistic. On the other hand, the nation faced the dazzling light of the world civilization of the nineteenth century, when she was awakened from her long slumber of peaceful seclusion. Zeal for keeping pace with the advanced nations of the world marked the temper of the new era. This meant an entire Renovation (*Isshin*) of national life and emancipation from all the usages, institutions, and policies established during the centuries of seclusion. Thus, the opening of the new era exhibited a striking combination of, and reaction between, these two streams of ideas and policies, Restoration and Renovation.

This double aspect of the ethos characterized not only the opening but the whole of the new age. There were ups and downs of the two tendencies, reactions, conflicts, and some

[1] The new era was named *Meiji*, *i.e.*, "Enlightened Government." The inauguration of a new era with a new reign was a long-established usage, and in this case the name was adopted as the motto of the new reign. The name is now used as the posthumous name of the monarch who ruled in that period.

amount of harmony; but the conservative tendency was never, particularly not in the beginning, a force directed solely to preservation, but always represented efforts to maintain national integrity for the sake of progress. In the sphere of social and moral ideas the radical tendency manifested itself in individualistic propositions, while the conservative control stood for national principles. This contrast and reaction were most clearly shown in educational ideas. The progressive tendency advocated scientific culture, chiefly for the sake of utility and individual promotion, while the moral control of life was mainly sought in the traditional virtues of loyalty and filial piety. A similar combination and reaction appeared in religious ideas, first between the inherited religions and the newly-introduced Christianity, then between anti-religious nationalism and religious universalism. Sixty years have passed, in this way, in a complicated alternation of opposing currents. But the general trend consisted in pursuing the course of progress in accord with the new situations; the problem amounted to how progress could be achieved without prejudicing the inherited virtues although consolidating the foundations of national life.

The opening of the new era brought an air of emancipation to the whole nation. Though the Samurai class were the chief agents in supplanting the old régime and establishing the new, their open-hearted acceptance of the new situation was shown in the wholesale adoption of the new civilization, in a remarkable contrast to the anti-foreign movement which had raged only a few years before. There was a period of bewilderment yet it passed in the course of less than a decade, and the general direction to be kept was clear. Shocks and irritations were manifold, yet they worked to stimulate new vitality. After a thunderstorm, as it were, the atmosphere was full of exhilarating ozone and the sunlight beamed through the dark clouds still lingering. The Imperial Throne was made the banner of the new age, and a declaration was issued in the name of the young Emperor, giving expression to the vigorous aspirations for renovation and progress. The first years of the era of Meiji were marked by freedom of aspiration and breadth of vision, such as might have made even the most progressive spirits of later years envious.

The declaration was made in the form of an oath taken by the sovereign early in 1868, before the " heavenly and earthly deities of the country." It proclaimed in bold terms the political and social programme of the new régime. The proclamation consisted of the following five articles :

1. Councils widely convoked shall be established, and all affairs of State decided by public discussion.

2. All measures, governmental and social, shall be conducted by the united efforts of the governing and the governed.

3. The unity of the imperial and the feudal governments shall be achieved ; all the people, even the meanest, shall be given full opportunities for their aspirations and activities.

4. All absurd usages of the old régime shall be abolished and all measures conducted in conformity with the righteous way of heaven and earth.

5. Knowledge shall be sought for all over the world, and thus shall be promoted the imperial polity.

Not undeservedly is this often called the Magna Charta of New Japan and its inspiration guided the policies of the new era. Although the councils for discussing State affairs first meant assemblies composed of representatives of the feudal states, the idea became a first step towards the parliamentary system.

In the same year the capital was removed to Yedo, modern Tōkyō. This step, though apparently of no great significance, was a sign of the desire for innovation, because it was a matter of great daring to abandon the time-honoured imperial residence and to start a new political life in a fresh capital. It had been an audacious proposal, when first suggested, but it was carried out without much obstruction.

The renunciation of a long tradition of more than a thousand years was thus achieved.

The policies of innovation determined upon were further pursued with vigour and efficiency during the ten years after the Restoration, and were consummated in the subjugation of an insurrection undertaken by a reactionary section of the Samurai class in 1877. When the Shōgun had resigned, all feudal states were brought under the direct control of the central government. Later, the title of feudal lord was modified to that of governor, and the hereditary governors were finally replaced by the officials appointed by the government. Thus the feudal régime was definitely abolished, and all the prerogatives granted to the Samurai class were similarly abrogated (1869-71). Although the title Samurai was retained, social distinctions were abolished, and even the classes of outcasts were granted social and legal equality. This idea of legal equality took practical form in the compilation of new penal and civil codes (1870).[1] The inauguration of the public school system (1872), as we shall see presently, had the same aim of giving all sections of the people an equal chance of being educated and attaining promotion. The establishment of the military service system by conscription (1872) was a measure for promoting national integrity and at the same time a decided step towards equalizing all the classes of the nation. In these bold measures, incentives and models were derived largely from Western nations, but it must also be noted that they were supported by the ancient idea of the equality of all people under the sole sovereign, as well as reinforced by the development of the new situation of national unity.

As the stimulus from the outside was a strong incentive to all these reformatory measures, the same influence soon

[1] See J. H. Longford, *A Summary of the Japanese Penal Codes* (*TASJ*, vol. 5, part II) ; J E. de Becker, *Elements of Japanese Law* (*TASJ*, vol. 44, part II).

made itself felt in the sphere of ethical ideas and in the rise
of the new science. In contrast to the morality of subserviency, the inspiration of the new age came from the ideas
of freedom and utility. The new science, which had gradually
been introduced by a few scholars since the eighteenth century,
now swept away the rule of Chinese science and Confucian
ethics. The old science was denounced as dull stupidity and
Confucian teachers were branded as *fuju* " rotten literati,"
while the *jitsu-gaku*, or " substantial learning " of the West,
was encouraged as the sole means of achieving progress.
The new science thus introduced included physical sciences,
chiefly applied sciences, and social sciences—ethics, sociology,
and jurisprudence. Montesquieu was translated and his
theory of government exerted a good deal of influence upon
the formation of governmental systems. Mill's *Utilitarianism*
and several other books of similar tendency were translated
in the early seventies. We shall see later how these importations influenced the ideas and policies of those years ; what
we have to note here is a combination of those new ideas
with some Confucian principles. The Samurai leaders of the
new age were all educated in the atmosphere of Confucian
ethics, and it was the practical aspects of Confucian ethics
that were adapted by them to the utilitarian ideas of the
new science of morals. This combination was later to exhibit
its effects in an anti-religious attitude on the part of the
authorities in governmental and educational circles, an
important clue for understanding many phases of religious
problems.

# RELIGIOUS POLICY AND PROBLEMS

*Religious Policy of the New Government*

THE first step taken by the new government in regard to religion was an attempt to establish Shinto as the religion of the State. The restoration of the pre-feudal institutions was understood to imply, among other things, a re-establishment of the theocratic idea as embodied in the institution of the *Jingi-kan*, or National Cult Department. Although the Department had been, even during the earlier imperial régime, an institution for ceremonial observance, having little to do with matters of really religious or political significance, the leaders of the new era, mostly Confucian Samurai and Shinto nationalists, deemed its rehabilitation a matter of vital importance. The Department was given the highest position among the government offices, and Shinto was proclaimed the national cult or State religion. This meant at the same time a vigorous suppression of Buddhism, because it was a foreign religion and had flourished under the protection of the Shogunate Government. All privileges granted to the Buddhist clergy were abolished and a large part of the properties belonging to the Buddhist institutions was confiscated. A reign of persecution was started. Buddhists were driven out of the syncretic Shinto sanctuaries which they had been serving for ten centuries or more. Buddhist statues, scriptures, and decorations in those temples were taken out and set on fire or thrown into the water. The " purification " of the Shinto temples was achieved and the severance of Buddhism and Shinto ruthlessly carried out, thus bringing to an end Ryōbu Shinto, which had ruled the faith of the nation for ten centuries.

At one time it seemed as if Buddhism would be swept away by the persecution, but the danger brought Buddhist leaders to united action, a state of affairs impossible during the previous three centuries on account of the prohibition of any interdenominational union. In the official circles too, some realized that an entire suppression of Buddhism was neither desirable nor possible, and the Government was induced gradually to modify their religious policy.[1] The National Cult was replaced by an Ecclesiastical Board (*Kyōbu-shō*), in 1872, under which a central board of preachers was to superintend religious instructions. The authorized system was called neither Shinto nor Buddhism but the " Great Teaching " (*Dai-kyō*), and its principles were formulated as follows :

1. The principles of reverence for the (national) Deities and of patriotism shall be observed.

2. The heavenly Reason and the Way of Humanity shall be promulgated.

3. The Throne shall be revered and the authorities obeyed.[2]

All religious teachers were required to preach within the limits of the formulated principles, the preachers being osten-

---

[1] Among the Buddhist leaders who worked strenuously at this critical moment and exerted their influence upon the government, the following names may be mentioned : Ekidō (died 1879), a Zennist ; Nisshū (died 1891), a Nichirenite : Tetsujō (died 1891), a Jōdo man ; Dokuon (died 1895), a Zennist ; Sessō (died 1904), another Zennist of the Sōtō school ; Unshō (died 1909), of the Shingon sect ; Mokurai (died 1911), of the Shinshū. These men worked in various ways to further the Buddhist cause.

[2] This decree " in three articles " represented a proverbial ideal of good, strong government, and the government of Meiji was, at its beginning, eager to carry out their measures in three articles :

(1) The morality of the five human relationships shall be observed ;
(2) Widows, orphans and other helpless ones shall be aided ;
(3) Those who commit the crimes of robbery, incendiarism, murder, shall be executed.

These were proclaimed on the official notice-boards throughout the country.

sibly nominated by the Government.[1]    The State religion was
thus kept nominally under the supervision of the Ecclesiastical
Board, but in reality Buddhists gradually superseded the
Shintoists.    The Board was abolished in 1877, and the
Buddhist bodies were granted autonomy.    Shinto was treated
in the same way, and its church bodies gradually emerged
out of the State religion, while the ceremonies in the court
and the communal Shinto cult were regarded as having
nothing to do with religious teaching, but as civic institutions.[2]

Thus subsided the frenzy of Shinto revival.    Even the
most fanatical of Shintoists recognized the infeasibility of
their plan, and the artificial injunction of religious and
moral teachings proved a failure.    Besides the fundamental
error in the attempt at restoring the old theocratic régime,
the causes of the failure were twofold : one, the tenacity of
Buddhist faith among the people at large, and the other, the
question of the freedom of conscience, which was called forth
by the discovery of the surviving Catholics and the new start
of Christian missions.    Indeed, these two factors later proved
to be the gravest issue in the religious problems of the new
era, in which the relation between Buddhism and Christianity
was destined to call forth deeper problems.

The impetuous revival of Shinto gave a severe blow to
Buddhism, but the loss in properties and privileges was
compensated by the reawakening of its leaders.    They
organized, as stated above, a union of Buddhist Churches,
which proceeded from resistance against persecution to further
promotion of their cause.    Instead of living in ease and peace,
as they had done during more than two centuries, the
Buddhists had now to work by themselves and to face the

---

[1] All preachers were called " teachers " (*Kyōdō-shoku*) and were brought under
the same control.    Actors and story-tellers were placed, for a while, in the same
category, theatres and vaudevilles were regarded as means of moral teaching.

[2] This distinction between the two kinds of Shinto, the national cult and
religious bodies, is kept even now as a matter of official interpretation.    Cf. D. C.
Holtom, *The Political Philosophy of Modern Shinto*, *TASJ*, vol. 49, part II. 1922.

difficulties arising out of the changed situation. A group of enterprising Buddhists started, in 1872, on a trip of investigation round the world. One of them visited Jerusalem and India.[1] As a result of this trip, Buddhist education was reorganized and some Buddhists began to study Occidental philosophy and Christianity. No sooner were the Buddhists released from persecution and awakened to the new situation, than they found themselves confronted with formidable rivals, Christian missions. Their reaction to Christian missions took various forms, polemics by learned men, agitation by demagogues, and also reorganization of Buddhist institutions, ecclesiastical and educational. The attitude of Buddhism towards Christianity began by asserting itself as antagonistic.

### The Reappearance of Christianity

The opening of the country was soon followed by the arrival of Christian missionaries, both Catholic and Protestant. There were three principal *points d'appui* of their activity. At Nagasaki, in the west, Roman Catholics renewed their activity and discovered there the surviving Kirishitans who had persisted through the persecution and strict vigilance of over two centuries. Thousands of these Catholics were arrested in 1869, because the new Government not only still continued the prohibition of Christianity but was just attempting to establish Shinto as the national cult and to enforce conformity to it. This drastic step caused a protest by foreign powers, which, together with the unswerving fidelity of the Catholics, finally induced the withdrawal of the prohibition (1873). The second of the missionary centres was Yokohama, where Americans started propaganda with medical work. Under the influence of the Presbyterian, the Rev. John Ballagh,

[1] This was Mokurai, mentioned above. It is noteworthy that this was the first instance of a Japanese Buddhist visiting the original home of his religion. Mokurai went to India after his visit to the scene of Christ's ministry.

several young men formed a band of Christian workers who later became influential leaders. The third point was Hakodate, in the north, where a young Russian, Nicolai, had come to serve in the Russian consulate and later began missionary work. He attracted several Samurai from north-eastern Japan, and hence the Greek Orthodox Church has the majority of its adherents in those provinces.

In addition to the missionaries, the foreigners engaged in educational work became a source of inspiration. Captain Janes of the English School of Kumamoto was one of these, and the young men converted by him formed the famous Kumamoto Band, who became later the " apostles " of Neesima, to be spoken of below. Another educator was Professor W. S. Clark, in the Agricultural College of Sapporo, and his converts became mostly independent Christians.

The first success of Christian missions was a credit to the zeal of the missionaries, but no less a part in it was played by the earnest zeal of the neophytes. These enthusiasts were mostly young men of the Samurai class, and their idea in embracing the new faith consisted largely in an earnest aspiration to work out the spiritual resurrection of the nation in conjunction with the new political life. Their faith in Christ was concerned not so much with the doctrines of sin or redemption, as with the strength of character shown by Christ's life and death and by the perseverance of His apostles.[1] Their faith was more ethical than religious and wrought into their inherited Confucian ideals of honesty and fortitude ; their Samurai spirit was invigorated and rejuvenated by Christian inspiration. Their conversion met with obstacles and threats from the opposition of their parents and relatives, but these only tended to inflame their zeal, while their minds experienced a fresh life from the wide spiritual

[1] This statement is based on the personal testimony of some of them. The part of the New Testament which most interested and inspired them was the Acts of the Apostles.

vista opened by their new faith. The high tone and the broad spirit of the young Christians of those days may be seen from a declaration, for instance, issued on the foundation of the first Christian church by Japanese in Yokohama in 1872 :

> Our church does not belong to any denomination but is established solely in the name of our Lord Jesus Christ. Therefore, our sole authority is the Bible, and we deem all to be our brothers who believe in the Bible and live according to its teachings. All the members of this church should love all the members of the churches the world over as members of the same family. Therefore, we call our church the Church of Christ.

### Joseph Neesima

While the missionaries were starting their work in Japan, an earnest Japanese was preparing himself in America for the Christian cause. He was Joseph Neesima, who had managed to get into an American ship in 1864, at the risk of life, and studied at Andover through the fatherly support of Alphus Hardy, of Boston. Neesima's idea in attempting the adventurous passage had been to learn the secret of Western civilization, which he had supposed to lie in physical and military sciences but finally discovered in the Christian religion. So having acquired not only a knowledge of civilization but the enthusiasm of Christian faith, he returned to Japan in 1874. His mind was full of zeal for converting his countrymen to the same faith and thereby accomplishing real progress in the new age. He was supported by the American Board of Foreign Missions, but he had to face many difficulties. His spiritual conviction was embodied in the foundation of the Dōshi-sha, or the " United in Ideal," which was started in 1876 as a school of English and later became a theological seminary. The place which he chose for his institution was Kyōto, the stronghold of Buddhism, a courageous step thus to attack the centre of the old faith.

The difficulties met by this pioneer of Christian education were twofold. One obstacle was the opposition of Buddhists and the prejudice of the people at large.  As Occidental civilization became more welcome in a few years, however, his way became easier in this respect.  The other difficulty was perhaps more trying, the necessity to mediate between his fellow countrymen and foreign missionaries—a situation which became more acute as time passed.  His idea in founding the Dōshi-sha was to lay a firm basis for education in Christian morals, but at the same time he foresaw clearly the necessity of educating Japanese for the new civilization.  He welcomed the support of foreign missionaries but found their ideas of missionary work and education often in conflict with his own.  His position is stated in a memorandum presented to the American Board in 1879.  To quote in part :

Our people are making a bold stroke in educational affairs.  The Government institutions of learning as well as private schools are advancing above us.  If we do not strive to improve we shall be left in the lower strata of the educational system, and fail to get the best class of students.  Our good missionary friends have thus far tried to teach the Bible too much and neglected scientific teaching.  A number of promising boys were much disappointed and have left us to go to the schools in Tōkyō, where they will have no Christian influence.  We cannot afford to lose these promising ones.  We must tie them to our school by giving them a thorough, higher and professional as well as Christian education. . .  To my great disappointment some missionaries do not take enough pains to adapt themselves to our way in this important respect. . .  The chief reason is that they are still Americans.  Their habits, ideas, and imagination are all American. . .  Petty troubles arise now and then between them and our Christians.  They want to get too many foreign reinforcements instead of raising up native workers by their own hand.[1]

This utterance was a result of many heart-aching experiences, and similar friction proved later the cause of a painful rupture between his Japanese pupils and their American fellow workers.  The issue was general to Christian missions and schools ;  and the attempt to impose foreign ideas and customs as if they were integral parts of the Christian religion, as Neesima had foreseen, caused mission schools to

[1] A. S. Hardy, *Life and Letters of Joseph Hardy Neesima* (Boston and New York, 1891), pp. 227-28.

alienate themselves from the nation's needs. Moreover, this break between native Christians and foreign missionaries extended to the question of religious faith, and, as we shall see by and by, there came a serious rupture concerning theological problems within Neesima's institution itself.

Neesima's perseverance through trouble and annoyance was a testimony to his Samurai character and Christian faith, and within a few years after its foundation the Dōshi-sha became a great centre of Christian education in spite of its internal struggles. The greatest event in the development of this institution and in the progress of Christianity in that period was the enlisting of the " Kumamoto Band " under the banner of Neesima. These young men from Kumamoto, having passed through persecution and having taken a solemn vow to dedicate themselves to Christianity and to their country, flocked to the Dōshi-sha, became the first graduates of its theological seminary, and worked faithfully according to their vow. Thanks to Neesima's inspiration and to the honest zeal of these young men, Christianity was soon implanted in the soil of Japan.

Besides the difficulties mentioned above, Neesima had to face another problem, the prejudice of the nation in favour of merely technical instructions and its neglect of moral education.[1] He had to awaken his countrymen to the evils of a one-sided technical education and to the need of moral inspiration, while at the same time he was asking his foreign colleagues for more intellectual training and less proselytizing.

The current of the time favoured Christian propaganda, and the Dōshi-sha prospered. Encouraged by its growth,

[1] Zeal for the " substantial learning " brought undue emphasis on technical and professional education. In reaction to this an attempt was made in 1873 to formulate the moral principles of national life in a compendium of morals, written by Motoda, instructor to the Emperor. Motoda was a Confucianist, and Neesima's remark on " Chinese philosophy " refers to him and his colleagues. Though this compendium had little influence at the time, the same idea and principle found more advocates in educational circles in the nineties.

Neesima proceeded to raise it to a Christian university. The circular issued by him for raising a fund, in 1884, may be regarded as a report on the national education of the time, as well as an expression of his purpose of emphasizing the moral aspect of education :

> There are many who are seeking to improve the public morality on the basis of Chinese philosophy. But we cannot rejoice in their efforts, for the moral code of China has no profound hold upon the minds of men. All Oriental states are almost destitute of liberty and Christian morality, and cannot therefore advance rapidly in civilization. It is the spirit of liberty, the development of science, the Christian morality, which have given birth to European civilizations. . . We cannot therefore believe that Japan can secure this civilization until education rests upon the same basis. With this foundation the State is builded upon a rock. . . Resting on the old moral code of China, it stands upon the sea-sands, and, when rough waves beat upon it, falls to ruin.[1]

The same idea was expressed in an appeal to the American public on behalf of his institution. This document may be taken as typical of the thought cherished by many of the progressive men of that time, the thought backed, in Neesima's case, by an aspiration to Christianize Japan :

> Old Japan is defeated. New Japan has won its victory. The old Asiatic system is silently passing away, and the new European ideas so recently transplanted there are growing vigorously and luxuriantly. Within the past twenty years Japan has undergone a vast change, and is now so advanced that it will be impossible for her to fall back to her former position. She has shaken off her old robe. She is ready to adopt something better. . . Her leading minds will no longer bear with the old form of despotic feudalism, nor be contented with the worn-out doctrines of Asiatic morals and religions. . . The pagan religions seem to their inquiring minds mere relics of the old superstition.[2]

Whether correct or not, this was Neesima's firm conviction, inspiring him to develop his institution into a real university and to work out his ideals of intellectual training and moral edification. But while he was making these proclamations, his health was declining. He had returned in

---

[1] Hardy, *op. cit.*, pp. 241-42. The translation is by Neesima himself.
[2] Hardy, *op. cit.*, pp. 281-82.

1885 from a tour of America and Europe a sick man, yet he still worked indefatigably for his purpose, and with far fewer obstacles than before. Early in 1890 this pioneer Christian educator died. Neesima died just before the rise of the conservative reaction, and represented in his life and work the progressive tide of the Christian cause. The severe reverse which followed affected the Dōshi-sha itself, and the institution suffered heavily but is now prospering as a great centre of Christian education, though perhaps, far from the ideal aim of its founder.[1]

## " A Modern Paul in Japan "

The number of converts won to the Christian Churches in the seventies was not very large, yet most of them were a choice type of earnest youth from among the Samurai class. They were men of ardent zeal for the new life of their country and brought over to their new religion the precious gift of their moral heritage. Besides Neesima and several others, a man particularly to be remembered was Paul Sawayama, the pioneer of the " self-supporting missions " (jikyū dendō), i.e., independent from foreign aid. A youth of enthusiasm and sincerity, he was converted to Christianity after an acute spiritual struggle. Then he studied Christianity in America. On his return home in 1876, he started his ministry, having refused the temptation of a generous offer in official service. In those early years, Christian missions were all the work of foreigners ; the " native " workers and converts depended wholly upon the missionaries in all respects, looking upon their foreign teachers as a superior kind of men. Sawayama saw in this a fundamental fallacy of Christian work, in which slavish dependence was anomalously combined with a spiritual

[1] For the vicissitudes of Dōshi-sha, see Edward C. Moore, *The Spread of Christianity in the Modern World* (Chicago, 1918), pp. 168-70.

cause of high aims.  Thus he declared the necessity of spiritual freedom and worked himself on a self-supporting basis.  As his biographer says : [1]

His aim was to found a living Japanese Church ; to put within it such a spirit of growth and independence as should set it free from its slavish, feeble condition ; to make it a permanent power by the force of its own religious life.  This he thought should be the aim of every Japanese Christian.

The point at stake in the mind of Sawayama was not merely a matter of finance, nor of nationality, but ultimately an issue of spiritual life.  Not only does faith require a free spontaneous growth of itself, but love presupposes a certain amount of self-sacrifice, which is contradictory to dependence upon pecuniary aid from others.  So far as and so long as Japanese Christians depend upon foreign missions, their religion could not achieve a wholesome growth ; slavish following kills the life of religion.  This was his conviction carried out in his organization of a small self-supporting church in Ōsaka, the great commercial centre.  He declared his ideas before the Interdenominational Missionary Conference held at Ōsaka in 1881, but his fellow workers did not appreciate his plea, judging it at least premature.

Fully prepared to face the innumerable difficulties likely to arise out of his principle, Sawayama courageously carried out his idea as the pastor of his little church.  Not only in church affairs but in family life he lived a life of tribulation, suffering from poverty and the constant illness of both himself and his wife, and this was all in glaring contrast to the easy promotion enjoyed by many of his friends in official life.  To rejoice in tribulations, to live in patience, probation and hope, this was the inspiration Sawayama derived from his namesake Paul.  Here we cite a poem which he wrote to console his dying wife :

[1] J. Naruse, *A Modern Paul in Japan* (Tōkyō, 1893), p. 37.  Naruse was Sawayama's friend and helpmate.  We shall speak more of Naruse.

Spare Thou our lives or take them, Lord,
  Our deepest hearts at peace shall be,
Our earthly frames with glad accord
  To all Thy will, we trust to Thee.

  .         .        .        .        .

The bitter pains and struggles sore
  Through which our lives are passing now,
Thou knewest them, Saviour, all before :
  Thou leadest us ; to Thee we bow.

For all who strive to enter in
  Thy heavenly kingdom, Master, God,
Must walk with anguish over sin,
  The thorny path Thyself hast trod.[1]

He survived his wife only three years, and died in 1887. The church founded by him became an important one and his inspiration is still living in the self-supporting churches and their workers.

The prophetic insight of Sawayama's idea may be seen in the problems and vicissitudes of Christian missions in the following years, to be treated later on. But he was prophetic in another respect, in his pioneership in the education of women. His belief in the sanctity of the human soul induced him to see one of the greatest defects in Japanese life in the debasement of women. With this in view he aroused his fellow Christians to found girls' high schools, one in Ōsaka and another in Niigata. The man who helped Sawayama and worked in these schools was Jinzō Naruse, his friend from childhood and his apostle in more than one respect. For Naruse later, in 1900, founded the Japan Women's College, in face of oppositions and obstacles. There, in Naruse's institution, we can even to-day see Sawayama's

[1] *Ibid*, pp. 55-56. It is to be specially noted that Christian missionaries in Japan emphasized the " optimistic " traits of their religion in contrast to Buddhist " pessimism." This circumstance combined with the ethos of the time produced an easy-going optimism among the converts, and the gospel of suffering like Sawayama's was a very rare exception. As a whole, Japanese Christians, particularly Protestants, are far from understanding the meaning of the Cross.

spiritual heritage perpetuated, though the College is not
denominationally " Christian." [1]

.    .    .    .    .    .

The religious policy of the new Government had started
with a fanatical zeal for Shinto but ended in the virtual
grant of freedom of conscience.  The net result was a renewed
life of Buddhism and the progress of Christian propaganda,
though Buddhism had to await its real revival for more than
ten years.  The most prominent feature of the religious
movement in the eighties was the rise of Christianity.  A
number of mission schools were founded and prospered ;
Christian journals were started ; a Japanese translation of
the New Testament was completed in 1880, and of the Old
Testamant in 1888.  An attempt at amalgamating the Presbyterian and the Congregational Churches had failed, but a
union of the different Presbyterian churches was accomplished
as early as 1876.[2]  The extent of missionary work was shown
at the Missionary Conference held at Ōsaka in 1883 ;  130
churches, 70 schools of various kinds, and about 5000 converts,
within the Protestant denominations.  Though the prejudice
of the people at large against Christianity was still strong,
the attitude of the Government was one of tolerance, even

---

[1] A worthy disciple and friend of Sawayama, Naruse (d. 1919) inspired his
college with a fervent spirit of religious faith, leaving free to every girl student
her choice of adherence and her interpretation of the master's ideas.  Naruse
emphasized the " self-support " and independence of spiritual life, his religion
consisted neither in creed nor in church organization, but in faith and love, in
a life of prayer—praying " to whom " was regarded by him as an idle question.
About a fortnight before his death, in spite of his serious suffering, he wrote down
in large letters—he was an excellent calligraphist—the mottoes of his college.
They were :
        Faith penetrating the innermost depth (of soul).
        Life of mutual service.
        Spontaneity and creativeness.
   All this was an amplification of Sawayama's life principle, and is the spiritual
legacy of these two men.
[2] A complete union of the Presbyterian churches was accomplished in 1890,
and that of the Methodist churches in 1907.

of encouragement in some quarters, because they highly appreciated the amount of educational work done by the missionaries. A period of far more rapid progress was awaiting Christian missions, and complete freedom of conscience was confirmed by the Constitution promulgated in 1889.

# A DECADE OF EUROPEANIZATION

*Utilitarian Ideas and the New Educational System*

WE turn back to the beginning of the seventies, when the old learning was being given up and the new " substantial learning " eagerly encouraged. This idea implied an irresistible tendency towards utilitarianism and individualism. Opportunities for free activity under the new régime, the wholesale denunciation of the old ideas, and the attractions of the imported civilization, naturally gave a strong impetus to the exaltation of individual welfare and of immediate usefulness, in contrast to the old culture of serenity and refinement. Education was regarded as a means of promoting man's welfare and science as a tool of personal advantage and social advancement. As a matter of fact, in every department of social and political life, men furnished with some knowledge of modern science were promoted to high positions. Men of " new knowledge " were almost idolized, and the ambition of every young man was to read the " horizontal writings " (*yoko-moji*) of Occidental books. In this, the thirst for knowledge played a great part, but personal ambition, chiefly promotion in an official career, was no less a stimulus. The nation as a whole asked eagerly for the benefits of the new civilization, and individuals aimed at taking part in civilizing work. The motto of the new era was " Enlightenment and Civilization " (*Bummei kaika*).

The most important of the measures adopted by the Government for progress was the inauguration of a system of universal education. Several foreign advisers were engaged

to organize a system, foremost among whom was David
Murray, an American, while the Japanese officials in the
work represented the French system. The result was a
combination of American and French systems. More important than the formal aspect of the new scheme was the
idea underlying the programme, which may be characterized
as utilitarian. The principles were proclaimed as follows :

Each individual is destined to live a happy life by promoting himself in
his career through success of his fortune and progress in his work. This can
be accomplished only by the training of self, the acquisition of knowledge,
and the development of ability ; and all this cannot be attained unless one
learns and is educated. This is the reason why the school is established.
Learning includes all that pertains to human life ; [1] knowledge about daily
business, training in speech, writing, and counting ; the training of the
Samurai, officials, peasants, artisans, merchants and followers of all other
occupations ; the knowledge of law, politics, astronomy, medicine and so on,
all this is learning. Only by doing his work with diligence and according to
his talent, can a man live a prosperous life. Thus, learning may be called an
investment for an advancing career, and therefore no one ought to remain
without learning. Those who lose their livelihood and are defeated in their
life incur that misfortune solely from their having neglected learning.

Learning has heretofore been regarded as the concern of those above the
Samurai rank, while peasants, artisans, merchants, and women were left
outside the pale of education. Even those who had the privilege of being
educated applied themselves mostly to the subtleties of letters and phrases,
and acquired hardly any practical knowledge. This was due to the harmful
tradition of the old régime and is the cause of the low level of our civilization,
as well as of failure and poverty. Therefore, every one should learn, and in
learning not mistake its aim and principles.

The leading part in the " new enlightenment " was taken
by political leaders. Their zeal soon elicited a responsive
echo from the people at large, who proceeded from the general
aspiration for the new civilization to an assertion of individual
rights and freedom. Although this stand for freedom and
equality proved later, towards the end of the seventies, to be
disagreeable to the authorities, it was in the first half of the

---

[1] This and the following passages were meant to emphasize the contrast with
the old conception of education as consisting in literary refinement and military
training exclusively for the Samurai class. Another emphasis was the necessity
of education without distinction of classes and occupations.

decade advocated equally by the Government and the people. Reforms in government, legislation, and education were started by the authorities and seconded by the people, always through the assistance of foreign advisers and teachers. Indeed, there was never a period in Japanese history when foreign assistance was so welcomed and made use of as in the eighth decade of the nineteenth century.[1]  Besides the political reforms effected, daily papers were inaugurated, societies of the " enlightened " were organized, and the people flocked to schools and foreign teachers.  In short, zeal for reform in social life swept the whole country.

### The " Meiji Six " and the " Co-operative Community "

The most important of the organizations of the " enlightened " intellectuals was *Mei-roku-Sha*, or the " Group of Meiji Six," since it was organized in the sixth year of Meiji (1873), the year memorable for the repeal of the prohibition of Christianity, for the adoption of the Gregorian calendar, and several other decided steps in innovation.  The " Meiji Six " comprised the most advanced men of the time who became spokesmen and leaders of that period so eminent in the ardour for progress.  Another group of more radical and younger progressives was the *Kyōson Dōshū*, or the " Co-operative Community," aiming at reforms on the basis of co-operative life, which was understood as a social co-operation of free individuals for the promotion of human welfare.[2]

[1] The memory of these foreign advisers has been much obliterated, partly wilfully, due to the conservative reaction in the nineties.  Their lives and services should be compiled out of the documents of the time, but unfortunately many of those documents stored in the government offices were destroyed by the fire after the earthquake of 1923.  The sources are therefore to be sought in the native countries and families of those foreign workers.

[2] The list of the members of these two groups may almost exhaust the names of those who, during the seventies and the eighties, continued to play great parts in progress and reform.

Among the members of the Meiji Six were : Fukuzawa and Nakamura, of whom

Some of these liberals later fought for political liberty, while most of the Meiji Six worked as peaceful educators or writers. The semi-monthly journal published by the Meiji Six represented the most progressive views and widest knowledge of the time, and its influence was immense in waking up the nation to modern civilization. It was in this journal that Romanized Japanese writing was first proposed, the necessity of a universal language was explained, the freedom of the press and of speech was demanded, the bearing of climate upon civilization was treated, and so on. The Co-operative Community also published its organ and diffused the knowledge of Occidental civilization, chief stress being laid on political and economic discussions. These groups started public speaking, quite unknown before except for Buddhist sermons. Every effort was made to awaken the people to political liberty and social progress.

The most prominent among the leaders of the new age was Yukichi Fukuzawa (1834-1901), one of the promoters of the Meiji Six. His knowledge of modern science and civilization was derived not only from Dutch and English books, which he had begun to study in the fifties, but also from his repeated journeys to Occidental countries, even before Meiji. He devoted his whole life to education, as a writer of popular

we shall presently speak ; Arinori Mori (or Murrey), the young organizer of the group, who later carried out educational reform as the Minister of Education ; Rinshō Mitsukuri, one of the earliest pioneers of Western science ; Amane Nishi, a Confucianist and Comtist, and the translator of Mill's *Utilitarianism* ; Shigeki Nishimura, also a Confucian Comtist, who later organized an ethical society of rather conservative tendencies ; Hiroyuki Katō, later President of the University of Tōkyō, an advocate of the theory that right is nothing but the right of the stronger, and a champion of anti-Christian polemics ; Kōji Sugi, a statistician who conducted a census in a province, for the first time in modern Japan ; and several others.

Among the "Co-operative Community" were Tatsui Baba, the hero of the vehement political movement for a parliamentary régime ; Renjō Akamatsu and Seiran Ōuchi, progressive Buddhists ; Fumio Ryūkei Yano, political leader and writer of several political novels of great influence ; Kentarō Kaneko, later a member of the committee for drafting the Constitution, now Privy Councillor ; Masakazu Toyama, educator and sociologist, a champion of the social reform movement in the eighties, and once Minister of Education.

books on various subjects and as the founder of the school
Keio Gijuku (now a university).   A strong exponent of
democratic principles and utilitarian ideas, he published in
1872-76 a series of pamphlets bearing the title *Admonitions
to Learning*, which aroused immense interest, both among
his admirers and opponents.   In the opening he says :

> Heaven has created mankind neither to rank one over others nor to
> subordinate one to others.   All men (and women) are furnished with the same
> dignity without any distinction, and every one is destined to live a free life of
> activity, by exercising both mind and body, so that he may show himself
> worthy to be, as he really is, the superior of all creatures.   Man is provided
> to live a prosperous and comfortable life by making full use of all gifts of
> nature, clothing, abode, and food, and to live a free life without molesting
> others.

This was quite a novel gospel of freedom at that time.
The essay proceeded further to explain differences of abilities
and fortunes as due to differences in the attainment of useful
knowledge.   The sale of these essays and other books of
Fukuzawa was so enormous that he was able to start his
school with the money so obtained, and the influence of his
writings was a great torch of progress.   The school founded
by him in 1867 grew by rapid strides and his influence was
extended through his pupils, chiefly to politics and business.
His moral influence was extensive, and his motto " Self-
respect and Independence " inspired many minds as a new
revelation.   His democratic way of living and his noble
personality attracted so much admiration that he was called
the " Sage of Mita "—Mita being the district of Tōkyō where
he lived and where his Keiō institutions were built.[1]

Another remarkable man in the group of the Meiji Six
was Masanao Keiu Nakamura (1832-91), a Confucianist who
became an admirer of English gentlemanhood during his stay
in England.   He taught his ethical theory of reverence

[1] Cf. W. L. Behrens, *Fukuzawa Yukichi, Author and Schoolmaster* (in the
Transactions of the Japan Society of London, vol. v) ; Miyamori, *A Life of Mr.
Yukichi Fukuzawa* (Tōkyō, 1902).

towards Heaven, or the Creator as he called it, and emphasized the importance of practising this faith in human relationships. He combined his Confucianism with Christian theism which he professed to advocate, although he was never baptized nor did he believe in the Trinity or in miracles. His chief interest in Christianity was in its ethical teaching, and he believed in God's blessing upon the virtuous, *i.e.*, in the unity of virtue and happiness. In this respect he was an intuitionist and utilitarian at the same time.[1] He produced a translation of Mill's *Liberty* and of Martin's *Evidences of Christianity*, and this latter inspired some Confucianists with enthusiasm for Christianity. But the greatest influence exerted by Nakamura was through his translation of Smiles' *Self-Help*, which found a wide circulation and impressed many people with the necessity for diligence, endurance, self-respect, and personal initiative.[2] Although Nakamura was not a pure individualist in theory, his popular teaching encouraged the free development of individual character. He worked as a professor in Tōkyō University and as director of his own school, and was one of the most revered men in Japan when he died in 1891.

### Fight for Political Liberty and Frenzy for Social Reform

The decade of the seventies was a period of emancipation marked by the free play of liberal ideas. The feudal system was largely dissolved, and several armed risings of the discontented Samurai succumbed before the force of the growing unity of the nation. Then the fighters for political liberty

[1] Confucian ethics was an intuitionism in that it laid the ultimate moral sanction in "conscience," the reflection and realization of the cosmic reason in the human mind.

[2] The book has become a classic in modern Japanese literature, and one of the stories in it has been dramatized.

proceeded to combat the clannish influence in the government and to promote a constitutional régime. The agitators derived their inspiration from the political ideas of English Parliamentarianism, as well as from the histories of the French Revolution and American Independence. The word "*jiyū*" (liberty) charmed the people like a spell, and the theory of the natural rights of man found a hearing even in the remotest corner of the country. The English Magna Charta was circulated in facsimile reprints ; the name of Rousseau was repeated like that of a saviour ; Patrick Henry was well known to many and his words " liberty or death " became a slogan. The Government tried to suppress these movements, but the high-handed measures only provoked so much irritation that some of the agitators had recourse to arms. However, the imperial declaration (issued in 1880) promising the inauguration of a parliamentary régime after ten years quelled the disturbance to a certain degree, and the agitators turned their efforts to preparing for the coming parliament.

Fierce agitation had subsided but polemic and propaganda concerning liberty and human rights still continued. Many political novels appeared in rapid succession glorifying heroes of liberty or independence, legendary or ideal.[1] In 1882 a book appeared condemning the theory of innate rights and it inflamed the controversies anew. The book was entitled *A Theory of Human Rights* and its author was Katō, formerly of the Meiji Six group, who had once been a liberal but had gone over to the other side. The " new " theory presented by him was that all human rights were not innate in human nature, but an outcome of the struggle for the " right of the

---

[1] One of these novels, written by Yano, of the Meiji Six, took its material from the stories of the struggle for independence of Thebes. Epaminondas, the hero, became a very popular hero, and young men imitated his speeches as recorded in the book. Another, by Shiba, depicted in series the struggles for liberty in Spain, Egypt, India. The opening scene was laid on Bunker Hill, and the story o2 American Independence became widely known and read with enthusiasm.

stronger." This was derived from the German theory of social evolution claiming to be a consequence of Darwinism, opposing the French school standing for innate rights.[1] Though the discussion was academic in appearance, it had a practical bearing upon the political situation of that time. The appearance of German influence in political ideas heralded by this book was a very significant fact, because the theory was backed by the partisanship of the Government circles for the German ideas of politics, administration, education, and science. This leaning of the authorities was vigorously put into practice, in the drafting of various new laws and in encouraging German science in the only university then existing. German influence was thus systematically implanted into government and education, and it was supported by military men as well, so that its effects were to appear more and more in various directions.

In the course of the eighties, political agitation and the discussions on human rights were gradually transformed into frenzy for social reform. Reform (*kairyō*) meant in those days attempts at transforming the modes of social and daily life into Occidental fashions, which were identified with civilization. Social leaders and educators preached a metamorphosis of the nation, and the people followed their advice, replacing old customs by Western ones. Dancing-halls were supported by the Government, theatrical performances in English became the order of the day in higher schools, proposals were made even for adopting English as the official language, and inter-racial marriage was encouraged for the purpose of " reforming the race." Every item of social life was to be reformed, to undergo a process of *kairyō*. The idea underlying all this was quite simple, that by imitating

---

[1] Katō depended much upon Iehring, Hellwald, Bluntschli and other German scholars, and later published his theory in German—*Der Kampf ums Recht des Stärkeren* (now out of print).

Western manners the nation could be ranked as a civilized
one and therefore achieve the desired revision of her treaties
with foreign powers on a footing of equality.   The method
was rather childish but the zeal was earnest, and therein
was shown the national ambition to stand abreast with
other nations.

Social reform meant nothing but Occidentalization, and
Christianity was naturally regarded as one of the necessary
conditions of civilization.   Christian churches were crowded
even with those who cared little for religion, and became a
sort of fashionable place where the " enlightened " men and
women met and listened to the sermons delivered by missionaries—preferably in English.   An eminent educator of that
time said : [1]

> Though there are not wanting on the one hand those who use the tongue
> and the pen to show that there is a personal God . . . and on the other, those
> who advocate the adoption of Christianity from a purely political motive,
> there is not . . . anyone who puts enough of stress on the importance of the
> Christian organization as a civilizing agency.

And the same author explained what he meant by this :

> In the following three respects the influence of Christianity on the
> improvement of society is very great : (1) the gathering of men and women
> in a church once every week ; (2) the church music ; (3) the marriage and
> funeral service.

This was quite typical of the idea underlying the zeal for
social reform, or " improvement of society."   Missionaries
corroborated this conception of the Christian religion as an
instrument of civilization, and the churches prospered with
converts who deemed themselves civilized persons just because
of their church-going.   Within a few years, in the last part
of the eighties, the number of converts increased by tens of
thousands, and most missionaries looked forward with confidence to the conversion of the whole nation.

[1] The writer was Toyama, formerly of the Meiji Six group.  The English is his
own.  But curiously enough, he sometimes attacked missionaries as the fathers
of ignorance.

## Counteracting Forces

While Christian missions were progressing with amazing success, counteracting forces were preparing to arise. Buddhism had seemed to have been nearly swept away by the current of the time, but it was too firmly embedded. Non-Christian and even anti-Christian influences were entering Japan from the Occident, and the people had finally to realize that not all civilization was Christian. Mill was followed by Herbert Spencer ; Darwin became known together with Huxley, and the conflict between Christian dogma and the Darwinian theory of evolution was introduced into Japan. Public lectures on Darwinism were given at the University of Tōkyō as early as 1878,[1] and many a young scientist of that university ridiculed as fables the Christian dogmas of creation, man's fall, and so on. One of them said :

I object to sending out missionaries, on two most grave grounds ; first, because they are the fathers of ignorance, and secondly, because they are enemies of free religion.

In addition to agnosticism and evolutionism, Hegelian philosophy was introduced in the eighties,[2] and it worked through the students of the university to arouse a new vitality in Buddhism. Thus the University of Tōkyō, the only institution of the kind in those years, became a centre of non-Christian or anti-Christian influence. These counteracting forces, however, were to appear more vigorously at the end of the eighties.

Meanwhile, a grave division appeared within the Christian movement itself, a danger to its cause more serious than external foes. The year 1887 was marked by the introduction of the " liberal theology " and allied ideas by the arrival of

[1] The lecturer was Professor Edward S. Morse ; he was accused by the missionaries of " preaching immorality."

[2] The agent was Professor Fenollosa, who also called attention to the precious heritage of art in the life of the Japanese.

Unitarian Missions from America (invited by Fukuzawa) and German General Evangelical Missions. These missions were denounced by the others as heretics, but they evoked in the minds of many Christians doubt as to the meaning of the Trinity, the authority of the Bible, and similar points of doctrine, which had been taught by the orthodox teachers as a matter of course in Christian faith. Those who had accepted these teachings without questioning realized, to their surprise, that there were dissensions even among Christians in the West. More thoughtful men had, since the appearance of Darwinism, been questioning the validity of several dogmas, and now they found that there was something besides and beyond what they had been taught by the missionaries. The body most " infected " by the new influence was Neesima's Dōshi-sha. One of its members attempted a new interpretation of the " inspiration of the Bible " ; another proceeded further to study German theology and finally produced a partial translation of Pfleiderer's *Philosophy of Religion*. When Neesima, the mediator between the young radicals and the conservative missionaries, died, a conflict broke out which was nearly to shatter the structure of the Dōshi-sha institution as well as of orthodox Christianity.

When Darwinism and allied streams of thought frustrated the smooth progress of Christian missions, and the liberal theology threatened the integrity of the Church, the missionaries were at a loss how to cope with the situation. The old-fashioned th ology and Christian evidences in which they had been educated proved powerless in face of the new forces. The University of Tōkyō was " purified " of missionary teachers ; young Buddhists studying there were arising to oppose Christianity with the weapons newly acquired ; the welcome extended indiscriminately to the missions was rapidly declining in fervour. Meanwhile dark clouds of nationalist reaction were gathering on the horizon to bring a thunderstorm on the Christian work and the Westernizing tendency. The hopeful prospect of Christianizing Japan was entirely lost and the optimistic Christians experienced a great disillusionment.

In order to understand the meaning of this great reverse to the Christian missions, we must see the significance of Japan's ambition of revising her treaties with foreign powers. The treaties of trade and commerce had been based on terms of inferiority on the part of Japan, and all foreigners residing in Japan, according to the provisions of the treaties, were not under the jurisdiction of Japan but of their respective consuls, protected by rights of extraterritoriality. Since the beginning of the new era, it had always been an ardent desire of the Government and people to abolish the anomalous situations created by the foreign consular jurisdiction within Japan. National pride as well as the inconveniences involved gave a strong impetus to this attempt at treaty revision. In fact, the zeal for adopting Western religion, science, jurisprudence, and other matters, was partly a manifestation of this hope and ambition. When this ardent expectation was disappointed through the repeated suspension of the negotiations with foreign powers in 1887 and 1889, the people vehemently resented the arrogance of the Western powers. Sad reflection followed impetuous resentment and the outcome was a strong national movement.

# CONSERVATIVE REACTION AND
# RELIGIOUS PROBLEMS

## The Nationalistic Reaction and Buddhism

THE sweeping movement of Europeanization necessarily provoked a reaction, and the resentment broke out furiously on
all sides, and " Down with frivolous Europeanization ! "
" Keep to our national heritage ! '"" Japan for the Japanese ! "
became the watchwords of the time. The pioneer in this
movement was a group of young Buddhists and others who
had been educated in the anti-Christian University of Tōkyō,
and their journal *Nippon-jin* (" The Japanese ") became a
beacon light of the nationalistic movement.[1] The " Japanese "
group was seconded by similar organizations, such as the
*Son-ō Hō-butsu Daidō-dan*, or the " Corporation for Adoration
of the Throne and Reverence towards Buddha " ; the *Nippon
Kokkyō Daidō-sha*, or the " Association of the Great Way, the
National Religion of Japan," and so on.[2]

All these, as can be seen from the names, were not simply

[1] The group was called the *Sei-kyō-sha*, or " Politics and Religion ", though
not a religious body but a group of nationalists. Its motto was " Preservation of
National Heritage " (*Kokusui Hozon*), and this sounded to many minds like a new
revelation, as if hidden and forgotten treasures were being recovered. The journal
was started in 1888 and continued to exist until 1923, under the editorship of
Miyake. He is not a Buddhist nor a religious man but a thinker of a striking type,
combining sharp insight and cynical sarcasm. Of another member of the group,
Enryō Inouye, we shall speak presently.

[2] The leader of the " Throne and Buddhism " was Ōuchi, who had been a
member of the Co-operative Community. His motto was only a modification of
the " Union of the State Law and Buddhist Religion " much in vogue before the
fourteenth century.

The leader of the " Great Way " was a military man of Zen training, General
Torio. He emphasized the unity of Buddhism, Confucianism, and Shinto, in the
national life of Japan.

religious bodies but represented a combination of ethical, political, and social ideas, aiming at the exclusion of foreign influence and the exaltation of national tradition. To these banners flocked not only Buddhists and Shintoists, but also Confucianists and agnostics, priests and lawyers, professors and students, making common cause against Europeanization and Christianity. Their attacks upon Christianity, partly making use of the newly borrowed weapons, were based more on social and political reasons than religious. In fact, many Christians of the time were themselves responsible for that kind of criticism, because their adherence to Christianity was not so much motivated by religious faith as by social or political considerations. Both parties stood nearly on the same plane, and real religious discussions were to appear later on. At any rate the blow to Christianity was effective and many dubious converts deserted the Church. The prospect of wholesale Christianization proved a delusion.

The anti-Christian movement was, however, not mere chauvinist propaganda but it involved the high aim of bringing back the mind of the nation to the precious heritage fostered by the three religions of Japan. Thus the movement proceeded to take the form of reviving those religions, especially Buddhism. The road for this had been prepared by the discovery by some Buddhists of a kinship between Buddhism and some phases of Occidental thought. To their surprise and delight, the young Buddhists found that the Buddhist conception of the world as a perpetually flowing process and the continuity of Karma had anticipated the Darwinian theory of evolution ; that the dialectical method of Buddhist philosophy in analysing all conceptions and dispelling the idea of permanent entity was quite congenial to Spencerian agnosticism ; that the Hegelian logic of reaching a higher synthesis over the concepts of being and non-being was exactly the kernel of the Tendai doctrine of the Middle

Path.[1]   Whether correct or not, these ideas provided a strong incentive to a conviction that Buddhism was not a mere relic of the past but had a mission for the future.   Young Buddhists proceeded to attack Christianity, chiefly its dogmas, with weapons both inherited and newly acquired.   Buddhism experienced a rejuvenescence through its philosophical revival, which was to pass subsequently to a deeper phase of religious faith.

*Nationalism and the Question of Education* versus *Religion*

The nationalistic reaction involved educational questions too.   The wholesale adoption of Occidental culture and the encouragement of the " substantial learning " had swept away nearly all traditional moral discipline.   The zeal for emancipation had partly accomplished its task and consumed itself when a return to moral training was considered.   As early as 1873 a compendium of moral instruction had been compiled by a Confucian scholar, intended as an authoritative teaching of morals.[2]   But this book had remained almost unnoticed until 1886, when a new scheme of education was proclaimed, wherein special emphasis was laid on national principles of education.   The fundamental principle of morality adopted in this reform was the Confucian conception of

---

[1] A great part was played by the influence of Professors Morse and Fenollosa, referred to above.   The ethics of Karma was discussed by Huxley in his *Evolution and Ethics,* which was later translated into Japanese.   The affinity of Buddhist philosophy with a phase of Hegelian philosophy was taken up by Enryō Inouye, one of the " Japanese " group.   His book *Bukkyō Katsu-ron* (" An Essay on the Vitality of Buddhism " or " To Invigorate Buddhism "), published in 1890, insisted on this affinity and exercised a great influence upon the young generation.   A college was founded by him for training Buddhists in philosophy.

[2] The compiler of the Compendium was the Confucian moralist Motoda, referred to above.   It is understood that the sovereign himself, being mindful of the moral life of his people, asked his instructor to formulate ethical principles.   The book was entitled *Yōgaku Kōyō,* " Principles of Instruction for Youth."   Motoda continued as the instructor until his death in 1890.   For the lectures given by him in the presence of the Emperor, see *TASJ,* v. 51 (1912).   It is to be noted also that Neesima, the Christian educator, made his appeal for moral education two years before the proclamation of the new educational system spoken of here.

reverence towards proper authorities. This was a reaction against the one-sided emphasis on intellectual education and utilitarian ideas; and this implied also a reinstatement of the authority of the State as against individual freedom. In this exaltation of the State and the suppression of the individual, the German theory of the *Staat* exerted great influence, the theory that the State is the source of all authority and the highest goal of moral life. The education of man not for his own sake but for the sake of State, this idea found a conspicuous embodiment in the Normal School, the so-called " fountain-head of national education," which was ruled by rigid, almost military discipline. Obedience, Comradeship, and Dignity were inculcated as the cardinal virtues of the schoolmaster; the result was a peculiar combination, on the part of the men trained there, of simple subserviency to the authorities and ostentatious formality in manner and thought.

After the conservative reaction had fully displayed its ardour and spent its force, a certain amount of equilibrium was restored; the radicals realized their delusion and the conservatives could not remain merely reactionary. Those who stood for the preservation of the national heritage never opposed a sound progress of the nation to take her stand among the civilized nations of the world. The Buddhists reorganized their schools and colleges, and Western science and philosophy were introduced into their curricula. The national Constitution proclaimed in 1889 took up a position midway between extreme radicalism and reactionary oligarchy. Many forms of innovation survived the fall of Westernization in general, such as the ardent study of foreign languages, the emancipation of literary style from old conventions, and these were to achieve further development in the following years. Christianity had lost many of its adherents, but those who remained faithful proved to be genuine and thoughtful

Christians, though lacking the vigour and enthusiasm of the first period.  In the gradual restoration of equilibrium each party proved to have gained something sound and of comparatively permanent value.  The last decade of the nineteenth century opened thus with a bright prospect of stabilization.

This stabilization or a guidance to it was expressed in a formulation of the moral principles of national life in 1890.  It was called the " Imperial Rescript on Education " and was proclaimed as the authoritative standard of moral ideas and discipline.  The foundation of national life was therein concentrated to the cardinal virtues of loyalty and filial piety, the former being the whole nation's devotion to the Throne and the latter the pivot on which family life should turn.  The background of these virtues, together with all other personal and social virtues, was taught to lie in the remote origin and long heritage of national life, while the universal validity of these virtues was no less emphasized.  Solemn in its expression, broad in its principles, and dignified in its style, the document was worthy of a proclamation from the Throne for the sake of the whole nation.  It is no wonder that it was accepted in reverence by all sides, except by a small section of Christians who regarded it as an infringement upon the authority of their Bible.  This last point was naturally subjected to attacks, and this trouble was aggravated by a narrow interpretation of the document by some conservatives who began to make use of the rescript as their weapon against religion in general and Christianity in particular.

One of the immediate effects of the educational reform of 1886 was the exclusion of religious influence from the school, the idea being that religious universalism was incompatible with nationalistic ethics.  Although this measure of exclusion had the merit of keeping the school free from sectarian strife, it worked to make antagonism towards religion almost a creed of the educational circles. The majority of the teachers identified religious faith with superstition, or regarded it as tolerable only for the sake of the common people—a survival of the Confucian attitude. This denunciation of religious influence was in many cases extended to other ideal phases of life, such as art and literature, as these seemed to the nationalists to be signs of sentimental degeneration or effeminacy. These teachers took pride in being rationalists, regarding their adoration of the State almost as a religion, a religion of patriotism. Most of them did not consider themselves Shintoists but they were at one in attacking Buddhism and Christianity.

A fierce polemic ensued during several months in 1891-92 between Christians and those who interpreted the Rescript in their own nationalism. The occasion was given by some Christians denying any authority other than the Bible, as stated above. Attacks on these men were made by the educational circles, and a professor in the University of Tōkyō, T. Inouye, criticized the Christian doctrine of universal love by arguing that Christian principles were incompatible with the teaching of nationalism. He formulated his points in a book called *A Conflict between Religion and Education*, emphasizing the opposition between the Christian idea of love and the national virtues of loyalty and filial piety.

The question had a far-reaching bearing on the contest between religion and nationalism, or between idealism and positivism in general. Neither party, however, was far-sighted enough to see the depth and ultimate issues of the question; the polemic developed into the question as to which was superior, the Rescript or the Bible. Bigoted Christians emphasized the sole authority of the Bible, while the conservatives denounced them as traitors to the nation. But most Christian apologists defended themselves by trying to show the compatibility of Christian ethics with the virtues of loyalty and filial piety, provided that the basis of these virtues be sought beyond the merely traditional ideas.[1] The Buddhists joined the conservatives in their attack on Christianity, hardly realizing that the same accusations might in time fall upon themselves. Thus the polemic was fought in confused camps, gradually declining into trivial objurgation. No decisive outcome was discernible, yet one point was pretty clear, that the Christians gradually shifted their position explicitly or implicitly, admitting more or less the place of national ideas in or beside religion. The biased denunciation of " heathenism " was mitigated, and the polemic marked a step in the naturalization of Christianity in Japan. On the other hand, some of the nationalists realized the lack of deep spiritual foundation in their own position.

### Changes in Religious Problems

The impetuous reaction had subsided, calmer reflection called forth a revaluation of national ideas, while religious questions were shifted to a more fundamental consideration of the meaning of faith in human life. In other words, nationalism was no more a mere reaction, nor religious problems mere controversy between native and foreign religions. While the questions at stake were being shifted in this way, the war with China (1894-95) called forth a rise of national hopes and ambitions. The success of the war came as a revelation to the nation, but the feeling of exultation was disturbed by a painful humiliation caused by the intervention of the three European powers in the terms of peace.

While the nation was eagerly engaged in the post-bellum adjustment, great apprehension for the future of Japan and of the Far East was aroused by the aggressive policies in China of the powers who had intervened in the name of

[1] One of those who clearly pointed out the ultimate issue of the question was Hajime Ōnishi, a fine thinker and Christian philosopher, who died young in 1900.

peace. The famous cartoon of the " Yellow Peril " designed by the German Kaiser deeply shocked Japan. Moreover, when the designer of the cartoon proceeded to assert himself high-handedly in China, the Japanese people were impressed with the sense of a grave danger, a " White Peril " under the cloak of Christianity threatening Asiatic nations ! Religious problems became involved, and many thinkers in educational circles began to view all religions with a suspicious eye.

The antagonism of nationalist ideas to religion was clearly demonstrated by a group of thinkers whose banner was *Nippon Shugi*, " Japanism." It was composed of heterogeneous elements, of positivists, agnostics, sociological advocates of the sheer struggle for existence, yet its contentions represented fairly well the attitude of the nationalists. They found a common platform in exalting the national ideals of Japan, which they interpreted as the glorification of the State and the rejection of all spiritual ideals aiming at anything beyond it. The State or national life, they taught, is the only firm ground on which the individual could base his life, and the object to which he should dedicate everything. The national heritage of the Japanese is represented by the three virtues, which are : energetic life, esteem for the present and actual, and the observance of purity—all in irreconcilable antagonism to the " obscurities " taught by the non-national doctrines of all and every religion.

In taking up this attitude, the Japanists were against individual initiative or universalism of any kind. Some of these men stood for a re-establishment of Shinto as the religion of State, while Shintoists who had once joined Buddhists in reaction to Occidental influences dissolved their alliance and proceeded to a decidedly anti-foreign activity. But some of the Japanists were too intelligent to be dragged into blind anti-foreign agitation, while the gulf existing within the group became more and more evident. The

Japanist group was dissolved in less than two years after its organization in 1897. At any rate, Japanism was typical of the time, though only a passing phase. It could in no way satisfy the yearnings of the individual soul. An antithesis to Japanism and nationalism in general was to manifest itself in an outburst of individual aspiration. In fact a prominent Japanist himself changed his views and later became a pioneer of individualism.

While the educational leaders were formulating the anti-religious principles of " national morality," some Buddhists and Christians were facing a grave problem, graver than the question of one religion *versus* another, namely religion *versus* non-religion. The first instance of the connection between the two religions was shown in a meeting of liberals from both sides in September, 1896.

The meeting was announced as merely a social gathering for exchanging opinions. Yet the proposal made a sensation and aroused criticisms from all sides, being generally regarded as a hazardous undertaking. Opposition, ridicule, even threats were heaped upon the plan, yet the meeting was held, there being about fifty persons present, old and young, Buddhists and Christians of various denominations, and one Shintoist. Some expressed their belief in the common cause of the two great religions notwithstanding doctrinal difference ; some even went so far as to look forward to a co-operation of all religions in social work ; none of them doubted the necessity of a free and candid exchange of opinions.

There were several circumstances which made the rap-prochement represented by this meeting possible. Both Buddhists and Christians trained in the historical or comparative study of religion had begun to take a broader view of religious truths. The way had also been paved by those who had alienated themselves from orthodoxy and regarded religious faith not so much as a matter of dogma as of the spirit. An example was given by the Congress of Religions held at Chicago in 1892, while the rise of the common adversary namely, anti-religious nationalism, gave a direct impetus.

Besides these circumstances, however, the more significant reason for the rapprochement was the position which the two great religions occupied in Japan, that of being on an equal footing of freedom and independence. So long as the foreign missionaries behaved towards Japanese, whether converts or not, with an air of superiority, their propaganda could but be an attempt to impose something upon the inferior " natives." The counterpart was the attitude of simple acceptance or mere obedience, often verging on slavishness, on the part of the converts. While this state of inequality prevailed, the Christian religion could not achieve a wholesome development in the soul of the Japanese. Accordingly, Paul Sawayama, referred to above, had fought for freedom and independence ; that was more or less attained in the course of the ninth decade on the part of a few independent Christians. Considering that an independent spirit is the first condition of candour, it is evident that a meeting aiming at candid expression was possible only in a comparatively free atmosphere. They were keen to examine their faith not as a matter of mere acceptance but as a vital problem of their own spiritual life. These independents never forgot to dissociate the fundamental tenets of the Christian faith from European or American traditions and idiosyncrasies as brought over by the missionaries. This led them to do justice to the soul of the Orient, of which Christianity itself was an heir, and from which Japan derived inspiration chiefly through Buddhism. Of course, they were still far from definitely grasping the spirit of the East, and they always questioned whether the two great religions flowing out from Asia were entirely incompatible. We shall see a further development of this idea of an Oriental interpretation of Christianity, but suffice it to say here that this free spirit of some Christians was instrumental in opening a way of communication between the followers of different religions.

One of the indirect results of the meeting was the organization of an ethical movement known as the Teiyū Ethical Society. It was composed of Buddhists, Christians, and other liberals, who were dissatisfied with the actual conditions of the organized religions and were against mere nationalism. Their purpose was not to attack religion but to fight sectarianism. They hoped to elucidate certain fundamental principles underlying various religions and ethical teachings which could satisfy the individual soul and fulfil the needs of social life. In emphasizing the necessity of interpreting human life in idealistic terms of humanity, the Teiyū ethical movement aimed at broadening the spiritual outlook of the Japanese to something beyond both nationalist morality and theological dogma. The initiative was taken by Yokoi, a former disciple of Neeshima, while the leading spirit was Ōnishi, a Christian philosopher affiliated to the Unitarian movement, who had always stood for the universal ideals of religious faith. Another leader, Takayama, once an advocate of Japanism, being repulsed by the narrowness of his comrades in the Japanist movement became a champion of individualism. The Ethical Society continues to exist but it has entirely changed its constitution ; yet the idea it stood for in the last years of the nineteenth century was representative of a tendency to resist the tide of nationalism and to emphasize the deeper spiritual meaning of ethical problems and religious faith.

## Popular Religions and Social Work

While educational leaders were dictating their official teaching to the nation and religious leaders discussing the question of religion in face of non-religious nationalism, the common people were left to themselves. The rise of industry and commerce brought with it the disturbance and distress accompanying an industrial revolution. The popular mind, always prone to superstition and open to appeals to instinct and emotion, now turned for help to popular religions promising immediate help and spiritual blessings at the same time. Some of these originating in the last years of the Tokugawa régime had persisted beneath the surface, and now in a time of stress after the war with China they came to the front. Some of them consisted in little more than divination and sorcery, together with certain obscene cults, and their activity was only ephemeral. But some others amounted to a simple teaching of purity of heart which might be called popular theism.

The most widespread and enduring of these popular religions was the *Tenri-kyō*, whose origin was described at the end of the feudal régime. Its rise to prominence in the eighties, the period when the nation was in a frenzy of Europeanization, surprised the intellectuals, and its far-reaching influence manifested itself in the nineties. Its teaching can be reduced to a pure and simple faith in the divinity as the creator and ruler of the world, the faith that purges the human soul from all impurities. The Creator has made the world for the benefit of all men, a world where men live by mutual help and in the all-embracing grace of the divinity. A practical inculcation, therefore, is that a man must never regard his possessions as private but as for common share. On the other hand, it teaches an established order of moral retribution in which every individual is assigned a definite place, to trespass which is simply the sin of greed. Consequently, the primary requisite for enjoying the divine grace in full is to purge oneself from all stains and sins and to open one's heart unquestioningly to the command of the divinity.

In teaching the exclusively mental origin of all diseases, Tenri-kyō exhibits some resemblance to Christian Science, and its method of mental cure plays a great part in its influence. In short, it filled in gaps left by other religions and appealed to the instinctive mysticism pretty universal to mankind.

Another popular religion rather similar to Tenri-kyō was *Konkō-kyō,* the religion of the " Golden Light," derived from the name of its divinity, Konjin or Konkō, the god who was worshipped in an unorganized form as an awe-inspiring mighty ruler of the hidden aspects of life. The founder, the peasant Kawadé (1814-83), took up this belief and purified it by emphasizing the necessity of the purity of heart in worship. This religion came up to the surface later than Tenri-kyō and has since made great progress. The two are similar in character, in combining spiritual cure with moral teaching and inculcating direct spiritual communion with the deity. Their adherents are found mostly among the lower classes ; Tenri-kyō has its followers chiefly among the peasants, while Konkō works more in commercial towns. In the beginning both did not carry on much organized propaganda, but individual members worked in personal proselytizing, more through cure and relief than preaching. It is quite otherwise now, forty years or more after their public appearance, and their missions are going across the seas.

The sudden rise of popular Shinto disclosed one lack in current religion, the direct appeal to the heart of the people, especially the lower classes. Another gap remained ; both Buddhists and Christians had been doing more or less charitable work for years, but social work in the proper sense remained for the Salvation Army to inaugurate, which entered Japan in 1895. Its first conspicuous work was the fight for emancipation of enslaved women ; though this campaign was only partially successful in its direct aim, its influence was far greater in arousing the sense of social justice among thoughtful people. The ideal of social justice was applied also to the denial of private ownership, by men outside religious bodies, mostly men of socialist tendency.[1] These and other similar questions were to arise more vigorously after the war with Russia about ten years later, but the movements and ideas stimulated by the Salvation Army worked to transfer the zeal of religious leaders, especially Christian, from direct evangelization to social work, and to-day we see all religious bodies working along some lines of social work.

One point to be noted in connection with the social movement was the promulgation of a new code of civil law in 1898. This law, together with other laws, being based mainly on the legal ideas of the Occident, differs from the old Japanese ideas in recognizing more fully the rights of the individual. The family and the rights of its head are preserved to a large extent, but individual rights play a greater part than before, to such a degree that the conservatives deem the code detrimental to the time-honoured family system of Japan. Another important point is the confirmation of monogamy, an indirect influence of Christianity, which has almost transformed the family life, particularly of the upper classes.

We can now review Christian missionary work, since the proselytizing practically came to an end in the first decade of the present century. Opinions differ, naturally, but the following points may be mentioned : that the missions had been the chief agents in introducing modern ideas, up to the time of the national reaction towards the end of the eighties; that since then, or even earlier, other streams of Western ideas were flowing towards Japan, even to antagonize mission-

---

[1] One of the pioneer socialists, though of a rather academic type, was R. F. Yano, formerly a champion of political liberty. His book, *The New Society*, published in 1902, was perhaps the first one of its kind written in Japan.

ary work ; that the development of the national educational
institutions gradually encroached on the educational work of
the missions ; that since the beginning of the present century
the evangelizing work has made little progress especially in
comparison with social work, both Christian and non-Christian;
that many changes in the moral and religious life of the nation
are taking place with little help from foreign missions.[1]   We
shall presently see how the spiritual agitation of the present
is taking its own course independently from missionary work
in the regular sense.   In short, an important aspect of the
Christian movement in Japan is the endeavour to emancipate
itself from foreign control, though many Japanese Christians
still think it necessary to have foreign aid.   Some Christians
eagerly desire the " restoration of Christianity to the Oriental
consciousness," on the ground that Christ himself was an
Oriental and the Occidental civilization is not entirely
Christian.   The question amounts to how Christianity can be
naturalized and grow out of the people's own soul.[2]

[1] The influence of Tolstoi is one of the instances of Christian ideas introduced
entirely apart from the missionaries.   More will be said about Tolstoi.
[1] Cf. R. Allier, Le protestantisme au Japon (Paris, 1908) ; E. C. Moore, The Spread
of Christianity in the Modern World (Chicago, 1919), pp. 141 ff.

# SPIRITUAL UNREST AND THE RISE OF INDIVIDUALISM

*Spiritual Agitation among the Youth*

THE religious agitation exhibited in the rise of the minor sects was a precursor of the rising tide of spiritual aspiration in general. The stress of economic difficulties passed for a time, yet the search for spiritual support continued among the younger generation. The official system of ethics was not only unsatisfying but its pressure aroused a spirit of revolt on the part of the sensitive youth. The more rigidly were the principles formulated and the more insistently were they inculcated, the deeper the discontent and the graver the opposition. The schoolmasters themselves were not sure of the value of the work imposed upon them from above, from which they were allowed no deviation. Not a few of them wanted something more directly appealing to the human heart yet had no choice but to hold their posts, being hypocrites, as some confessed. The neglect of the individual was the fundamental defect of the educational system, and the reaction against this was shown in the demand for freedom and also in the insistence on spiritual aspirations. " We have asked for bread and have been instructed merely in the theory of making bread "—this utterance by an ardent individualist, Takayama, found sympathetic echo in many quarters. In this way the first years of the twentieth century were marked by the rise of individualism and the increase of spiritual agitation.

Yearning for something broader or deeper than the official

ethics, searching for an enduring light beyond nationalistic principles, yet being not satisfied with any of the current religions, sensitive young men and women struggled and often fell into a desperate agony. The word *hammon* (spiritual trouble and agony) represented this period of storm and stress. An extreme case of *hammon* was that of a sceptic of seventeen years who killed himself by jumping into a great waterfall, leaving his last words inscribed on the trunk of a tree near by, wherein he ridiculed human life as a meaningless trial not worth enduring, a riddle never to be solved by religion or philosophy.[1] In his eyes his fellow-beings who were living without any conviction in the real meaning of life were simply pitiable, and for him death was the only solution for not being a hypocrite or coward. This took place in April 1903 ; many young people were deeply moved, some admired his audacious consistency and followed his example. This was an extreme case, but the idea and mood shown in it were typical of the youth of that time, so far as the prevailing unrest was concerned.

In the tension of the spiritual atmosphere changes were of frequent occurrence. An extreme sceptic was often transformed into a sentimental pietist, a rationalist into a mystic. There were hardly any among those troubled hearts who did not pass through various stages of doubt and hope, despair and consolation. Buddha and Christ, Hōnen and Nichiren, and several other religious figures were reviewed in new lights, often in arbitrary subjective interpretations, mostly in melancholy self-introspection. Resort was also had to modern individualists, such as Tolstoi, Nietzsche, Kierkegaard, Ibsen. Instances of extreme sentiment and behaviour can be cited at length ; there was lack of balance but there was the ardour

[1] The scene was the sublime waterfall of Kegon near Nikko, which hence became a favourite place for suicide. Another became famous later, the awesome crater of Mount Asama.

of aspiration ; the heart was over-sensitive but sincere and earnest to the utmost.

Among the typical representatives of the time, the first and most prominent was the case of Takayama, who had once been a champion of nationalistic Japanism and had denounced all religions as mere superstition. But the ideal leaning of his innate heart reasserted itself and led him in quite an opposite direction. He became a pronounced individualist, and confessed without reserve all his spiritual troubles, announcing himself to be in spiritual whirlpools. He became thus the mouthpiece of the troubled souls who were cherishing similar questions and passing through similar struggles.

Early in 1901 Takayama published an essay entitled " The Beautiful Life," which aroused great enthusiasm among the younger generation and stirred the indignation of the conservatives. His idea expressed therein amounted to this, that man's true destiny consists in a " beautiful life " lived according to pure human nature, free from the fetters of social convention and unhampered by ideas of interest and benefit. Life is valueless without sincerity, and sincerity can be secured only by freeing oneself from ulterior considerations, by simply following the voice of one's own pure conscience, innate nature or " instinct," as he called it. The Good is nothing but the Beautiful, wherein man lives an untrammelled life like the flowers in the fields. In thus identifying the Good and the Beautiful, Takayama spoke like a poet or a philosopher of the type of Plato ; in denouncing social conventions and ethical theories, his voice was like that of Rousseau or Lao-tse ; in the exaltation of individual freedom and of heroic audacity he became a " Nietzsche of Japan," as he was called by his admirers.

But the Nietzschean " Superman " was too brutal to be the final ideal of Takayama's tender heart. A man who had once been an admirer of Byron and Heine, and whose heart was moved by Chikamatsu's love-tragedies, could not rest satisfied with the domination of a strong will.   On the other hand, he who had advocated Japanism and had seen something of the nation's spiritual heritage, could not remain for ever a mere individualist, or " egoist," as he sometimes called himself.   Moreover, some religious aspiration had been sown in his heart by his reading of the Bible, and a certain influence from his study of Buddhism remained in his soul. At last he found a spiritual guide who fulfilled all his demands and yearnings, national and individual, poetic and philosophical, religious and social.   This was Nichiren, the prophet of the thirteenth century, whose influence wrought a thoroughgoing transformation in Takayama.

Converted to Nichiren's religion, Takayama mastered within a short time the doctrine of his master and derived profound inspiration from his life, finding the clue to the understanding of Nichiren in the intrinsic connection between his teaching and personality.   The first essay he published on the subject was a powerful study delineating Nichiren's career in reference to his prophetic zeal, as shown in his conviction in the remote origin of his mission as revealed by Buddha himself.   The next writing drew a parallel between Nichiren and Christ, especially in respect to their dignified aloofness from earthly powers, in which Takayama saw the kernel of veritable spiritual leadership.   His most inspiring writing was a beautiful letter simulating Nichiren's thought and reminiscences during his exile in Sado, in which the writer happily combined religious zeal and poetic imagination, the powerful style of an essayist with the melodious language of a poet. The letter became the beacon of a Nichirenite revival, to which flocked men and women, old and young, seeking for spiritual inspiration and charmed by Takayama's style, as well as drawn by Nichiren's strong personality.

This awakening of interest in the prophet of the thirteenth

century was not simply a religious movement but a many-sided upheaval of idealism, hero-worship, patriotism, romanticism, all combined in most of the enthusiasts. Indeed, Nichiren's personality and teaching were so comprehensive that both individualists and nationalists, religious men and poets, could derive inspiration from them; in addition, Takayama's own many-sided individuality and his candid veracity attracted many types of men and women to the Nichirenite revival instigated by him. The work done by this apostle of Nichiren within about a year, between his conversion in November 1901, and his death in December 1902, had far-reaching effects. Takayama never lost the fresh vigour of youth even in his illness. In every step of his varied career he was always straightforward and ahead of his time. Thus he was an embodiment of the youthful spirit of the age, in his struggle and his final aim. He stirred and inspired latent yearnings in the heart of youth, his early death made him ever one of them, and he became thus a pioneer of spiritual agitation to follow. His tomb stands in the precinct of a Nichirenite temple which commands a grand view of Mount Fuji across the Bay of Suruga, and the place has now become a place of pilgrimage, where the grandeur of nature also inspires the pilgrims in conjunction with Nichiren's lofty ideals and Takayama's enthusiasm for the prophet.

### A Buddhist Pietist and a Christian Mystic

Parallel with the Nichirenite revival there was a pietist revival in Buddhism initiated by Kiyozawa. He was a strong dialectician of the Hegelian type and had played a part in the philosophical rejuvenescence of Buddhism in the nineties. He was also a man of stoic temper and lived a very austere life, which could vie with that of any monk in rigour and purity. His spiritual struggles were not so striking as those of Takayama, yet we can discern in his writings and confessions how earnestly he tried to temper his logical mind with his inherited faith in the grace of Buddha—he was born in a Shinshū family.  He did not undergo a marked conversion, yet it must have been a very difficult task for him to moderate his stoic rigour through the devout meekness of a pietist.  He emphasized in his philosophical essays the antithesis between relative and absolute, particular and universal, and endeavoured to attain a higher synthesis of the two aspects of idea and life.  His Hegelianism, though partly a result of his study under a Hegelian teacher, was not a product of mere intellect but involved a personal striving to transcend the limited self through absorption into the bosom of the Absolute.  We see in his life an example of the conflict between intellect and sentiment ;  the effort to reconcile these two and to live in pious devotion.  The final result he attained was a religion of absolute dependence on the grace of Buddha, implying the elimination of self.  As a philosopher Kiyozawa spoke constantly of the finite and infinite.

> The unity of the finite with the Infinite is attained either by the development of the internal capacity of the finite or by the assistance or grace of the external actual Reality. . . . The Infinite being the One, we must take it either for the One of potential capacity or for the One of actual reality . . . *and so on.*[1]

This is cited not so much for elucidating his idea as to show what kind of abstract thinker he was.  It was a long process by which he transformed his abstract theory of the Absolute into a living religious faith.  Ten years later we find him no longer a theorist but a devout believer in the " Infinite."

> The Infinite illumines all quarters and is embracing us into the same illumination.  We experience that the Infinite Light (Amitābha) is guiding us and that we are living in delight within the Infinite Light.  We believe that all other beings also are being embraced by the same Infinite Light and therefore that they are all our fellow beings.[2]

---

[1] Cited from the authorized translation of his *Skeleton of a Philosophy of Religion,* written in 1892.

[2] From an article written in 1902, *The Illumination of Faith in Buddha's Power.*

This life of devotion and delight he called the " Spiritual Life," in which one eliminated self and freely admitted the grace of the Infinite Light. Thus Kiyozawa instilled his stoic virtue with devotional piety, he inspired his disciples with a religious ardour combined with calm self-renunciation, and he lived with them in monastic simplicity in the midst of the bustle of Tōkyō.

Kiyozawa did not much appear in public but his inspiration of his few disciples produced various types of men. All of them emphasized to an extreme degree the omnipotence of Buddha's grace, the sinfulness and finiteness of man, and therefore the necessity of self-abnegating dependence on Buddha. All this was in accord with the tradition of Shinshū pietism, but these men were eminent, more than many other pietists, in fervent zeal and the personal element. Books and journals published by them contained meditations and prayers which might easily be taken for those of Christian pietists or revivalists. Kiyozawa died in 1903 ; his influence developed in various directions—simple piety, strong revivalism, working among the abandoned, and even wanton naturalism.

The fervour of personal religious experience penetrated into Christianity. While many Christians were engaged in the questions of creed and church polity, some went to the depth of religious faith of more or less mystic type. The clearest instance was that of a Christian mystic who " saw God " in a vision. This was Ryōsen Tsunashima who, having once been a thinker of rationalist tendency, became a Christian by himself after a period of struggle. He belonged to no Church but was attracted by the mystic side of Christianity, as he was also in sympathy with Oriental mysticism. Yet he was never content with mere contemplation but desired a personal realization of divine light. Finally he attained an intimate contact with divinity, in which he realized the ecstatic joy of a religious life, but when he reached this

climax he was a sick man, and his last days were devoted to
imparting the delight of his mystic experiences to others in
talk and writing.  He describes his experience thus :

'Ah !  That was indeed a serene night !  I was writing something with my
pen, by the light of a lamp.  I cannot now know what was the commotion of
my mind, but sudden and instantaneous was the change.  In a moment my
self had become a self which was no more my former self.  The motion of
the pen, the sound of writing on the paper, each and all, being transformed
into an absolutely brand-new and unimaginable in terms of anything else,
became an illumination before the eyes.  This lasted only a few minutes, as
I thought ; yet beyond all words and descriptions was the invading consciousness for the time, something like a shock, or a bewilderment, or a rapture, as
if I had met face to face a spiritual living being—a great being majestically
arising out of the deep and serene abyss of infinity. . . .

In this way I have met God, seen God.  To say *meet* or *see* is still too
superficial and external to exhaust the consciousness of that moment.  It was
a confluence, a union of me with God ; at that moment I myself became
almost melted away into the reality of God.  I became God.  Thanks are due
for that, direct and straight from God, this amazing and surprising consciousness has been given me. . . .

Blessed is one who believes without seeing, but more blessed is the one
who believes by having seen. . . .

By thus having seen God, I have felt surging out of the depth a
consciousness that "I am a son to God";—an incomparable glory on
earth. . . . Ah! I am a son of God and I must live like a son of God. . . .
Is not God, whom I have met face to face, abiding beside me and extending
around me His invisible arms ? [1]

This marked the third and highest moment of Tsunashima's
mystic vision during the year 1904.  On its publication this
confession aroused various criticisms but it also influenced
other yearning hearts to a similar tendency.  Though not
many had so vivid an experience as Tsunashima's, the spiritual
undulation, so to speak, propagated itself without regard to
distinction of creeds or denominations.  Whatever the physio-
logical or psychological explanation of a case like this may be,

[1] Tsunashima, *Byōkan-roku* (" Notes in a Sick-bed "), published in 1905, pp.
370-88.  This book was followed by another, *Kaikō-roku* (" The Returning Light "),
in which he expressed further his delight in mystic experiences and also reviewed
various other mystics.  Cf. Anesaki, *The Religious and Social Problems of the
Orient*, pp. 18-20.

it embodied the yearnings of sensitive youth in a period of spiritual agitation. At any rate, Tsunashima left behind him a record of vital religious experience, ending his life in ecstatic joy in 1908.

Takayama, Kiyozawa, and Tsunashima, these three represented the stream of spiritual aspiration, each in his own characteristic career and manner. Takayama started with a sentimental romanticism and, having passed through nationalism, arrived at a fervent faith in Nichiren's prophetic religion. Kiyozawa first struggled against self, a rigorous logical mind, and finally surrendered himself to the grace of the Infinite Light. Tsunashima also surrendered his rationalism to mystic experience and imparted his ecstatic joy to others. Kiyozawa's inspiration was the gospel of piety and meekness and Tsunashima's that of mystic immersion, while Takayama represented the spirit of effort and emulation.

The spiritual agitation or craving was by no means limited to these striking instances but was widespread among the youth of the time. Unions of young Buddhists came into prominence, with various principles ranging from rationalism to sentimentalism, some aiming at a philosophical reconstruction of Buddhism, others fighting against traditionalism, others forming little groups for pious devotion. Christian churches began anew to be thronged by young seekers after spiritual truth, and some of them proceeded to the audacious task of forming a new Christianity. Religious essays and books of devotion, both Buddhist and Christian, were published in increasing numbers.[1] The divinity of Christ was discussed in conjunction with the inherence of Buddha-nature

---

[1] The author may be allowed to state that his writings shared in the movement of the time. His study on the aspects of Buddha's personality, historical and religious, though a scientific one, had some bearing on religious questions. *Fukkatsu no Shokō* (the " Dawn of Resurrection ") stood for the fight of religious spirit against the over-emphasis on science for the interpretation of life. His diaries of a trip in Italy was perhaps the first book which made known St. Francis of Assisi to the Japanese public.

in the human soul.  " The bankruptcy of science " was supported by an " alliance of religion with art and poetry." Spiritual faith was emphasized as against official ethics and conventional morality.  Pleadings in favour of " naturalism " against traditionalism had a religious tinge or ran to an extreme of sensualism—of which we shall see more.  On the other hand there was strong protest against the " degenerate effeminacy of religious mysticism " denounced as a neuropathic phenomenon.  Yet the sway of religious craving was incontestably strong during the first decade of the present century.  The writings of ancient Buddhist leaders, especially of Nichiren and Shinran, were re-published, the inspirations derived from them were viewed in a fresh light.  Epictetus, Augustine, Eckhardt, Carlyle, Fechner, and others found translators or admirers.  In the midst of this agitated atmosphere of religious spirit the war with Russia (1904-5) broke out, and though religious topics were more or less overshadowed for the time being, the spiritual struggle was destined to reappear in the years after the war and later, more and more in conjunction with the social agitation consequent upon the advancing industrialization of the country.

# SOCIAL UNREST
## SHARPER ANTAGONISM BETWEEN RADICALS AND CONSERVATIVES

### *Post-bellum Agitation and More Individualism*

WHEN the war with Russia came to an end in 1905 the general uneasiness increased. The moral effects of the war were very different from those of the war with China ten years before. This latter had been the first experience of the kind for the Japanese and a frenzy of excitement had been aroused over the victory, while the war of 1904-5, on a far larger scale though it was, was faced in a comparatively serious and tranquil attitude. Enthusiasm for the immediate issues of the war never eclipsed the graver problems. Serious consideration of moral and religious questions, readjustment of educational institutions, besides economic and political questions, were the features of the period. But a perplexing situation was caused by political and social circumstances. The liberal but often unprincipled policies of one cabinet were followed by the narrow reactionary measures of another; and an alternation of hope and disappointment was the effect produced upon the minds of the people. The penetration of militarism into educational institutions, a natural accompaniment of war, particularly instigated a turbulence of ideas, and often a spirit of revolt. Extreme individualists appeared and young people were easily captivated by radical ideas. Moreover, the period was one of financial stress, and the economic situation was aggravated by congestion of population and the resultant difficulty of life. This found reflection in the mind of the rising generation, as they faced the question of bread and of the spiritual needs at the same time.  The spirit of revolt and the pressure of conservative paternalism reacted upon each other.

Irritated sensibility manifested itself in extravagant tendencies.  There appeared several who declared themselves to be prophets and saviours of the world.  Their characters were various, some moderate and others decidedly megalomaniac, just as their contentions were diverse.  But they had one point in common, that they regarded all existing religions inadequate for the guidance of the age. Some Christians came forward to denounce their Church and its dogma, expressing an ambition to restore Christianity to its original purity, or else the conviction that another Christ was to appear   Herein was shown the influence of Tolstoi combined with stimulus derived from the revival of Nichirenism.  Most of them emphasized the immanence of divinity in man, and proceeded further to an assertion that divine nature could be realized even in the instinctive life of man—a combination of a biological idea and some aspects of Buddhism.  One significant fact in this outburst of religious self-assertion was that many of these " prophets " were ex-Christians.  This fact, together with other indications, shows the influence of Buddhism upon Japanese Christians, some of whom characterized it as the " pressure of the Oriental consciousness upon Christianity."  Buddhism also produced men of similar types but they were less bombastic, though the impact of naturalism was to manifest itself more strongly about a decade later.  The activity of these pretenders proved ephemeral in most cases, ceasing in a few months or years ; but there were a few who persisted longer and worked assiduously at propaganda.[1]

---

[1] One of them was Toranosuke Miyazaki who called himself " Messiah-Buddha " and published several writings.  One of them is *My New Gospel*, translated into English by a Christian writer, Takahashi.  Miyazaki died in 1929, enduring a life of penury and struggle.

Another feature distinguishing the last part of the first decade was the rise of what was called naturalism. Though its expression was chiefly limited to the sphere of literature, it represented a strong stream of thought operating against the authorized teaching of ethics and religion. The artificial method of imposing official ethics upon the youth worked, as we have seen, to arouse a spirit of discontent and even revolt among the young people of independent spirit. The impatient among them demanded total emancipation on the contention that the genuine " natural " meaning of life could be realized only in a full play of the instinctive nature of emancipated individuals. Theorizing or arguing did not suit their temper ; to expose life in its naked reality seemed to them the only method of arriving at a satisfactory solution of human problems, because all entanglements were understood to arise out of artificial means of control. By " naked reality " were meant the actualities of life stripped of all conventionalities, and the literature produced for this cause aimed at a relentless exposure of all compromise and hypocrisy. The literary movement was, in its negative aspect, a bitter protest against every kind of authority, and was on its positive side a declaration of emancipation of the individual. This movement of individualism and naturalism prepared a way for the rising of socialism as an idea, which was destined to take more practical forms in consequence of economic agitation during and after the World War.

Naturalism in literature by itself was not an enduring force, but it was a phase of a larger issue and a deeper current of thought, the biological view of human life which was beginning to control the mind and life of the people to a large extent. After the war with Russia, the Japanese people began to think of their own destiny more seriously than before, the ideal of being a civilized nation having been partially attained and being no more so strong a motive force as in

the preceding century.   The expansion of national interests
in the Asiatic continent, the rise of industry on a large scale,
these brought to the nation a considerable degree of self-
confidence as a civilized power in the modern sense, but the
same causes tended to make her share the travail of industrial
civilization and feel the relentless nature of the struggle for
existence, both at home and abroad.   The burden of taxation
consequent upon heavy armaments fell upon every home.
The economic prosperity, both real and apparent, made the
accumulation of wealth more and more one-sided ; the clash
of class interests manifested itself in labour troubles, class
legislation in Parliament, and so on.   All this caused the
people to think of life, both national and individual, as an
arena of sheer struggle and competition.[1]  Life viewed from
this angle seemed supported by Darwinism, or to be supplemented by the Marxist idea of class war ; theory and fact,
idea and actualities, reacted mutually to endorse each other.
Naturalism in literature was only a vanguard of this tendency,
whose effects were shown more and more in the second decade
of the present century and continue to exert its influence to
the present, in no way abated but enhanced.

All these forces working to break down traditional ethics
and social conventions were later to burst out in conjunction
with the agitation brought about by the World War.   Even
preceding the war, an air of uneasiness prevailed, as shown in
the reaction between the conservatism of the ruling class and
the demand for emancipation on the part of the unprivileged.
In 1911 the Government convened a meeting of religious

---

[1] Herein is an instance of the power of popular interpretation, or misinterpretation, of a scientific term. \The phrase, " struggle for existence " was translated
into Japanese by a phrase, *seizon kyōsō*, which means " competition for subsistence "
and may mean sheer competition, bloody contest to the neglect of other considerations.   The complaint of Darwin himself concerning a similar misinterpretation of
his theory found here an illustration.   The phrase was freely used in daily life,
giving the impression that there was nothing else in life, and this idea borrowed
from a biological theory exerted evil effects upon the ideas and life of the people,
awake as they were at the time to the burden of life.

leaders representative of Buddhist, Christian, and Shinto
Churches, and asked for their co-operation in ameliorating
the situation, thereby implying the fight against radicals.
The representatives expressed their readiness to make efforts
against social evils and to raise the spiritual level of the nation.
Similar attempts were repeated by succeeding cabinets,
but the official declarations of the church leaders bore little
fruit.

### The Death of the Emperor Meiji and the Growing Uneasiness

An unexpected event marked a step in the growth of the
general uneasiness. In July 1912, the serious illness of the
Emperor was made public, to the consternation of the whole
nation. The ruler, who remained silent and seldom appeared
in public, was nevertheless an object of great confidence and
high reverence among the people. Not only his firm rule
combined with his dignified aloofness, but his sentiments
made known through his numerous poems, always impressed
the people with deep trust in his person. When the serious
announcement was circulated, the pious devotion of the
people to him manifested itself in fervent prayer for his
recovery. Prayer meetings were organized everywhere, and
even otherwise non-religious people joined in them. When
the illness became more and more serious, many people
assembled in front of the imperial residence, first waiting
anxiously for any information, then kneeling down on the
ground sobbing or praying. The spacious park was spontaneously transformed into a campus of great revival meetings,
so to speak. Everyone offered up prayer or performed some
sort of religious service according to his or her fashion ; each
group organized its own religious ceremony ; murmur of
praying and chanting filled the air from earliest morning to
late at night. It was an inspiring but pathetic spectacle, the

varieties and confused states of prayer or services showing a sad lack of unity among the people in religious faith. Nevertheless the occasion was a significant demonstration of religious fervour as well as of the patriotic spirit concentrated in the person of the ruler. No one who had witnessed the scene could forget it and any religious revival could hardly surpass it in intensity and extent.[1]

When the death of the beloved monarch was announced, early on the morning of 30th July, sorrow darkened hamlet and hall. Emotion for the deceased sovereign surged like a tidal wave. Days passed in profound mourning and in further idealization of the late ruler. The funeral ceremony took place in September, and the day saw the whole country like one great religious service. The sense of solemn sorrow was aggravated by the suicide of General Nogi and his wife at the moment of the departure of the funeral procession from the imperial palace. Whatever may be said of this tragic event, it affected the minds of the people like a magnetic storm, infinitely deepening their pious reminiscence of the dead sovereign and his faithful general, modest, resolute, strong in himself. Hence the imperial mausoleum near Kyōto and the memorial shrine close to it in honour of Nogi became immediately a great centre for pilgrimages.

Traditional reverence towards the sovereign played a great part in the religious ardour shown at that time, but no less was the force of the personal magnetism of the deceased ruler, while the sense of solemn gravity was much deepened by the apprehension of how the vacancy produced by his death could be filled. It was a real crisis when the people were deprived of the symbolic figure with whom they identified all the glories and achievements of his reign.

Moreover, this change of reign took place when the course of national life was reaching a stage when it must take turn,

[1] See Plate XXI.

PLATE XXI

PEOPLE FLOCKING TO THE ESPLANADE OF THE IMPERIAL
PALACE AND PRAYING FOR THE RECOVERY OF THE
EMPEROR

Last Days of July, 1912

when the new life of the era of Meiji had nearly achieved its task and was facing the deeper problems of the new civilization. Indeed, it is impossible to overestimate the amount of progress achieved in the half-century of the past era, yet it was after all an age of transition and as such left many problems behind it. A feudal state had been transformed into a constitutional state, an Asiatic nation into a world power, an agricultural society into largely an industrial one ; but the constitutional government, industrial régime, universal education, these new factors of national life had yet to grow and to achieve full naturalization. Contented life had yielded its place to effort for progress, family control to individual ambition, traditional learning to scientific culture ; but the real meaning of these forces of civilization was still not quite firmly grasped by the people, to be defined and amplified only through further struggle. What does progress mean ; does civilization necessarily bring happiness ; wherein lies the aim of human life ; these and similar questions remained little touched, except by the individualists above cited, while the problems of capital and labour, of democracy, of social reconstruction, were agitating beneath the surface. The people in general were still unaware of the coming difficulties but the change of reign gave a certain amount of ominous suggestions to the changing phases of social life. It is no wonder that minds so long under the spell of progress and almost intoxicated by the glories of the new age were bewildered at the apparent end of that glorious era and began to question about the future of the nation.

It was not otherwise with the official representatives of the organized religions. The Buddhist leaders who gladly accepted the rôle of tools of the Government [1] and the Shinto

[1] One instance out of many was this : when pious Buddhist peasants had hesitated to engage in sericulture because of the killing of silkworms, Buddhist preachers were commissioned to encourage it, justifying the killing for the sake of the export of silk, therefore of the nation's wealth.

teachers concentrating their efforts on the sanctification of traditions and the glorification of the nation's sucesses could not realize the underlying forces of social problems, nor anticipate anything contrary to their easy-going serviceableness to the ruling classes backed by their glorification of the régime. The Christian leaders were not very different. They worked first as the civilizing agents who adopted Christianity as an integral part of the new civilization and, therefore, had always rejoiced at the changes wrought in that direction. They were firm in the conviction that modern civilization was identical with their religion, this being particularly the case with Protestants who branded the Middle Ages of Europe as simply a dark age and considered, with little questioning, the Reformation as the fountain-head of everything good and modern. None of them ever suspected the explosives contained in modern civilization or in Christianity having to face dangers in its Occidental home. How then could these religious leaders think critically of the civilized reign or anticipate the coming of something else ? The angles were different but the optimism was the same. But the times were changing, new forces were arising, and the meaning and destiny of the new civilization was being questioned by the minority who were sensitive enough to think of the other side of life and civilization.

# THE WORLD WAR AND AFTER

*Social and Moral Effects of the World War*

WHILE the Japanese nation was being entangled in social unrest and political instability, the World War broke out in Europe. Japan had experienced two wars fairly recently, which stimulated national self-consciousness and brought on many new problems ; but the disasters and miseries of war were not brought home to the people at large, since the battle-fields were far away from the homeland. The third war, too, at least in its first stages, seemed to the people a matter of distant lands, notwithstanding Japan's official share in it. They were indifferent to the various issues raised by the war, such as the combat between militarism and democracy, the question of international justice or of the self-determination of nations, the problems of peace and social reconstruction. Moreover, the biological view of human life applied to international relationships found an easy-going acceptance among the intellectuals, while indignation against the Occident's aggression in the East induced the people to discredit the pleas of the Allies and sometimes, in reaction, to sympathize with the German claim for " a place in the sun." [1] But later, the collapse of the great empires, the final outcome of the war and its aftermath, these could not fail to produce profound impressions upon the Japanese. The people little grasped the meaning of the situation and problems, yet the gravity of the situation and its troubles finally became evident to everyone,

[1] Cf. Anesaki, *Japanese Views on Present International Problems*, in the *Centenary of the University of California* (Berkeley, 1919).

and the seriousness of social and moral problems began to demand deep reflections.

The first point in this respect was the social unrest called forth by the changes in economic conditions. Because of the favourable position occupied by Japan during the war, her industrial and commercial prosperity made remarkable strides. The war boom produced many *nouveaux-riches*, so-called *narikin*,[1] and brought tremendous changes in life and ideas. The extravagant luxury of the rich *entrepreneurs* provoked heavy demands from the labouring classes; the one-sided accumulation of wealth, never before paralleled, was co-incident with an astonishing rise in the cost of living; the heavy expenditure on the army and navy was in flagrant contrast to the miserable resources of schools and other institutions for culture and public welfare. The uneasiness of the educated classes rose in a high tide, the misery of the poorer classes increased apace; labour strikes became frequent; socialist propaganda found easy acceptance; and finally the rice-riots of August 1915 made everyone realize the seriousness of the situation. The reactionary Terauchi Cabinet fell in consequence and the nominally liberal Hara (assassinated in 1921) took the rein of government, but the sharp antagonism between reactionaries and radicals was never assuaged. The demands for change and reconstruction so alarmed the conservatives that their nervousness became almost morbid. Any expression of radical ideas was suspected of connection with Bolshevik propaganda, for the Russian Revolution became a perpetual nightmare to the privileged classes. Prosecutions for *lèse-majesté* grew more numerous from year to year. Expressions of a leaning towards socialism, communism, or the like, were indiscriminately treated as potential cases of high treason. The Shinto religion and

---

[1] The word " *narikin* " was taken from a term in Japanese chess, its Occidental equivalent being a pawn raised to the dignity of a queen.

" national ethics " were used against such " foreign ideas "
and reactionary fanatics were mobilized for fighting the
" dangerous ideas."

The frequency and extension of labour strikes brought
in their train the rise of labour organizations. No period
before had witnessed in Japan so many publications on the
labour movements, Marxism, syndicalism, social reconstruction, and so on, as the ten years following the Great War.
With the coming of a serious economic depression in 1921,
the labour movement seemed to have subsided, but the stand
taken by the controlling political parties in favour of the
propertied classes worked continually to instigate broils
beneath the surface. The scandals in official and financial
circles exposed one after another, all on a larger scale than in
earlier years, could not but arouse the resentment of the
public. The desperate steps taken by the quick-tempered
radicals were exhibited in the cases of assassination of men in
high positions or in attempts on them. In these ten years
the agitation changed its aspects in one way or another, but
the general situation remained nearly the same, except that
measures taken by either side became more and more erratic
and violent. The cleavage between classes, both in industry
and agriculture, became more marked, and the general
situation was one of serious ferment and agitation.

### Outburst of Instinctive Forces in Religion

The fermentation was not limited to the political and
social arena, but went down to the very root of human life,
the turbulence manifesting itself in the demand for a wanton
emancipation of the instinctive aspects of human nature.
An irritable and pugnacious temper marked the social movements, and consideration of the instincts for self-preservation
and perpetuation played an important part in the discussions

on moral and religious problems.   Many problems were
reduced to that of food or sex, and naturalism was no
longer limited to the sphere of literature.   Herein we see a
recurrence of the conflict between instinct and reason which
we noted in the moral conflict of the seventeenth century ;
but now the outburst of instinctive nature had more social
bearings, being interwoven with the struggle between classes
and the changing social order.   In speaking of these situations
we have now largely to give up the use of the historic past
and to use the present tense to connect the recent past with
the present.

One outstanding feature of the spiritual and social ferment
is the general discredit of all the existing religions, including
Christianity, and the appearance of new movements ranging
between impetuous revivalism to calm self-renunciation.   No
matter how wide the gap between the various types is, common
features can be discerned in them all ; that spiritual problems
have been brought into closer touch with social, particularly
economic, considerations ;   that the intuitive or instinctive
nature of religion is emphasized in antagonism to doctrinal
and ecclesiastical systems.[1]   On the social side, more or less
communistic ideas are common to the new religions ;   a
fairly universal emphasis is laid on the instincts, either for
the justification of human passions and inclinations which
used to be called sinful, or some kind of attempt at their
transformation, or even justification.   Herein we discern an
insurgent upheaval of the religious instinct embedded in the
depths of the soul, which is taking advantage of the opportunity of social agitation and spiritual ferment to express its
discontent with the traditional religions. Many of these new
forces are crude in expression and extravagant in their pre-

---

[1] As we have seen, this amounts to a distinction between the religion of " personal
test or contact " and the " doctrinated " and " ecclesiasticated " religion.   There
was a similar contrast drawn in the thirteenth century.

tensions, but there is within them the vigour of nascent vitality. Some of them are extremely individualistic and sentimental, but many representative leaders have, after having passed through stages of spiritual convulsion, attained some insight into the mysteries of life. In short all this amounts to a bold challenge to traditional beliefs, a call for a complete revision of spiritual values, and for a thoroughgoing reconstruction of human life, individual and social.

A rich soil for spiritual turbulence is found in the field of the Shinto religion, partly because it appeals most to the instinctive aspects of a religious mind and partly because its unorganized form is favourable to any variety of ideas and practices. A typical representative of the crude expression of religious aspiration is the Ōmoto religion, which means the " Great Fundamentals," pretending to reveal the mysteries of life, especially of the national life of Japan, the divine mysteries long obscured and suppressed by the wanton tyranny of the privileged classes since the very beginning of the " Age of the Gods."

The movement was started by a woman fanatic who believed herself to be the prophetess of the gods and wrote down the divine messages in automatic handwriting during more than twenty years of her " god-possessed " life. Gradually, dissemblers and fanatics flocked around her, and when, during the World War, uneasiness about the outcome of the war began to overtake some people, especially military and naval men, the propounders issued various predictions warning the nation against a foreign invasion. The predictions, though always worded in ambiguous terms, amounted to saying that the whole country would be devastated and that the only place saved would be Ayabé, a little town in central Japan, destined to be the centre of the new world order ruled by a theocracy of the Great Fundamentalists. Besides appealing in this way to the apprehensive fear as well as to the patriotic pride of the people, they practise a kind of mental cure by hypnotism combined with exorcism, which they call " divine possession," a practice common to all Shinto movements.

Ōmoto-kyō was once suppressed by the police authorities but its leaders are never disheartened, continuing to work along the same lines.[1] They pretend to have followers even in China and Korea, where there are, as in Japan, many souls ready to fall victim to similar predictions and " miracles."

The assertion of the instincts can be found no less in Buddhism and Christianity.    Buddhism as an aggregate of church organizations is hopelessly degenerate, yet not without signs of spiritual vitality.    There was a revival of Nichirenism, as we have seen, several years ago ; on the part of many of its enthusiasts, it amounted to a religion of hero-worship, which remains still a force in the religious life of the Japanese. But many of the followers of Nichiren have narrowed down the horizon of Nichiren's spiritual vision to the limits of chauvinistic patriotism.    Thus, the movement has subsided to a great extent, but it is yet to be seen whether Nichiren's profoundly religious ardour will inspire coming generations.

The wane of Nichiren's influence was followed by the rising interest in Shinran's piety.    In fact, Shinran's religion of absolute faith in Buddha's grace involves full recognition of all kinds of human weakness or sinfulness.    Though not quite justifying or advocating sins and passions, he emphasized that we could be saved even without purging ourselves from the depravities of human nature, because of the overwhelming strength of Buddha's saving power.    This aspect of Shinran's religion could easily be used to endorse the naturalistic or biological view of human life, and there have been in recent

---

[1] The founder's pretension to have direct communication with the gods was interpreted by her followers to mean her descent from the primeval deity.   This fanatical claim was a step forward to a revolutionary political ambition.   Later, a similar pretender appeared in the camp of the Tenri-kyō, and he was prosecuted in 1928.

years various signs of this combination of pietism and naturalism. The modern followers of Shinran start from a full sense of the innate wickedness of human nature. This might seem an attitude of confession, but these men deny the necessity of remorse or contrition. In view of the all-powerfulness of Buddha's grace, no effort on the part of man is called for, they hold, either for the sake of life or for salvation. On the contrary, they proceed to the joy of cancelling all sins and obstacles through the all-embracing mercy of Buddha. All vile darkness vanishes, according to them, before the universal light of his love, the love which can and ought to be experienced even by the most sinful beings. It is only one step from this joyful faith to a kind of glorification of human passion, and, in fact, the new power of Shinranism lies in the free delight in life even in vice and passion. To cite from one of the typical representatives of this movement :

"Religion is nothing but yearning of a defective being after perfection. The humility of the soul by which it confesses without any reserve the barrenness of self full of falsehood, bewildered, and troubled—this humility makes us aspire for the absolute reality which is rich, true, and stands beyond all commotion for ever. The lonely cannot bear to remain alone, but ardently longs to be joined to an eternally beloved—that is religion." [1]

But this is not all. Reality or love, they say, is not an abstract principle, it is nothing unless personally experienced by everybody. Again, that experience needs no training in higher types of culture or contemplation, but lies just in love, the very carnality of every human being. Love is best exemplified by sexual love, latent as it is in every man and woman, but only brought forth to actual experience through contact. Love is a union of both flesh and spirit, and those who are the best and most fervent lovers in life are best

[1] Hyakuzo Kurata, *Starting-point of Love and Cognition* (in Japanese), pp. 85-86. He is the author of a very popular drama in which Shinran plays the rôle of acknowledging, and almost justifying, human weakness, especially the sexual instinct. English translation by Glenn W. Shaw, *The Priest and His Disciples* (Tōkyō, 1922).

entitled to be embraced into Buddha's love. This is the religion of Shinran, according to his modern followers, and this amounts to securing the love of Buddha through love for other beings—certainly love of all kinds but especially sexual love. There are various other points to be noted in these tenets, but suffice it to say that they emphasize what they call " pure experience," identifying it with " genuine love," thereby identifying instinctive love with religious faith, and thus they see genuineness only in the life of prime instinct. This form of religious faith is surely sentimentalism, but, being something more than a mere play of sentiment, seeks to penetrate to the very root of the individual soul and it discovers there something beyond the individual.

Another variety of Shinranism evidencing more social consideration with communistic ideas is represented by Tenkō Nishida and his " Fraternity of One Lantern " (*Ittō-en*).[1] After having experienced various vicissitudes of fortune, Nishida entered into a new life of non-possession and service for others, basing his life on the conviction that the " Universal Light " of Buddha's grace would induce all to a life of mutual confidence and service. The fraternity is open to all who will give up their possessions, whether material wealth or intellectual attainments, and be ready to serve without demanding any return. " Give and take " is, according to Nishida, the root of all troubles, while " work in demanding nothing " is a test of faith, absolute trust in the all-embracing grace of the " Light." For the Light penetrates only into the heart of those who have given up the idea of self and possession. In the life of their community there is no rule of discipline, except a sincere devotion to the Universal Light and joyous work done for anybody who asks for it. The fraternity lives

---

[1] " One Lantern " is derived from a Buddhist legend, that among thousands of lanterns dedicated to Buddha the one lantern brought by a poor woman outshone all others. " One Lantern " means, therefore, services done by people with no possession, *i.e.*, the principle of non-possession.

in a cottage, which may be erected at any suitable place, and their life is sustained by free gifts from the sympathizers. However, Nishida's further ambition is to organize a kind of co-operative industrial system on a communistic basis, and a start has already been made. He calls this organization one for " Propagating the Light." [1] It remains still a question how far " One Lantern " can propagate its light. At any rate the personality and life of Nishida are noteworthy as a product of a profoundly religious nature working in reaction to the social agitation of the day.

Christianity cannot remain unaffected by the general movement of emphasizing the intuitive aspect of religious life. A section of young Christians share that tendency with Buddhist sentimentalists, standing for the assertion of free individuality. There are, among them, some Tolstoians, mystics, advocates of naturalism, admirers of Shinran, and so on. Let us hear one of them. On explaining the reason why he deserted the Church, he proceeds to elucidate his idea as follows :

" And the solution (of the problems of life) is offered by Love, the pure instinct of attachment. In love I enfold others, as I am enfolded by others in love ; and thus I and others make up a life beautiful in texture, by weaving together the woof of self with the warp of others. The better and more profoundly the inner self is developed, the better and the more profoundly is the external world enfolded into itself. The whole life is thus perfected. There is in this no sacrifice, nor duty, but only the privilege to be grateful.

"Christ enfolded into his supreme love all mankind. . . . Was it not he who said ' Love thy neighbour as thyself' ? he who loved himself with a love greater than any other son of man that he might give himself away the more and become a self vast enough to enfold all mankind. That he exhorted men to follow him shows how convinced he was of the possibility on the part of all men, even the mean and foolish like myself, of treading the same pathway with him." [2]

---

[1] Another organization with a similar scope is led by a theosophist and its title is the " Heavenly Flower." We may expect the rise of other similar movements.

[2] T. Arishima, *Love Enfolds without Reserve* (in Japanese), Tokyo, 1920, pp. 131, 133, etc. This writer inherited great wealth but it was an agony to hold it. Finally he distributed his landed properties among his tenants, so that they should organize

This brings us to an attempt at humanizing Jesus, not a solitary instance but more or less a tendency. In 1921, appeared a book of 1500 pages bearing the title *Shin-yaku*, i.e., " The New Testament," an imaginary story of Jesus. Its author, Ebara, attained fame at one stroke through this book. In it the author sets out the human aspects of Jesus' personality and life. He is depicted as a man of fine sensibility guided by ecstatic visions and auditions, uncertain as to his own destiny and the import of his experience. Emphasis on sex is strongly shown in the author's way of handling the inner secrets of Jesus and many other persons appearing in the stories, thereby pointing out the discrepancy between the Law and Love. Another striking point in the book is the author's sympathetic attitude towards Judas Iscariot. The betrayal is depicted as his experimenting, so to speak, with Jesus, with the idea that the Kingdom of God could be tested only through this experiment. While the other disciples were still holding the traditional conception of the Kingdom, and while Jesus himself was not yet quite clear as to his own destiny, Judas somehow caught an insight into the necessary consequences of Jesus' teaching. In a latter book bearing the title *Resurrection* Ebara goes further, even so far as to say that the title implies not so much the resurrection of Christ as that of Judas, the modern man free from convention and hypocrisy.

This book of Ebara, in its attempt at humanizing, or as some might say desecrating, Jesus, finds its milder companion in another life of Christ written by Mushakōji, the Tolstoyan and founder of a communist settlement, the " New Community." There Jesus is represented as a simple human

a co-operative society. However, being discontented with his life, he found a solution in love, love of a lady journalist, and ended his life in joint suicide with her, in 1923. This caused a great sensation, and hot discussions on the case were only overshadowed by the disaster of earthquake and fire in the same year, three months after his death.

being of pure heart. If we may call the Jesus of Ebara a
man of spiritual passions, that of Mushakoji is a man of childlike simplicity and divine purity. Jesus penetrated into the
heart of man through his love of his Father, and thereby
reached the innermost depths of the human soul. To cite a
passage from Mushakoji :

> " I cannot bear thinking of mankind *minus* the being of Jesus  There is
> nothing more comforting in the world than that Jesus and Buddha have
> appeared. I cannot live without thinking of them . . . I am here alone but
> can hear Jesus' words, can converse with Buddha, and similarly with Gœthe,
> Whitman, Rodin and many others.
>
> " O Jesus ! What vigour I derive from admiring you ! . . . Pity this
> little brother of yours ! . . . I am yet too little to converse with you as a
> friend, but hope to be finally one day a friend who can talk with you without
> any reserve. In these days I feel I know more and more the truth of what
> you have spoken." [1]

This is not the place to examine these views on Jesus, but
what is to be noted is that these are an expression of the
radical ideas cherished by the youthful spirit to disentangle
itself from all convention and formalism and to attempt a
revaluation of all values. These writers, together with their
numerous followers and admirers, are not satisfied unless
everything is reviewed in a new light emanating from their
own heart and soul. [2]

### The Present Status of the Organized Religions

The emphasis on the instinct of love, almost replacing
faith by it, marked the chief feature of the religious movement in the second decade of this century. But this move-

---

[1] Mushakōji, *Jesus* (in Japanese, published by " The New Community,"
Tokyo, 1920), pp. 219-20. The settlement of the " New Community " is in the
province of Hiuga, the ancient home of the Japanese.

[2] A similar remark may be made of Kanzo Uchimura, a veteran preacher and
independent thinker with a great following. Though insisting on the truth of
orthodox teachings such as miracles and the second advent, he emphasizes personal
experience. He may be called an orthodox mystic.

ment mostly took hold upon young people who had no denominational allegiance, while the organized Church bodies
hardly manifested any reaction towards it explicitly, neither
for nor against. Their attitude was simple indifference or a
certain amount of ridicule towards the " fungoid " growths
of religion. The people in general were similarly indifferent.
Yet that many are not satisfied with the regular teachings
of the organized religions can be seen from the fact that
almost any religious or semi-religious propaganda promising
immediate benefits together with spiritual blessings finds
more or less following. Indeed, Japan to-day is full of such
new teachings ranging from chauvinistic types of Shinto to
individualistic methods of health and healing. No one can
see whether or not any of these will achieve any amount of
wholesome growth.

Meanwhile, social changes became accelerated in proportion to the vicissitudes of economic prosperity during and
after the War. An abnormal boom was rapidly followed by
a period of panics and depressions in the years after 1921,
culminating in the great panic of 1927. The situation was
aggravated by the earthquake of 1923, of which the moral
shock was not less than the material loss. Dark clouds still
linger and signs of a dispersal are still undiscernible. The
large amount of unemployment, more especially in professional
circles, has been working to arouse a keen sense of intellectual
proletarianism which is now attacking the university students.
These and similar difficulties cannot but produce deep and
far-reaching effects upon the moods and ideas of the people,
not to speak of the many impacts of radical social ideas from
the outside, largely due to the aftermath of the war including
the several political revolutions in Europe and Asia.

Under these circumstances sensitive youth would not
rest content with the mere play of idea, whether naturalism
or pietism or anything else, but wishes to think and behave

in the more tangible ways of social agitation.   This, however, is not merely due to the effects of the war but is a consequence of the industrial revolution which has transformed many phases of Japan's national life.   Quite naturally, it is almost impossible for the organized religions to cope with the situation, Christianity not being an exception.   This leads us to a consideration of each religion in face of the critical juncture.

First, Christianity has always, since the beginning of the new age, been eminent in social work and its leadership still rests on that, in spite of the rather insignificant number of its converts.   Without enumerating the fields in which Christian social work displays its activity and some amount of its achievements, it suffices to say that the names of the Salvation Army or of Toyohiko Kagawa, the Christian socialist, alone tell the important places of Christianity in the social work of new Japan.   The churches and many missionaries do not fail to follow their steps.   Yet the chief defect is that the Christians are too much divided.   The Churches are almost all mere importations, including the titles, organizations, methods and teachings, which, in many cases, have nothing to do with the interests or needs of the Japanese.   The missionaries who still play an integral part in many of the Churches are often too much representatives of their respective nationalities ;  they identify their own national manners, habits, even prejudices, with the Christian religion ; the converts, even ministers and bishops, retain the contentions and methods of the divided churches.   Even Catholic missionaries often uphold their own nationalities, if not more than their Mother Church.   This is the reason why there have appeared so many independents who alienated themselves from the Church, not because they lost their faith in Christianity but because they saw in the churches rather an impediment to its true mission.

A defect much graver than division is that the problem of the Christian religion or church is at stake in the Occident, not less than in Japan. Many people call modern civilization Christian, but it is evident to every unbiased observer that Christianity is not taking the lead in civilization but is struggling to accommodate itself to it. Japan's problem lies partially in how to be a modern nation in contrast to her past, but it lies in a higher degree in her facing the problems arising out of the industrial régime introduced and nearly naturalized. It is, therefore, no wonder that Christianity is not a solution but a problem in Japan, the Christianity that is so bitterly attacked by socialism, a natural product of modern industrialism, and also the Churches which are criticized in their homes as being too much tools of the capitalists. Moreover, although the " conflict between science and theology " is regarded by liberal Christians as a matter of the past, these liberals have still to combat Fundamentalists, while the Catholic Church is condemning " modernism " as persistently as ever. How then can Christianity, of whatever colouring it be, offer a perfect solution to the Japanese people of the relations between science and religion ? In addition to this most Japanese would gravely question the dogmas of creation by fiat, of original sin, of vicarious redemption, of apostolic succession, and so forth. It will take a long time, at least, for Christianity, by convincing the Japanese of the truth of these tenets, to carry the people across the whirlpools of human life and social problems.

Concerning the disease of division, nearly the same remarks apply to Buddhism. It is hopelessly divided and each branch of Japanese Buddhism remains faithful too much to the subtleties of its ancient teaching, not simply the spiritual legacy of its founder but much more its traditions and conventions accumulated during the centuries of its existence. Ecclesiastical Buddhism, represented by its sects and sub-sects amounting to nearly sixty, still retains much of the indolence it acquired under the high patronage of the government which it enjoyed during the past three centuries. The reinvigorated Buddhism of several revivals and various social works is almost entirely the work of those outside the organized bodies, or of those who have revolted against them. In social work modern Japanese Buddhism has derived much stimulus from Christianity, which it has taken as a model, but it must not be forgotten that the deeper motive comes from the original soul of the religion and the models of past ages.[1] Yet it is questionable whether Buddhist activity is sufficient to cope with the grave situation of the present. Besides, although Buddhism has shown much elasticity in its attitude towards modern science, perhaps more than Christianity, its weakness in face of the industrial régime is too evident to need comment.

Lastly, in considering Shinto we must distinguish two categories in its working. One is the official cult of the State, supported by the Government and the communities, the other is the Shinto bodies furnished with church organizations and treated on the same footing as other religious bodies. The official interpretation is that the Shinto of the first category is not a religion but a part of public institutions. Therein emphasis is laid on the sanctity of the Throne, and its practical efficiency is sought in making the local sanctuary the centre of the communal life, with which are associated the local organizations of young men and women. In recent years much effort has been spent in enforcing this official Shinto as a weapon against " dangerous thoughts " ; but its efficacy is doubtful, to say the least, because it is mostly in the hands of political leaders much guided by conventions and ex-

---

[1] Some Christian observers see the one side only, the aspect of mere imitation. That their observation is superficial can be seen by examining the details of the work as well as the careers and confessions of the workers

pediencies.[1]  In fact, there is much artificiality in the conventional interpretation that this Shinto is not a religion, but there is some truth too, both because the exponents of the theory are men who are anything but religious and because their sincerity is not unquestionable.

The second category comprises thirteen sects and their adherents are officially given as amounting to respectable numbers.   But these religious bodies, except two or three, are very questionable ones in which sorcerers, diviners, dubious bigots live parasitic lives, and of which the constitution is quite ephemeral.   Evidently, little wholesome influence can be expected from these organizations.   Yet it is to be noted too, that a few exceptional ones are manifesting a fresh vitality, a continuation and extension of the popular religions in a nascent state which appeared in the last stage of the feudal régime.   It is still premature to predict their future and it goes without saying that even the best of these are far from mastering the situations arising out of the industrial régime.

These observations may sound rather pessimistic.   But the other side of the situation demands our consideration, that the modern civilization of the world, and of Japan too, is in itself a problem.   If not subscribing to Spengler's theory of the decline of the Occident, or to the Marxists' curse of capitalistic industry, every one must realize the difficulties involved in the consequences of modern industry, in the meaning of democracy, and in the true mission of science. The point in question amounts to this : [2]  World civilization, which entered upon new courses with the fresh motive forces of

[1] There are some individual thinkers who try to give a new interpretation on this national cult.  Most of them import too much their own new ideas, often borrowed from Occidental thought, and their interpretations are often far-fetched and artificial.

[2] Behind this remark is the author's view of the problems of modern civilization for which see : *An Oriental Evaluation of Modern Civilization* in *Recent Gains in American Civilization*, edited by Kirby Page.   New York, 1928.

PLATE XXII

A

B

GATHERINGS OF THE FOLLOWERS OF THE TENRI-KYŌ AT THE
FORTIETH ANNIVERSARY OF THE DEATH OF ITS FOUNDRESS (1926)

A. The " Teachers " bowing before the Memorial Mirror
B. The crowds outside

enterprising spirit three or four centuries ago, is now demanding another inspiration of reinvigorating motives, a revision
of all values, and higher ideals.  Japan is, indeed, facing two
problems, one of carrying through her transition from a
mediæval state to a modern, from a feudal régime to an industrial, and the other of facing the grave crisis inherent in
the newly introduced civilization.  If the reformatory inspiration is to be expected from religion, no matter whether
organized or not, or from religious idealism, the question for
Japan may amount to whether or not some of her spiritual
legacies, or of their renewed manifestations, or a phase of
her new religious life arising out of the contact with Christianity and modern civilization, could contribute to a broader
and higher solution of the present difficulties.  The Congress
of Japanese Religions held in Tōkyō in June 1928 passed a
resolution expressing the conviction of the participants representing all the religions existing in Japan that the present
world crisis could be solved only through religious idealism.
Perhaps this term was used largely in opposition to Marxian
materialism, while the import of the word idealism or faith
was as varied as the denominations of the participants, having
little definite meaning in it.  Moreover, to be convinced of
something does not necessarily coincide with a readiness to
carry it out, nor can too much faith be put in a mere resolution.
Yet anything short of it could hardly express the present
need, even in a very general way, if there is any idealism or
striving after ideals in the religious soul of Japan which could
be an inspiration to the immediate future.  What this idealism
or religious motive should be, whether or not it could be
efficiently reinvigorated, all this must be left to the observation
of future historians.

# INDEX

ABHIDHARMA-KOSHA (Kusha), 94
Abode of the gods (Takama-no-hara), 308
Abraxas, 125
Achala, 96
Acts of the Apostles, 338 n.
Adhishthāna (Kaji), 128
Admonitions to Learning, 352
Adoption, 84
Age of the Gods, 88, 397
Aggressive propaganda, 230
Agriculture, agricultural life, 22-23, 29, 32, 34
Ainus, 2, 204
Air and moon, air and stream, air and waters, 86 n., 108 n., 228, 293
Air-rhythm, 213
Akamatsu, Renjō, 351 n.
Ālāya (cf. Unconscious, Store), 95, 132
Allier, R., 374 n.
Ama-no-Yasugawara, 28
Amaterasu (see Sun-goddess)
Ame-no-Minaka-nushi, 24, 268, 309
America, 321, 342, 343
American Board of Foreign Missions, 339, 340
American Independence, 354
American system of education, 349
Amita-Buddhism (cf. Jodo Buddhism), 187, 191, 194, 211 n.
Amita or Amida, Buddha, 68 n., 147-49, 151-52, 160, 169, 170-87, 198, 262 n.
Analogies, cosmological, 239
Ancester worship, ancestral deities, 11, 69, 99, 100, 222
Ancient Learning (cf. Kogaku), 278-79
Andover, 339
Anesaki, 37 n., 54 n., 62 n., 77 n., 98 n., 114 n., 117 n., 119 n., 129 n., 150 n., 152 n., 187 n., 188 n., 189 n., 191 n., 200 n., 209 n., 222 n., 228 n., 270 n., 297 n., 382 n., 383 n., 393 n., 408 n.
Animal, Beast, a resort of transmigration, 90
Anjiro (see Yajiro)
Annam, 90
Annen, 146 n.
Annunciation, Fraternity of, 249
Ansai school (cf. Yamazaki Ansai), 320
Anti-Christian movement, 360-62, 365-66
Anti-foreign movement, 308

Anti-religious attitude, 333
Apostates, Kirishitan, 252, 253
Arai Hakuseki, 270-71
Ara-mitama, 40
Archismati, 96
Architecture, 76, 97, 154
Arima, 252
Arishima, Takeo, 401 n.
Aristocratic régime, Oligarchy, 96, 134 f.
Arms, swords, bows and arrows, 38
Armstrong, R. C., 270 n., 302 n.
Art movement of the Ashikaga period, 224-28
Ārya-deva, 205
Asama, Mount, 376 n.
Ashikaga, régime, period, 215, 219, 222, 223, 244
Ashikaga Yoshimasa, 226, 254
Ashikaga Yoshimitsu, 222-23, 224, 226
Ashikaga Yoshinori, 230
Asiatic continent, 5, 11
Asiatic morality, 342
Asanga, 94
Assassination, 394, 395
Aston, W. G., 87 n., 289 n., 297 n.
Asura, 71 n.
Atkinson, J. L., 306 n.
Ātman, 209
Augustine, 384
Augustinians, 250 n.
Awaré, 156-57
Ayabé, 397
Azuchi, 244

BABA, TATSUI, 351 n.
Bakin, 297
Ballagh, John, 337
Banishment of Kirishitans, 249
Bankruptcy of Science, 384
Bashō, 291-92
Beautiful life, 377
Behrens, W. L., 352 n.
Being and Non-being, 113 n., 114
Bhaishajya-guru, 148 n.
Bhāradvāja, 91
Bible, 159, 358, 364-65
Bīja, 95
Biography, 189
Biological view of human life, 387-88
Bizen, 315

411

# 416 INDEX